RULE BRITANNIA

BREXIT AND THE END OF EMPIRE

RULE
BRITANNIA

DANNY DORLING & SALLY TOMLINSON

\B^b\

Biteback Publishing

First published in Great Britain in 2019 by
Biteback Publishing Ltd
Westminster Tower
3 Albert Embankment
London SE1 7SP
Copyright © Danny Dorling and Sally Tomlinson 2019

ISBN 978-1-78590-453-0

To Bronwen, Danny's mum, who taught him what the Suez Crisis meant when he was more excited about the idea of pyramids than power games, and to Sally's children, their partners and her grandchildren, who are all citizens of the world, including Europe.

CONTENTS

LIST OF FIGURES AND TABLES

FIGURES

TABLES

ACKNOWLEDGEMENTS

Many thanks to Ailsa Allen for drawing up all the graphs and maps in this book so carefully and to Claire Hann for helping ensure that the final manuscript was internally consistent and presentable! Thanks to Olivia Beattie at Biteback for taking this project on when there were already so many 'Brexit books' out there. We promised this one would be different, and we hope it is. We are extremely grateful for her editorial advice and especially for her editing the final text so diligently, diplomatically and deftly.

Our profound thanks for help with this book are also due to all those who commented on earlier chapters, including Becky Alexis-Martin, Shaista Aziz, Dimitris Ballas, George Davey Smith, Alison Dorling, David Dorling, Philip von Hausenchild, Stacy Hewitt, Benjamin Hennig, Aniko Horvath, Sebastian Kraemer, Carl Lee, Bill Lodge, Chris Lynch, Deborah Outhwaite, Jan Rigby, Paul Scarrott, Robbie Shilliam, Brian Tomlinson, Dariusz Wojcik and Vicky Yiagopoulou. Rebecca Carter of Janklow & Nesbit valiantly found us a publisher when all were heartily sick of considering any more writing on Brexit. We don't hold any grudges against those publishers who turned the opportunity down, save to say – if you are reading this now it probably did better than you thought possible. Thanks also to all our other family and friends who argued from both sides of the Brexit divide, but who are still talking to us.

We are also grateful for all the thoughts of the people who turned up to our public lectures during the writing of this book in Bath, Belfast, Birmingham, Bristol, Cambridge, Cardiff, Changchun, Cheltenham, Coventry, Dublin, Durham, Edinburgh, Eton, Groningen, Guildford, Hay-on-Wye, Hong Kong, Hull, Leamington, Leeds, Liverpool, London, Loughborough, Manchester, Newcastle-upon-Tyne, Northampton, Ottawa, Oxford, Portsmouth, Sheffield, Stoke-on-Trent, Swansea, Weston-Super-Mare, Weymouth, Winchester, York and several smaller towns and rural villages. Apologies for only making it the once to Scotland while writing this book, but you seemed to know very well what you were doing north of the border without our intervention or thoughts!

Finally, we should thank all those who gave permission for the photographs they took to be included, their song lyrics to be quoted or for their images to be included. The artist Joseph Kelly very kindly allowed us to reuse his illustration as a frontispiece here. It was first included in the 2016 March/April issue of *Strike!* magazine. Benjamin Hennig allowed us to reproduce his maps shown in Figures 1.3 and 3.3; the Royal Mint gave permission for Figure 2.1 to be included; Trinity Mirror, Mirrorpix, and Alamy Stock Photo for Figure 2.4; the Jewish Museum for 4.3; the British Library for 4.4; Allan Warren for 6.1; Wasi Daniju for 6.2; Ian Burt for 6.3; Andre Burdett for 6.4; Daniel Watson and Emma Foster for 6.5; Zoe Norfolk for 7.1; Steve Bell for 7.2; *FE Week* magazine for 7.3; Matthew Elliott for 7.4; Daniel Gordon Watts for 8.1; and Alasdair Rae for 8.2 and 8.3. We are very grateful for all their help.

Illustration by Joseph P. Kelly
The authors are very grateful to Joseph for permission to use this image.

INTRODUCTION

*Empires, in common with most other historical events,
leave behind them after-images ... There is no one
version of the British imperial myth.*

– BERNARD PORTER, EMERITUS PROFESSOR OF
HISTORY, UNIVERSITY OF NEWCASTLE, UK 2015[1]

Books on Brexit, on how and why parts of Britain voted to
leave the European Union, fell hot off the press in late 2016,
saw a resurgence during 2017, and then appeared a little more
slowly throughout 2018 as the public's appetite waned and we all
became less and less sure of what was happening and what might
happen. In the heat of the moment, in the month or the year of
the event, emotions are often still running too high to see clearly.
Sometimes you have to wait a little time before you can know
what really happened.

Why Brexit? Once you have children, you realise that the
answer to 'Why?' is never simple. Whatever your reply, the child
can almost always ask 'Why?' to that. And then, of course, there
are the questions of who did what to whom, where, when, how,
and by how much. Above all, we want to highlight what will be

seen as important in retrospect. What was it all about? What did it all mean?

Jo Cox MP was murdered a week before the EU referendum in June 2016, by a man who, when asked for his name, replied, 'My name is death to traitors and freedom for Britain.' Many racist attacks and more killings followed the vote.[2] In the aftermath of the referendum, government spending was diverted from health and social care towards paying for Brexit, in ways that will have foreshortened many other lives. So, given some breathing space, an obvious question to ask is whether one reason for a narrow majority voting to leave the EU was partly that we were now finally hearing the 'language of the unheard'[3].

Those dedicated to recovering national sovereignty, to taking back money supposedly spent in the EU, and removing immigrants, certainly claimed that the referendum was the voice of the previously silent majority, the largely unheard masses.[4] Did people feel they had not been listened to sufficiently? Or are there many more explanations as yet hardly explored?

Some of the dozens of books that were published in the immediate aftermath of the referendum promised the full story of the political manoeuvring that got the UK to this point, and others promised to make sense of the vote, with a couple of tomes focusing on the supposed evils of immigration and Islam. One or two suggested that Britain would eventually not leave Europe[5] and even change its mind quickly and choose to Remain, and that it would actually be this that would make Britain great again.[6] Others showed signs of their authors adapting and responding to rapidly changing times in interesting ways.[7]

This book tells a different story. We have had the benefit of a little more time to stop and think. Here we argue that part of the reason the Brexit vote happened was that a small number of people in Britain have a dangerous, imperialist misconception of our standing in the world, and that this above all else was the catalyst for the process leading up to Brexit, especially for those arguing most fervently for Brexit.

In this book we suggest that once Brexit happens, we will be faced with our own Dorian Gray-like shockingly deteriorated image. Of course, we cannot be completely sure what a post-Brexit Britain will look like until long after we leave the EU, or fail to properly leave, but the flailing, erratic attempts at negotiation to date do not inspire confidence in the dawn of a new British Empire. Looking into the mirror, people often see what they want to see, especially if that mirror is largely angled by a tabloid press and a patriotic BBC telling them what they want to hear. The reality can be strikingly different.

Here we suggest that in the near future the EU referendum will become widely recognised and understood as part of the last vestiges of empire working their way out of the British psyche. Other European countries had already been shedding their (smaller) empire mentalities immediately following the Second World War, but Britain found it hard to come to terms with the reality that, by the late 1960s, foreign country after foreign country had escaped the clutches of the British – some peacefully, others as a result of ferocious conflicts. Almost all those with any substantial populations that remained colonies by 1969 would gain independence in the 1970s.

The post-war creation of the 'New Commonwealth'[8] had been much more than a rebranding, although in Britain few acknowledged that point. Despite importing former colonial labour from the late 1940s onwards, Britain began to get into serious economic difficulties once it had lost control of almost all its colonies. But, worse than that, its people had inherited a colonial mentality that would have repercussions for decades to come.

Images of domination and pride in the empire, illustrated by maps with lots of pink on them, adorned classroom walls into the 1960s; often they were still there in the 1970s. Books continued to be written even well into the twenty-first century extolling *How Britain Made the Modern World.*[9] Such writing covered up the real story of how, out in the big wide world, British influence and dominance had diminished. Governments of all political preferences either felt unable to explain this fact to the British population or did not themselves recognise this new reality. Instead, they clung to a pretence that much of the old empire could be held on to by force.

National Service, by which some two million young men were conscripted into Britain's armed services between 1946 and 1962, was used to force many young British men to fight colonial wars.[10] The experiences of these men shaped the attitudes of their generation. As one RAF flight controller explained, 'We had Empire Day at school and we all thought empire was a marvellous thing. When Britain chose to give her empire away we were all rather saddened. The colonial people had all the blessings of British colonial rule and look how casually they dismissed them.'[11]

When the British public did vote to stay in the European Economic Community in 1975, there was a vague feeling that since the old empire was 'going, going, gone', another alliance was better than nothing. Flippantly, people were told that maybe the price of Danish butter might come down. Later, much later, *The Brexit Cookbook* hit the bookshops with its promise that:

> Scotch eggs and trifle built the greatest Empire the world has ever known until the EU forced us to eat Danish pastries and pizza. But now the kitchen tables have been turned. We've taken back control and can cook what we blooming well like. So, put down your croissant, stop chomping on your ciabatta and cook something properly patriotic for a change with *The Brexit Cookbook*![12]

There was also some rejoicing when it was revealed that the television programme *The Great British Bake Off* was being screened in 196 countries and the format copied for home-grown shows in twenty of those countries. Britain can still offer culinary cultural gifts to the world, it was said!

It also offers great confusion, not least in the use of the term 'Britain'. In this book, we adopt the common shorthand of Britain being synonymous with the sovereign state of the UK, but we never refer to Britain as a country. Strictly speaking, Britain is made up of four countries, three of which constitute Great Britain with the fourth being Northern Ireland. If you are already confused or annoyed by this, you are not alone.

In *Rule Britannia*, we try to provide an honest appraisal of the importance to the Brexit decision of Britain's origins; the British Union of separate countries; Britain's overseas endeavours; the manufacturing of tradition; the establishment and often brutal running of the empire. All this is folded into an assessment of our changing relationship with Commonwealth countries and the story of how badly we treated people from the Commonwealth in the past, even through to the 1970s and 1980s, and, remarkably, still today. Laid out like this, we then see how similar that older racism is to how the British often think of and treat people from Eastern Europe today.

Both of us saw the racism of 1970s Britain, and sadly, this is not so different today – although it is often a much older group of people who are most racist now. Thankfully, there are fewer racist murders than in the 1970s, perhaps because it is no longer skinheads leading the racist charge but men with a similar lack of hair, now due to age, typing out bile on the comment sections of newspaper websites. So many of those bigoted men today would have been the same age as or might even have been the very same skinheads who were in the National Front in the 1970s.

David Cameron still sports a fine head of hair, but he has lost most of what reputation he once had for competence. Despite the continual clamour of complaints he received from his EU-hating opponents, David Cameron did not have to promise a referendum in the Conservative manifesto in 2015. But he and his friends in government concluded it was worth the risk. They could see that if they did not promise the EU rebels their referendum then the Conservative Party might tear itself apart, that the UK Independence Party (UKIP) would take even more votes from the Conservatives, and that Labour might then have gained power in 2015. In the event, UKIP disintegrated, with their votes going mainly to the Conservatives; there was some speculation that erstwhile leader Nigel Farage would stand for a Northern Irish Democratic Unionist Party parliamentary seat.[13]

Furthermore, the long Brexit referendum run-up and debate became a useful distraction from the reality of austerity. In any case, once the EU referendum result was declared, David Cameron immediately quit as Prime Minister, with his family wealth of well over £10 million intact.[14] He then charged up to £120,000 for speeches[15] and re-joined White's Club, the 'gentlemen-only' club he had resigned from on becoming PM.[16] He left a woman to sort out the mess.

In this book we are not arguing that any soft/hard, in/out or maybe position would have been preferable in hindsight. Instead, we want to suggest that Britain will be diminished by the process of trying to leave the EU whichever way it does it, and that there is no welcoming empire, Commonwealth or other set of countries ready to quickly embrace new trading and other relationships with Britain. We suggest that an adjustment like this was always on the cards.

Partly, if not largely, because of failing to come to terms with its loss of a huge empire, the UK had been ramping up economic inequality since the late 1970s, reaching a point where the gap between rich and poor in Britain was wider than in any other European country. When India, and then most colonies in Africa, won their freedom, the British rich found themselves suddenly becoming much poorer. They blamed the trade unions and socialists in the 1970s. To try to maintain their position, from 1979 onwards they cut the pay of the poorest in a myriad of ways and vilified immigrants in the newspapers they owned or influenced, while managing to hold on to some of the pomp and ceremony that their imperial grandparents had enjoyed.

Something had to break, and, in the end, it was a break with the EU – it was Brexit. It is true that Brexit was partly the language of the unheard – the masses cocking a snook at the demands of their overlords – and there were some who actually believed the propaganda that problems in health, housing and education were due to immigrants, and some who really thought 'their' country was being taken over by colonial and EU immigrants, by refugees from anywhere, or even by Islam. But there were many others who voted Leave out of hope. They just hoped for something better than what they had.

The British had been distracted from the rise in inequality and the consequent poverty that grew with it by decades of innuendo and then outright propaganda suggesting that immigration was the main source of most of their woes. Without immigrants, they were told, there would be good jobs for all. Then they were told, at first in whispers, and later through tabloid headlines, that without immigrants their children could get into that good school, or the school they currently go to would not be so bad. Without immigrants, they could live in the house of their dreams, a home currently occupied by immigrants who have jumped the queue and taken their birthright. 'We' (always 'we', always 'us') need to cap net immigration to the 'tens of thousands' and then all will be so much better. All this was said to distract people from looking at who was actually becoming much wealthier and who was funding a political party to ensure that the already wealthy could hoard even more in future. Or, as Alex Massie of *The Spectator* wrote in 2016:

If you spend days, weeks, months, years, telling people they are under threat, that their country has been stolen from them, that they have been betrayed and sold down the river, that their birthright has been pilfered, that their problem is they're too slow to realise any of this is happening … at some point something or someone is going to snap.[17]

FIGURE 0.1: THE MOST GENEROUS POLITICAL DONORS FROM THE RICH LIST OF 2018

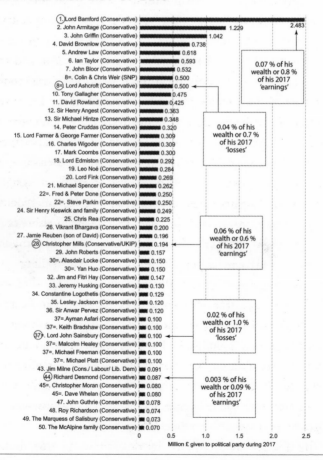

Note that the text boxes have been added by the authors based on the Rich List data.[18]

The reality was that Britons *had* had their country stolen from them, but not by immigrants – by the rich. We illustrate this above with a table taken from the Sunday Times Rich List 2018, showing that many of the rich people listed have donated money to the Conservative Party – a party that over the years has produced policies which have increased economic and social inequalities and given rise to huge injustices, some of which are only now being revealed. Most of these men encouraged a Leave vote. The largest donation, by Lord Bamford, was of £2.48 million.[19]

In this book, we include many snippets that make up a jigsaw, such as the table above. Combining all this, we try to explain where the British are now, how they got to this point, and what they can expect from the future. This includes the British problem of tolerating gross inequality, which helped fuel the Leave vote; our lack of sustainable economic growth compared with other developed countries; Britain's dearth of non-financial exports; and, in turn, the people's reliance on imports from EU member states.

We try to explain why the British (and especially the English) have such a dangerous misconception of their national identity, by spending a great deal of the pages that follow focusing on the British education system, which, despite a certain modernisation in recent years, has its roots in nineteenth-century ideas about race and the class system.[20] The majority of people who voted Leave were taught what they know of British history in the 1940s, 1950s and 1960s. We argue that the British education system has helped produce a homogenised and corrupt elite who are often descended from the architects of empire, and who too often make claims for British exceptionalism. They are also easily wrong-footed due to their collective ignorance of, for instance, the importance of the Irish border.

The first country colonised by the English in 1169, Ireland, turned out to be incredibly important, but there was almost no whiff of English understanding of this until late 2017. In December 2017, the *Daily Telegraph* had to report that one key Northern Irish political party – the Democratic Unionist Party – was refusing to co-operate in Prime Minister May's dealings with the EU leaders[21] and holding out for a hard Brexit with no compromise.[22] The Republic of Ireland is, of course, staying in the EU, where, for the first time in 800 years, it may well soon be in a stronger political position than Britain.[23] It was not just in Northern Ireland that there was dissent within the Union. Only a little later, on 15 May 2018, the Scottish Parliament refused to give its consent to passing the main piece of UK Brexit legislation.[24]

Many British people's understanding of their empire's past and their country's future, and how Britain is now viewed by former colonies and the rest of the world, is largely myth and nostalgia. This misunderstanding has been fuelled by an elitist education system that extols military patriotism, heroic deeds and public service. Britain is still mainly stuck in a mythical past, especially in its history and geography teaching, and this is often reinforced through popular literature, music and film.

The British may not really think that 'Britannia [will] rule the waves' again, as they sing annually on the Last Night of the Proms in London, but in 2016 and 2017 through to mid-2018 it was still considered plausible to have a public debate about how Britain – if it stays as four countries – could be ever 'Greater' in future, despite a diminished and diminishing position in the world. There was at that time very little discussion of exactly how the UK currently is supposed to be a force for good in the world. Until very recently, that was so often, as documented in so much fiction and film, just assumed to be the case. Britain could be much better, but it would be folly to equate improvement with greatness.

Finally, we consider what good can come of all this. Can parts or all of the United Kingdom become less racist, hermetic and imperious? Can the British learn to have much greater actual humility, not the faux-humility where they pretend to be humble while harbouring a national narcissism whose time now has to come to an end? Out of the ashes of Brexit could, should, and perhaps will come a chastened, less small-minded, less greedy future. There are good reasons to be hopeful. What we had before was not that great: a set of countries often just too unequal, too bigoted and too chauvinistic for their own good.

Briefly, the chapter outlines below illustrate our views of what has happened and may happen to these divided countries of a no longer United Kingdom. Other people will have different views. But you are unlikely to have heard the arguments made in this book put together in quite this way before – with the benefit of a little more hindsight.

CHAPTER 1: WHY BREXIT?

Whatever the final outcome of the Brexit vote, Britain's place on the world stage will likely be much diminished in the process. Already, Britain, and especially its politicians, has been losing face in so many ways, with Theresa May pleading for more respect from other European leaders in September and October of 2018. At home, social services were falling apart due to austerity cuts, with death rates rising among infants and the elderly since 2014. State school budgets were being slashed. Fewer homes were made available to those who needed them; street homelessness rose rapidly and growing numbers of children were spending each Christmas in bed and breakfast accommodation, an entire family in just one room. Some long-promised money was found for the NHS on its 70th anniversary date in June 2018, but even then Mrs May couldn't then say where it would come from. In hindsight these were desperate times.

By the time you read this, the claims and counter-claims about Britain's greatness that were so much the norm in 2017 and 2018 should have greatly diminished. This rhetoric was never going to improve the image of Britain in the eyes of much of the rest of the world's people, who looked at us, sighed, shrugged and waited for us to grow up and get over it. But there has been an upside. The British have been learning a great deal about themselves as a result and there is so much more to learn. Above all else, we need to recognise how firmly Britain, and even Brexit, has had its roots in the British Empire.

In this introductory chapter, we provide a considered and il-lustrated analysis of the Brexit vote. The Scots and Northern Irish mostly did not vote for Brexit, and neither did most Londoners, nor the majority of the young. What did these four groups have in common? Perhaps it was a rather different understanding of British history: less jingoistic, more realistic. And who were most of the unheard who could only express their anger at the current system through the referendum? How badly off were they, where did they live, which social groups were they from? How did men and women differ in their voting, and why? Read Chapter 1 to find out – it is staggering how little of this part of the story is well known.

CHAPTER 2: BRITAIN'S IMMIGRANT ORIGINS

In Chapter 2, we point out some of the myths, revisit Britain's actual immigrant origins, including the immigrant origins of its royal families, and briefly explain why the British began setting up colonies and trading posts, which included an infamous global slave trade and the looting of India by the East India Company.

We include a new map of the empire showing the dates of acquisition and independence from empire, using circles to show the respective population size of the colonised countries. We note the nostalgia for empire, picturing Chris Patten looking with concern at his daughter's tears as Hong Kong was returned to China in 1997. The 'Mother Country' has for decades been becoming less and less important to the rest of the world. All of Britain's social classes, whatever their views and votes on Brexit, are going to have to adjust to new realities.

The chapter ends with an image of Britain's contribution to the EU Border Force on the Greek island of Lesbos and asks: how did it come to this? How did we come to think that sending a warship to the tiny Greek island of Lesbos was an appropriate response to families fleeing Syria to seek asylum? Who might have wanted such a picture to be broadcast? In whose interests was it to make it appear as if the UK was under threat from mass migration of people with darker skins or different religions?

CHAPTER 3: FROM EMPIRE TO COMMONWEALTH

Chapter 3 looks at some of the beliefs and myths underlying British imperialism, which from the mid-nineteenth century onwards were bound up with social Darwinism – beliefs that the white Anglo-Saxon 'race' was superior to all other races and peoples, and that hierarchies could be constructed of inherently superior and inferior groups of people. Just at the height of the power and spread of the empire, it was Charles Darwin's half-cousin Francis Galton who tried to provide a 'scientific' basis for selective breeding. A young future psychologist, Cyril Burt, sat on the ageing Galton's knee as a boy (he lived nearby). Later, as the empire became a Commonwealth, Burt supported spurious theories about IQ and ability, his influence unfortunately extending to the 11-plus examination in the UK via the notion that some children are genetically superior in 'educability' to others. It is also unfortunate that our leading Brexit politicians and their advisors also believe that they are much superior in intellect to others. And it is intriguing just how many of them are white but were born in the less-white parts of the former empire, or are closely connected to people once high up in the outposts.

Despite the passing of the age of empire and of the most virulent British supremacist rhetoric, the search for Galton and Burt's superior golden children goes on in Britain today in a way not seen in any other country on earth. We show the distribution of students admitted to Oxford, the university with which we are both most closely associated today. Many of the elite politicians that Oxford and other 'top universities' produce still denigrate poor people, despite accepting, when asked, that their degree of poverty – even when in work – is intolerable. Many British politicians still blame families for their children living in poverty, or not doing well at their often-underfunded schools.

When politicians urge people to be 'a bit more patriotic', they do not understand that many people do not want to be patriotic about a country that treats its working and unemployed people so badly, that holds out so little hope to its underprivileged young people, and that currently has a Prime Minister who has assured us she would be prepared, if necessary, to agree to a nuclear war, and (unlike almost all other countries in the world) is prepared to waste billions of taxpayers' money to be able to do so. We end this chapter with an image from a century ago, from 1918, that is worth bearing in mind today. The prevention of future world war was one of many reasons for nurturing a community across Europe that developed into the European Union.

CHAPTER 4: HIGH INEQUALITY
AND IGNORANT POLITICIANS

Chapter 4 suggests that it is not such a good idea to appoint Foreign Secretaries whose judgement is so lacking that they quote from a racist poet while at a sacred Buddhist shrine, as Boris

Johnson did. The past couple of years have revealed that it is essential to more fully understand Britain's imperial past if we are to understand what Brexit is most deeply about. So many of the British have never really understood why they were once so rich, and so find adapting to becoming normal very difficult. Many racist Victorians helped conquer and make money out of imperial countries – Cecil Rhodes in South Africa and Rhodesia being the inescapable example. They were often just 'men of their time', but their influence lingers on.

It is worth also noting that Britain's universities are still an attractive destination for students from Europe and around the world, but this may change as fees, funding, visa problems and racism deter overseas students.

School and university rankings dominate government thinking in Britain, as part of a national introspection. Britain is not good at thinking about itself except in competition rather than co-operation with other people and countries. In reality, Britain currently has a very poor record when it comes to investment in health, housing, education and other indices of inequality when compared to other European countries, all of which have recently made greater social, health and economic progress than Britain has.

CHAPTER 5: THE FANTASY AND FUTURE OF FREE TRADE
In Chapter 5, we begin with economists and their arguments over free trade. A large number of British economists, both past and present, have extolled the notion of free trade, but mostly when it has been in England's favour, preferring protectionism as soon as this does not seem to be the case. Those who casually assume that no trade under EU rules can bring big benefits under World Trade Organization (WTO) rules do not know their trade history. The Brexit-supporting group Economists for Free Trade need to have a greater understanding of trade, while other groups are

hampered in their efforts by our own politicians, who appear to be not only ignorant of our past but suffering from a crass disregard for standards of decency. The pro-Brexit Initiative for Free Trade, for instance, could have done without the then Foreign Secretary turning up to its launch to claim that Libya would be a great tourist destination 'once they had cleared the dead bodies away'.

The British are still seen as being good at banking, although there are some caveats when they require the government to bail them out. But we note that banking, unlike mining and farming, can be done anywhere, not necessarily in the City of London. The British were good at arms dealing, especially from the mid-nineteenth century, when the empire was expanding. The arms trade, often with countries whose governments have many recorded human rights abuses and few moral qualms, will sadly probably continue. Services will continue to be many times more important than manufacturing, despite promises of a future high-tech manufacturing bonanza. The British may also continue to be good at spying, since espionage is needed more than ever now in the digital wars now beginning around the globe.

CHAPTER 6: HOW NOT TO TREAT IMMIGRANTS

This chapter suggests that there is a long history of British governments and the British public being hostile to immigrants, despite the fact that many past and present politicians have immigrant origins. In the nineteenth century there was some toleration of richer expatriates, mill-owners such as Friedrich Engels and his author friend Karl Marx, and the young Michael Marks, who set up a shop with his friend Thomas Spencer. But the Aliens Act in 1905, intended to restrict Jewish immigration, translated a dislike of foreigners and immigrants into official policy.

The creator of Sherlock Holmes, Arthur Conan Doyle, was undoubtedly a racist and helped fund an organisation that tried to prevent Jewish immigration and wanted to 'stop Britain being a dumping ground for the scum of Europe' – sentiments which appeared to resonate in the EU referendum.

Although in the twentieth century all political parties colluded in anti-immigrant legislation, the classic 'nasty' remains Enoch Powell and his Rivers of Blood speech – although we note that in his Wolverhampton constituency the River Tame was actually flowing with industrial waste and dead cats, which he was apparently not bothered about. Powell was also a fervent believer in national sovereignty and was anti-European, and he would have been delighted with the Brexit vote.

CHAPTER 7: IMPERIALLY ROOTED
EDUCATION AND BIGOTRY

In Chapter 7, we document the current sorry bunch of politicians that have put Britain in the mess it is now in. The country is facing one of the most important decisions in its history, but it appears to be led by people whose overwhelming self-interest, hypocrisy and hubris surpass the record of most other politicians in Britain's very long parliamentary history (and there have undoubtedly been some rotten ones).

We make no apology for naming names and checking the backgrounds of these people, whose record may be dubious but whose callous disregard for the condition of their country, its people and the greater good has been becoming clearer by the day. Their stories should be recorded as part of the history of Brexit.

In contrast, we also write in this chapter about Clement Attlee, Churchill's Deputy Prime Minister during the Second World War, who was derided as unimpressive and untalented before he took office in 1945 and created a welfare state and healthcare system which rightly made Britain the envy of the world. To use the collective noun, the present disappointment of politicians have gone a fair way to reversing all that, and Britain is becoming more of a joke than a country to be envied.

CHAPTER 8: A LAND OF HOPE AND GLORY?

Penultimately, in Chapter 8, we begin to sound a positive note by pointing out that Britain is not on course to create another empire. We claim that what went wrong with Britain was largely a product of being led by people who did not want to contribute to the general good of the country. Many went to schools which had been designed to produce men who could run an empire. These schools are still instilling feelings of superiority today, but with no empire to absorb the urges that creates. A small coterie of mainly rich and privileged people mouthed slogans about improving social mobility while producing policies that actually ring-fenced the wealthy and made most of the population poorer. After the Brexit referendum, these people tried to convince us that it was poorer northern Labour supporters who swung the vote to leave the EU, whereas it was huge numbers of Tory voters in poorer Tory areas voting Leave that did it.

Was it, as Robert Peston so eloquently wrote, that people wanted to give a bloody nose to these posh boys who had created so much more inequality to the benefit of only a tiny few? Or was it the many other reasons put forward so effectively by the Leavers: too few good employment opportunities, too many immigrants, loss of border controls, European courts very occasionally having the effrontery to suggest (usually correctly) that our courts were not being just? What about the retired in Spain, the borders with Gibraltar and Ireland, the Channel Islands and other tax havens – had Brexiteer leaders done any homework on those? How good is a tax haven when your country becomes poorer and an outcast from where the action is? Or were a few people, who had a lot of money to spend on securing the result they wanted, not thinking about that and just wanting to be in the limelight and have the opportunity to indulge in splendid jingoism?

CHAPTER 9: WHY NOT BREXIT?

We think Brexit is a disaster, but there may be silver linings to the huge dark cloud. We revisit the map created by Freddy Heineken, the Dutch beer magnate who envisioned a Europe of seventy-five regions – which unfortunately did not quite give Yorkshire its perennial wish to be independent! We end by suggesting that Britain can build on its reputation as a reasonably successful multiracial and multicultural set of countries, maybe a bit battered now but improving, including with a royal dual-heritage marriage.

In or out of the EU, there are things the country can be good at, but we cannot be 'Great' in the way we were once so great at domineering. Britain cannot be top dog again. However, the British might even learn that not being top dog does not actually matter, and in many ways it can be preferable to be more normal. As it says on the lid of this little tome: Brexit is about the end of empire, and that, above all else, should give us hope for the future because at some point we really do have to begin to come to terms with who we are, what we are worth and where we have come from. Brexit could be the reality check required.

CHAPTER 1

WHY BREXIT?

The years of the long recession have brought with them a nostalgia
for a time when life was easier, and Britain could simply get rich
by killing people of colour and stealing their stuff. All of this is
made possible by lies: the lies many of us were told about what our
great-grandparents were up to in India, the lies we told ourselves
when we decided not to look too closely, the lies we told the peoples
we subjugated: Britain is a country built so firmly on deceit,
dishonesty and backstabbing that the symbol on our national
flag is not just a double-cross, but a triple.
— ADAM RAMSAY, MARCH 2017[1]

What is to be done? Do we just have to somehow get through 'Brexit: the death agony of empire' and eventually come to our senses?[2] Let's work our way backwards and then forwards again to try to get to the answer. Back in 2016, Theresa May promised a patriotic red, white and blue Brexit, but what we are getting is the pink, cream and aquamarine version. At first, May had been positively gung-ho about what Brexit would achieve for Britain. She had been following on David Cameron's lead when, in 2011, he had claimed he had 'an opportunity to begin to refashion the EU so it better serves this nation's interests'.[3] So why such a patriotic initial stance, and then such a desperate climbdown? Almost two years after the Brexit vote, she was writing apologetically in the *Sunday Times*: 'Trust me: I'll take back control but I'll need your help.'[4] She still promised to take back control of our borders, our money, our laws, our trade, our social and tax policies, but now she claimed that Brexit would be an opportunity to develop relations with fast-growing nations around the world, 'and in doing this we will put the values that make us great as a nation at the forefront: openness, tolerance, diversity and innovation'. 'As a proud Unionist and Prime Minister of the whole United Kingdom,' she continued, 'I am clear that … there will be no hard border between Northern Ireland and the UK' and, paradoxically, possibly no single market and customs union. Theresa May's tragedy is that she wanted to remain in the EU but was forced to implement some kind of exit. A tragedy for the UK may be that some of those in government (for it was the government who proposed the referendum) had no intention of explaining to the public what the EU did or did not do, and the vast majority of the general public are only just beginning to find out.

Throughout and shortly after the Brexit campaign, it was pointed out by a few of the most prescient academics, when commenting in their blogs, that 'present in the discourse of some of those arguing for a Leave vote was a tendency to romanticise the days of the British Empire, a time when Britannia ruled the waves and was defined by her racial and cultural superiority'.[5] That, at least, was the thinking that was gathering strength as to why the UK may choose to leave. But, at the time of the vote, its result was simply greeted with shock by most media commentators, and explanations centring on empire were largely ignored. Why Brexit? Why now? Why had the electorate of the United Kingdom voted on 23 June 2016 to recommend ending the state's membership of the European Union? Two years after the UK joined the European Community in 1973, it confirmed its membership in a referendum, with 67 per cent of those who voted opting to stay in. By 2016, the proportion in favour of remaining in the EU had dropped to 48 per cent, a fall of nineteen percentage points. Why this shift in opinion?

Brandishing the campaign slogan 'Vote leave, take control', the Leave side in 2016 secured a narrow majority (1.3 million), 51.9 per cent of the 33.6 million who voted. Some 13 million registered voters did not turn out at the ballot boxes, and, on top of that, a further seven million eligible adults were not even registered to vote in 2016. They were disproportionately 'the young, flat-dwellers, especially renters; members of ethnic minorities; [and] recent movers'.[6]

Many people chose not to register to vote for a wide variety of reasons, mostly not laziness. Some fear debt collection agencies, whom they know are allowed access to the electoral register, even including access to those who request anonymity on the public roll. Others may think they are likely to be living at an address for only a matter of months, or they are partly homeless, such as staying temporarily with a friend, so they can hardly register to vote where they currently sleep. In London alone, there were 225,000 people aged 16–25 'sofa-surfing' in other people's homes in 2016 and many hundreds, at times thousands, sleeping rough on the city's streets.[7]

People who were poorer or younger were not most likely to vote Leave; they were most likely not to vote at all. Most of those who did not register to vote, or did not vote if registered, were of an age or in social and economic situations that would have made it likely they would have voted Remain had they had a vote and used it. Then, on top of that, the voting figures do not include the millions of mainland EU citizens and British sixteen- and seventeen-year-olds who were not allowed to vote because of earlier political decisions to dismiss their legitimate interest in the outcome. Young people aged sixteen and seventeen had been allowed to vote in the Scottish independence referendum in 2014, but were excluded from the EU referendum in 2016.

It was initially reported that it was younger people who voted overwhelmingly for Remain. Some 73 per cent of voters aged 18–24 were reported to have done so, according to Lord Ashcroft's exit poll. But then, when the turnout figures became known, it turned out that this apparently high figure represented only around a quarter of all 18–24-year-olds, as only a third of people of that age voted on the day (see Figure 1.1). There was controversy over this estimate, with some evidence later suggesting that 64 per cent of young people claimed to have voted, as compared to 90 per cent of older electors who said they could recall voting in the referendum.[8] Of course, this recall data is not reliable: apparently far more people can remember voting than actually voted in June 2016!

Given that turnout among the young tends to be low, it will certainly be the case that the youngest age groups had the largest proportion of non-voters. Figure 1.1 suggests that 64 per cent of 18–24-year-olds abstained, which in turn reduces the total share of the electorate voting for Remain in that group to 26 per cent, with those who voted Leave representing 10 per cent of all those aged 18–24.

Once turnout is factored in, it becomes clear that it was not the young who were most in favour of Remain, but people aged 35–44. In fact, as a share of the electorate, fewer young people may have voted Remain than even those aged 65 or over! This is because so many of the young did not vote, or could not vote because they were not registered.

Where there *is* a clear age gradient, however, is in the proportion voting Leave, which rises steadily with age. Figure 1.1 makes this very clear.

**FIGURE 1.1: VOTING BY AGE GROUP
IN THE 2016 EU REFERENDUM**

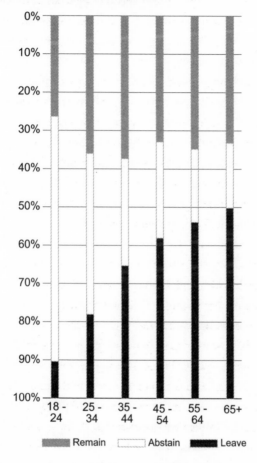

Data from Lord Ashcroft Polls combined by the New Statesman
with information from Sky Data.[9]

What is remarkable is how little is known about what actually happened, almost three years after the event.

In total, just over a quarter (28 per cent) of the entire UK electorate decided not to vote in the 2016 referendum. This is lower than in general elections, where in so many constituencies voting is practically pointless, but not that much lower. The turnout could well have been a decisive factor in the final result, partly because there were so many non-voters and partly because those who chose not to vote are thought to have been more likely to choose Remain. Electors were less likely to vote in areas where Remain support was revealed, in retrospect, to have been strongest.

However, it is worth remembering, before worrying too much that just a few factors could have drastically changed the result, that a victory for Remain, unless massive, would only have been temporary. There would have been call after call for a second referendum following a narrow Remain win. As much of the rest of this book explains, those who most wanted Britain to leave the EU, and had the money to help make that happen, were not especially influenced by ideas of democracy or fairness. They believed in destiny. They desperately wanted Britain to leave. But even they were shocked that Leave won on the first attempt. In a way, it was a little too early for them. They were not prepared for their victory, and did not know what to do with it. So why (and where) did they win?

The regional distribution of the vote is shown in the next graph (Figure 1.2). The geographical distribution of votes across the regions and countries of the United Kingdom is shown here as it compares to the UK average. Abstentions were highest in Scotland and then London, the two parts of the UK that were most strongly Remain. The next highest number of abstentions were in Northern Ireland, the other part of the UK best known for having a majority vote Remain. Had turnout in London and Scotland been nearer the UK average, this story would be very different; at the very least, the events of today would all have been delayed by a few years.

FIGURE 1.2: VOTING BY REGION
IN THE 2016 EU REFERENDUM

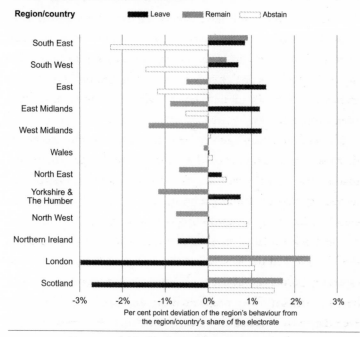

Region/country ■■■ Leave ▨▨▨ Remain ⬚⬚⬚ Abstain

Per cent point deviation of the region's behaviour from
the region/country's share of the electorate

Data provided by the Electoral Commission on turnout
by vote by country and region.[10]

Abstentions were lowest in the south-east, but there Leave and Remain were neck and neck. Next lowest were abstentions in the south-west (Leave majority), the east (largest majority vote for Leave), and then the East Midlands and West Midlands. In short, the Leave vote was 'got out'. There is much more that was not clearly seen in the immediate aftermath of the vote. For instance, in great contrast to the surprise expressed at the time over its Leave majority, Wales was actually the least unusual part of the UK, with its shares of Remain, Leave and abstentions being almost equal to the total UK shares. The south-east, in contrast, had a much lower proportion of people abstaining than average.

This is still not widely understood almost three years after the referendum itself.

Figure 1.2 shows the extent to which people in Britain were more or less likely to vote Leave, vote Remain, or not turn up, all as compared to the UK average. The measure on the horizontal axis is the share of the electorate in each region or country as it differed from the UK average proportions. The regions and countries are ordered from those in which abstention rates were the lowest – the south-east of England – to the area with the highest proportion of abstentions – Scotland. It is now believed that abstentions were highest in the three regions and countries where people were least likely to support Leave partly because people there more often thought the result was a foregone conclusion.

If you are going to remember one fact from this chapter, then remember this: because of different levels of turnout and numbers of registered voters, most people who voted Leave – by absolute numbers – lived in southern England. Furthermore, of all those who voted Leave, 59 per cent were middle class (often labelled as A, B or C1), and only 41 per cent were working class (labelled as C2, D or E). The proportion of Leave voters who were of the lowest two social classes (D and E) was just 24 per cent. One of us published these statistics not long after the vote, in the *British Medical Journal*,[11] but that did little to quell the middle-class clamour to try to 'blame the working class'.

Middle-class Leave voters were crucial to the final result. This was because the middle class constituted two thirds of all those who voted, partly due to their higher turnout rates. However, voters' class or region mattered less to the overall result than the personalities of those who led the campaigns. Within two weeks of the Leave win, Boris Johnson, Michael Gove and Nigel Farage had all given up their immediate UK political leadership ambitions or had been forced to by others. The repercussions of the outcome were as unexpected as the result itself. No one, especially Vote Leave campaign director and all-round political strategist Dominic Cummings – of whom we say more in the chapters that follow – had the ability to foretell the future in early 2016.

Immediately after the event, most commentators quickly realised that the vote in June 2016 would become a divisive element in the United Kingdom's politics for years to come. Thus, it was surprising that there was not a closer examination of the voting patterns. Such an inspection is essential to make more sense of the underlying divisions in society that need to be both understood and addressed. Close examination of the vote is also vital, if we are to know the likely future route of politics in this country. At the time of the result, many people wondered whether it was down to complacency among life's winners, and particularly in those areas where it was most assumed that Remain would prevail. So, was it complacency that led to this outcome?

It is possible to see the result less as a protest vote and more as the result of five key factors: a particular lack of voting in London; a relatively low turnout in Scotland; a similarly low turnout among the young; the denial of the vote to those aged sixteen and seventeen; and the exclusion of those who had the most interest of all in the outcome: the citizens of Europe who lived in the UK but were not born in the UK. Increasingly, new interpretations of the result see it as telling the British, and everyone else living in Britain at this time, about what was really going on in these islands, and most importantly what was in many people's minds and imaginations; especially in the minds of those who were allowed to vote, were registered to vote, and were inclined to vote.

In late 2017, four economists, Federica Liberini, Andrew J. Oswald, Eugenio Proto and Michela Redoano, examined newly released detailed survey data on the Brexit vote.[12] They concluded that unhappiness with life did influence the vote, but that 'the key channel of influence was not through general dissatisfaction with life. It was through a person's narrow feelings about his or her own financial situation.' They also found that the result was not entirely caused by the old. As they said in conclusion, looking at the carefully selected and weighted sample of voters they had to study: 'First, despite some commentators' views, Brexit was not caused by the attitudes of old people. Only the very young were disproportionately pro-Remain.' The analysis of their samples differs from that reported in Lord Ashcroft's exit poll (used in Figure 1.1 above), but it is worth noting that, when ignoring turnout and just concentrating on the exit poll, the greatest variation in support for Remain is between the youngest group (73 per cent) and the next youngest (62 per cent). Those in older age groups were far less positively Remain. And overall the young were not enthusiastic enough to outweigh the rest. But the result was close enough on that particular day for many variations to potentially have reversed the outcome.

Later in this book (in Chapter 6), we present more evidence that it was middle-class voters in Middle England areas that predominantly voted for Leave in the largest absolute numbers – the numbers that mattered. However, the paper written by these four economists also suggested that it was that subset of voters who were most likely to affirm that financially they were finding it quite difficult or very difficult to get by, who were most likely to vote Leave. As the economists explained, 'Feelings about income were, in these data, a substantially better predictor than actual income.' It was not the poor voters but the averagely off voters who *felt* poor that mattered most. A huge amount of research has now found that people on average incomes in very economically unequal countries, such as the UK, tend to fare badly and feel especially hard done by as a result of that economic inequality.[13]

A year earlier, two political scientists had produced interesting results that differed in some important ways. Matthew Goodwin and Oliver Heath wrote a paper for the Joseph Rowntree Foundation entitled 'Brexit vote explained: poverty, low skills and lack of op-portunities'. They did this in August 2016, just a few weeks after the vote.[14] They used data from part of the British Election Study: in particular, that collected from 31,000 people questioned via the in-ternet. These people were asked how they thought they would vote in May and June of 2016, each being asked to speculate on their own behaviour just a few weeks before the actual poll was held.

What Matthew and Oliver found of most importance was a very strong interaction effect whereby people with university de-grees or A levels who also lived in more affluent areas were 30 per cent more likely to say they would vote Remain than that same group of people who were living in poorer areas. They also found an effect of income and poverty, but it was not as strong as this interaction effect. The interaction effect meant that two things had to be in place for someone to be very likely to vote Remain: they had to both have good educational qualifications and live in an affluent area. Affluent people with many qualifications living in poorer areas, it transpires, often saw more clearly that all was not good in Britain in 2016.

At this point, it helps to introduce a map (see Figure 1.3). The map of the Brexit vote (whatever the projection used) is remarka-ble because it does not look like any other map of Britain's elector-al or social geography. For a start, Scotland clearly had a different enemy to worry about. For the Scots, the dominant institution taking away their sovereignty was based in London, not Brussels. Scotland was solidly Remain without any area of great exception. That is why every area in Scotland in the map below has a dot in it. The cartogram shown below resizes each voting area according to the total electorate living there. This helps explain why the out-come was frequently, but wrongly, blamed on the working class in the north of England; a traditional map makes the north look so much larger than it really is.

FIGURE 1.3: VOTING BY LOCAL AUTHORITY AREA IN THE 2016 EU REFERENDUM

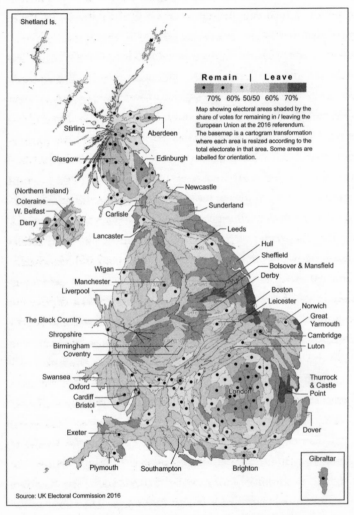

*Areas voting majority Remain have a dot placed in them,
with the strength of the vote shown by shading.*[15]

The next thing to point out is just how few areas voted for
Remain. The proportions of people who voted Remain in Remain

areas were much higher than the proportions of people who voted Leave in Leave areas. The map is drawn with area in proportion to population. It reveals that most areas of England and Wales voted majority Leave (areas with no dots in them), but only narrowly so. In the north, the exceptions are few and far between: the university towns with the most students – Newcastle, Lancaster, Leeds, Liverpool and Manchester – voted Remain. More areas stand out in the south, with central London, Oxford and Cambridge as the summits of Remain. However, even there, parts of suburban London were majority Leave, all around Oxfordshire was majority Leave, as was almost everywhere west and south of Swindon, bar the university towns of Bristol, Cardiff and Exeter.

You might look at the map and think it was poverty that mattered, but there are many very poor areas in London that voted solidly Remain, as well as much if not most of Liverpool and Manchester. Similarly, there are some areas with quite low rates of poverty, in Essex in particular, that were solidly Leave. It was not deprivation 'what done it'. On 25 June 2016, the brilliant academic and analyst Alasdair Rae showed that the correlation between voting Leave and constituency deprivation indices was just 0.037.[16] It was barely positive. In other words, there was very little evidence that the more deprived an area was, the more likely its residents were to vote Leave.

There are many other interesting analyses as to who voted in the referendum and why. One theory that hit the headlines suggested that fat people were responsible. Peter Ormosi, an Associate Professor of Competition Economics at the Norwich Business School (University of East Anglia), posted a blog on the London School of Economics website at the very end of June 2016 entitled: 'The weight of Brexit: Leave vote is higher in areas of higher obesity'.[17] Peter reported correlations of 0.80 (very high in comparison to the deprivation correlation of 0.037). He then speculated that because 'neurotic people are more likely to have [eating] disorders', then it is possible that the correlation he found reflects those neuroses. Not surprisingly, this did not make him very popular in certain circles. As one voter retorted: 'I am quite trim and voted out of the undemocratic EU ruled by unelected commissioners.'[18]

On 30 June 2016, ITV reported the news as 'UEA research claims link between obesity and Brexit voters'.[19] On 1 July, the *Daily Express* ran the headline 'Outrage after academic says Brexit voters were probably FAT',[20] reporting that 'the jibe is the latest insult fired at leave voters already labelled "stupid" and "Little Englanders" on social media sites'. No newspaper asked why the correlation was so high and what it could really be telling us. Areas in which people tend to be thinner are often very similar to each other in many other ways.

Peter Ormosi managed to produce one of the best examples of why correlation is not causation. He used public health data to suggest that the more obese people there were in an area, the more the area voted Leave.[21] Many other analyses showed that the fewer immigrants there were in the area, the more people voted to leave, in both working- and middle-class areas. The village in the Cotswolds where the trimmer one of the two of us lives was very much pro-Leave, for example, and is home to almost no immigrants from overseas. So, was a part of this correlation due to immigrants being more likely to be thinner than the more settled, more sedentary population? But immigrants from the EU did not vote at the referendum; they were not eligible. So skinny Spaniards and svelte Italians were not themselves going out to vote Remain to make these correlations so strong.

The very strong relationship between the number of local immigrants and the likelihood of an area voting Leave was also shown to have mattered greatly very early on. On 18 July 2016, the appropriately named Mario Cortina Borja, Julian Stander and

Luciana Dalla Valle wrote a brief but highly informative paper titled 'The EU referendum: surname diversity and voting patterns'. In it, they included a figure showing that in both England and Wales the more people there were in an area with unique names, the fewer Leave voters there were; but in Scotland there was no such relationship. Areas with many people having a unique name tend to be areas of high immigration from a disparate set of places of origin.[22] We will return to the geographical clues in the vote, as to what mattered most in terms of local influences, in Chapters 6 and 8. Here, we turn back to the national campaigns.

The national media matters. In May 2017, a study was released of the 14,779 newspaper and magazine articles that had mentioned the referendum in the run-up to the vote over the final ten weeks of the campaign. It concluded that:

- Coverage of immigration more than tripled over the course of the campaign, rising faster than any other political issue.
- Immigration was the most prominent referendum issue, based on the number of times it led newspaper print front pages (there were 99 front pages about immigration, 82 about the economy).
- Coverage of the effects of immigration was overwhelmingly negative. Migrants were blamed for many of Britain's economic and social problems – most notably for putting unsustainable pressure on public services.
- Specific nationalities were singled out for particularly negative coverage – especially Turks and Albanians, but also Romanians and Poles.[23]

To maintain support for Leave requires maintaining fear of immigrants, but how will that be done as net immigration begins to fall?[24]

CONCLUSION

What has happened since the referendum? Almost immediately, support for Leave dipped below Remain, but not by much. At the very end of 2017, polling company BMG revealed that Remain had only managed to draw ahead of Leave in February of that year, almost ten months after the actual vote. However, BMG's head of polling Michael Turner pointed out that 'digging deeper into the data reveals that this shift has come predominantly from those who did not actually vote in the 2016 referendum, with around nine in ten Leave and Remain voters still unchanged in their view'.[25]

What really lay beneath all this? As Ian Jack pointed out in early 2018, we now know that in January 2016, '43% of British people believed the British empire was a good thing and only 19% a bad thing, with 25% believing it was neither. Furthermore, 44% felt that Britain's history of colonialism was something to be proud of and only 19% felt it should be regretted.'[26] It was not that Leave voters were fat. It was not that Leave voters were poorer, or more stupid, or cleverer. It was that they thought quite differently on many issues from most Remain voters – especially Remain voters with a degree or A levels who lived in more affluent places where all was relatively fine.

Statistical analysis is never enough. We need to know to what extent ideology and understanding played a part. How might those understandings change in the years to come as we learn more about ourselves and our history, and as Brexit – in whatever form it takes – changes our position in the world? We may learn more about gender from the vote, about how British men and British women differ, especially in middle age. As Ipsos MORI pointed out, 'A very small majority of women voted to remain, while men voted to leave. The biggest gender differences were among the AB social class and among those aged 35–54, among both of whom women were eleven points more likely to vote to remain than men.'[27]

What is it that most differentiates middle-aged men from middle-aged women? Could it be that the men are more frustrated with their lot for some reason? What mattered was not the reality of who was faring worse, but who felt that they were faring worse than they *deserved*. Men and women in the past were educated very differently from each other. Men were routinely taught that they deserved more than women: better jobs, higher pay, more respect. Or maybe women tend to be more risk-averse? Leaving the EU would be a big step into the unknown.

Some men are, of course, delighted with the Leave vote, especially those who played a large part in bringing about the result. One of those is Dominic Cummings, the so-called mastermind of the Brexit campaign, set to be played by Benedict Cumberbatch in a Channel 4 television drama about the referendum to be aired just before the actual departure in March 2019. We will see more of Cummings later.[28] The 29 March point of departure is now widely predicted to be a day of reckoning, regardless of what transition deals may or may not be agreed by then. As one academic put it in spring 2017, 'Articulating and responding to the divisions that were laid bare by the events of 2016 will be the primary challenge of tomorrow.'[29] Tomorrow has arrived.

CHAPTER 2

BRITAIN'S IMMIGRANT ORIGINS

The United Kingdom of Great Britain and Northern Ireland came into being in a series of treaties between its constituent nations, England and Wales in 1536, with Scotland in 1707 and with Ireland, thus formalizing its long-standing occupation, in 1801. Not dissimilar to other nation states, its creation involved political, administrative and imaginative efforts.

— Tariq Modood and colleagues, 2012[1]

INTRODUCTION

British history is currently greatly contested and that long-running debate partly explains the Brexit referendum.[2] There was an ancient Roman province called Britannia, but its female personification, the goddess Britannia, had disappeared as a symbol in Britain for almost 1,500 years until she was revived shortly before the 1707 Act of Union.

In the fifth and sixth centuries, following the fall of the Roman Empire, what we now call England was carved out by immigrant warlords to make tribal territories. A few were Saxons. Others were Vikings, Angles, Jutes, and Danish kings, who fought each other repeatedly.

Rather than never (never never) being slaves, as the chorus of 'Rule Britannia' implies, many ancient Britons were slaves of the Romans, the Vikings and the Danes and then for many centuries they were vassals of the feudal Normans. Much British land is still owned by the invading families who were clustered around William the Conqueror in 1066. A Dutch stadtholder replaced the King of England in 1688. However, it was not long before British emigrants began invading other countries – though of course they never saw themselves as immigrants when they did so.

The British Empire beyond these islands was built up by an immigrant people, who, as they took control of more and more provinces overseas, began to create and embellish yet more patriotic myths about those from 'home'. Then, as the empire declined, these myths of Great Britain lingered on and were further bolstered to help those trying to hold on to a greater and greater share of a shrinking national pie.

IMAGINATIVE EFFORTS

Tariq Modood is putting it politely when he talks of 'imaginative efforts'. In October 2017, the then leader of UKIP, Henry Bolton, claimed that 'in certain communities the indigenous Anglo-Saxon population is nowhere to be seen'. Like so many of the most fervent supporters of Brexit, Henry was born in an outpost of the former empire, Nairobi in Kenya. He is a former lance-corporal of the Royal Hussars. He has also worked for the British Foreign and Commonwealth Office, including in Afghanistan.[3]

A few months before Henry Bolton made his Anglo-Saxon claims, the Odinist Fellowship wrote to the Church of England demanding reparations for the oppression of the Anglo-Saxon nation by Christianity. The Odinists believe in the god Odin, and that Anglo-Saxons migrated to become the dominant group in

Britain in the fifth and sixth centuries. This, however, is untrue. As Duncan Sayer, a Reader in Archaeology, explained in 2017:

> In the US, this mixed-up medievalism is associated with the white supremacist alt-right who use Anglo-Saxon and Viking motifs. But archaeological research, which examines ancient DNA and artefacts to explore who these 'indigenous' Anglo-Saxons were, shows that the people of fifth and sixth century England had a mixed heritage and did not base their identity on a biological legacy. The very idea of the Anglo-Saxon ancestor is a more recent invention linked closely with the English establishment.[4]

Sayer went on to explain that it was not until the sixteenth century, as the myth of Britain was beginning to be established, that the term Anglo-Saxon was used at all. Those who lived in the British Isles were a far more mixed bunch than simply being mainly Anglo-Saxon. However, the Anglo-Saxon myth later became politically useful, especially during the First World War, to try to downplay anti-German sentiment over the German (British) royal family – they were also Anglo-Saxon and so apparently just like 'us'. On the Anglo-Saxon myth, Sayer concluded:

> Today, the term Anglo-Saxon is a convenient label for those opposed to future immigration. While it collectively describes some post-Roman and early medieval culture, it has never accurately described a biological ethnicity nor an indigenous people. The DNA evidence points to an integrated people of mixed ancestry who lived side by side. Anglo-Saxon ancestry is a modern English myth – the English are not descended from one group of people, but from many and that persists in our culture and in our genes.

All this is not ancient history. In Oxfordshire in the 1970s, all state school children were required, once a year, to build Anglo-Saxon houses out of lollipop sticks, with fake thatch on top made from straw. (Shrewd parents kept the model house stored away so that the next sibling could tart it up and bring it into the school in a later year.) Returning to Oxfordshire a few years ago, with young children, one of us was amazed to find this myth-making about the ethnic origin of the English is still continuing, as if nothing had been learnt since the 1970s. To this day, Oxfordshire school children still make an Anglo-Saxon model house every year so that they can imagine some fictional history to relate to; though today, of course, most of the parents of those children, if not the children themselves, never came from the county of Oxfordshire – they are migrants, mostly from elsewhere in the UK, increasingly from elsewhere in the world.

It is time we packed that 'Anglo-Saxon' house away for good.

THE LAST THROES OF EMPIRE THINKING

Our contention is that the EU referendum showed up the last throes of empire-thinking working its way out of the British psyche.[5] We suggest that Britain had only joined what became the EU in the 1970s because the old British Empire had fallen apart. Country after country had won independence and escaped from the control of the British by the late 1960s. No one had explained to the British that Britain had become rich by exploiting the land and labour of colonised countries.

From the mid-1970s onwards, Britain began to get into serious economic difficulty, worse than the crises in other countries at the time because of the double whammy of no longer receiving what was in effect tribute from so many colonies that had so recently been trapped in the empire.

When others are forced to buy your expensive goods rather

than making their own or buying from cheaper countries, they are paying tribute. When you destroy the textile industry in one continent, after enslaving people from a second continent and forcing them to pick cotton in a third continent to be woven in Manchester, all to make a profit, you are receiving tribute. Your wealth is built up through great military power and controlling a monopoly. Nations can become addicted to receiving tribute and addicted to the idea of not having to do very much to be rich. Then, when the former colonies are no longer forced to buy your Manchester cotton, nor all your other empire produce, the flow of tribute ends. The attempts to reboot tribute via a banking 'Big Bang' eventually failed. In the November 2017 Budget, it was revealed that national debt would not return to 2008 levels until 2060 (and that's assuming there are no further recessions)[6] and British families were experiencing 'the longest period of continuous falls in disposable incomes in over 60 years'.[7]

Whatever kind of Brexit occurs – hard, soft, or even a cancellation and staying in the European Union – Britain will be much diminished by the Brexit process. Already the British have lost face in a multitude of small ways. More additional money had to be found to pay for Brexit in the November 2017 Budget than could be found for the NHS.[8] On the same day as that Budget, we also learnt that Britain would lose its special place on the International Court of Justice for the first time since the court's inception in 1946.[9]

The arguing and making of claims and counter-claims about its national status has not improved the image of Britain in the eyes of much of the rest of the world.[10] But there is an upside. The British may well learn a great deal about themselves as a result of what they are going through. Not least that Britain, and even Brexit, has its deepest roots embedded firmly in the ashes of the British Empire.

It is not hard for modern-day Britons to be a little confused over who they are or where they have come from. Many were born abroad but are now British. Even more have at least one parent who was born abroad, and yet more have at least one grandparent who was an immigrant. Thanks to the British Empire, London is now the most ethnically mixed large city in the world.[11] It is the real global melting pot – the biggest of big apples.[12] New York pales in comparison, yet celebrations of Britain's multicultural global supremacy are few and far between. There are, for instance, no British national museums devoted to immigration or to the empire and its associated atrocities.[13] In contrast, there are many museums devoted to, or touching upon, slavery in Britain, the largest being in Liverpool. The slave museums may be popular with some benefactors because of the Conservative myth that their MP William Wilberforce abolished slavery in 1833. It was hardly abolished as far as the living conditions of many slaves were concerned, but a lot of slave-holding families became exceedingly rich from the compensation Wilberforce helped to arrange.

In the USA, people's histories of immigration are celebrated and the birthplaces of both parents and grandparents are recorded in American census forms, but this is not the case in Britain. This is partly because the empire was once seen as a single indivisible entity: individual countries of origin within the empire were considered irrelevant. Exact numbers are therefore hard to estimate, but very few people will have only British ancestors stretching back to pre-empire days.

The Parliament of Great Britain came into being when the Act of Union between Scotland and England took effect in 1707. Before then there was no Britain, at least not as we know her today. Britain's namesake, Britannia, the goddess, first appeared on Roman coins around 119 AD but disappeared as a symbol on coins in Britain for almost 1,500 years until she was revived shortly before that Act of Union.[14] (In 2017, a particularly warlike Britannia was designed by Central St Martin's student Louis Tamlyn to grace the royal mint's five-ounce gold coin. Following the Brexit vote, the worth of the gold in the coin rose to almost £8,500 as the value of the pound dropped.)

FIGURE 2.1: THE BRITANNIA 2017 UK FIVE-OUNCE GOLD PROOF COIN

Reverse design by Louis Tamlyn, a student at Central Saint Martins: 'Britannia is arguably the oldest and most famous symbol of Britain'. We are grateful to the Royal Mint for permission to reproduce this image.[15]

It is worth thinking a little more deeply about why the symbol of Britannia was revived shortly after 1707, the purposes for which it is used today, and just how important the empire was in creating what we think of as today's 'British' identity – which has so little to do with the island of Britain. As the BBC explained in

February 2018, 'Modern Britons trace just a small fraction of their ancestry to the people who built Stonehenge.' This is due to a very effective, almost rampant, continuous immigration. That process of constant immigration involved virtually the entire replacement of the 'indigenous' population around 4,500 years ago by one of the first of so many invasions.[16]

Today, Britannia is a patriotic symbol that can be used to create a largely artificial sense of nationhood and of the rightful position and destiny of the peoples who now live in the British Isles. In short, Britannia is used for propaganda and the creation of a myth. This deception is at least 300 years old. For instance, every statement in the song 'Rule Britannia', penned a few decades after the Act of Union, is untrue:

> When Britain first, at Heaven's command
> Arose from out the azure main;
> This was the charter of the land,
> And guardian angels sang this strain:
> 'Rule, Britannia! rule the waves:
> Britons never ever ever will be slaves.'

Britain has an incredible legacy of myths, tales and songs used to spin a national myth that is very different from the reality. Later came 'Jerusalem', the song that became known as the unofficial anthem of Britain. It was adopted by Women's Institutes in the 1920s. Three eminent composers had a hand in putting William Blake's 1804 poem to music in 1916. 'Jerusalem' was intended to stir up patriotic feelings during and after the First World War.[17] It is not an ancient song. It was a poem revived and recast when it was thought that a renewed sense of patriotism was required. Again, we suggest you ask what the logical answer to each couplet is:

And did those feet in ancient times
Walk upon England's mountains green?
And was the holy Lamb of God
On England's pleasant pastures seen?
And did the Countenance Divine,
Shine forth upon our clouded hills?
And was Jerusalem builded here,
Among these dark Satanic mills?

The answer to each question in the lyrics above was and remains 'No'. What Blake actually intended his poem to be about can be debated. He certainly mentions the terrible injustices faced by the enslaved workers in textile mills – those 'dark Satanic mills'. However, during the First World War, it was interpreted as being triumphant. King George V wrote that he preferred the song to the national anthem and in March 2016, on its centenary, David Cameron suggested it should take the place of 'God Save the Queen'. He was not joking.

BRITAIN'S IMMIGRANT ORIGINS

The Angles were a Germanic tribe who invaded what became known as the 'land of the Angles'. The Jutes and Saxons, two other Germanic tribes, also invaded. Saxon and Danish kings then fought each other repeatedly. Eventually, Cnut or Canute (1016–35) imposed taxes and married a Norman lady. Four kings later, Harold was defeated by William the Conqueror in 1066 and all the 'English' (not British until much later) royal families thereafter were of Norman French, Dutch or German extraction.

The Normans, whose main base was in France, expanded their empire into Ireland, colonising that province in 1169. Then, in 1282 under Norman (English) King Edward I, they conquered Wales, annexing the principality. Ever since then, the heir to the

English throne has been titled the Prince of Wales, deliberately denying the Welsh their own dynasty. But the English were also subjugated. The rulers of England were not English; they did not speak English but French. They did not look like typical English people of the time, who were more often blond; the elite generally had dark hair.

The Normans and their friends who controlled the land of the Angles (Angle-land, as in Eng-er-land) in the centuries after 1282 tried repeatedly to invade and conquer the Kingdom of Scotland. And they repeatedly failed. Henry VIII married his sister to the Scottish king, but it took two more centuries to secure the 1707 Act of Union with Scotland. There had been attempts before to combine England and Scotland, but all had failed. Much later, the Victorians would try to rename Scotland 'northern Britain', which took myth-making a step too far; it never caught on.

So why was the Act of Union finally successful in 1707? It was not due to an English liking for the kilt, which in fact only came into its own after the Act passed. Indeed, Parliament considered banning the kilt in 1715 as 'on a windy day, or going up a hill or stooping, the indecency of it is plainly disclosed'.[18] No, the answer is that there was finally something worth coming together over – and that something was the new empire that was being created overseas. War at home was too costly a price to pay when it became clear there were such great spoils to be won abroad. Initially those spoils were realised by raiding Spanish galleons; later by the taking of colonies. A little greed can lead to much evil.

An (imperial) United Kingdom was resisted by rebel forces. There was an attempt at Scottish independence with the Jacobite rising in 1745, decisively defeated in 1746 at the Battle of Culloden, and still viewed by many Scots as a disaster. Similarly, some Welsh nationalists still see the 1282 conquest as a disaster. Invasions in Scottish and Welsh history are resented, whereas the English attitude to the Battle of Hastings is often very different; indeed, some texts even celebrate it. For the English, 1066 is taught as part of a glorious history stretching back into folk memory. Apparently, according to a very recent and popular GCSE textbook, 'The Normans were foreign invaders taking over a proud country with a strong identity.'[19] Quite how history textbooks published in 2016 know of the pride that English folk felt for England a millennium before is not clear. The first decent survey of England was not conducted until 1086, and even then, the Domesday survey was more concerned with counting wealth than people. We continue to write utter fabrications in school textbooks for our modern jingoistic purposes.

What rubbish we so often still teach our children. Brexit might just be the trigger we need to more widely recognise this – there is hope! We still teach them a history of adventurers and explorers, when the reality is usually far less exotic, mostly concerning thieves and murderous pirates. What later became called the British Empire started with greed for gold and the need for food. Some historians claim the antecedents of the empire began when English fishermen got as far as Newfoundland in the 1540s to fish for cod to feed the English Navy. It also began with avarice: during Queen Elizabeth I's reign, English aristocrats sponsored many pirates to steal from the Spanish and Portuguese. And, finally, accident played a part. The first overseas colony began with a shipwreck in 1609 on Bermuda, which is now one of just over a dozen UK overseas tax havens.

Between 1609 and 1707, it had become clear to those running England and Scotland that they could do far better exploiting people in these faraway places than attacking each other. The last of the major invaders of the British Isles, the Dutch, who had been living in the richest and most powerful country in the world before the British Empire emerged, invaded England in 1688.

That invasion was rebranded 'The Glorious Revolution', in one of many misrepresentations of 'British' history, pandering to the egos of the English, who like to pretend to themselves that they have never been defeated in (almost) 1,000 years.

Following the 1707 Act of Union, the creation of a new myth of Britannia and Britain began in earnest in the newly merged nation, as those ruling it wanted the people to believe their monarchs were sovereign by some kind of divine right – sovereign because their families had always ruled. The family tree that attempts to prove this point gets quite complicated. There is an enormous dose of illegitimacy, secrets, lies and deceit in the lineage of the British royal family, which will be familiar to the avid reader of modern history, but which we do not yet teach routinely in our schools. In any case, the ancestral chart certainly doesn't answer the question a child might ask: how can you have always ruled something which has only just been created as a geographical entity? The song 'Rule Britannia' was a poem set to music by Thomas Arne in 1740. The poem was written by the Scottish playwright James Thomson, who was subsequently given a pension of £100 a year by the then Prince of Wales in return for demonstrating such patriotism and skill at early propaganda.[20]

Notably, the Prince of Wales in 1740 was Frederick Ludwig of Brunswick-Lüneburg, a grandson of George I, the elector of Hanover. Frederick had been born in Germany in 1707 when 'Great Britain' was being created. He did not set foot in England until 1728. This is not much dwelt on in traditional history books (see Figure 2.2).

The newly christened British, or at least those who were quickest to accept their newly created history and new united identity, began founding colonies and setting up trading posts. The West Indies was swiftly populated by a vastly expanded, infamous global slave trade, at which the British excelled. The East India Company began the looting of India and exporting opium and its addiction to China. The early empire appeared to begin falling apart when those colonists that the English thought were just 'a rabble of farmers' in the thirteen American colonies defeated the British Army and won their war for independence in the early 1780s. From then on, the British became far more vicious in their dealings with their colonies. They had learnt that they could lose them, could lose the empire. Britain's formative identity was as the heart of an empire.

FIGURE 2.2: THE 'BRITISH NATION' FROM 55 BC TO 1912 – THE MAKING OF A MYTH

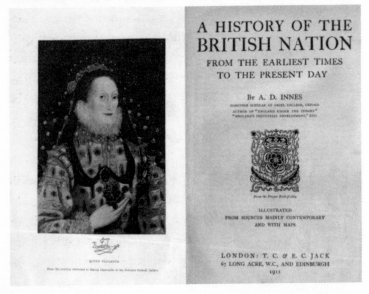

Presenting Britain as if it were a nation, and one with a much longer history.[21]

The Britain we know today is not a country. It is a collection of four small countries, which the BBC calls nations. Great Britain is the term used for the collection of just three nations, and also for the largest island of the British Isles. It is a remnant of an empire; it is all that is left. Together with three Crown Dependencies and fourteen small British Overseas Territories, mostly being tax havens, it is the shattered remains of a once great – if short-lived – empire. Some of the British still like to describe the empire as just one small part of a long and glorious history of the British nation.[22] But there never was a British nation or a 'Great Britain' before empire; it was a cold, damp, backward, unimportant archipelago. The British needed a fabricated royal family tree, in which infidelity was ignored, and they needed legends of imperial glory, of knights and round table, to control those below them – and to provide an image of legitimacy.[23]

So, what has all this to do with Brexit, you might well ask. National identity shapes our politics, and that matters greatly when thinking about Brexit. How the British see themselves matters enormously in determining voting behaviour, and what matters most is how the English view themselves and England, as they made up by far the largest group of voters in the EU referendum. A survey by YouGov for the BBC in 2018 found that, in England, Conservative voters were much more likely to say they are proud to be English (77 per cent) than those who supported Labour (45 per cent) or the Liberal Democrats (42 per cent). Pride in identifying as English was weaker among the young (45 per cent) and stronger among the old (72 per cent). Three quarters of Leave supporters in the Brexit referendum reported a high level of pride in being English; among those who voted Remain that applied to less than half.[24]

BEING BRITISH

The most interesting part of the British Isles is the island of Ireland – interesting because in so many ways it isn't part of Britain. However, it contains a group of people who think they are absolutely British and who are ultra-patriotic, but many of whose ancestors were previously Scottish (not even 'northern British'). Ireland, the first country to be colonised by the English (Normans) in 1169, was subject to exploitation, derision and famine over the centuries. It has an inglorious history, a history which may not help Theresa May, the British Prime Minister at the time of writing, who depends on Northern Irish DUP votes to keep her in power and to keep her Brexit process going.

Most older white English people, including the supposedly well educated, know little about the reality of the empire into which their grandparents or great-grandparents were born, or how it transformed into a Commonwealth. In 1949, the Commonwealth had just eight members. Many countries came and went as they gained independence, fell out of favour or came to dislike the association. By 2009, when Rwanda joined, it had become a Commonwealth of some fifty-three states, thirty of which are still home to fewer than three million people each. In contrast, black and Asian people tend to be better educated about the empire and its exploits, as are most of the Irish and the Scots. The English were mainly taught at school about things like Henry VIII's six wives and (if attending a Catholic school) his possible syphilis, but not much about what really happened in the empire that later evolved out of his daughter Elizabeth's plundering.

To be fair to the people of Britain, there was an awful lot of former empire to know about and a few remote places are still included, such as the Falkland Island Dependencies. In 1982, when Argentina invaded the Falkland Islands, many English people initially thought that they were Scottish islands! Hardly anyone in Britain knew then that they were also called *las islas Malvinas* or that, as Antonio Castillo explains, 'the first buildings in Las Malvinas – or the Falklands as the British call the islands in the South Atlantic – were houses made of stone and were built by Argentinean hands',[25] They also did not know that, in 1833, the British 'ethnically cleansed' the islands, expelling Argentineans after invading the islands. Today, people living on the periphery of Britain, and those whose forefathers were cowed in previous colonies, often have a better knowledge of the history of Britain than those who live in Middle England. Those on the periphery more often know how much of that British history was not great but shameful. This includes fairly recent history. Think, for instance, of the Chagos Islanders, expelled from their homes by the British government in the 1960s so that the Americans could build an air base on the islands. The British, or more particularly a few of the English, kept on taking away other people's homes and rights, right up to the present day.

The Scots and Irish mostly did not vote for Brexit, nor the Welsh in Welsh-speaking areas of Wales, and neither did most Londoners, nor the majority of the young. Did these five groups have anything in common? Did these people tend to have a rather different understanding of British history, perhaps less jingoistic? As it becomes better understood that the key vote for Leave came from the English home counties and the narrow band of counties that surround them, the imperial legacy of colonisation and the failure to decolonise the English school curriculum may become more and more obvious. Universities may be more alert now to students from all backgrounds who want to decolonise the curriculum by demanding a better education with a greater representation of non-European thinkers. But British universities still have so much to learn. People in the university in which we both work even defend leaving the statue of a despot on the highest plinth looking over the public high street rather than moving it indoors and adding a plaque explaining that it was once there and why it was ever carved.

The debate about removing statues of colonisers, especially Cecil Rhodes at Oxford, will not go away and will eventually be won. During 2017, students and academics at Cambridge were in discussion about the teaching of post-colonial English literature, which drew national attention, resulting in racist and sexist abuse on social media and in some of the mainstream media. The whole episode was carefully documented and explained by Maev Kennedy in 2017.[26] However, other journalists are less careful, mistaking the views of a single student as representing a group, for instance. In 2018, the removal of a portrait of Theresa May at Oxford following student protest was not because, as *The Sun* claimed, it offended 'de-colonial scholars'.[27] In truth, May's role in the creation of a hostile environment for immigrants, the Windrush scandal and the heightened sensitivities during the Brexit process were far more important than concerns about decolonialisation, which in the course of the protests was mentioned by only a single student. In fact, the portrait was most upsetting to staff within the department who did not like having to walk past it, especially some who were EU but not UK citizens. (On the other hand, it could be argued that mounting the portrait makes clearer the complicit role of the University of Oxford in producing politicians like May, and her many predecessors.) Brexit brings to the fore a great many issues previously brushed under the carpet. Exactly what do we have to be proud of about Britain or its Prime Ministers?

However Brexit is resolved, whatever is done now, Britain's status in the world and in Europe will inevitably be much reduced, even if the UK somehow stays in the European Union. It will be difficult for the English, fed on so much past imperial propaganda, to accept a reduced place in the world after Brexit. The Scots, who suffered deindustrialisation first in the mid-1970s, have had longer to get used to the new global realities. Brexit partly came about because some were finding it very hard before the vote to accept Britain's current status as not special compared to other countries. They were hoping to put the 'Great' back into Great Britain. The whole idea of being just one of twenty-eight

European states, and of having to co-operate and compromise, rather than lording it over them, had never gone down well with the manufactured British psyche. No other state in Europe prefixes its title with a word like 'great' except the Grand Duchy of Luxembourg, and there they don't insist on being called grand. There is no 'Team GD' representing the Grand Duchy in sporting events.[28] In no other country can you read books such as Rosemarie Jarski's *Great British Wit: The greatest assembly of British wit and humour ever*, in which the author feels she needs to tell us both that she is British – presumably because of her surname – and also that she has a bulldog called Adolf.[29] What could be more British than that?!

Many people in Britain, especially the Scots, are now learning that they are not part of something that is especially 'Great'. This understanding in Scotland came about through decades of English abuse, from the early introduction of the poll tax to the English ignoring deals made during the Scottish independence campaign. The Scots voted to stay in the UK after they were promised greater respect if they did. The Scots were assured that remaining in the Union was the only way to guarantee their membership of the EU. Then the English voted to exclude them from the EU and showed no respect at all!

Across all of the UK, some 60 per cent of all those voting for Brexit were aged over sixty and had mostly started school between 1930 and 1960 – too young to have served in the Second World War but imbued with the idea that the British (rarely the Allies) had won that war simply because they were great. They included those men who did National Service between 1946 and 1962, who were pressed into fighting colonial wars, and who had been told that people fighting to reclaim their own countries for democracy were the enemy.

The British thought they had done something in World War II

that no other European nation had been capable of doing, and Churchillian oratory entered the national psyche. These older people came from a generation that was schooled to feel superior to British 'colonials', other Europeans and all other foreigners. Almost all of this generation had experienced an ethnocentric jingoistic curriculum in which 'men of renown' had conquered and plundered countries inhabited by heathens apparently in need of missionaries. The victims were depicted as uneducated savages, primitive people, a smattering of cannibals and other natives; so much so that even 'natives' became a derogatory term. The British were implicitly and explicitly taught myths of empire. In 1948, an *Empire Youth Annual* described an exciting train journey from Delhi to Lahore without once mentioning the horrors of the previous year's partition when many thousands of people were massacred along that single route in the refugee crisis created by Britain's botched division of India.

The high point of the celebration of empire came long after its point of greatest economic dominance, which peaked around 1897. In the 1920s and '30s, notions of free trade were abandoned and 'imperial preference' was imposed, which required British greatness to be emphasised. It was at the very point that empire was beginning to fall apart that ideas of British exceptionalism began to be most strongly developed. The Empire Exhibition in London in 1924 was aimed at persuading people to buy the empire's goodies and not 'foreign muck'. A life-size statue of the Prince of Wales made of Canadian butter melted at the event. However, other aspects had a much longer shelf life. The official caterer for the Indian Pavilion of the Empire Exhibition eventually opened the first Indian restaurant in Britain. But today the balti (northern Pakistani) food he served may be in peril due to British immigration officials denying visas to balti chefs.

A character in Andrea Levy's appropriately titled book *Small*

Island,[30] visiting the Empire Exhibition and seeing an African woman skilfully weaving cloth, was told, 'They are backward, we've got machines to do that' and 'They only understand drums.' Later in the book, her black friend tries to tell her husband about his arrogant assumption that he is better because he is white: 'You want to know what your white skin makes you? It makes you white. That's all. No better, no worse than me.' But the message is incomprehensible to a man who is convinced of the superiority of British whites over all 'coloureds' and all foreigners. It is not just the right wing in Britain who think they know better than foreigners.

SOVEREIGNTY

There are many people on the left of British politics who argue that the EU is a neoliberal club that blocks the introduction, for instance, of socialist policies. Others on the right simply object to the British not having full control over all aspects of what happens within their borders. They promote a hostility to globalisation and the avowed progression to a European federalised super-state. But they also have a tendency to believe in a Great Britain that could better manage its own affairs. In this context, it should be pointed out that the year of the EU referendum was not the EU's finest hour. The refugee crisis, the aftermath of the global financial crash and the European debt crisis were not being handled well.

The EU is very far from a perfect union, but its left-wing critics rarely point out that the UK has become far more neoliberal than the rest of Europe, and that many of the progressive developments that were occurring on the Continent were (and still are) not found in Britain. That is worth repeating again. The most innovative forms of education, the best-funded healthcare systems, the highest quality of housing, the greatest job protection and productivity, and the lowest rates of poverty are all found in parts of the mainland of Europe, not in Britain.

When those on the left of British politics try to point out Britain's failures, they are often labelled unpatriotic, with increasing undertones suggesting that such talk verges on treason. The left need to remember that the right have traditionally blamed them for Britain's decline. The right blamed Britain's economic difficulties on trade unions at home in the 1960s and then on those Arabs and their oil in the 1970s, but in reality, a key reason for the country's economic woes at the time was the loss of tribute by way of unfair trade arrangements from the rapidly shrinking empire.[31]

The city of Rome could no longer be quite the same city after the Roman Empire collapsed. Similarly, London – the single largest and richest city on the planet not so long ago – fell into what Patrick Wright called 'ruins' in his prescient 1991 book on Britain at the height of the Thatcher years.[32] London had become 'ruined' by 1991 because the money had run out. A new way to bring money in was then found, no longer through the tribute of unfair terms of trade, but by becoming the supreme financial juggler for the world. The 1986 Big Bang of the City of London was born out of the ruins. The Big Bang was shorthand for deregulation, initiated so that enormous profits could be made – profits large enough to emulate the tribute of the past. For the following twenty-two years, the City laid golden eggs for the British (or rather, the southern English) until, in 2008, the banks fell apart and almost bankrupted the UK. They fell apart because they had been so poorly regulated. Then something new was needed, and the next escape plan was to go it alone; a brave new Britain throwing off the shackles of Europe.

There is a great irony to wanting so very badly to leave a club that the British had so recently wanted very much to join. Back in the 1960s and early 1970s, the British had repeatedly asked the members of the forerunners of the European Union for permission to join and repeatedly they were turned down. These rebuffs were especially painful as Britain had had the chance to be involved during the early days, and had opted not to. Eventually, on 1 January 1973, the British were finally allowed to join the Common Market. They then held a referendum to confirm that membership on 5 June 1975. Politicians such as Margaret Thatcher campaigned for the UK to join, partly because, back then, most of Europe was politically further to the right than the UK. Of all the large European countries, only Sweden (which was not even an EEC member at the time) had lower income inequality than the UK in 1975. Ever since that initial referendum, many of the old empire diehards have been working to try to reverse that decision. Now they seem to have got their way, and what has followed has been described as all-out war between politicians.[33]

Few people today believe that Brexit is a marvellous opportunity to renew our imperial contacts. But it was not long ago that the UK Independence Party was telling us that 'outside the EU, the world is our oyster, and the Commonwealth the pearl within'. UKIP was starry-eyed about the old empire. Boris Johnson began to fall off his bike with enthusiasm for world trade outside the EU. He was countered by David Cameron's argument about 40 per cent of our trade being with the EU and the difficulty of doing deals with the rest of the world. However, Cameron's motives for promising and, unexpectedly, having to have, an EU referendum were sufficiently dubious to make him appear untrustworthy, allowing Johnson to sound statesman-like in comparison.

Of the more than 100 former colonies, protectorates and dominions once ruled by Britain (depending on how you count them), fifty-two eventually transformed into the Commonwealth, while some remain as British Overseas Territories and Crown Dependencies. Thirty of those are not very significant for trade, having populations of less than three million or so, but fifteen operate as tax havens. Hardly any of the other European overseas territories are tax havens (see Figure 2.3). The empire has largely gone. What remains today is chiefly significant because of its international tax avoidance/evasion industry.

FIGURE 2.3: EU OVERSEAS TERRITORIES AND OUTERMOST REGIONS 2018

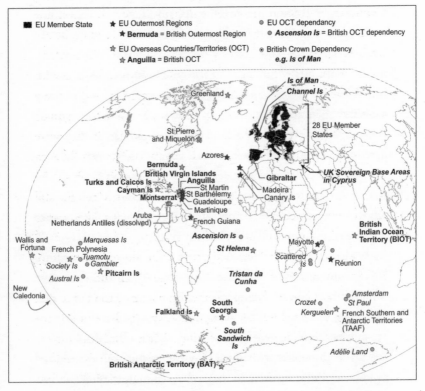

The British Overseas Territories and Crown Dependencies are labelled in bold.[34]

As we write in November 2018, in the very near future Britain will have three choices: it could return humiliated to the European Union by not actually leaving at the last minute; or it could only partly leave (soft Brexit and a long transition) and so lose power and influence while still having to abide by the rules; or it could bail out very fast (hard Brexit). None of these are good choices any more. If that last option is chosen, then persuading former colonial countries to sign trade deals will be difficult. You only need to look at other trade deals to see that.

The Trans-Pacific Partnership was negotiated between the USA, Japan and ten other Pacific Rim countries, including five Commonwealth countries. President Trump tried to cancel this trade agreement, but the rest decided to carry on without the USA, anticipating that a change of US President will result in the USA eventually joining. Canada has already done a deal with the EU which is being ratified by every EU country and in some cases by regional parliaments. The UK would have to negotiate trade deals with each of its larger former colonies, if they were agreeable. Later in this book, we ask what would be in it for each of them? We ask what Britain now produces that is so special that its former colonies will desire it, and whether Britain still represents a particularly important export market for them, rather than being an inconveniently faraway place.

As we said at the very beginning, even before the EU referendum, Britain's importance in the world was diminishing and it is set to diminish further regardless of whether Britain leaves the EU or not. It was partly a fear of this fall in importance that fuelled events in the second decade of the twenty-first century. When a hard exit from the EU was first mooted, all manner of weird imperial world-dominating fantasies were revealed by some of those campaigning to leave. Some simply hoped to rely on negotiating trade agreements, just like all other members of the World Trade Organization, but other Brexiteers, such as Owen Paterson, even suggested that the UK would impose no WTO import tariffs on goods coming in while still accepting them on exports.[35] When older Conservative Brexiteers talk of such possibilities, they often sound like a Pathé newsreel from the Empire Marketing Board, extolling the benefits of British trade. Younger Conservatives are more likely to be Remainers.

In case you were not aware of what it used to do, the Empire Marketing Board produced seventy-two reports over ten years, recommending imperial trade. Included in these were 'A Book of Empire Dinners', 'A Calendar of Fruits and Vegetables from the Empire' and 'Why Every Woman Should Buy British' (meaning British Empire). A recipe included with this last missive described how to make the King's Empire Christmas Pudding, to be cooked entirely out of empire ingredients. There was also a professorial chair in Imperial Economic Relations installed at the London School of Economics, funded by the Empire Marketing Board.

EMPIRE EDUCATION

It is often rightly said that black history is not well taught in British schools, but the same is true of white history. English people rarely know much of their real history, having been taught a version which was largely manufactured in the time of the British Empire. School curricula were then changed and began to present an ever more glorious past to try to justify how large the empire was becoming and how owning it was Great Britain's rightful role.

To this day, British school textbooks are still very one-sided because of the legacy of empire. Many older people are shocked that someone has the effrontery to title a book: *Inglorious Empire: What the British Did to India*, as the Indian politician and diplomat Shashi Tharoor chose to call the 2017 UK Penguin edition of his 2016 *An Era of Darkness: The British Empire in India* (first published by an Indian publishing company, Aleph, in India). With hindsight we can see that we need to review our perspective. That particular book is simply being honest from its title onwards. We should not be so shocked by the truth.

Young adults and school children today, despite being less experienced, tend to understand more than their parents or grandparents do about Britain's place in the world. They include those students we mentioned earlier: the ones who fancy decolonising education through introducing non-white literature, and toppling statues of Rhodes in Oxford. Others have called for looted statues on campus to be repatriated, such as the golden cockerel of Jesus College, Cambridge, originally stolen from Nigeria.[36] Even the leader of Her Majesty's opposition is now calling for all children to be taught about the grave injustices of empire.[37] However, the majority of people under fifty have only a hazy idea of what the empire and Commonwealth were all about. Even worse, the majority over fifty have a fanciful memory of what empire was all about. Some think it was glorious, a great achievement. This is hardly surprising considering that they were repeatedly told it was so.

In the early 1960s, the map of the world in British classrooms still had a quarter of the land coloured pink as it 'belonged to Britain'. Geography and history books then extolled the empire, and immigrants were – as Robert Winder put it in the title of his 2004 book – 'bloody foreigners', even as colonial immigrants were arriving to prop up the British economy.[38] Understanding why the majority of older people in England and Wales voted to get out of Europe is impossible without an understanding of our past empire-centred education.

It has taken the British a long time to adjust to their loss of territory, and a great deal of adjustment is still needed. One little girl, who will now be an older woman, told researcher Rob Jeffcoate in 1979, 'Once we owned the whole world, but now we've only got a little piece. I think there are too many coloureds in our country.' A thirteen-year-old boy told Lord Swann's Committee on 'Education for All' in 1985 that 'the foreigners take our homes, our jobs, our food and even our women'. These views were common among young white people in Britain in the 1970s and 1980s. As that generation has aged, their opinions have often changed little and are still reflected in much mainstream media.

The younger generation in Britain now benefit, in most schools, from being taught a less jingoistic history. From Bermuda (as we have mentioned) being claimed following a British shipwreck in 1609 through to our reluctantly handing over Hong Kong to the Chinese in 1997 (tears were shed), all the countries of the empire were variously conquered, taken over or handed over to the mighty British, often using bribes to the local elites. The British Empire's real high point, in terms of world dominance, could be said to have been long before the 1920s and 1930s years of empire celebration – instead being around 1897, just before the shock of the Boer War when large numbers of potential recruits were actually found to be too undernourished to be soldiers. Some flag-waving nostalgists still see that time as Britain at its best. The low point, though still with no acceptance that the empire was gone, was perhaps the handover of Hong Kong in 1997 (see Figure 2.4). Prince Charles looks on, bewildered. Chris Patten, later a staunch defender of Oxford's Rhodes statue, comforts his crying daughter. The picture was widely used in British media at the time, and over many more years since, to appeal to those harking back to a supposed golden age of empire. In hindsight, it seems unlikely that the girl was crying for the empire. No teenager enjoys having to move home, especially if they are going out with an Australian surfer called Alex while in Hong Kong.[39]

To understand the British, we have to understand how their great-grandparents, grandparents and parents benefited from what was in effect the plunder of a quarter of the world by one country. Fortunately, there are now many books that do this and in the endnotes to this book we have referenced a few. What is less well known is how the teaching of geography and history in schools has been so biased in past decades that it has left the older generation with a very false impression of how Britain gained its wealth. Do some of those who voted Leave imagine such riches are again possible? Even ardent Remainers sometimes suggested it was possible for Britain to become the richest country in the world again, as George Osborne claimed would happen by 2030 if only the country kept to his 'long-term economic plan'. There were fantasists on both sides of the Brexit debate. The past, present and likely future of Britain was not, is not and will not be what they currently imagine.

FIGURE 2.4

Outgoing Governor of Hong Kong Chris Patten comforts members of his family: Alice, Kate and Laura (wiping away tears) watched by Prince Charles as the royal yacht Britannia *sails from Hong Kong and the sun finally set over that outpost of empire in June 1997. © Trinity Mirror / Mirrorpix / Alamy Stock Photo. Reproduced with permission.*

THE HUMANITIES

The British have relied on cheap labour, both abroad and from abroad, for as long as there have been British people (which is not very long in historical terms). Ireland is the only country in the world to have a population smaller today than in the 1830s. Its population was used as very cheap labour in England, especially after the 1845–50 famine when the British government let the Irish starve; a million died and two million emigrated.

Understanding why the Irish will be so resolute about the rights they have won requires understanding a different version of British history from that traditionally taught in British schools. Brexiteers appeared unconcerned about what might happen to the Irish border until the government needed to rely on DUP votes and could not so easily abandon the North of Ireland. During the summer of 2018 it became clear that no obstacle could be put at the Irish border of any kind – it was, in fact, no longer a border! Many will ask if it would be easier if the North of Ireland were to re-join the rest of Ireland. Just as they ask in Scotland if now is the time to leave the 300-year-old union, and an economically sinking English ship. The debate about whether England is sinking or just settling a little is addressed in later chapters. Here we consider how the identities of the British have been fabricated, and the effect that is having now.

To understand Brexit, we have to revisit the geography textbooks in use in schools up until the 1960s, which told school children, including some recent migrants from former colonial countries, that

> under the guidance of Europeans, Africa is steadily being opened up ... Doctors and scientists are working to improve the health of the Africans, missionaries and teachers are educating the people ... The Europeans have brought civilisation to the peoples of Africa ...whose standards of living have been raised by their contact with white people.[40]

This is a very different story from that told by the descendants of the 10,000 or so Kenyans killed during the 1950s uprising against colonial rule.

So how can the current generation of school and university students – and all the rest of us born after overt colonialism – understand the empire, how Britain now fits into the world, and the importance of the EU? Statutory guidance for the study of history still demands that students should know the history of our islands as a chronological narrative, and also 'how Britain has influenced the wider world'. This approach is now seen by many contemporary historians as being something of a whitewashing of the Key Stages and GCSE curricula.

When he was Education Secretary in 2013, Michael Gove was forced to backtrack on his original ideas for the national history curriculum – 'rote learning of patriotic stocking fillers', according to the Regius Professor of History at Cambridge[41] – but what he did manage to change was what he termed 'the proper narrative of British History – so that every Briton can take pride in his nation'.[42] This most recent myth-making is still extremely controversial, and says a lot about Gove and his beliefs. It may also explain why he became a leading light among those campaigning to leave the EU. He may not know that he is a peddler of myths, but he could ask the experts if he is in doubt.

Historian Deana Heath has noted that Britain's national history curriculum still manages to avoid tackling the actual impact of empire on either the colonised people or the colonisers. As Simon Schama put it, much of our teaching is still '*1066 and All That* but without the jokes'. Schama was referring to a book first published in the 1930s that parodied bombastically patriotic histories and was part of the beginning of trying to better understand where the British came from. However, as the excerpt we included at the beginning of this chapter illustrates, GCSE textbooks today try to imply that even before 1066 there was great English patriotism. Such talk of a national identity rarely withstands scrutiny. We could come up with examples from books still being given to British school children today, but thankfully in general they are not quite as bad as older textbooks. There are grounds for hope, at least when it comes to the broader curriculum, though less so when we think about how we understand British trade.

It is a matter for debate as to who will want to trade freely with the UK if we go it completely alone, out of both the customs union and the single market. If the Brexit referendum felt very much like the last death throes of empire, when even many Brexiteers were not expecting to win, the post-referendum period was even more surreal, and then the proceedings became bizarre, with the Conservative Party negotiating with itself while attempting to negotiate with the EU. Fighting within your own side is not a good negotiating stance. To understand how the British got so much so wrong you need to go back to their schools, colleges and universities; to what they were taught of history and how they were not taught even their most recent history well. This alone is a huge topic; one of us has recently written a whole book on it, *Education and Race from Empire to Brexit*, to be published in March 2019. But for the argument being made, here we do need to make a few points about the teaching of geography.

Geography is still a subject concerned with colonial domination – it is just of a different kind today. As a recent leader article in *The Times* put it, 'Geography is the middle-class route to the top.'[43] They could have added that the same held true back when it indirectly trained young men to become colonial officers. Today, the most affluent of young people – even more affluent than those who go to university to study music or classics or philosophy – are sent to study geography. They go on disproportionately to become bankers, financiers and now even Prime Ministers. Where one of us teaches, for instance: 'Of the 204 students on the course, 192 are from the three higher social groups and more than half of those are from private schools.'[44] And that may be a relatively good record in comparison to geography departments in some other British universities today. However, at this current historical high point of economic inequality, universities appear to have a lot to answer for in terms of what they have produced, especially the universities at the very top. The role universities play in constructing Britain today is more important than ever. Hardly anyone who has not been to university today gets near a whiff of power. But what was taught in elite universities in the recent past differed greatly both from what is taught today and from what was then taught at other institutions. Our leaders disproportionately attended Oxford and were taught at a time when many of its tutors were remarkably out of touch. Still sunning themselves at Parson's Pleasure, for instance.[45] For the tutors of their times, the '60s certainly weren't swinging, and the '70s and '80s might as well have been the 1870s or 1880s in terms of modernising the curriculum. If you wanted to learn how the world was changing, you had to be educated away from Oxbridge.

THE PRIDE OF THE ELITE

Oxbridge, and especially Oxford, played a key role in Brexit. Leading Brexiteer MPs Boris Johnson (Balliol), Jacob Rees-Mogg (Trinity) and Michael Gove (Lady Margaret Hall) were educated there. Dominic Cummings, 'brain of Brexit', went to one of the university's least socially diverse colleges, Exeter. Privately educated Dominic would have fitted in well at Exeter. Only a minority of its students were state-educated, and only two colleges – Magdalen and Trinity – admit fewer state school students than Exeter recently managed according to the 2018 Oxford University Admissions report. Remarkably, it is still the case that in most years in these particular colleges, and several others, there are no black students or just one solitary black student.[46]

Oxford students are told that they are at one of the 'two best universities in the world', according to a league table published just 56 miles away, in London. Note that the Oxbridge student body includes only a minority of 'privileged hooray henrys', and many students who attend neither start off like that nor end up that way. However, Oxbridge (and especially Oxford) does either encourage or collect higher levels of self-satisfaction than average. In 2018, a whopping 57 per cent of Oxbridge undergraduate students reported that they are either completely satisfied with their life or score 8 or 9 (out of 10) on a measure of such satisfaction, and exactly the same proportion believe that the things they are doing with their life are 'completely worthwhile'.[47] This contrasts with 10 per cent fewer students having such feelings in other leading British universities and 59 per cent of young adults in the UK being anxious and fearful about their future in 2018, the highest proportion ever measured.[48] Why are Oxbridge undergraduates still so smug when most other young people of their age are not? It could be because we are living in the most economically unequal place in Europe. These kinds of rates of self-satisfaction are generally only found in places like Texas, among the most unequal states of the USA, where to get by you need to think of yourself as deserving.[49] Only a very small proportion of undergraduates at Oxford were born overseas; almost all are English. And, notably, no leading Brexiteers went to Cambridge. Cambridge concentrates on the sciences, on evidence and fact.

We have to go back to 1913 to find the last peak of economic inequality in Britain – the time of the last pinnacle of frequent displays of self-assured extreme smugness[50] – and even further to understand many current attitudes, and especially the contemporary behaviour of the English elite. To understand what is happening, we need to go back to the public schools of the nineteenth century, which nurtured the rulers of empire. The *Contemporary Review Journal* told the public schools in 1899: 'British rule of every race brought within its sphere has the incalculable benefit of just law, tolerant trade and considerate government'; it was seen as the duty of the British to provide competent rulers.[51]

The headmaster of Harrow School agreed with the *Contemporary Review*, telling the Royal Colonial Institute in 1895 that 'the boys of today are the statesmen, generals and administrators of the future ... In their hands is the future of the British Empire.'[52]

Upper- and upper-middle-class boys at public schools were encouraged to believe in an ideal of selfless imperial service, a sense of racial superiority and imperial chauvinism. This faith was nurtured by the development of social Darwinism and claims of a genetic white British superiority over non-white races, as expanded on later in this book. If you wonder whether a British sense of superiority and the belief that we have a duty to rule over the world still matters today, then ask yourself this question: what do you and others see when you look at *Protector*, the ship of the UK Border Force docked in Lesbos to keep the refugees out and intimidate them, less than a year after three-year-old Alan Kurdi was washed up dead on the Turkish shore? Does the image make you proud?

FIGURE 2.5: BRITAIN'S ROYAL NAVY MESSAGE TO FAMILIES AND CHILDREN FLEEING SYRIA

UK Border Force patrol vessel Protector *docked in Lesbos, April 2016. Photograph taken by Danny Dorling*

As one historian of empire, T. O. Lloyd, put it, 'By the 1860s British opinion simply regarded the Empire's black and brown subjects as natural inferiors.'[53] Such arrogance was still on full display among our politicians almost 150 years later. Perhaps the legacy of empire could partly explain their ardent belief that we would be so much better off if we were completely in charge of ourselves (and others) again?

It is not just the more expensively educated who may have been taught that the British are somehow naturally superior and don't need to co-operate. The values underpinning the public school curriculum percolated down to the middle-class grammar schools and the elementary schools of the working classes. The British class system and gross economic inequality is designed to make those at the top feel superior and those at the bottom feel inferior. But after that early lesson in their station in life, what better means to raise their morale than by convincing them that at least they are superior to everyone else in the world? In an *Oral History of Working-Class Childhood and Youth*, one elderly respondent commented, 'Froggies, Eyties, Dagoes… the only way we'd describe them was that they was all beneath you.'[54]

Through the more jingoistic elements in the school curriculum, juvenile literature and, later, films of books (including *Tarzan* and *The Jungle Book*), the lower classes were encouraged to believe in their economic, political, social and racial superiority to the rest of the subjects of empire. A little earlier, *The New Century Geography Reader on The British Empire* (published around 1902), explained to British school children that 'the Hottentots are stupidly barbarous people with yellowish brown faces, black woolly hair, flat noses and thick lips'.[55] This racism helped deflect attention from the school children's own precarious position in the economic structure. Sport was used in a similar way, to get crowds to gather to cheer a local football team rather than demand a decent wage. Football grew as the empire grew, fastest in the industrial towns that made the most empire produce. But wages at home could rise as long as there was an empire to exploit. The domestic underclass could become the imperial over-class, and all British classes could unite in national patriotic superiority. This rotten alliance still exists in the twenty-first century and goes some way to explaining the xenophobia, racism and hostility that is such an obvious part of our British heritage but now awkwardly co-exists with multiculturalism and a diverse society.

THE FALL: FROM ONE CANAL TO ANOTHER

The Suez Canal was the British Empire canal. Britain's might was ridiculed by the Suez Crisis of 1956 and its financial sector exposed as similarly incompetent by the release of the Panama Papers sixty years later, showing the extent of the tax avoidance and evasion among Britain's elite. The Paradise Papers of 2017 showed there would be more and more to come. For those alive today who were born in Britain, the stories of our lives have largely been a story of having to realise that the British are no longer top dog. Finally discovering that so many of the wealthiest and most influential in Britain are effectively cheating on the mother country by refusing to pay their proper taxes has been hard for many to accept. How has this come to be? Think of the Last Night of the Proms, loyally broadcast every year on the BBC, and the crowd singing those words paid for by a German prince in 1740. Look again at it:

> When Britain first, at Heaven's command
> Arose from out the azure main;
> This was the charter of the land,
> And guardian angels sang this strain:
> 'Rule, Britannia! rule the waves:
> Britons never ever ever will be slaves.'

No line, including subsequent verses, of 'Rule Britannia' holds water. Heaven did not command it be created, the sea around was usually not coloured azure, there was no original charter (indeed, there is still no constitution), there were no singing angels, no rule of the sea and we Britons were often slaves. Other nations had been and became more blessed. British tyranny was defeated around the world as its empire collapsed, yet every year in the Albert Hall in London at the end of summer the British sing this song, and 'Jerusalem', and of course 'Land of Hope and Glory'. So, all together now, let's end by singing a verse of that today and see how it feels:

> Land of hope and glory, Mother of the free
> How shall we extol thee, who are born to thee
> Wider still and wider, shall thy bounds be set.
> God who made thee mighty make thee mightier yet.

In many ways, Britain today is more a land of doubt and hatred than one of hope and glory. A place becoming ever more bounded, weak, small, powerless and globally less important. No wonder the country is completely split on Brexit and so much else. Its people do not know what or where they are now. But it is not their fault. It is not even the fault of their leaders, who were misled through their education, which has served them too so poorly. And it is not the fault of those of us who teach in such universities, as we did not teach them; and anyway, it is not the fault of their university teachers, but who taught *them*. It is the fault of empire.

That is what happens at the decline and fall of an empire; so much ends up leading back to it when the ghosts of the past remain unconfronted. When its people fail to adapt, an empire mentality remains for a long time. Especially when it is not clear to many people in the UK by whom or what the empire was defeated. Britain's former position at the centre of the greatest empire the world has ever known has become a poisoned chalice. Who would have known the effects would still be reverberating today, with such dramatic effect in the mother country?

CHAPTER 3

FROM EMPIRE TO COMMONWEALTH

Douglas Carswell, the sole UKIP MP during the referendum, was
raised in Uganda; Arron Banks, who bankrolled UKIP and the
xenophobic Leave.EU campaign, spent his childhood in South
Africa, where his father ran sugar estates, as well as in Kenya,
Ghana and Somalia; Henry Bolton, the current head of UKIP,
was born and raised partly in Kenya; Robert Oxley, head of
media for Vote Leave, has strong family ties to Zimbabwe.
One can only speculate about how much impact these formative
years had on their political outlook (Carswell attributes
his libertarianism to Idi Amin's 'arbitrary rule'), but it
would be odd to conclude they didn't have any.
— GARY YOUNGE, FEBRUARY 2018[1]

INTRODUCTION

It has taken the British a long time to adjust to their loss of territory, and a great deal of adjustment is still needed.[2] Unlike politicians brought up and educated in other countries, much of the ideology underpinning the views of many British politicians reflects the assumptions of empire. This includes the widespread belief that there is a need to educate their apparently more gifted children in England separately from their peers. At the extremes of these beliefs are some of the leading Brexiteers, often raised in positions of great privilege in former colonies.

Much of what we discuss here is from just outside living memory from the period when Britain joined the European Community in the 1970s. The new Commonwealth was presented to people in Britain in 1949 in such a way as to suggest that there had been a continuation of empire, and that the British Empire had been particularly benevolent for those who were ruled by Britain.

We need to understand how the stories that were constructed in 1949 led to the British not really understanding the Suez Crisis of 1956, and not realising what was actually going on during the 1960s and 1970s when country after country gained formal independence from Britain. The British were losing what had once been captive markets. It was not that British workers were particularly unproductive in the 1960s and 1970s, but that those who employed them did not understand why it was becoming harder and harder to sell abroad. It was becoming harder because the British had never before had to really compete to sell their products. Her Majesty's loyal subjects abroad purchased them at high prices.

Both authors of this book are white, and English, and so it is easier for us to make these points in a country that is still so racist and so extremely sensitive to any criticism of its jingoist stupidities. However, the most apposite descriptions of what has transpired have not come from the white English; they (we) have been too close to see. We have had to be told these truths most clearly by those who are so often said to never quite fit in.

It is not just senior law lecturer Nadine El-Enany[3] or journalist Gary Younge who have pointed out the home truths that needed to be told. When the journalist Afua Hirsch made similar points, she quickly realised that:

Britishness – at least this patriotic, defensive, glory-addicted version of it – seems to be in a highly fragile place. It cannot withstand being problematized or critiqued. Many of those I've raised this with feel aggrieved that someone who was apparently 'allowed' into Britain's educational and professional establishments should feel anything other than gratitude ... I am accused of 'coming here' and 'attacking our culture'.[4]

As Hirsch goes on to point out, 'The fact that Britain is also the country made possible by the labour, wealth and culture of my antecedents still hasn't actually sunk in.' It will take a great deal of spade work to get a better understanding of the position and unfabricated history of Britain to sink in to the British. So, we might as well start digging now and dig deep.

SINKING IT IN

As Nadine El-Enany explains in a damning article on how little the British understand the British: 'Britain's drastic manoeuvre away from the EU is intricately connected to its imperial history, one that it has long refused to confront and acknowledge for the brutal legacy that it is. Britain's unaddressed and unredressed colonial past haunted the recent EU referendum and prophesied its outcome.' She continues by pointing out that it is no coincidence that Nigel Farage (former and many-time UKIP leader) said he preferred migrants from India and Australia over Eastern Europe – Farage preferred a fanciful reincarnation of empire. She explains the ignorance of Liam Fox, Secretary of State for International Trade, who is unaware that Britain has to be ashamed of much of its twentieth-century history[5] – a man who epitomised what Paul Gilroy has described as the 'embarrassing sentiment' where colonial times are romanticised in an 'unhealthy and destructive post-imperial hungering for renewed greatness'.

How do we best understand views such as those of Liam Fox (on whom more later) and earlier Conservatives such as Enoch Powell (on whom much more later)? It helps to start with the generation alive in the years before Powell was born.

In the nineteenth century, the British suffered from a peculiar double whammy that was not entirely their fault. The first stemmed from being top dog at the time, and the second from Britain being the birthplace of a particular set of scientific breakthroughs. Until the middle of that century, all animal species had been considered immutable, part of a divine cosmic order, and (for Christians) humans had been thought of as especially distinct, made in the image of God. To be told you are a species of ape and a distant relative of a gorilla takes a bit of getting used to. Evolution was not – and is often still not – an easy sell.

For many people, the realisation that we had evolved to become human would result in some humility. It brings us down to earth. However, for a few of the British, the publication of *On the Origin of Species* (subtitled: 'by Means of Natural Selection, or the Preservation of Favoured Races in the Struggle for Life') resulted in a very different response. At that time, Britain owned the greatest empire the world had ever known. The British lorded it over so many peoples that it went to the heads of a few. Of the present 193 members of the UN, Britain conquered or invaded at least 90 per cent (171) of them.[6] Either this was just grossly unfair and very wrong, or there was a justification for it. Fortunately, science had just produced a possible answer: the British could be viewed as part of a superior race. Many in the British elite came to believe that the British were personally the pinnacle of humanity, and particular families in Britain were at the very top of that pinnacle. Others, such as Enoch Powell, despite being 'only two generations out of the Welsh coalfields',[7] latched on to this belief and came to see themselves as superior to almost anyone else in the world. Try to imagine believing this about yourself. How might you behave?

With the publication and widespread acceptance of *On the Origin of Species*, suddenly there was an apparently much sounder justification for both Britain's class structure at home, with all its rigid demarcations, and its colonial success abroad. No longer a product of divine right or birthright, the elite had a plausible explanation for Britain's place at the top, as well as its internal, extremely hierarchical social structure. Given the choice of accepting that their treatment of other people was monstrous or justifying it by selective biblical quotes, or by a scientific theory, the choice must have appeared to many at the time to be obvious. They chose a particular version of science to explain their and their country's newly accrued wealth. There was potentially a problem due to emigration – what to do with all the 'expats', especially their offspring if they had mixed with the 'natives'? – and the question of how to classify some people no longer technically British, but that could be solved by broadening 'British' to 'white Anglo-Saxon' – that ever so convenient mythical subset of white – and, if necessary, 'English-speaking' and 'Protestant'.

In 1859, when Charles Darwin published *On the Origin of Species*, he did not think carefully enough about its subtitle, of what the implication might later be of the words 'the Preservation of Favoured Races in the Struggle for Life'. Darwin was not an especially brilliant thinker. Indeed, he was quite slow at times; in many ways he was a very normal person.[8] Within decades, the repercussions of his thinking could be found worldwide. In 1898, a sterilisation law was introduced in Michigan and twenty-four male children were promptly castrated for epilepsy, imbecility, masturbation and weakness of mind.[9]

The effects of that poor choice of subtitle in 1859, compounded by existing racism and amplified afterwards by some of the worst

British bigots in human history (some of whom we touch on in later chapters), were enormous and swept around the globe. By the early twentieth century, abuse was rife among those who believed in biological determinism and the dangers of a defective population. Winston Churchill, Home Secretary in 1911, believed that a system of labour camps, sterilisation and even euthanasia were ways of dealing with the 'feeble-minded'.[10] By 1924, a 'Racial Integrity Act' was being passed in the state of Virginia that defined someone as 'coloured' if they had one non-white ancestor. This was despite us all coming out of Africa! The Act was accompanied by a Sterilization Act based on the 'Model Eugenical Sterilization Law'.[11]

Around the globe, statutes were passed forbidding relationships between white women and non-white men (and, less often, the opposite). Artificial races, almost all newly imagined and ranked in a supposed order of racial fitness, were defined as realities in much of Africa, in the rest of the Americas, across Europe, Asia, Australasia – all around the world. Even the *partial* legal dismantling of this cruelty and stupidity took over a century, from 1859 to 1959, to make any headway. But then, after battles in the 1960s, '70s and '80s, South Africa elected its first black President in 1994 and the USA followed suit in 2008. People everywhere began to realise that everyone was in some way mixed, all had a differing ethnicity, and there was only one human race, one species.

FAVOURED RACES IN THE STRUGGLE FOR LIFE

By 'races', Darwin meant different but related species and geographically isolated subspecies. When he mentioned race, he often meant different species of pigeons and tortoises and mockingbirds, not people. For him 'natural selection', that phrase used in the other part of his long subtitle, included understanding the advantages of species living together constructively. The life he described was not always a struggle and there was a huge amount of chance involved.

Darwin realised that over time the nature of species could change and that, particularly on islands, this could result in different species evolving more quickly. When he was developing his theory, it was only slowly being realised that climate could change dramatically and that there had been an ice age. Darwin did not know anything about plate tectonics, which would not be discovered for another century. They would eventually explain how some animals and plants had spread and why the climate influencing a land mass might change over very long time periods. Darwin had to do a great deal of guessing, and when we guess, we make mistakes.

Darwin was no radical. He did realise that siblings could be very different from each other and thus that any hereditary benefit of having apparently able parents is not always (or even often) bequeathed. Because of this, he was very much opposed to primogeniture, the English habit of leaving land and wealth to the first-born in the family. But he was hardly a modern man. He thought the practice subverted natural selection of the fittest person to cultivate the land. As he once memorably said, 'Primogeniture is dreadfully opposed to natural selection; suppose the first-born bull was made by each farmer the begetter of his stock.'[12] Unlike his far more enlightened contemporary, Alfred Russel Wallace, Darwin didn't worry as much about the cows as the bulls. Wallace not only contributed as much as Darwin to the theory of evolution, but was also a very early feminist. But because he was not a wealthy man many of his ideas were ignored.[13] Victorian notions of British superiority hampered the rate at which the British learnt and adapted, and helped bring about the end of empire. Farming successfully today is, of course, not a matter of brute strength to plough, survive and produce the biggest bulls. The cattle we rear in our farms are the product of very unnatural selection. They are not at all like wild cattle. We forget that *On the Origin of Species* was the first stab at explaining a new idea, it was not a bible.

FIGURE 3.1: DARWINS, WEDGWOODS, GALTONS AND BARCLAYS FAMILY TREE, 1573–1914

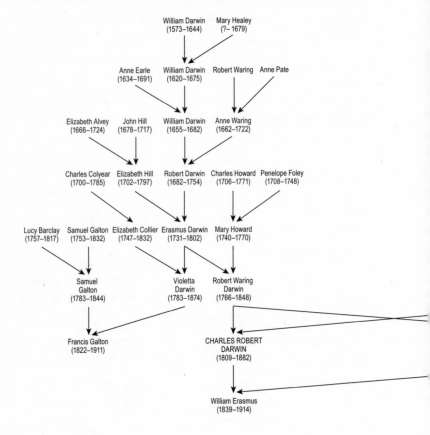

*Drawn as a hybridisation network, a 'path diagram',
rather than as traditional family tree.[14]*

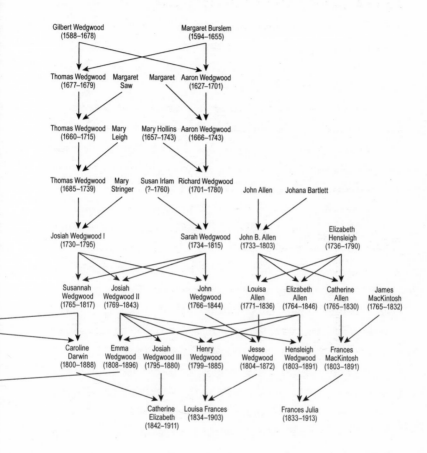

History doesn't record whether Darwin also ever wondered why God appeared to be inordinately fond of beetles, as J. B. S. Haldane is once thought to have remarked. However, Darwin himself was remarkably fond of beetles.[15] He was English. He liked collecting things. It was his obsession with collecting specimens, not his wonderful mind, that helped him contribute to the discovery of the process of evolution. It was also the monies he had access to, which came from being born into a rich family in the richest nation of the world, that helped him buy so many specimens from other collectors. Darwin had married into the wealthy Wedgwood family, those of potteries fame. Much of Britain and the empire was persuaded it needed china plates and tea cups, not made in China, but in Britain.

A major problem for the English in Darwin's time was that so many of the elite were inbred. This, of course, worried Darwin. The diagram above shows why he was especially worried, but the full harm that such excessive inbreeding can cause was not fully known in his time. In Darwin's era, in his social class, cousin marriages occurred 4 per cent of the time (1 in 25). Darwin himself was married to his cousin. Such marriages occurred far more frequently in areas where gentry were sparse, such as among the Darwins and Wedgwoods, and that resulted in many medical problems. Partly as a result of improved knowledge about the problems of inbreeding, in the 1930s in Britain, the proportion of inter-cousin upper-class marriages declined to 1 in 600 and then 1 in 25,000 by the 1960s.[16] We know so much more now than we did when the British Empire was at its height. For instance, we now know that the English elite were very far from genetically superior due to inbreeding.

After 1859, Francis Galton, half-cousin to Charles Darwin, began the task of trying to provide a 'scientific' basis for selective breeding. His aim was to improve the genetic inheritance of the human race. Galton believed the English elite were superior. He believed that the English lower classes and most other people on the planet had ineducable minds, that those lower orders were overbreeding and producing defective people who were a danger to what he regarded as 'the British race'. Galton helped to make it acceptable to believe that the people colonised by the British had inferior intellects. All of this matters in the complicated story that this book is trying to recount because, in 2016, many of

Galton's ideas, or at least the germs of his ideas, still seemed to be held by leading Brexiteers in the debate about the future of Britain. Michael Gove, Boris Johnson and Dominic Cummings, in particular, mention or allude to their pet theories about IQ and the inheritance of ability, and genetic potential. They and so many others of their ilk do this rather too frequently for it to be incidental to their support for the Leave campaign.

It is not hard to find a direct line from Galton's beliefs in the advantages of selective breeding of humans through to selective schooling today, where 'better' children are kept carefully away from other children, so they will not only not learn together but also not mix socially and, later, not breed together. Writing on the issue in 2018, academics Stephen Gorard and Nadia Siddiqui explained that:

> The United Kingdom, among others, has spent 20 years or more including pupils with special educational needs and disabilities into mainstream schooling. The argument was that whatever specific provision was needed could be provided in most mainstream schools, they could be taught separately for some tasks, and that it was better to allow them to socialise and gain educational experiences with their non-SEN peers. It is hard to see why exactly the same argument does not apply to the most able students in each area.[17]

Hard to see unless you understand that some people still believe today what Galton believed 150 years ago.

In his books *Hereditary Genius* (1869) and *Inquiries into Human Faculty and Its Development* (1883), Galton advocated selective re-production and used the term eugenics – derived from the Greek *eugenes*, 'a person hereditarily endowed with noble qualities' – as a science which would preserve what at the time were thought to be the best inborn qualities of the population. He argued, as did many other members of the British elite at the time, that just as genius and talent were inborn, and confined largely to privileged families, so low abilities, mental defects, delinquency, crime, prostitution, illegitimacy and even unemployment were the product of inherited tendencies that had become concentrated in the lower classes. He argued for the kinds of sterilisation that were later enacted in Virginia, in Nazi Germany, in Sweden, in India, and in many places elsewhere across the world.

We too easily forget today that Francis Galton's biographer, Karl Pearson, claimed in 1892 that 'no degenerates or feeble-minded stock can ever be converted into healthy and sound stock by the accumulated efforts of education, general laws or sanitation'.[18] We have generally forgotten that Marie Stopes, recently *The Guardian* newspaper's 'woman of the century',[19] promoted contraception to counter 'the reckless breeding from the [lower classes] and the semi-feebleminded, the careless who are proportionately increasing in our community', but such ideas were widely spread by Galton and then his acolytes such as Pearson.

THEY KNOW NOT WHAT THEY DO

Karl Pearson's belief that improving sanitation, or introducing better laws on how people should be housed, or providing better education for the masses, could never result in a better educated and healthier population, was completely wrong, but it was also a product of his upbringing and circumstances. His mistakes were not entirely his own fault. Some British academics remain impressed by Pearson because he invented new statistical techniques, but, just like Darwin, he was in the right place at the right time, with the right peculiar obsessions to achieve those innovations. Karl Pearson proved through his own example how it was possible to be clever but still stupid.

Being simultaneously 'ever so clever' and at the same time 'extremely stupid' is a trait the British elite came to excel in. Believing that you are the descendants of the most superior of human races, which themselves are the most superior of all animals, is a good recipe for delusions of grandeur. There have been those who have at various times questioned whether this superior attitude is the best approach. The British habit of condescension leads to undervaluing skilled workers by viewing many as second rate. For instance, in 1916, Sir Michael Sadler (an alumnus of Rugby School and Trinity College, Oxford, and later Master of University College, Oxford) lamented that, unlike Germany, Britain does not make good enough use of its 'second grade intelligence'[20] (its workers). Even while suggesting that such workers should be more respected, Sadler couldn't help but condescend. He was not unusual in still calling those he thought were not like him 'second grade'. He did this at a time when the social Darwinist and eugenic theorists were busy trying to demonstrate the intellectual inferiority of the working classes. In the century that followed, the vast majority of scientists, and later most university students, would come to have at least one grandparent who had been working class. No one is 'second grade', but a few people are embarrassing fools.

A hundred years after the comment about second-grade intelligence was made by Professor Sadler, the then Mayor of London (more recently Foreign Secretary) Boris Johnson declared that 'as many as 16 per cent of our species have an IQ below 85, while about 2 per cent have an IQ above 130'. He presumably thought that his was at the higher level. A popular newspaper reported this as 'Thickos born to toil'.[21] In fact, it was Johnson who was being a little slow, but at the same time appearing super-confident and able (at least to those of his friends and supporters who were easily impressed). Johnson did not understand that IQ distributions are specifically defined to always find 16 per cent with an IQ below 85 and 2 per cent with an IQ above 130, regardless of actual performance or ability. Johnson didn't understand many things. Fortunately, ability later in life is largely not inherited from your parents, so whatever failures may be innate in Boris, will hopefully remain with Boris.

Eugenics is now largely discredited. No one today wants to be labelled a eugenicist. IQ is not a measure of overall ability, but simply a narrow test of a particular kind of logical reasoning. Many people could be trained to do well in most tests, especially IQ tests. There are a few children who are unusually nerdy. Johnson isn't one of them; Pearson probably was. However, the nerds are never clever across the board. The nerds are often very bad at aspects of life that do not require nerdiness, such as empathy. Luckily, they usually do not pass on their nerdiness to their offspring,[22] as evolution may very likely have limited the spread of nerdiness due to the disadvantages that come with it. Similarly, and this is Galton's worst nightmare, we have known for a long time now that nerdy children are usually the product of parents who are not especially able.[23]

Francis Galton's life's work was erroneous. But he was much worse than a waste of time; he helped propagate a myth of Great Britain among its Great British hereditary families. It is a myth that is especially kept alive in many parts of the Conservative Party today, where people believe that a few deserve to be rich because they have inherited the more able genes of their more able forebears. No wonder it was the Conservatives who were riven by debates over Europe. They come from a political party more obsessed than any other (apart from the Democratic Unionist Party)[24] with weird outdated ideas – such as seeing British people as somehow both very unified internally, but also distinct from most other European people.[25]

If you are interested in how eugenics was found to be wrong then consult Chitty 2007;[26] Gillborn 2008,[27] 2016;[28] Hearnshaw 1979;[29] Kamin 1974;[30] Gould 1996;[31] Montague 1975;[32] Rose 2014;[33] Tomlinson 2017;[34] and Evans 2018[35] among hundreds of others. The very latest genetic research finds that, at most, 'raw parent–child correlations in education may reflect one-sixth genetic transmission and five-sixths social inheritance'.[36] In other words, it is massively mostly nurture (not nature) that matters. Those who suggest a greater genetic influence than this tend to have particular axes to grind and tend to have been looking for such incorrect findings, not stumbling upon them.[37] In 2018, nails were still having to be repeatedly hammered into the coffin of the idea that some racial groups are more able than others.[38]

Unfortunately, in Britain today, many of those who consider themselves top dogs and have the power to influence the lives of the rest of the population also sincerely believe in their own superior intellect and intelligence, and know little or nothing of all the work just listed. For all their acquisition, display and cultivation of social and cultural capital, they are an embarrassment. They make statements that should, on reflection, shame them, but they believe so strongly in their own superiority that they rarely question their own ability or knowledge. They do not suffer from impostor syndrome. They do not doubt that they should be at the top. They tend to be extremely narcissistic.

At this point it is worth taking a breath, stepping back and then taking a good long look at a contemporary human geography map of what were once the countries of the British Empire (Figure 3.2). How could people in a set of countries as small as the United Kingdom come to think of themselves as fit and able to rule over so many others? Delusions of grandeur are essential to rule over an empire. A people have to fool themselves, and be fooled, into believing that they are special enough to rule over huge multitudes of others. The lies that are told to create that necessary delusion can persist long after the empire has gone. To be most convincing, those who teach and tell the lies have to believe them to be truths. If it had not been the British, however, it would have been another European state that would have been the centre of the largest empire of the world. It was Britain partly, if not largely, by chance.

FIGURE 3.2: A MAP OF THE BRITISH EMPIRE WITH AREA IN PROPORTION TO CURRENT POPULATION

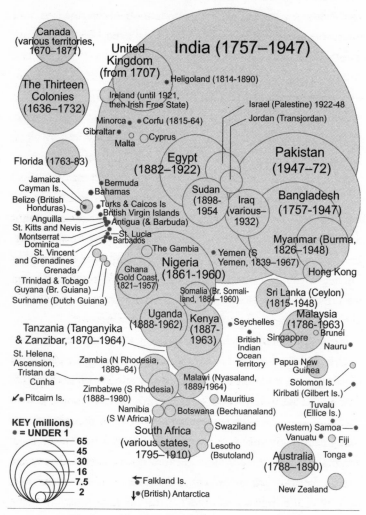

The dates when some areas were claimed and rescinded from the British Empire are given in brackets.[39]

When you looked at what makes up most of the former British Empire today in Figure 3.2 and considered how small Britain is, did you think Britain was more significant, and if so, why? Was it how you were brought up? How you were nurtured? Were you ever shown a map like this at school? Were you ever told the stories we are telling here? What did the people you grew up with believe?

Nurture is an unfortunate word because it could just mean education or training. In fact, it is the entire social environment in which you are brought up, which includes kindness, caring, opportunity, wealth, expectation, culture, and good and bad luck (chance events) – so much more than just education and training. Nature and nurture interact, but overall what matters most in becoming seen as competent is *to whom, when and where you are born*. History and geography are by far the most important determinants of overt ability. For instance, being born in Britain today is now *less advantageous* than being born elsewhere in Europe when it comes to being free to think intelligently and imaginatively. We know this from international tests of ability in problem solving, mathematical and literacy acumen.[40]

Being born female 100 years ago was a massive impediment to being allowed to be clever. Later, however, a higher pass mark would be set for girls in the 11-plus examination because they were doing too well! Today, being female means you are more likely to do better at exams and be regarded as able, even though you still may not make it into the upper echelons in business, or even academia. Other factors change far more slowly. Even today, where you are born in Britain, which part of town you live in and how well-off your family is profoundly affect the chances of your being considered clever, as does your ethnicity. We all hold dear a set of largely unfounded prejudices. If you do not believe us, think about what you believe about the ability of the young. Do you think that standards have slipped, and they are not taught as well at school as you were? Even though British children now rank towards the bottom of many league tables of ability, they are still (on average) much more able than their parents. On average, each generation born since the Second World War has been allowed to be more able than its parents or grandparents, as provision has been made for young people to stay on at school until, first, age sixteen and, later, age eighteen. Known as the Flynn Effect, ability at passing IQ tests is going up steadily all over the world, and the results have to be periodically recalibrated to maintain the preordained average of 100 for each generation. And if you want a challenge, try explaining that to the man who was until recently British Foreign Secretary, Boris Johnson, who is in danger of going to his grave never fully understanding how IQ tests work and what their purpose was.[41]

THE BRITISH AND THEIR STRANGE SCHOOLS, AND SCHOOLS OF THOUGHT

University – A school, where all the arts and faculties are taught and studied, and where, in the view of some news-sheets and political hacks, there are seditious lectures against Brexit.
– HARRY EYRES AND GEORGE MYERSON, 2018[42]

In Britain today, the interminable arguments over selective education are based on the belief that children are born with their potential ability already determined: some will be very able, others average, others less able, others disabled. The children of the less well-off are seen to have limited potential.[43] That, regrettably, is true; however, they are not limited by their genetics but by the society in which they have had the misfortune to be born.[44] In contrast, countries with more equal education systems around the world, including almost all of the rest of Europe, have better-functioning economies and appear to produce a happier, healthier, more able, more productive population. Among the countries of the

OECD (Organisation for Economic Co-operation and Development), only Chile spends more on private education than do the British. In Britain, that money is spent mostly by just a few of the most affluent of the southern English. In stark contrast, most affluent countries have hardly any selective private education. The majority of OECD countries spend *most* on the education of children who find school more difficult. They do this through higher state education spending for those who need it, not private spending on those who mostly don't need extra help.[45]

Some of those who consider themselves elite can often be rather dim. They talk of themselves as 'privileged' to have been selectively educated, whereas the real privilege is to be educated among *all* your peers. How can you understand other people if you have never properly mixed with them? The 4th Viscount St Davids (aka Rhodri Philipps), a descendant of Richard the Lionheart, never mixed much as a youngster.[46] Philipps was jailed in 2017 for racially abusing Gina Miller, the businesswoman who won a legal challenge over a parliamentary vote for Brexit after Article 50 was triggered. He had described her as 'a boat jumper' and went on to say, 'If this is what we expect of immigrants, send them back to their stinking jungles.' It is unfortunate that many of the elite were educated at 'exclusive' English schools where so much of the ethos still seems stuck with the imperial mentality. Philipps was educated at Worth School, Sussex.[47] He was the offspring of a British viscount who married Augusta Victoria Correa y Larraín Ugarte, from Chile. He was perhaps unlucky to have been born to parents from two of the world's most unequal OECD countries; it might not be entirely his fault that he is as he is.[48]

The old British canard about the inherent ability of children is a comforting myth. It comforts those who are uneasy with the degree of inequality they see but would rather seek to justify it than confront it. The myth of inherent potential helps some leading politicians in Britain justify to themselves why they are privileged and why they are in their jobs. They call other, normal, people 'underprivileged' when often the normal are, in many ways, more fortunate than them. It is actually a privilege not to have been sent to a boarding school or taught old-fashioned arrogant ideas. It is a privilege to get to know your mum and dad as you grow up rather than seeing the nanny and house master as your substitute parents.

In early December 2017, all the members of the government's Social Mobility Commission resigned. Their chairman claimed that 'failing to deal with the inequalities that fuelled the Brexit vote would simply lead to a rise of political extremes'.[49] In fact, an obsession with social mobility doesn't deal with inequality; social mobility is just about trying to get a slightly different group of people to the top. In contrast, focusing on reducing inequality has always increased social mobility. One of Britain's problems before the Brexit vote was a lack of recognition of the importance of inequality, along with a denial of economic inequality's effects. Tolerating very high rates of economic inequality causes widespread misery. However, this remains disputed, especially by leading Brexiteers, despite inequality being consistently associated with so many acute social, economic and political problems.[50] Just one of the many problems the British have is the amount of money they spend attempting to retain the advantage of a small elite whose children are seen to deserve their privilege. That requires their parents to prevent too many lower-class children joining their group, going to their schools, their universities, taking their jobs and buying similarly impressive homes.

The latest OECD-reported Gini index of income inequality for the UK is 0.360 for the year 2015, up on 0.356 in 2014 and higher than that reported for any European country other than Lithuania.[51] The Gini measure of inequality can be bewildering. Here is a helpful way of thinking about it. Imagine a country made up of just two households: one has an annual income of £25,000 and the other £75,000. The difference between them is £50,000. Divide that by the total of their incomes (£25,000 plus £75,000) and you get a ratio of 0.5. That country would have a Gini of 0.5, similar to Mexico today. That same measure of all possible differences, averaged over all possible pairs of households, is, according to world-leading statisticians, 'numerically close to the Gini'.[52] As we write, the highest (worst) recorded Gini in the world is 0.623 for South Africa. Chile is at 0.545, Brazil is estimated at 0.515 but not properly measured, the USA is at 0.490, Turkey 0.404, Russia 0.376 and Israel 0.346 (a fraction lower than the UK). The UK is part of an unsavoury group of highly inequitable states. In contrast there is Iceland (0.246), Denmark (0.256), Finland (0.260), Norway (0.272), Austria (0.276), Sweden (0.278), Germany (0.289), France (0.295), Switzerland (0.297) and the Netherlands (0.303) – all normal European countries. The UK is not normal, and many widely held views within the UK are also not normal. Living with high inequality seems to make some people more stupid, especially the affluent.

Many parents who consider themselves much above the average believe that their children will inherit part of some greater potential and, most importantly, that other people's children will not. These beliefs create and sustain inequality in society and allow for the creation of high levels of ignorance across populations. Britain did not become one of the most economically unequal countries in Europe by accident. A small group of people wanted that to happen and they worked hard to achieve their aim, to create a society of winners and losers. This small group overlaps closely with the group that led the Brexit campaign. If you want to find the modern-day equivalent of Karl Pearson, then look up the theories and background of one of the leading Brexit campaigners, Dominic Cummings.[53]

Dominic Cummings believes he is very intelligent, and that intelligence is distributed along a bell curve with a few people like him at the top end of it.[54] He also maintains that an individual child's performance is mainly based on genetics rather than the quality of teaching, while simultaneously damning the quality of teachers.[55] Later on in this book, we will look more closely at the mysterious figure of Dominic Cummings. Dominic is often presented as a Professor Moriarty-like genius, or as one commenter put it, 'a man in a constant state of awe at his own strategic brilliance'.[56]

The bell curve idea suggests some rationality in a process of originally labelling children as idiots and imbeciles at the lower end, and as gifted and highly able at the other end. The idea that such a curve exists still resonates globally in education and with politicians and the public, alongside the notion of limited potential and expectation. Indeed, when New Labour replaced Clause IV of its constitution in 1994, it asserted that the party wished 'to create for each of us the means to realise our *true potential*, and for all of us a community in which power, wealth and opportunity are in the hands of the many, not the few' (emphasis added).[57] Younger readers might be interested to know that the original Clause IV, seen as the soul of the Labour Party, drafted in 1917 and accepted in 1918, began with the words: 'To secure for the workers *by hand or by brain* the full fruits of their industry…' (emphasis added). It thus included a eugenic distinction between two types of worker, which was hardly surprising as Sidney Webb, its author, was a eugenicist. That eugenic tradition was maintained by Tony Blair when his new Clause IV was adopted in 1995, with its promise 'to create for each of us the means to realise our true potential' and consequent implication that those true potentials varied greatly. A wartime coalition government passed the 1944 Education Act, which proposed dividing children up according to ability at the age of eleven. Eugenic thinking is widespread.

In September 2016, the then new Conservative Prime Minister Theresa May had announced a return to the policies of selection of children for English grammar schools, which were originally intended to give only around 20 per cent of children an 'academic' education. The fact that now between 40 and 50 per cent of children obtain qualifications sufficient to gain a university place was apparently irrelevant! Not many people know that it is in fact harder now to get into university than it was in the 1980s; the grade requirements are higher, children must study for longer and jump through far more hoops.[58] As with New Labour's new Clause IV, Theresa May believed[59] that some children (children like her of course) had much more potential than others and they should be sought out at an early age and educated differently. At university, May herself was 'groomed ... for the Final Honours School'[60] by her tutor, who spotted what she *thought* was Theresa's potential early.[61]

The grammar school policy was more popular among older people in Britain, often the same people who had voted for Brexit. Most of that generation had been brought up to believe in a hierarchical system: individually they were often told that they were inferior to many other people in Britain, but that Britain itself was superior to other countries. Grammar schools are also popular with some people who cannot afford private education but believe that society is so competitive that their children must be educated at a school that can ensure their 'rightful place' in society; something that can be most easily achieved by sending the hoi polloi (the many) to second-rate schools. Their children in most cases today gain a grammar school place not by fair competition but by expensive private tuition, or advantaged parental tuition, training them in how to do well in the 11-plus exam.

The lobby for grammar schools will not go away any time soon and it overlapped very closely with the lobby for Brexit. There are many parents, including very many from minority groups associated with recent migration, who are 'aspirant' for their children and are keen to prepare their children for the 11-plus examination for a grammar school place. It is of course a lobby that is, in reality and in greatest effect, really calling for many more secondary moderns, for schools that keep the lower orders low. What is the point of sending your children to a grammar or private school if later they have to 'compete' with children from good comprehensives who know more about life than your children do? No wonder so many Conservatives hate comprehensives.

When tests revealed that the British did not perform particularly well among affluent countries internationally, the Conservative Party proposed that a return to grammar schools was what was needed. A return to 'the good old days'. The British government was trying to use those international comparative tests to back up its own divisive education policies, suggesting that Britain's poor performance showed a need for increased selectiveness in schools.[62] However, that same data Theresa May relied on shows that it is precisely because the British (along with the Americans) teach in a competitive, test-based, league-based, constantly ranking system that Britain produces the least well-educated 24-year-olds in the rich world. What the data from the OECD shows is that states which encourage greater competition between schools end up with worse results overall, with children learning how to pass exams but not how to retain what they have learnt just a few years after taking those exams. Exams really matter in very unequal countries because different jobs pay such different salaries and wages. Our poor performance in the international leagues is largely a product of the underlying economic inequality in the UK. To be better requires less divisive education, but that is hard to achieve while still tolerating very wide income inequalities.

If the UK government had really wanted to improve social mobility and access to high-quality education for the most able pupils, then as a very practical measure they could have argued for the introduction of tuition fee grants covering the fees of part-time, usually poorer, students at university. At a cost of £2,721 a year, these are in fact cheaper to give out than the government subsidy for the current Open University tuition fee, which costs the government £2,864 a year per student.[63] Part-time student access to universities, the number of part-time students arriving, has more than halved since 2012 in England as a direct result of fees rising by 247 per cent. The UK government increased university fees in England so much in that one year, tripling them to become the highest fees in the world, because Britain had become a land of inequality and not opportunity. There was resistance in Wales and Northern Ireland and complete opposition in Scotland. In fact, grants are cheaper than tuition fees in the long term, in part because the government so rarely recoups the fees in full. But rather than taking this into account, or listening to the arguments from the smaller countries, the government tried to move the agenda even further towards education extremism and talked of re-introducing many grammar schools. So far, they have thankfully largely failed.

When it comes to education, there are constant distractions from the major problem of economic inequality. The right wing became over-reliant on the concept of a 'white working class' (as if black people are not so often working class). They then used this term to undermine the critical importance of the consequences of gross economic inequality and the poverty and economic disadvantage it causes. They did this by trying to add virtually non-existent discrimination against white British people as a factor they would like to be considered. Working-class people are discriminated against in Britain, but there is no special extra discrimination against white working class as distinct from the working classes among other ethnicities. The myth of white working-class discrimination has led to misleading BBC headlines such as 'Poor white schools "destroyed" by rankings'.[64] The truth is that education all across England has been severely harmed by ranking schools and attempting to get them to compete, like gladiators in a cage. The ultimate outcome of the ranking system is that some schools are shut down as failures so others can be lauded as beacons of upwards mobility. All the rest must fruitlessly attempt to emulate these paragons in a race that clearly, mathematically, is unwinnable by all but a small minority. This is exacerbated by the idiocy of schools being compelled to enter pupils for GCSE examinations when they are either recently arrived refugees or totally unprepared (usually) working-class children. Some of these children are now voting with their feet and refusing to go to school and sit for two hours in an incomprehensible examination environment. The school, of course, will be penalised for low outcome scores. The alternatives to the English system can be found all across Europe, in those countries where children on average all do better at school, where schools don't compete but collaborate, and where people understand why publishing school league tables makes the situation worse. There are very few private schools on the European mainland and they are mainly reserved for the less able children of the very wealthy.

When the average educational score of people aged 16–24 in each country is compared to income inequality in that country, the results reveal that economic inequality harms thinking ability across entire populations. Inequality brings out the worst in us. The USA is the only other large rich nation that is more economically unequal than the UK, and it shows.

In the United States, by the year 2015, the best-off tenth of households enjoyed an average annual income of $439,883 a year, some 18.75 times more than the $23,460 a year that the average of the poorest tenth of households survived on each year. Racism allows this inequality to be tolerated. Vastly disproportionate numbers of poorer children in the USA are not white and they perform worst of all in OECD international tests. The USA now has the worst level of income inequality in the rich world, and produces the least-able children by international measures for wealthy countries. Britain ranks second on such measures.[65] And yet both countries supposedly lead the international university league tables! But no university league table actually measures what undergraduates are able to do. They are all about the brand, and the ability to market that brand.

The social values that are responsible for gross inequality in income extend to education, with inevitable consequences, bolstering segregated education systems and harming the thinking of both rich and poor who grow up in such divided societies. Our British children are not dense, any more than American children are, but the current educational systems in both countries are unusually stupid in comparison with other, more equitable countries. Today, Harvard, Yale, Princeton, Oxford and Cambridge are not symbols of the pinnacles of great achievement, but of the folly that comes before the fall. Countries with really good universities don't feel the need to boast. In late 2017, protesters complained that prominent work being conducted at the University of Oxford was still proclaiming a 'racist, hackneyed, and fictional trope about the nature of pre-colonial societies'.[66] This was followed by the release of the following statement by Oxford University Africa Society on 19 December 2017:

> Oxford only retains three Black full Professors, yet a number of academics willing to publish works of colonial nostalgia ... Therefore, the Africa Society calls on University of Oxford's administration to increase resources and programmes dedicated to fostering diverse,

pluralistic and decolonial scholarship including the meaningful study of history and legacies of colonialism and imperialism.[67]

The university's Africa Society then went on to quote Innocent Gangaidzo, a former student who decades earlier had linked the issues of colonialism raised earlier in this book with current issues in British education. Why is British university teaching still so behind the times when these problems have been pointed out so many decades ago? As Gangaidzo explained:

> The colonial era really did produce a catastrophic dislocation of the lives of common people. All those wars of self-defence, bitter rebellions, millennial uprisings and a million individual acts of protest were set aside airily as the mere product of benighted savagery, perverted superstition or natural foolishness. All those new urban slums, miseries, moral squalors were explained, when they were explained at all, as the outcome of African fecklessness, incompetence or worse. And so with the post-independence upheavals, excellent institutions, it was said, had been provided – whose fault but African incapacity if they now failed to work?

THE SEARCH FOR THE GOLDEN CHILD

Universities like Oxford may be so slow to learn from their students because some in those universities believe they have a eugenic mission. Oxford is the most elite university in the UK, taking young people from even more affluent backgrounds than Cambridge and producing far more Prime Ministers than Cambridge (though the latter admittedly did produce Nick Clegg, once titled Deputy Prime Minister). Cambridge dominates in the sciences and the production of Nobel Prize winners. Oxford dominates in pomp and ceremony; philosophy and classics.

The map in Figure 3.3 illustrates the home locations of

UK-domiciled students who recently won a place at Oxford University. The cartogram in Figure 3.3 shows the same information, but every area is drawn in proportion to population rather than land. (It is a continuous population cartogram in which every area still connects with all its original neighbours correctly and does so in such a way that lines of longitude and latitude meet at exactly 90 degrees everywhere on the new map despite being now curved. Don't worry at all if this makes little sense to you, unless you are very young and should have benefited from the general rise in the ability to do abstract thinking!)

FIGURE 3.3: HOME LOCATIONS OF UK STUDENTS AT OXFORD UNIVERSITY IN 2012

Each point is the home location of a student at Oxford University in 2012. The entire UK-resident undergraduate population is shown on both the equal area map and the population cartogram of the UK. Points are slightly perturbed to protect anonymity, and not shown in Northern Ireland on the conventional map for the same reason.[68]

In Figure 3.3, it becomes clear that many times more young people from some neighbourhoods in Britain arrive in Oxford than from others. Just over 2,700 dots represent one year's intake at Oxford. Only a tiny number drop out, so almost all of these students graduate. If all things were equal, Oxford's students would come from a much wider set of geographical areas – the dots would be far less clustered on the population cartogram. Studies in the sociology of education have long pointed out the different educational outcomes by location and type of school attended. High A-level grades are more likely to be 'a signpost to your street, school and socialisation' than to your inherent ability.[69] Private schooling and parental wealth still provide major avenues into the 'good' universities. From some parliamentary constituencies, such as Sheffield Central, on average only a single child goes to Oxford each year. From others, such as the most affluent areas of London and a few hotspots of great wealth outside the capital, dozens 'come up' with great regularity each year. The areas with no dots on the cartogram are those from which not a single child came to Oxford in 2012 – and from which not a single child comes to Oxford in most years.

The clustering on the map is also far too pronounced to be explicable simply by where school pupils who secure the highest grades at A level live. While high A-level results are clustered together, it's to a far lesser extent than this diagram would indicate, and many other factors are at play. Other research by the authors, produced for internal Oxford University debate, has confirmed that. Almost all other countries show that it is possible to have a much more geographically diverse set of children attending top universities in a country; but to achieve that, you have to treat all children far more equitably throughout their school careers, have a less entrenched university hierarchy, and be open to the idea that academic potential is not preordained at birth. The best example in the world is found in Finland and the Scandinavian countries. But when it comes to education, Britain is as different from a place like Finland as it is possible to be.

England's national public education system developed a good half-century behind those of many other European countries, the general view being that the labouring classes did not need education. Countries like Finland were similar, but took a very different turn from the 1950s onwards. They also greatly benefit today from not having felt the need to establish an educational system able to produce leaders who could run an empire. Finland has no grand, and ever so private, public schools. In England and Wales, elementary education was made free for the masses only in 1891, and then with a state grant of just 10 shillings a year per child! Currently, government in the UK expects all potential workers to reach minimum levels of literacy, numeracy, problem solving and digital understanding.[70] However, the persistence of Victorian values in Britain has held its children and universities back.

In 1886, a Schools Inquiry Commission suggested that 'the different classes of society, the different occupations in life, require different teaching'.[71] The assumption was that only the upper classes would produce children capable of high educational attainment. Over 100 years later, lower educational achievement is still often attributed to feckless parenting of supposedly lazy, drink- and drug-taking working-class benefit scroungers. But, stop for a moment: whose parents do you think actually consume the most cocaine, drink the most champagne, suffer the worst liver disease, are not reliant on work because they receive an income from their capital and property, and pay a nanny or public school to try to parent their offspring?

EMPATHY AND UNDERSTANDING

Britain is a country of opportunities but only for a few; it is a country of drudgery for the many, and misery for a growing minority. Even those who enjoy great opportunity have to leave if they wish to live in a less divided society. The map and cartogram in Figure 3.3 showed which areas of residence give you a chance of attending the most elite university. For the most elite street, the odds from birth begin to approach 50:50. In contrast, there are other streets where a newborn baby is far more likely to enter prison than university or college shortly after their eighteenth birthday, and many areas where often being out of work is still quite a likely future, due most importantly to being born in the wrong postcode, and therefore going to the wrong school in the wrong town or city.

In Britain in 2018, people were out of work most often where there was a lack of work, not because they were feckless. The real level of unemployment in Britain, when properly measured, was 2.3 million, not the 800,000 reported by the government.[72] While national government claims to have brought unemployment down to new lows, and says that people who can't find work are not trying hard enough, the reality is that your chances of finding any work depend mainly on where you live. Then, on top of your geography, your chances of finding well-paid work depend on your social background – what kind of family you were born into. As Britain became more and more divided in the run-up to summer 2018, your parents' social class and where you were from grew greatly in importance.

For those out of work and those in low-paid work in England and Wales, there was a 14 per cent increase in the use of bailiffs by local authorities between 2014 and 2017, to collect the local taxes that poorer people increasingly could not afford to pay. Bailiffs were used 1.38 million times by local councils in the financial year 2016/17.[73] British social and economic policy since 2010 has been particularly influenced by the Conservative Party's ironically named think tank the Centre for Social Justice. It would be far more accurately called the Centre for the Spread of Mistruths. The centre has worked hard to blame the victims of inequality and, subsequently, austerity for their own woes.

In 2008, the Centre for Social Justice (CSJ), an organisation created by the ardently pro-Brexit MP Iain Duncan Smith, produced several reports which included CT scans of the supposedly 'deprived brains' of children, apparently caused by maternal neglect. For an example, see the cover of a 2011 paper entitled 'Early Intervention, Smart Investment, Massive Savings'[74] by MP Graham Allen in a report which claimed to contrast the brain of a 'normal' three-year-old child with a 'neglected brain', with the words 'costs to the taxpayer' beside it. The latter CT scan was taken from a US paper[75] and showed the brain of a child following 'severe sensory-deprivation neglect', described as 'minimal exposure to language, touch and social interactions'. However, that paper itself pointed out that other chaotically neglected children did not in any case demonstrate such changes.

The Allen report was implying that severe neglect is widespread and a significant drain on the system, which isn't the case, and also that a smaller brain, or a brain that hasn't properly formed, is a common result of cases of neglect, which the US paper it quoted found was false. The number of children in the UK with such brain changes is negligible and furthermore they would have automatically been taken into care when they became known to the authorities. The supposed costs of a damaged brain included low attainment, welfare benefits, drug and drink abuse, teen pregnancy, violent crime and a shorter life. The Centre for Social Justice simply got it completely wrong. That report is an example of Conservative politicians deliberately propagating a myth.

The children of the elite, from whom Conservative think tanks tend to draw their staff, are still educated separately. Arguably, this makes them less empathetic and more complacent about their apparent privileges. Such people are currently driving education policy in England – it is no wonder that the country is in such a sorry state.

It has been argued that it is a lack of empathy among their leaders that induces Conservative regimes around the world to enact policies that harm their people so much more often and more deeply than their more progressive counterparts. Looking just at suicides, one study of 100 years' worth of data for England and Wales concluded that of all the suicides that had taken place, 'roughly 35,000 of these people would not have died had the Conservatives not been in government. This is one suicide for every day of the century, or more appropriately, two for every day that the Conservatives ruled.'[76] Thirteen years after that finding, when the Conservative government of 2015 released a report on the 40,680 people who had died within a year of receiving an adverse decision on their benefit claims, its researchers argued: 'These isolated figures provide limited scope for analysis and nothing can be gained from this publication that would allow the reader to form any judgement as to the effects or impacts of the Work Capability Assessment.'[77]

Current government policy in England aims to ensure that by 2020 all schools will be semi-privatised academies or free schools, and competition between schools is to be greatly encouraged. In contrast, in his award-winning book *Finnish Lessons*,[78] Pasi Sahlberg notes that although changing to a successful education system takes time and needs government support, a system based on competition, denigrating teachers, with semi-privatised schools and business management (running schools as a business) is the very opposite of the key to success. The belief that all young people can learn, with no assumptions that hereditary or social factors will limit the potential, characterises the Finnish system, and so many other systems in the affluent world that are all radically different from that pursued in the UK and USA. In all the more equitable countries of the world, geographical location is not a key to higher education destination, and there are no elite groups asserting that some children are inherently less capable of learning. Everyone there does so much better as a result.

RACIAL SUPERIORITY, PATRIOTISM AND BREXIT

Unfortunately, the British and to a large extent the Americans have ignored the lessons of those who have repeatedly explained why they are not inherently superior to others. In 1927, the biologist Raymond Pearl, one of the earliest critics of the eugenic movement, wrote that: 'I frankly do not see the usually alleged cause for eugenic alarm, for the reason that history demonstrates, I believe, that the superior people of the world have always been recruited from the masses, intellectually speaking, in far greater numbers than they have been reproduced by the upper classes'.[79]

As the geneticist Eric Turkheimer has pointed out, if 'all other sources of variation between people are accounted for then everything is heritable'.[80] But of course other sources of variation have huge impact and so we are left with very little that is heritable, and what is inherited is the result of the random mixing of two sets of genes producing a pretty random outcome. In fact, it is an almost completely random outcome.[81] What matters most to the vast majority of people is how they are treated after they are born (and also during their development in the womb), not their particular genetic makeup. For instance, his genes may have possibly made Jeremy Corbyn an unusually kind man, one not predisposed to be greedy, but it was events around him that propelled him to become leader of the Labour Party, not his innate ability. Corbyn is not an especially gifted public speaker; he was not born with a trait for great charisma, or an innate flair for getting others to trust him when perhaps they shouldn't. But no party leader, no Prime Minister that Britain has ever had has been particularly special as a person. And at least Corbyn understands that when Plato originally suggested children could be divided into those who were gold, silver, iron and brass, as God had fashioned them, Plato was talking *without* the benefit of thousands of years of subsequent understanding, research and scientific discovery.[82]

Genes only matter greatly when everything else hardly matters at all, and that hardly ever happens because more crucial factors intervene. It may be the case that the vast improvements in mass education that have occurred are now producing far more educated people than it is assumed can be accommodated in a digital global economy, and this may be yet another contemporary reason for the perpetuation of myths that attempt to support inequality. The idea that most people can be educated and participate more equally in democracies continues to be a problem for – that is, a threat to – those who see themselves as superior. However, do not lose heart: as Adam Smith explained in 1776, the difference between a philosopher and a street porter 'seems to arise not so much from nature as from habit, custom, and education'.[83]

The British ignored what Adam Smith knew about education, what Raymond Pearl explained, what thousands of educationalists have tried to convey in recent decades: that the golden children are a fantasy.[84] There are no super-genes. We are not led by extraordinarily able people – that is obvious. The 'British race' is not a race. It is a collection of mongrel invaders and other immigrants that owes its most recent manifestation to the Huguenots (1572), the Dutch (in 1688), the Irish (1840s), the Jews (1880s), and all those from the Caribbean, the countries of Africa, the Indian subcontinent, and every corner of former empire and then Europe who came and came and came. For example, the area with the greatest concentration of immigrant children as recorded by recent British censuses has been Hyde Park in London. And the birthplace of the largest group of these foreign-born children was the United States of America. More generally, they were the immigrant children of international bankers.

Britain has not become 'polluted' by joining the European Union. Leaving it will not bring about some great new era of superiority where an inborn British ability and predisposition to trade, to earn, to invent and to invest will cause the country to be great again once the British genes are freed from supposed EU restraint. Like so much myth-making, these ideas are destined, alongside Empire 2.0, for their place in the great dustbin of stupid ideas in our history. And, while we are about it, something to add to the mix for that dustbin is patriotism.

Patriotism, referred to by Samuel Johnson in 1775 as 'the last refuge of the scoundrel', is often a strange quasi-religion based on artificial national boundaries, generally the result of wars and myths. Samuel Johnson's biographer, James Boswell, later clarified that Johnson's line wasn't meant to condemn all patriotism, but only 'that pretend-ed patriotism which so many … have made a cloak for self-interest'. Johnson himself thought that he practised a true patriotism.

Patriotism is often seen as obligatory if you are born within particular boundaries. You are expected to adopt it if you choose to move to Britain, but it is something you should apparently never lose if you move away or even die: 'There's some corner of a foreign field that is for ever England. There shall be in that rich earth a richer dust concealed.' Every English politician, including Labour Party leader Jeremy Corbyn and Green Party leaders Jona-than Bartley and Caroline Lucas, is required to claim that they are patriotic. With many versions of patriotism,[85] this can come close to being forced to claim that you are a bigot, 'a person who has strong, unreasonable beliefs and who does not like other people who have different beliefs or a different way of life'.

Theresa May, in saying, as she did in July 2016, that she would be prepared to push the nuclear button, stated that she would be prepared to slaughter hundreds of thousands of people in a nuclear war. And so did Donald Trump. But no one called the people in white coats to take them away. They should have done. Saying you would be prepared to commit a holocaust is not the act of a sane person. Such beliefs, held by people with such power, are completely unacceptable – unless, of course, you believe the lives of foreigners don't count because they are an inferior race. If the UK does not acquire some more able political leadership quickly, we may still be blaming others for our poor educational outcomes, our schools, our housing problems, our low wages, our underemployment and our trading problems for years to come – unless we learn more about ourselves now. False patriotism is a dangerous cloak to wear.

FIGURE 3.4: ONCE A GERMAN, ALWAYS A GERMAN

British Empire Union. 'Once a German, always a German. Remember! Every German employed means a British worker idle. Every German article sold means a British article unsold.' Poster by David Wilson, printed on the Strand in 1918 and sold in London.[86]

The poster in Figure 3.4 was produced by the British Empire Union after the First World War. It is a good example of some very false patriotism. In the fascists' view, it was the dastardly Germans who, when they had finished skewering babies and threatening women, took British jobs. This supposedly patriotic message[87] did not help ordinary people, who found that the jobs and houses they had been promised by their government did not materialise in the 1920s. Notions of patriotism and national superiority will not, and never have, put the 'great' back into Britain. Great Britain is the largest island of an archipelago of islands. It is not 'great'. It is not unimportant, but neither is it (or its Queen) particularly happy or glorious.

In the centre of the poster in Figure 3.4 is an image of the grave of the British nurse Edith Cavell, now well known for saying on the night before her execution by German firing squad on 12 October 1915, 'Patriotism is not enough. I must have no hatred or bitterness towards anyone.' The British fascists quickly tried to adopt her for their cause despite her refusal to indulge in hatred. They even put her grave in their posters, but she was no bigot. As a nurse during the First World War, she saved the lives of soldiers from both sides without discrimination. Presumably her views on patriotism were not common knowledge in 1918. A statue was erected to her in London in 1920 inscribed: 'For King and Country'. A version of her last message was not added until 1924, following a campaign led by Dick Sheppard, subsequently the founder of the pacifist Peace Pledge Union. Today, war with Germany is unimaginable. Today, Edith is remembered for telling us that 'patriotism is not enough' on the very night before she knew she was to be killed. Today, as always, there is great hope that we will learn from our mistakes and become better people.

We have a lot to learn. When a country loses at war, its people quickly learn from its errors. The British have not lost a war for a very long time. The British elite have never had to confront their belief in eugenics in the way the German elite had to. They have not had to address the failures of their prestigious selective private schools, schools of the kind that are rare in the large majority of more equitable affluent countries worldwide. The British have inadvertently chosen to learn about themselves through the process of Brexit. It is a better way to learn than going to war.

CHAPTER 4

HIGH INEQUALITY AND IGNORANT POLITICIANS

Brexit is intricately connected to Britain's unaddressed and unredressed imperial past.

– Nadine El-Enany, November 2017[1]

The questions are obvious. Who are we? What does 'we' mean in a state that encompasses four different nations? Where have 'we' come from? What diverse and contested histories have shaped 'us'? Where are 'we' going – and where do 'we' want to go? The answers are a different matter ... But the England of frivolous Etonians, the swollen House of Lords and the London-based elite is not the only England.

– David Marquand, June 2018[2]

INTRODUCTION

The British, and especially the English, are not good at thinking about themselves except as being in competition with other peoples and countries.[3] Today, that competition is most obvious when it comes to the football World Cup, but in the past it also concerned industrial prowess. Sport is a useful distraction today. Britain currently has a very poor record of investment in industry, and in health, housing, education and other measures of inequality, when compared to almost all other European countries. Despite not being so continuously competitive, these other countries have recently made greater social and economic progress, seen life expectancy rise faster, and their people fare better overall than the citizens of the four countries of the UK.[4]

When Britain joined the European Community in the early 1970s, Sweden was the only large European country to have lower income inequality than the UK. By the time the British chose to leave the European Union, they had the highest income inequality of any country in Europe. That was not because of the EU; the British did that to themselves, largely by themselves. American bankers and Australian-born newspaper tycoons played a part, but essentially the British engineered this unwelcome change themselves. They did this with the help of Margaret Thatcher and the right wing of her party, with the help of Tony Blair and his *New* Labour, and a few like-minded 'patriots' and their newspapers. At the very same time, all other EU countries, even including those where inequality increased, managed to become relatively more equitable places to live than Britain.

The British are in a very bad place. The last time pay fell as much as it has fallen recently was during the 1860s and 1870s.[5] Death rates have risen, with about 120,000 more deaths occurring between 2010 and 2017 than would have occurred had the UK been better politically managed.[6] But it has not been well managed, and so life expectancy in the UK has stalled in a way that, like pay falls, has not been seen since the 1860s. It is projected that an extra million years of life will be lost by 2057 if these trends are not altered.[7]

This chapter concerns the persistence of an imperial mindset in Britain. It is a mindset that suggests that pay cuts simply require the application of a stiff upper lip for a few years. It is a mindset that implies that if mortality rates are rising, that is just a cost to be borne. It is a mindset that is undermining Britain's chances of trade success post-Brexit. It is a mindset that works well when you are living in the most powerful country in the world and need to keep your confidence high to impose your will on others. But it is a mindset that is highly damaging to society and to each individual that holds it in the decades after the empire has ended. Fortunately, we can see that over time the English are learning to move away from seeing themselves as so very great (Figure 4.1).

FIGURE 4.1: HOW PROUD OR EMBARRASSED ARE YOU ABOUT IDENTIFYING AS ENGLISH?

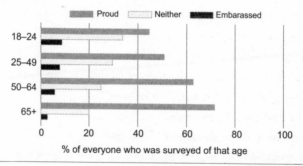

Results of a survey of people in England carried out in May 2018.[8]

Fewer than half of all 18–24-year-olds in England are now proud of being English. Given this, and given that the young are traditionally the most rebellious, there are some questions to be asked and answered. Why don't the British rebel against their leaders? One answer is that they have been taught that their leaders have incredible intellects (especially the Etonians), so it is folly to pooh-pooh them and, of course, the English are seen by so many within England as being naturally superior. There is a geography to this tendency. When surveyed in May 2018, some 90 per cent of respondents in Lincolnshire and the Midlands felt strongly that being English was something to be proud of, but less than half the populations of towns such as Liverpool and Manchester were proud of being English. Perhaps it was the young in large university cities who were least likely to be proud of being English because they are now being taught a little more about the truth of England's colonial history than the old or their counterparts in Lincolnshire and most of the Midlands.[9]

TAKE UP THE WHITE MAN'S BURDEN
Take up the White Man's burden –
Send forth the best ye breed –
Go send your sons to exile
To serve your captives' need;
To wait in heavy harness
On fluttered folk and wild –
Your new-caught, sullen peoples,
Half devil and half child.
– Rudyard Kipling, 1899[10]

It may not be such a good idea for British politicians to show off their knowledge of Kipling's poetry, as the British Foreign Secretary, Boris Johnson, started to do in 2017 on an official visit to the Shwedagon Pagoda, the most sacred Buddhist temple in Myanmar. Fortunately, the British Ambassador quickly stopped Johnson's impromptu recital, preventing him from further embarrassing himself and his country and further diminishing the status of Britain in the eyes of the Commonwealth.

Joseph Rudyard Kipling, journalist and poet, was born in Bombay (now Mumbai) in 1865. He was awarded the Nobel Prize for Literature in 1907, but even in his lifetime his poetry was regarded as propaganda for imperialism, with an added and very distinctive racial bias. His 1899 poem (of which a stanza is shown above) had originally been written for Queen Victoria's Diamond Jubilee but was then replaced by another of his poems. It was later rewritten to support the USA's (for Kipling, still Anglo-Saxon) colonisation of the Philippine Islands.

The life of Kipling's friend Cecil Rhodes (1853–1902) had epitomised taking up 'the White Man's burden'. The phrase is now referred to with some irony. In four words it highlights how deluded the British had become about their empire by 1899. They described it as a burden, when it was actually giving them unjustified luxury. Almost all the older buildings of Britain's great universities were built from the spoils of empire. They were funded by gifts from plantation owners to build libraries at All Souls, Oxford, or by voluntary penny levies on the workers of Sheffield to build a university for their grandchildren, the pennies indirectly coming from sales of metal work abroad. Once you start to look, and follow the money back, a huge amount of our infrastructure, from municipal sewers to royal palaces, can be traced back to financial sources that would not have existed but for the British Empire. Of course, not all of the British benefited. Hardly any of the grandchildren of the workers of Sheffield ever went to university, and that library at All Souls is often very empty.

Before his death, Rhodes had paid for the building of the Honoured Dead Memorial, an ancient Greek-styled monument in Kimberley, South Africa, to commemorate the British who had died defending the city during the Siege of Kimberley in the Anglo-Boer War. Inscribed on that memorial is the following poem, written by Kipling:

This for a charge to our children in sign of the price we paid
The price we paid for freedom that comes unsoiled to your hand
Read revere and uncover for here are the victors laid
They that died for the city being sons of the land[11]

When the poem speaks of 'our children', it means the children of the British invaders in Africa. When it speaks of freedom, it is the freedom of the British to invade and colonise foreign countries against the wishes of the local people. When it says that freedom was achieved unsoiled, the words are a lie, as too was the claim that the British invaders were the sons of the land they took from others. The British soldiers had mostly been born in Britain.

Why did the British rewrite history as they did? Why did they inflict their oddly Anglo-centric schooling on so much of the rest of the world? Recent detailed work has now discovered that even at the very time of the greatest expansion of the British Empire there was something very odd about the British. Some researchers, looking in detail at the behaviour of colonialists, have 'even suggested that imperialism ... was [a] real mental disorder; they explained the behaviour of British colonialists in terms of status anxieties, sexual hang-ups, and feelings of insecurity'.[12] The suggestion was that the empire-building fed these insecurities – but also that the building of empire was initially partly caused by them. From Clive of India to Lawrence of Arabia, with hundreds in between, it is a very odd set of characters who make up the list of British Empire heroes. Building an empire, just like fighting in a war, can lead to serious mental ill health. Poor mental health can hardly be cited as a justification for colonialisation, however.

Britain is such an unequal and unproductive country today precisely because of its imperial legacy, which required the establishment of an elaborate class structure, creating status anxiety and all manner of phobia, including sexual inhibitions, awe of the upper echelons and disdain of the lower classes and the 'natives'. While the British Empire is long gone, we are still living through its legacy today. Without a clear understanding of what the Empire was about, we cannot properly understand ourselves today. So, let's take a little time to remember Cecil Rhodes with more honesty than most do.

After spending only one term at Oriel College in Oxford, where he enlisted in the Bullingdon Club,[13] Rhodes, aged twenty, joined the white man's rush to exploit gold and diamonds. He acquired the huge open-cast mine at Kimberley. There, he would apparently spend hours gazing into the pit where 'thousands of naked Africans filled one-ton iron ore buckets with blue earth'.[14] These were the 'new-caught, sullen peoples, half devil and half child' as described in Kipling's poem. By the age of twenty-two, Rhodes was a billionaire controlling 90 per cent of the world's diamond output and in 1890, aged thirty-seven, he became Prime Minister of the Cape Colony.

Rhodes believed that the Anglo-Saxons were 'the finest race in the world', and that an expansion of the British Empire should include taking back the American colonies. He pioneered the use of the Maxim machine gun, the weapon most associated with British imperial conquest.[15] His men used it to slaughter Africans; they used slave labour and they set the scene for apartheid in South Africa. Almost all older people in England have been taught very little of this history, but the young know a little more of it – or have a sense of it – hence they are less proud to say they are English, with all the connotations that brings for them.

Both Rhodes and Kipling were big supporters of the 1899–1902 Anglo-Boer War between the British Empire and Dutch settlers, when the British turned refugee camps into concentration camps in which about 26,000 Boer women and children died.[16] The Boer War was a particularly nasty conflict in which the normal rules of engagement were frequently broken. Arthur Conan Doyle, reporting on the war, was worried that the British used deadly expanding dumdum bullets against the former Dutch settlers, bullets that were 'never intended to be used against the white races'. They were banned by the Hague Convention in 1899. But Conan Doyle and those he supported also had concerns over immigration into Britain. The imperialists were very happy to go abroad and do whatever they wished, but they were often hugely concerned about the idea of others coming to Britain. At the turn of the twentieth century, racist concerns about 'alien immigrants', especially Jews, were rife. The figure of John Bull was frequently used to personify the portly freeborn Englishman who feared that his way of life would be tainted by the arrival of others. Ironically, John Bull was originally a figure of derision when first drawn in cartoon form in 1712, the equivalent of the pejorative term 'gammon' used first as an insult in 2012 to apply to white right-wingers who are said to turn a deep gammon pink when angered.[17]

**FIGURE 4.2: 'JOHN BULL' LOCKING THE DOOR,
DAILY EXPRESS, FIRST PUBLISHED IN 1901**

ANOTHER OPEN DOOR.

NOTICE.
DESTITUTE
ALIEN
IMMIGRANTS
WILL PLEASE
KEEP OUT

JOHN BULL :—"I think it's about time I closed it."

An early example of tabloid press xenophobia, stoking fear of those from Eastern Europe.[18]

Arthur Conan Doyle, best known as the creator of Sherlock Holmes, was a racist, an antisemite and a proto-fascist.[19] He helped fund the British Brothers' League, which was set up in 1902 with the slogan 'England for the English', to prevent Jewish immigration and 'stop Britain being a dumping ground for the scum of Europe'.[20] East End of London Conservative MP Major Evans-Gordon became closely allied with the league, and together Conan Doyle and Evans-Gordon were instrumental in the introduction of the first immigration controls and regulations through the Aliens Act of 1905. In a statement before the House of Commons, Evans-Gordon said, 'Smallpox and scarlet fever have unquestionably been introduced by aliens within the past few months, and ... trachoma, a ... cause of total loss of sight, and favus, a disgusting and contagious disease of the skin, have been and are being introduced by these aliens on a large scale.'[21] In 1902, the ophthalmologist F. A. C. Tyrell had reported that Jews were 'peculiarly prone to trachoma' and suggested that it was 'largely a disease of race'. All this fuelled the early fears about immigration to Britain.

The Aliens Act gave the Home Secretary overall responsibility for immigration and nationality matters. Ostensibly designed to prevent paupers and criminals from entering the country, one of its main objectives was to stop Jewish immigration from Eastern Europe. Campaigning in favour of the law, Evans-Gordon said, 'Not a day passes but English families are ruthlessly turned out to make room for foreign invaders,' and 'The rates are burdened with the education of thousands of foreign children.' Problems with health, housing and education were all claimed, as now, to be caused by immigration.[22] A little later, the league was absorbed by Oswald Mosley's British Union of Fascists. There were intimate connections between the thoughts and actions of Cecil Rhodes and his friends and the origins of fascism in Britain.

Before he died, Cecil Rhodes set up a scholarship programme to bring English-speaking young men from abroad to Oxford University. They in turn were then to bring 'the whole of the uncivilized world under British rule'.[23] The scholarship continues to this day, though now some young women are also recipients, and increasingly the scholars are not white. However, you will not find much mention of Rhodes's original aims on the website of the Rhodes Trust itself, which in October 2017 said:

Established in 1903, the Rhodes is the oldest and perhaps the most prestigious international graduate scholarship programme in the world. Cecil Rhodes's vision in founding the Scholarship was to develop outstanding leaders who would be motivated to fight 'the world's fight' and to 'esteem the performance of public duties as their highest aim', and to promote international understanding and peace.[24]

Ironically, given all the rhetoric about not rewriting history, that particular little bit of history has now been deleted from the Rhodes Trust website. However, the endnote attached to the quote above gives the wayback machine web reference to let you see how the page was edited during 2017 and 2018. It is, of course, encouraging that whoever was in charge of the website in 2017 realised that talking about Rhodes's vision as something to emulate was perhaps misguided.

To find Rhodes's true intentions, you need to read his 1877 *Confession of Faith*,[25] in which he explained: 'It is our duty to seize every opportunity of acquiring more territory and we should keep this one idea steadily before our eyes that more territory simply means more of the Anglo-Saxon race, more of the best, the most human, most honourable race the world possesses.' It is sometimes said that you should not judge people in the past by the morality of today. However, long before Rhodes was behaving so outrageously, many people had been teaching peace and understanding and were behaving far more morally than he was. There were also many critics of the idea that 'the Anglo-Saxon race' was superior to others. Writers in the *Manchester Guardian* attacked Rhodes in the 1890s. Even by the standards of his day, he was considered a particularly virulent racist. Today, Rhodes and his kind represent some of the worst of human behaviour. If this were better known in Britain, there would be less rose-tinted nostalgia for the empire. The statue of Cecil Rhodes that still stands high above Oxford's High Street signifies how badly educated the British elite remain about their past. One day, when the elite in Britain are better educated, that statue will no longer stand in that prominent spot and Rhodes's name will be taken away from many other places and buildings. It is simply a matter of time, determination and equality.[26] A very economically unequal nation, such as England has become, can be very slow to see the direction in which the wind is blowing. Great inequality leads to such particular blindness.

And what of the argument that removing the statue would amount to rewriting history, the central line used by its supporters? Moving a statue indoors, just like deleting a webpage on the Rhodes Trust website, does not remove a person from history. Rhodes shouldn't be celebrated. He should be remembered. But we need the most prominent spaces for our new statues. History is always being written.

ARCHITECTS OF EMPIRE

Rhodes House in Oxford was, like the Honoured Dead Memorial, designed by the architect Herbert Baker. There is a thread that runs from the imperialism of Rhodes and Kipling, through to the education given at Oxford throughout the twentieth century, and on to today's rampant inequality, and it is a thread that continues to hold strong today. In 1951, Stuart Hall came to the UK from Jamaica to take up one of the Rhodes scholarships. Hall was not the first non-white Rhodes scholar – that was Alain LeRoy Locke in 1907 – but he was one of very few. Times then were changing, and Stuart Hall would spend his academic life changing them, demonstrating the links between racial prejudice and the media, and how New Labour operated only on the 'terrain defined by Thatcherism'.[27] But those who thought you could have too much change were also desperately trying to turn the clock back and reinstate white British superiority in 1951.

In 1941, when it still looked as if Britain could lose to a German invasion, George Orwell wrote about how the class system was hampering the state's ability to fight effectively. He also turned his ire on the left in his own country and suggested that their lack of patriotism might be harming the war effort. In 'The Lion and the Unicorn', Orwell wrote:

England is perhaps the only great country whose intellectuals are ashamed of their own nationality. In left-wing circles it is always felt that there is something slightly disgraceful in being an Englishman and that it is a duty to snigger at every English institution, from horse racing to suet puddings. It is a strange fact, but it is unquestionably true that almost any English in-tellectual would feel more ashamed of standing to attention during God Save the King than of stealing from a poor box.[28]

Of course, within a few years of 1941, intellectuals across Europe had learnt to be ashamed of their own nationality – and none more so than the Germans. The English still stood to attention during 'God Save the King' by the 1960s and '70s, with a slight but growing sense of embarrassment. But they stopped stealing from the poor box, abolished the poor law, and put a welfare state in its place. People no longer had to rely on charity to survive. Charity hospitals were replaced with NHS hospitals. The country became more equitable from 1941 through to 1978. But the sniggering at English institutions had stemmed from a real embarrassment, since many were not very good.

George Orwell died in 1950. And later, much later, those he had opposed began to dismantle the welfare state, started stealing from the poor box again, and stood proudly to attention as the national anthem was played. When 'Team GB' won medals at the Olympics, they were partly funded by the National Lottery, which operates by giving false hope to the poor – in effect, a stealth tax on the working classes. The working classes were beginning to be divided by again spreading the lie that their problems were caused by immigrants.

In Britain in the 1950s, many factory owners, often backed up by trade unions, supported the colour bar that prevented any black men from working in factories, including the car factory in Oxford back when Stuart Hall was studying in the city.[29] Ordinary people agitated against the introduction of civil rights in America in the 1960s. Many of the men who joined the National Front in England in the 1970s, following its creation in 1967, were marginalised and fearful individuals – bullies who were themselves scared. They wanted to protect white racial advantages at both a collective and an individual level. All this is very recent history but so poorly known by so many. Both the authors of this book experienced the tail-end of those days. The National Front was finding it hard to accept that women and people who were not white were gaining respect and beginning to be treated in some quarters as equals. And then economic inequality began to grow wider again in Britain and we began to see the rise of a new set of more ignorant politicians, ones who had not had to fight in world wars started by arguments among imperial rivals.

All the time, progress is balanced with backwards steps and resistance to change. In 1968, a young Bill Clinton arrived in Oxford on a Rhodes scholarship. He would later become President of the USA (1993–2001), and a young Stansfield Turner, another Rhodes scholar, would become director of the CIA (1977–81). Britain may have lost control of the original thirteen US colonies, but she could still exert influence in other ways. A slew of later world leaders would pass through the doors of Rhodes House, and in Oxford they would mix with aspiring British politicians. All these people would travel to Oxford and find themselves at the heart of England, in a country that from the late 1970s onwards was becoming ever more unequal with every year that passed and ever less productive economically – in comparison with other European nations.

SO MUCH CHANGES IN A CENTURY, AND SO LITTLE

Boris Johnson arrived in Oxford in the autumn of 1983, having earlier attended Eton. David Cameron arrived, also from Eton, two years later. Britain does have a global reputation for being good at university education, and Oxford University has much to be proud of – but it also has a lot to answer for. A well-remembered joke in the 1980s series *Yes Minister* was when the minister worried that 'we must do something for the universities' and his permanent secretary, Sir Humphrey, replied soothingly, 'Of course, Minister, both of them.' The other university, of course, was Cambridge. No other university was then seen as worthy by the elite, not even the ancient Scottish ones – well, they were Scottish.

Despite all the pessimism, the British now have a more highly educated population than they did in the 1880s or 1980s, with over 40 per cent of British children now becoming students in some 123 universities (depending on how you count them).

Many other young adults go to university a little later or join the Open University, an institution sadly now subject to severe funding cuts. However, despite the cuts, almost half the young population will soon have a university degree; too many for the current number of graduate-level jobs, which may be one reason why school exams have been made harder – reducing university intake, it is thought, will then reduce competition for those jobs. This is not clever thinking.

The world has changed and may be on the verge of very much changing for the better. In the UK we could well have reached peak inequality, but that is exactly the time when everything is open to change. Today, the UK government spy centre GCHQ advertises in newspapers for cyber spies while Members of Parliament ask universities to spy on the activities of their lecturers. Not all the most intolerant are from Oxford! In October 2017, Chris Heaton-Harris, graduate of Wolverhampton Polytechnic and the Conservative MP for Daventry, found time to write to all university Vice-Chancellors asking them for the names of any professors teaching European affairs 'with particular reference to Brexit', adding, 'If I could be provided with a copy of the syllabus … I would be much obliged.'[30] One can only assume that he wanted to name and shame those who did not share his particular view of Brexit and to 'out' the Europhiles. He was compared to Joseph McCarthy, the American senator who ruined many lives in the 1950s by accusing people of being communists. He might be interested in a copy of this book.

Despite the rapidly increasing tuition fees (£1,000 introduced in 1998, £3,000 from 2004, then a whopping £9,000 per annum from shortly after 2010, and £9,250 from 2017) and much grumbling from students – rightly – as to whether they were getting value for money, by 2017, most UK and many EU students were still applying to study in Britain. However, when EU students find that after Brexit they might have to pay as much as other foreign students, they may not be so keen. As late as July 2018, ministers gave them an assurance they would not have to pay more. But, as with everything else to do with Brexit, that is not really guaranteed until everything is agreed.

Worldwide, university fees are highest in the most economically unequal of countries – in the USA, UK and Chile. They are lowest, often non-existent, in the most equitable of countries – such as Germany, the Netherlands and Finland. Universities in Britain could continue to be an attractive destination for EU and other overseas students, especially as the pound falls in value, except that the fees currently demanded are unaffordable for UK students in a country that is getting poorer. Free or very much cheaper higher education is on offer in so many other countries. As it stands, around one third of student fees in the UK are not being repaid, and the English system of most young people leaving home to attend university is financially unsupportable in the long run.[31] Going to university locally is more common in most European countries, and in the United States and in Scotland.

UK (or perhaps just English) universities may not remain so attractive when the realisation dawns that Brexit will mean the removal of both research money and the staff drawn from mainland EU countries, thus diminishing the quality of UK higher education. It is the unusually international nature of many UK universities that currently makes many of our centres of learning so attractive and creative (as well as the great advantage of all teaching being done in the language most well known among the affluent of the world). In some parts of the University of Oxford, especially those parts dedicated to global studies or international research, a majority of staff are from the European mainland. Many are anxious as to their future.[32] Furthermore, the UK is one of the largest recipients of research funding under the EU Framework Programmes (the current one being Horizon 2020), which distribute some €120 billion for collaborative research across EU countries, or about €20 billion a year.[33] The UK receives the largest share per head of all that research money.

So, following Brexit, how is the UK going to educate and train young people well at universities for a more advanced technological future? And what about the other 50 to 60 per cent who do not go to university, but whose secondary schools often rely on teachers from the European mainland (especially in London)? Brexit politicians and their advisors have not even begun to think about these issues. Instead, they worry about other aspects of Britain's standing in the world, about where Britain ranks and how we can rank higher. So, they talk of leading universities, the global race, of ambition and pride, but not of what it is that had made our universities so successful before the tuition fee rise and before Brexit.

David Cameron, convinced that he would win the vote to Remain, didn't think of the consequences when he decided to hold a referendum, and nor did Boris Johnson when he campaigned to leave. Both had been brought up with that over-confident imperialist mindset. Neither Cameron nor Johnson had much idea of what real life in Britain entailed for the vast majority of people, from university lecturer to car plant cleaner, let alone what Britain's history had really been about. Unlike younger state school children, Boris and David were not taught the unadulterated history of the country they grew up in, nor were they ever exposed to the reality of life for most people in the city they came to study in. They lived and learnt badly in a tiny, 'privileged', out-of-touch bubble.

The British do rank highly in the international education league tables for universities, although it is often their journalists and think-tank researchers who have had a hand in drawing up those league tables, and thus in deciding what counts and what doesn't. However, in international surveys of young adult ability, Britain does not rank highly in league tables of affluent nations comparing ability in literacy, numeracy and problem solving – despite having some of the world's most famous universities.[34] Perhaps it is relevant that those particular highest-ranking universities are still largely reserved for the children of the better-off and the much better-off. The British are very good at talking about just how good they are. They find proving it more difficult.

INTROSPECTION

National introspection and a constant concern with their ranking in the world is one thing at which the British excel, alongside the Americans. It was the USA and UK that spent the most money on their national Olympic teams and which were ranked first and second in the medals table at the most recent Olympics, held in Rio in 2016.[35] And yet the British are the most obese of affluent European nations and so their sporting prowess hardly reflects a pronounced national athleticism (though at least the Americans are fatter). Obesity rises in affluent nations as economic inequality, precarity and insecurity rises.

The British are also good at producing royals and politicians who say unfortunate things about 'slanty-eyed foreigners', 'piccaninnies' and Africans with 'watermelon smiles', as Prince Philip and Boris Johnson have managed to do between them. People who say such things can be found everywhere, but rarely in quite such elevated positions as they are so often found in British society. Arguably only the United States produces an even crasser set of politicians and celebrities.[36] There is little acknowledgement in British public life of just how unwelcoming Britain has been at some times to people from around the world (see Figure 4.3).

FIGURE 4.3: A CARTOON PRINTED IN 1905

"Britannia: I can no longer offer shelter to fugitives.
England is not a free country."

A cartoon printed in the wake of the 1905 Aliens Act. The text reads: 'Britannia:
I can no longer offer shelter to fugitives. England is not a free country.'
Reproduced with the kind permission of the Jewish Museum, London.[37]

As a result of so much historical self-promotion of 'the British race', the British often do not realise just how much they have relied on immigration in the past – nor how much we are reliant on it still today. For instance, we recently discovered that the British suffer from employing immigration officials who are far too keen to reduce numbers of visas for overseas students, and a Home Office that has been revealed to have produced false figures on students not returning home after their studies. It turns out that almost all overseas students who come to Britain leave when they finish studying here. Increasingly, they don't arrive in the first place. Australia overtook the UK as the second most common destination for overseas students in 2018, behind only the USA.[38] Britain is not as wonderful a place to live as some of the British imagine it to be. Students from overseas quickly return or find somewhere better to travel to, as do so many other migrants to

Britain. After both the 1991 and 2001 censuses, the British discovered that there were a million fewer people living in the country than they had believed because they had over-counted immigration and under-counted emigration.[39]

BEING PROUD OF BEING BRITISH

There are of course many things to be proud of about life in Britain: the absence of handguns; a propensity to queue in an orderly fashion; an intricate knowledge of and fascination with the weather; and an everyday acceptance of multiculturalism among a significant minority – rare in Europe – fostered by far more integration, especially in London, due to the city having been the centre of the largest empire on earth. But the British also rest on their laurels a little too much, believing that they already have so much to be proud of. For many, not being 'proud to be British' verges on treason, although thankfully the word treason was rarely used in the UK by the end of 2017. Instead, the *Daily Mail* referred to judges it does not agree with as 'Enemies of the people'.[40] If you doubt our words over the intolerance of the British, try wearing a white poppy on Remembrance Day – the poppy worn to remember all the casualties of all wars and to show a commitment to peace.[41] Intolerance of the British towards those they suspect of being unpatriotic currently runs at very high levels, further stoked up by Brexit.

The British tend to be proud of their industrial revolution, though are usually taught to be this way in school, rather than coming to this conclusion themselves. Spinning jennies, steam pumps and steam engines were not just invented by a Lancastrian (Hargreaves) and two men from Devon (Savery and Newcomen): they were part of a revolution that swept across Europe, with a huge number of similar inventions occurring at much the same time. However, it was the British who engaged in that revolution most voraciously. The change from charcoal (produced from wood) to coke (produced from coal) as fuel in iron ore furnaces led to a dramatic increase in coal mining and also immigration. The Welsh Valleys became the second most popular destination for immigrants in the world in 1890, after California.

The immigrants to South Wales came from all over the world, going down pits to dig out coal, in conditions just as dangerous as the then contemporary diamond mine at Kimberley, and almost as productive for the (English) owners. The English changed Wales irrevocably. These miners stayed in Wales, had children and became 'Welsh'. Hence the large majority of Welsh people cannot speak Welsh, because their near relatives never did. Wales is largely populated by recent migrants, almost all having arrived in just the last century and a half, or by their descendants.

The burning of so much coal meant that historically Britain emitted more carbon per person than the citizens of any other large country: 1,127 tonnes each since the start of the industrial revolution. Moreover, because carbon dioxide resulting from pollution can stay in the atmosphere for centuries, historical emissions are even more important than current emissions; they have greater aggregate effect.[42] Britain burnt its coal first and had extensive reserves to exhaust. You might say that such profligacy was all in the distant past, but over the past forty years, Scotland's North Sea oil has been largely squandered, to pay for 1980s tax cuts which mostly benefited better-off people in England, and which then encouraged economic inequality to grow further. This compares very badly with the Norwegian approach, where oil was and still is used to underwrite a sovereign wealth fund, and has been extracted more slowly as a result. Norway has also maintained high top income tax rates, which has discouraged vast disparities in pay between chief executives and workers.

The British might have a poor record when it comes to carbon pollution but they have been good at banking and financial services, despite some very dodgy dealing. Britain thinks it is the largest arms dealer in the world after the USA. At least, its officials say it is, though international statistics suggest it may only be sixth.[43] Britain also has some very impressive listening centres for spying on other people, but historically the British have not been good at unmasking their own upper-class double-agents. Today, banking, the arms trade and spying all rely on government promotion. Already, financial firms are relocating many bankers into mainland Europe, and London bankers' salaries are being cut. The European banking regulator lists the numbers of bankers paid over €1 million a year in each country in Europe. In the UK those numbers are now dropping, and not just due to the drop in the value of the pound! Furthermore, the Americans are now demanding that the British do not undercut them in the arms and aircraft trade, so future expansion of that somewhat sordid trade is unlikely. And Britain's role as America's eyes and ears in Europe will probably become much diminished, as, without access to espionage data from the European mainland, what interest should the USA have in the UK?

Throughout this book, we are asking: 'What are the British actually good at when it comes to trade?' – especially with regard to free trade, where Britain cannot oblige others to buy its goods and services. The answer, it turns out, is that Britain has fewer and fewer areas of expertise: no longer the old areas of shipbuilding, no longer textiles, no longer most eminent in banking; so perhaps the British should focus on higher education for overseas students, although, as we have seen, the shine has gone off some of Britain's universities with Brexit. Steel is still made in Britain as long as the pound is falling in value, though steel plants were recently mothballed when the pound briefly rose, and they may be again if a trade war with the USA cannot be avoided. A higher

25 per cent tariff on UK steel was imposed by the USA on 1 June 2018. However, even if that tariff is lifted, much of the steel we produce is used to make vehicle chassis, but most of the other parts for many of those cars come from mainland Europe.

It was in March 2018 that Trump first placed tariffs on steel and aluminium imports, claiming it would give jobs back to American steel workers – 'the backbone of America'. He had previously placed tariffs on imported washing machines and solar cells.[44] The Prime Minister was not amused: 'Theresa May attacks Trump's "unjustified" steel tariffs', reported *The Guardian* in June 2018.[45] Mrs May noted that 'it would have ramifications for the US defence projects'. The specialist steel imported from the UK is used in the US defence industry, and possibly even in the four F-35 planes made in the USA which recently arrived for the previously plane-less new aircraft carrier HMS *Queen Elizabeth*.

In the 1980s, Britain sent labour abroad to Germany – in the era of *Auf Wiedersehen, Pet*.[46] Could a post-Brexit future mean cheap English labour again going to the Continent? Labour where the British need work permits to enter and do not have the rights of other Europeans, where they might soon be paid less as second-class non-EU citizens, just as Turkish guest workers were once routinely paid less in Germany. This all looks more likely than the alternative, which is a great resurgence of British manufacturing. On 18 June 2018, it was announced that Britain could become a centre of excellence in the manufacturing of paper straws and that could, by 2019, create 200 jobs in a company, Transcend, that currently employs only twenty people. The jobs would be needed to supply paper straws, instead of plastic ones, to, among others, the 1,361 UK McDonald's outlets by September 2018.[47] This begs the question of how long it will be before the method of making paper straws is discovered in other countries with cheaper paper and cheaper people. It may be complex technology, but it can't be that complex. And patents don't help, as there is more than one way to make a paper straw.

The left's case for Brexit, aka Lexit, is that Britain could create 'socialism in one country' if it were free of European Union rules – although, of course, it would really be socialism in four countries. The case for Lexit weakened over recent decades as country after country on the European mainland became more economically equal than the UK: better at promoting its industry, targeting an area worth excelling in, providing welfare benefits for its people, funding its health services, building affordable housing with fair rent regulation, and teaching its children well in schools – where the school they went to mattered less and less over time. Most other European countries invest far more in their children, as well as their industry.

Britain has 'the weakest investment record of any G7 country'[48] – weaker than Canada, France, Germany, Italy, Japan or even the USA – and this is not because of its membership of the European Union. During the Brexit debates, Larry Elliott, *The Guardian*'s economics editor and Lexit proponent,[49] regularly pointed out the industrial weakness of Britain when he suggested that Brexit might be a good idea. However, he never explained why other countries within Europe managed to do so much better and still remain part of the Union. France, Germany and Italy all invest more in their industries; many smaller European countries have done even better. It is not that the EU itself has helped much. It only spends between 1 per cent and 2 per cent of all public monies in Europe, because it raises so little in tax.[50] The EU is hardly a federal super-state. But individual countries within the EU have made policy choices at the national level that have resulted in great social progress. The British keep looking for a quick fix instead. As a Downing Street policy board chief recently explained to Theresa May, in contrast to being progressive, the Tories and the government have come to look like 'a narrow party of nostalgia, hard Brexit, public sector austerity and lazy privilege'.[51] But what of those on the left who want out? We have some advice from a Dutchman for them.

IT'S TIME TO LISTEN TO THE DUTCH AGAIN

Earlier in this book, we mentioned how the Dutch arrived in the UK in 1688 and that this mattered greatly for British history, including the actual creation of Britain. Some 330 years later, one Dutchman is leaving – and he's not the only one. In October 2017, Joris Luyendijk made a heartfelt plea to the English in the pages of *Prospect* magazine. Joris is a journalist who was born and brought up in the Netherlands, but who has lived in the UK since 2011. He specialised in reporting on British banking. He asked the following questions:

> Why would you allow a handful of billionaires to poison your national conversation with disinformation – either directly through the tabloids they own, or indirectly, by using those newspapers to intimidate the public broadcaster? Why would you allow them to use their papers to build up and co-opt politicians peddling those lies? Why would you let them get away with this stuff about 'foreign judges' and the need to 'take back control' when Britain's own public opinion is routinely manipulated by five or six unaccountable rich white men, themselves either foreigners or foreign-domiciled?[52]

To try to answer Joris is difficult, but both of us are English academics who for many decades have looked at the changing social geography of the country, and how the English have been taught a particular version of their history. A huge problem is that many among us have still not accepted that our place in the world is no longer at the very top. We also don't understand that, for instance, across much of the European Union, regulations on goods have often been referred to as 'British regulations' because it was the British who in the recent past were particularly insistent on common and high safety standards across the Continent, something that we should have been proud of – but we were never told we had achieved this. The British succeeded in most of these efforts, becoming the health and safety champions of the Continent, but failed to spread the use of their strange-shaped but safer mains electrical plugs to any other European countries aside from Cyprus, Ireland and Malta (those three all being a result of British colonialism). Amazingly, the British believe myths about European regulations over the shape of bananas while not knowing the truth about all their regulations that have been imposed on others!

Had Joris been writing a few days earlier, he might also have asked why the British Ambassador had to tell the British Foreign Secretary to shut up when he started quoting Kipling in that temple in Myanmar. Was it because Boris Johnson didn't understand just how offensive it was for him to recite a poem that mocked reverence to a statue of the Buddha, and reminisced about a British soldier kissing a Burmese girl (too young to be called a woman), or because he supports Rudyard Kipling's British imperialist values? For Kipling, 'East of Suez' was where you could find relief from both the English weather and English morality (hence the girls).

Boris Johnson's imperialist stunt is unfortunately indicative of a wider issue. Almost two centuries ago, sometime around 1805, the artist James Gillray drew a cartoon of William Pitt and Napoleon Bonaparte desperately attempting to carve up the world, represented as a plum pudding (Figure 4.4). These days, the carving is done by trade deal rather than sword and gun. So where have the British got to with all those brilliant trade deals planned with the rest of the world after Brexit? It couldn't be that the brilliance was just a mirage, could it?

FIGURE 4.4: WILLIAM PITT AND NAPOLEON BONAPARTE DISSECT THE PLUM PUDDING

The Plumb-pudding in danger – or – State Epicures taking un Petit Souper by Gillray (1805). Text: 'The great Globe itself and all which it inherits is too small to satisfy such insatiable appetites.' Reprinted with kind permission of the British Library Board.[53]

In September 2017, with less than eighteen months before the leaving bell tolled, the EU's chief negotiator Michel Barnier told the world that the UK's approach to leaving the Union was 'nostalgic, unrealistic and undermined by a lack of trust'. Two weeks later, Prime Minister May suggested adding another two years before actually leaving, thereby prolonging the uncertainty and lack of clarity on trade deals. In mid-December 2017, both Boris Johnson and his fellow Old Etonian Jacob Rees-Mogg described a transition period as the UK becoming a vassal state of the European Union.

They probably deliberately used a term that only 'superior' people imbued in the finer points of empire would know – but were actually using it inappropriately. The British are choosing their fate, it is not being forced upon them, and the EU is not threatening to invade, which is what the subjects of a vassal state would fear.

In September 2017, Boris Johnson wrote an article suggesting that, after leaving the EU, the UK 'will be able to get on and do free trade deals … not least with the fastest growing Commonwealth economies, and build a truly global Britain'.[54] At the time, the UK was unable to make any progress on even the most simple of preliminary issues with the rest of the EU: what would happen over the Irish land border? Which of its financial commitments would the UK pay for after leaving? And what would be the status of EU nationals who were already living in the UK at the point the referendum had been taken in 2016? It seems deeply unlikely that Britain's leaders will be able to successfully negotiate highly complex trade deals with any speed when they are unable even to agree basic issues with their nearest neighbours.

Many of the chief Brexiteers have suggested that this scepticism amounts to 'talking Britain down', arguing that a positive attitude on the part of the general public will make up for a demonstrable failure of negotiation skills among our leaders. As the commentator Edwin Hayward tweeted in response:

> International law doesn't care about feelings, belief, positivity, optimism, or patriotism. It just is. Anyone who says that 'Brexit is failing because you don't believe in it enough' might as well be talking about fairies at the bottom of the garden, for all that their comment relates to the reality of our situation.[55]

The extent of Boris's ambitions and imagination was later judged by his comments at a dinner for Conservative Party donors, telling them that the Brexit negotiations were heading for 'meltdown' and that US president Donald Trump would have handled them better.[56] A few weeks later, the BBC reported him as having said 'Fuck business'[57] in response to a question about the concerns of so many businesses about the direction in which the negotiations were not going. The BBC rarely, if ever before, had reported the use of the word 'fuck'. By October 2018, however, 'Auntie' was reporting another Tory MP, Johnny Mercer, as having described Brexit as having become a 'shit show'.[58] One admittedly minor advantage of Brexit may turn out to be that the BBC learns to spell out swear words and stop pretending they don't exist.

Why did Boris start the swearing? Possibly the flamboyant interior of the Foreign Office[59] had gone to Johnson's head – no other ministry is so lavishly decorated, presumably designed to impress visiting dignitaries with the splendour of British imperial rule. Or perhaps he was motivated by nostalgia for what he had been taught were the grand days of empire and the pre-1973 Commonwealth, when former colonial countries were often still coerced into trading with the 'mother country'.

In autumn 2017, the Prime Minister appeared to be running around the world begging for trade deals with Canada – which had by 21 September just signed a deal with the EU after many, many years of negotiations following talks and pre-talks[60] – or with India, where so many still have rather negative memories of domination by the old East India Company. Some humility was obviously required. None was forthcoming. Within hours of Theresa May's autumn 2017 Brexit speech in Florence, the credit rating agency Moody's downgraded the UK's financial trustworthiness again.[61] That occasion is now forgotten, because her 2017 Conservative conference speech that soon followed it was even more disastrous. She lost her voice, said silly things, was dramatically interrupted by a prankster handing her a fake P45, and letters of the party slogan on the wall behind her started falling off. Even that awful speech has been overshadowed by the shambles of the Brexit negotiations that 'sort of' took place during the first six months of 2018. It should not be forgotten, however, because in that speech, while outlining her motivation for being Prime Minister, she explained that three of her cousins had become professors despite their (and her) grandmothers having worked in service. The only possible relevance of that remark was to try to imply that she had something akin to 'special genes', perhaps for fortitude and ability, making her up to the job.

But by June 2018, with nine months to go before the official leaving date and after two years of arguing, the then Brexit Secretary David Davis was in open war with the Prime Minister. This time it was over negotiations for a customs union 'backstop' to solve the problem of the border between Ireland (which was clearly staying in the EU) and Northern Ireland.[62] When the huge company Airbus tried to point out some of the problems, Cabinet minister Jeremy Hunt was called in to label their concerns 'inappropriate'.[63] Hunt's appearance may be best remembered for another utterance of a four-letter word, this time by a BBC news presenter mis-pronouncing Hunt's surname.[64] Theresa May's October 2018 conference speech saw her coming on stage to the tune of ABBA's 'Dancing Queen' and declaring that austerity was over. And the band played on.

AN EMPIRE STATE OF MIND

What on earth put the British in a position where they were so inept at negotiating as they appeared to be in 2018? Why could they not do a deal with the rest of the EU? Part of the answer is that the high days of empire were not about trade deals at all but were achieved through domination. The British made few deals and rarely stuck to those they did – the 1840 Treaty of Waitangi being a rare exception that still holds today, and even that is not taught in British history books. The main point of controlling an empire was, after all, to rob countries of their raw materials, food and – initially through slavery – labour.

All those merchants, financiers and industrialists who dominated trade from the seventeenth to the twentieth centuries were not exactly playing fair. Following early Spanish and Portuguese examples, slavery was introduced into the Caribbean by the British to grow and process the sugar that initially rotted the teeth of the aristocrats and traders. Writing on India in 2015, William Dalrymple concluded that for all the power wielded today by Exxon Mobil, Walmart or Google, they were tame beasts compared with the militarised East India Company.

Back then, foreign competition was curtailed by force. Oliver Cromwell pushed out European competition in colonial trade, with a Navigation Act in 1651, decreeing that all goods, slaves, food and manufactures were only to be carried in English ships and putting tariffs on foreign sugar arriving in England. Two further Acts followed shortly after his death, in 1660 and 1663.

In 1911, Rudyard Kipling and his co-author C. R. L. Fletcher produced *A History of England*, which included a poem by the former. This ditty splendidly linked trade with the superior British merchant and fighting navy. Starting off 'Oh where are you going to, all you Big Steamers, with England's own coal up and down the salt seas?' the poem went on to describe the food brought into the mother country from the empire. It continued:

> For the bread that you eat and the biscuits you nibble
> The sweets that you suck and the joints that you carve
> They are brought to you daily by all us Big Steamers
> And if anyone hinders our coming you'll starve.

Britain did promote free trade throughout most of the nineteenth century, but the British were in an overwhelmingly strong position to exploit it, as they could destroy domestic industries in other countries through flooding markets with cheaper goods. In New Zealand (where the Treaty of Waitangi was signed) to this day cotton sheets and towels are still referred to as 'Manchester' on retailers' shelves as a result of British dominance. But, formally, there was some genuine commitment to free trade, which changed in the early twentieth century.

By the 1920s, notions of free trade were abandoned and 'imperial preference' (a predecessor of today's 'buy British') was quickly ushered in. A plethora of organisations were created, devoted to extolling colonial trade and urging people to buy goods from the empire, including the 1924 Empire Exhibition in London, established to show off imperial goods, which attracted millions of visitors.

Universities also colluded in the celebration of empire and colonial trade. A Rhodes chair of Imperial History was set up in 1919 at the University of London, to celebrate the old rogue who had looted South Africa and the area then known as Rhodesia. Professor Halford Mackinder, one of the founders of the London School of Economics (LSE), who had set up a School of Geography in Oxford in 1899, developed a series of empire lectures for teachers in the 1920s. The Empire Marketing Board endowed a chair in Imperial Economic Relations at the LSE. All this was an attempt to create a narrative in which the British were depicted favourably and then teach that narrative to the young. But it was not true.

It all began to fall apart in the Second World War, especially when Britain depended on the USA to keep the food coming, and rationing had to be extended to July 1954. There was then a sharp decline in the UK economic growth as, one after another after another, the former colonies celebrated their independence and enjoyed the benefits of the liberalisation of trade. Independence came with growing insurrection when it became clear that Britain was no longer top dog. However, the people at home who lost out the most were the rich who had investments in the colonies, and so economic inequality within the UK fell as the rich became poorer and the poor won a welfare state.

The British elite blamed trade unions at home for their woes in the 1970s, but their economic woes were actually down to Britain's loss of bullyboy status worldwide. None of the current establishment, neither May nor Johnson, nor indeed any of their 2017 or 2018 Cabinet colleagues, appear to have learnt much of the true story of the inglorious empire[65] at school or at university. They, and much of the British media, appear to believe in a Great British superiority myth. They do not understand that the empire had made their forebears rich through exploitation and that once the empire was lost, the UK would inevitably become much poorer in comparison with other affluent countries. By GDP per head, in 1870 the UK was the richest large country in the world, becoming second to the USA by 1913, falling to fourth in 1950, eighth in 1973 and twelfth in 1989. It briefly rose to ninth by 2008 when the effects of the 1986 Big Bang and the subsequent unsustainable banking boom made themselves known, but has fallen ever since that date, dropping faster and faster with each passing year so that it will soon be outside the top two dozen, if current trends continue.[66] Brexit may well accelerate that process.

Since the late 1970s, laws such as rent regulations and re-strictions on reckless behaviour by the banks have been lifted. This allowed the rich and financial institutions to get richer by gambling with other people's money. When the gamble failed in 2008 they were bailed out by other people's money, too. It turned out that the banks had been relying on exploiting those with less money within the UK, as they could no longer exploit the colonies. There have also been a few successful attempts at new overseas ventures. One of the most successful British exports today is the TV show *The Great British Bake Off*. Initially, British baking was famous for showing what you could do with few ingredients during rationing. But the *Bake Off* has meant more flamboyance is encouraged today. Versions of the show are now screened in 196 territories. Thanks to the British concept, in the Netherlands judges on TV can now be seen 'nibbling baked breasts and sugar-dusted penises'.[67] Britain now leads the world in harmless innuendo about soggy bottoms. It's nice to be good at something harmless for a change. But the British have yet to get to the bottom of where they are from, and how they have been misinformed.

In the 1970s, when May and, later, Johnson were at school, a standard geography textbook was J. H. Stembridge's three-volume *The New World-Wide Geographies*.[68] In these 1970s textbooks, Stembridge stated that 'mankind is divided into three primary races, the Caucasian or White Race, the Mongolian or yellow race and the Negro race'. Xenophobic histories and geographies, and the memorising of Kipling's poems, was probably not the best education for understanding Britain's future world trade possibilities in the twenty-first century. What is still surprising today is how many people educated in the 1960s and 1970s will look back and say, 'I was taught nothing about the empire.' They were – but they didn't realise how much had been implicit.

WHERE TRADE REALLY HAPPENS

In March 2017, *The Times* newspaper reported that Liam Fox's plans were being derided by his civil servants as 'Empire 2.0'. It was pointed out that he had expressed particular colonial yearnings, tweeting a year earlier in March 2016 that 'the United

Kingdom is one of the few countries in the European Union that does not need to bury its 20th century history'. Adam Ramsay, who reported that tweet, also explained that 'since the end of World War II – which marked the beginning of the end of the British Empire – the UK hasn't really figured out how on earth to pay our way in the world'.[69] The Brexiteers were not just driven by folly: they were driven by shame over what they saw as the poor national trade record. Britain had joined the EU hoping to improve that record.

It is not just nostalgia that has got the British into trouble. One major problem is enormous ignorance of where Britain gets most of its imports from. The graph in Figure 4.5 shows recent data. India was only the 16th most important country from which Britain received imports in 2017. Similarly, Australia ranked outside the top 24 (it had ranked 22nd a year earlier) and Malaysia ranked 23rd. For the UK, the country that produced more of what the British needed than any other in 2017 was Germany, followed by the USA, then China and then a series of other EU and European free-trading-bloc nations, beginning with the Netherlands and ending with Poland. Figure 4.5 also shows that the total the British imported from the top six countries it trades with rose by $11 billion in the year to 2017.

The most ardent of Brexiteers really do suggest that a second empire is possible. In an attempt to sound up-to-date, they actually began to adopt that joke version of computer-speak to name it – Empire 2.0. What had started as parody became farce. *The Times* newspaper reported: 'Ministers aim to build "empire 2.0" with African Commonwealth'.[70]

Brexiteers often use terms like 'Anglosphere' or 'Global Britain'. And while they don't explicitly advocate imperialism, this is often what their wishes amount to in some (much watered-down) sense. However, the facts get in the way of plans for Empire 2.0.

FIGURE 4.5: IMPORTS TO THE UK IN BILLIONS OF US DOLLARS (2017)

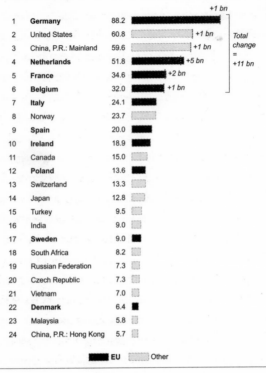

*International Monetary Fund estimates of 2017 trade
data showing ranking and change from 2016.*[71]

The data source used in Figure 4.6 revealed that in 2015, India, despite its huge population, was only the UK's eighteenth largest export market; by 2016, that ranking had dropped to twenty-third. By 2017 it had improved slightly to twenty-first, though still hadn't managed to reclaim its position from a year before Brexit. In 2019, we will know if it is back at eighteenth place or not. All this is despite the pound falling in value and it is becoming easier, in theory, to export.

Britain is no longer strong in manufacturing. Its record is poor when compared with many other European countries and has been getting worse over time. Britain exports less and less widely. Despite that, many Brexiteers think that 'Empire 2.0' is possible, presumably to arrive at the same time as Xbox 1 is replaced by Xbox 2 (made in China). This is a risible fantasy made possible only by the fostering of immense ignorance among a significant proportion of those educated in elite UK schools and universities.

Most manufacturing in the UK is relatively low-tech and driven by cost considerations. That which is high-tech, such as ARM in Cambridge, is now often owned by overseas investors, in this case the Japanese. Britain has also failed to invest in technology. The precursors to ARM chips were originally state funded and appeared in BBC microcomputers, but the British (especially the English) have preferred real-estate investment pipe-dreams to industrial hard work. It looked as if the rate of return on assets in Britain was greater if those assets were not industrial, so the British with money in the main moved out of industry. What the British do make, when it is not going to Europe, is going to the country which already has the largest trade deficit in the world and whose President says he wants imports cut – the USA.

It is worth saying it again: the destination for the most exports from the UK to any single country is the USA. But British exports to the USA were worth $6 billion *less* in 2016 as compared to 2015. Figure 4.6 shows the total then dropping again by $2 billion in the year to 2017. This is the latest data at the time of writing and refers to the situation before any tariffs were imposed by President Trump's executive orders. Figure 4.6 also shows that, in aggregate, the UK exports *massively more* to Western European countries than to the USA, after which most (but not that many) exports go to China, and then, in financial terms, the UAE. The UK currently exports almost ten times as much by value to Germany than India. However, exports to the top six countries in the last year grew by only $10 billion while imports grew by $11 billion, further widening the overall trade gap; despite the fall in the pound.

FIGURE 4.6: EXPORTS FROM THE UK IN BILLIONS OF US DOLLARS (2017)

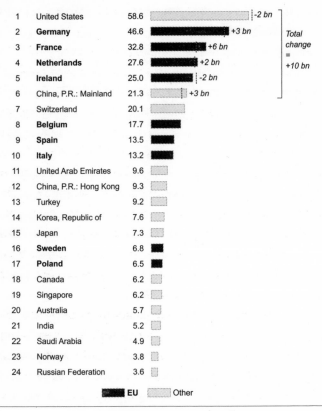

International Monetary Fund estimates of 2017 trade data showing ranking and change from 2016.[72]

The UK imports far more material goods than it exports – because it also exports 'invisibles', financial products. Invisibles cannot be seen, but they matter just as much as goods in monetary terms. The net invisible trade balance is the profit Britain makes by trading financial products or simply by acting as a conduit for trades in insurance contracts or currency conversions or the raising of capital that passes through the City of London. The greatest market for these invisible products is mainland Europe and if the banks are not 'passported' (i.e. allowed to operate in Europe) as completely as they presently are, that is also threatened. Let's face it, Brexit will not result in Empire 2.0, but in Empire 0.0 – a return to the days before the British Empire existed – which could be all to the good in the end. Eventually, every place that once had an empire learns to get over it. Even with passporting, the British banking sector has suffered a huge loss of reputation due to Brexit. But the unexpected Brexit result and, more importantly, the completely unexpected rapid last-minute swing in favour of the Labour Party at the June 2017 general election mean that what was once thought of as impossible may no longer be so. If the British people can vote for Brexit maybe one day they might also nationalise the banks. One of the main banks in New Zealand, Kiwibank, is nationalised. Perhaps now is a good time to begin to learn from former colonies about how to survive when you have to make your own way in the world.

Brexit, whatever it eventually comes to mean, will be about Britain learning how small a country it really is – how unimportant a trade partner it really is compared to the inflated propaganda about its imagined greatness. When you see Theresa May looking broken and Boris Johnson appearing to play the fool, you are seeing how Britain looks to the rest of the world.

WHERE REALITY LEAVES BRITAIN

So where does this leave Boris Johnson, the other Brexiteers, the Prime Minister and the future of UK trade deals? Since the EU takes 44 per cent of UK exports, as compared to 9.5 per cent to the Commonwealth, and the Indian Tata empire has recently effectively (via a merger with a German company) signed another trade deal with the EU, will Britain really get any imperial preference in trade deals?

As of November 2017, the government was still not letting on about what it thought trade and the economy would actually be like after Brexit. The shadow Brexit Secretary, Keir Starmer, had to use a 'humble address', an ancient parliamentary procedure not used since the nineteenth century, to try to find out what civil servants and their ministers believed might happen. Eventually, the closely guarded government impact assessments on fifty-eight sectors of the economy were leaked – and turned out not to be impact assessments at all, in the government's own meaning of that term, but a miscellaneous collection of documents of probably doubtful value but with very worrying implications. For example, on 18 June 2018, we learnt that 'UK-made parts for planes could be no longer valid and pilot licences could be defunct'[73] after 29 March 2019 if no complex deal is agreed. Negotiations for a separate deal for aviation were not allowed, as 'nothing is agreed until everything is agreed'. And this will include whether UK-made military aircraft can fly in mainland European countries, which is hardly reassuring news for the British arms trade.

All major British political parties still agree that selling arms is a trade that gives the country an economic boost, even if the partners and recipients are a bit dubious on the moral and human rights front. Labour under Jeremy Corbyn is becoming a bit more sceptical about the true value of the arms trade, and the Greens have always opposed it. In September 2017, Britain's Defence Secretary signed a deal to sell twenty-four Typhoon jet fighters to Qatar, and BAE Systems announced that it has orders on the books from the Royal Saudi Air Force, the Royal Air Force of Oman and the Kuwait Air Force. The Saudi deal has so far failed to materialise, but despite that, the rest of the world watches on and often thinks what a dubious and pathetic trade the British now try but fail to excel in.

So much for arms, or flying to foreign destinations, but what about food for the British, especially if the Brexit negotiations fall apart – will people go hungry or have to eat (even more) poorly? Many people in Britain eat very unhealthily already compared to what is common on the Continent. This is a small part of why life expectancy in Britain is low compared to the rest of Europe, especially Western Europe. Life expectancy for women in the UK is now lower than in Austria, Belgium, Cyprus, Finland, France, Germany, Greece, Iceland, Ireland, Italy, Liechtenstein, Luxembourg, Malta, the Netherlands, Norway, Portugal, Spain, Sweden and Switzerland.[74]

The World Trade Organization's trading rules are the default backstop if a hard Brexit were to occur. The questions this raises are many and worrying. With only world trade rules to protect British imports, will the British in future be getting chlorinated chicken, phoney corned beef and rotten avocados? A rational observer looking in from outside might at this point well ask: 'Can they make enough from selling arms and laundering dodgy money through their discredited financial institutions to pay their way in the future that is being planned?' Most farmers in Britain run small operations and can only survive because of EU-backed subsidies, especially those north of the Severn–Wash line. The future of farming in Britain has been cast into great uncertainty, as the UK may well not be able to afford to replicate EU farming subsidies in future, and at the same time fund its National Health Service and keep its taxes low for the rich and its inefficient industrial and service sectors as they currently are. Something is going to have to give.

Joris Luyendijk ended his piece in *Prospect* magazine on what he had learnt by living in Britain for six years with these wise words:

As for the EU, it is first and foremost a rule-based organisation. If the rules around Article 50 were bent to allow Britain back in on special terms, then the whole edifice is undermined.

Scotland should be let in if it wants, and Northern Ireland too. But England is out and must be kept out – at least until it has resolved its deep internal problems. Call it nation building.

Joris makes a good point. He could have added that all the MEPs from Britain would also then be retired, which removes the largest group of far-right MEPs in the European Parliament, as the Conservatives are to the right of mainstream European Conservatives and there are so many UKIP MEPs. He could have mentioned all the opt-outs that the British should not really have had in the first place. He could have mentioned how much better are the prospects for more joined-up-thinking in the EU without the UK. The British have yet to come to terms with themselves and what they have done. Until they do that, their future prospects are poor.

No country on earth has carved up so much of the globe and constructed so many other countries, often with the wrong borders in the wrong way and at the wrong time. Those who believe that the empire will rise again fail to understand that the British will now have to accept reduced economic status and heal the harm caused by so many decades of rising economic inequality and social division. They may never come to understand the ignominy of their position. They may always blame doubters, like us, or they may blame the Germans, or immigrants in some convoluted way – but never themselves. They may believe Britain has never lost a war, but it has certainly lost a battle – one which it was responsible for starting, before the negotiations on Brexit began. It never was in a strong position to negotiate.

The Brexiteers believed in 'the market'; believed that nations should be competitive, rather than co-operative; and insisted that there should be winners and losers (and that the mainlanders would get less of 'our' money). The British held a referendum and when 52 per cent voted out, they found that they had picked a battle with the EU that, on the evidence, they were bound to lose. The EU will soon recover from any impact of Britain leaving. The EU27 could even become stronger as a result of this separation from the belligerent British. It may be many years before a constructive attempt at nation building and soul searching in Britain finally starts. Or it could begin remarkably quickly, amid the ruins of the failure of Brexit. Those who predict the end of the EU, with the rise of populist votes especially in Italy, underestimate the ways in which all other European countries in the past accommodated far more easily the loss of their, albeit much smaller, empires.

Our Dutchman, Joris, is correct about the size of the mistake the British have collectively made; but does he know why they made it? To understand the true extent of the folly of the British, you have to be British, to have gone to school in Britain, lived and worked in Britain, and felt British all your life; but also know the many parts to the countries of Britain and what each is reliant on. You have to have properly mixed with people on these islands, people that lead such segregated lives, often with so little hope, often so patiently. You have to know what the British think their history is. You have to be able to look in as well as out. Only then are you in a position to explain why this could happen, because – to most of the rest of the world – what has happened is unbelievable.

WE HAVE SPENT TOO MANY YEARS DELUDING OURSELVES
At the start of World War I, Rudyard Kipling is said to have lobbied for his very short-sighted son, John (also known as Jack), to be allowed to sign up and fight, despite Jack being only sixteen years old at the time.[75] In September 1915, Jack is thought to have died, aged eighteen, having disappeared during the Battle of Loos. Loos was the prelude to the Battle of the Somme, and the

site of the first British experiment during wartime of the use of poison gas. Kipling suggested that he could hold his head up 'all the more' having sent his own child to war. But he sent him to such a terrible death and to endure so much suffering precisely because he had come to believe that holding your head up high and being at the pinnacle of power mattered so much.

My Boy Jack, by Rudyard Kipling

'Have you news of my boy Jack?'
Not this tide.
'When d'you think that he'll come back?'
Not with this wind blowing, and this tide.

'Has any one else had word of him?'
Not this tide.
For what is sunk will hardly swim,
Not with this wind blowing, and this tide.

'Oh, dear, what comfort can I find?'
None this tide,
Nor any tide,
Except he did not shame his kind –
Not even with that wind blowing, and that tide.

Then hold your head up all the more,
This tide,
And every tide;
Because he was the son you bore,
And gave to that wind blowing and that tide!

– First published on 19 October 1916 simultaneously
in *The Times*, *Daily Telegraph* and *New York Times*.[76]

Many will feel that his choice should be a source of eternal shame. But accepting your mistakes is the hardest thing to do if you have been brought up to extinguish self-doubt, to give orders to others and to lead from the front. If you have come to believe that yours is the earth and everything that's in it.

Rudyard Kipling and Jack Kipling were each victims of empire in their own way. It was not just the colonised who suffered; the colonisers too were hugely damaged, and that damage lasts a long time. It takes generations to become normal again. We British are still going through the process.

CHAPTER 5

THE FANTASY AND FUTURE OF FREE TRADE

Foreigners should be charged £10 to buy a visa to get into the UK once Britain has left the EU, the government has been told.
– European Reform Group of 100 Tory MPs,
23 December 2017[1]

Brexit nightmare: 17-mile traffic jams at the Dover border
– Headline, *Business Times*, June 2018[2]

INTRODUCTION

We have said a lot in the previous chapter on Britain's trade after Brexit. Will life stay the same, get better or get worse? That will depend heavily on the extent to which Britain's goods and services are desirable to other countries, and whether other countries will continue to be able to export goods and provide services to Britain without too much trouble.

In 2013, the UK government produced a series of Foresight reports on the future of manufacturing. Manufacturing made up just 10 per cent of the UK economy. In contrast, in Finland, manufacturing had grown to 25 per cent of its economy despite a series of failures at Nokia leading the telecoms company to sell its handset business to Microsoft. In Japan, manufacturing represented 20 per cent of the country's economy, despite two 'lost decades' of economic stagnation after the asset bubble burst in 1991. In Germany, it was well over 50 per cent larger than in the UK, at 15 per cent of the huge German economy. However, none of the British decline had occurred by accident. The reduction in manufacturing's share of the UK economy was an intentional strategy, one that harked back to Thatcher-era Britain, when the plan was to remove the UK's dependence on 'unsophisticated' manufacturing and move into services and banking. The strategy was known at the time to be high-risk. Today, it has backfired on Britain in dramatic fashion.[3]

After the loss of empire, a new way to bring in money needed to be found. No longer would Britain flourish by imposing unfair terms of trade on countries around the globe. Instead, it was thought, Britain could enjoy superior status by becoming the supreme financial juggler for the world. The 1986 Big Bang of the City of London heralded a new era. For twenty-two years, the City laid golden eggs for the country – until, in 2008, the banks fell apart. They fell apart because they had to. You cannot make more and more money out of doing less and less of productive use for ever. But that is what the plan is, if you aim to enrich a country mainly by concentrating on banking. Even in 1986, two of the Big Bang's authors forecast that it would come to be seen, when and if it resulted in 'scandals and liquidations', as the 'unacceptable face of unpopular capitalism'.[4]

So, when the crash of 2008 spelled the failure of Big Bang, the next grand plan to revive the British economy was to suggest going it alone – a brave new Britain throwing off the shackles of Europe. But in what will Britain suddenly trade in greater quantities outside of the EU? A detailed analysis of what the British now have to offer the rest of the world does not conjure up great confidence. Tourism can increase, although having to pay for a visa to enter the UK may not help. The British can try to draw in more overseas students to their universities, but high fees and a shrinking reputation for excellence may deter some potential students – especially compared to the now comparatively more affordable Ivy League universities of the USA. The international reputation of British banking is now tarnished. Within the EU, the UK was sheltered from some of these realities. Now the British may soon find out they need to tighten their belts even further as the comparative advantages they thought they had turn out to be a chimera, especially if their food is stuck in a 17-mile traffic jam at Dover.

To some extent, comparative advantage is built up over time through the accumulation of skills, capital resources and brand image. Sheffield steel is a case in point: it really doesn't make a great deal of geographical sense to produce steel in Sheffield today, but some companies still exhibit high levels of market competitiveness, as noted in the case of the special steel exported to the USA – though only when they are protected from below-cost steel imports from China or prohibitive tariffs imposed by the USA. Trade is never free, and freedom means far more than having the right to trade.

WHAT WAS FREE TRADE?

What are the British actually good at? One thing the British produce is an unusual number of economists, including those who later came, through their work, to define the academic subject. Adam Smith, Thomas Malthus and James Mill are remembered now, perhaps unfairly, for talking about the magical invisible hand of the market (Smith), the problem of poor people having too much sex (Malthus), and how India was a basket case until the British arrived (Mill).[5] Their ideas all had great influence, but none of those ideas have actually survived the test of time as much as those of their contemporary David Ricardo and his theories about free trade.[6]

David Ricardo, son of a Dutch stockbroker, was born in London in 1772. His grandest theory is now best remembered for a story about wine and wool in Portugal and England. Ricardo suggested that both countries would grow rich if Portugal concentrated on what it was best at – making wine – and England concentrated on wool and weaving that into clothing and carpets. The two countries could then trade their surplus stock, and each would have as much finished wine and woven wool as they could wish for, and would be far better off than had they not traded.

The magic of free trade was an idea that gained favour in England. It is a superficially convincing theory. England is wet, deforested and has a great deal of grass for sheep to eat. Portugal is relatively dry and hot, an ideal place for vineyards. You can even produce a few equations that suggest that all would be rosy if there was increased specialisation. The only problem is reality.

Almost 200 years after Ricardo and all those other male economists were eulogising about free trade being the wonder of the world, their ideas were debunked. In 1979, one of the first widely recognised female economists, Joan Violet Robinson, a professor at the University of Cambridge, explained: 'In reality, the imposition of free trade on Portugal killed off a promising textile industry and left her with a slow-growing export market for wine, while for England, exports of cotton cloth led to accumulation, mechanization and the whole spiralling growth of the industrial revolution.' When she wrote, Robinson was able to cite the evidence-based work of Sandro Sideri, unlike David Ricardo with his armchair (and evidence-free) theory of free trade.[7]

'Free trade benefiting all' was and remains just a theory. It is not a truth. It is one of many classical economic theories that are unsubstantiated yet somehow still gain credence. People may say that the EU is about free trade, but it was initially as much about promoting peace and preventing war. That is partly done by ensuring economies become interdependent – not because such interdependency is necessarily terribly efficient, but because we better understand each other if we work for each other and buy from each other. It is also much less annoying if a fridge made in Poland works in Spain, if a customer of a bank operating from Greece can use the cashpoints in Finland, and if you don't have to pay roaming charges on your phone anywhere in the EU.

The comparative advantage theory behind free trade is a theory that was later testable by events. In fact, when ordinary people did become better off, it usually turned out not to be due to more free trade. Usually, it was when they fought for and won increased rights and better wages. Organising rent strikes, forming trade unions, electing MPs who care about people like you improves your circumstances. Of course, much more can be made when coal is dug up to fuel mass manufacturing – but it is the fossil fuels that make that possible, not the mystical magic of free trade. The right wing don't like the truth about how living standards for most people in the world improved, and so they continue to repeat the 200-year-old myth of comparative advantage, and the idea that it was free trade that 'lifted all boats', as the growing wealth of the rich trickled down to the poorest of all – or so they mistakenly claim.

Brexiteers claim that when we leave the EU, free trade will increase, making Britain rich again. They put their faith in the market, free of state intervention, to improve Britain's economic prospects. They tend to see Britain's increased prosperity in the latter part of the nineteenth century as the result of the 1846 repeal of the Corn Laws, ushering in more free trade, rather than acknowledging the effects of the growth of empire abroad and the introduction of public health Acts at home. They generally favour as little state intervention as possible – other than measures to contain inflation, as inflation eats away some of the accumulated wealth of the rich. In contrast, in June 2018 Labour's shadow Chancellor John McDonnell proposed altering the central mandate of the Bank of England from controlling inflation to aiding productivity. He explained that inflation targeting had both helped precipitate the financial crisis of 2008 and, since then, exacerbated a deflationary bias. Private bank lending is skewed towards consumption, as the Bank of England now itself belatedly acknowledges, and to property speculation (which the Bank of England does not yet acknowledge), rather than investment. Giving the Bank a new and different mandate to direct and guide lending towards productive investment to raise both incomes and productivity is an alternative to the Brexiteers' belief that the market left alone is the solution.[8]

At the extreme, some of the more gung-ho Brexiteers claim that free trade in future will help even if other countries impose World Trade Organization tariffs on Britain but the British impose no tariffs in return. They forget that Britain already had free trade within the EU and losing that will not necessarily make it richer. Free trade is not good or bad: it is just far less free and less common than you might think. Economists overestimate the value of free trade.

Economists often make mistakes. Figure 5.1 shows various forecasts for growth in productivity in the UK since 2009 against the actual trend (the out-turn). Almost all the forecasts have been wrong, and the reason is not that the British didn't have enough free trade.

Recent research by two economists, Arnaud Costinot and David Donaldson, looking at seventeen types of crops grown in fifty-five countries, found that the places that produce more of one thing than another are not necessarily the places that have the greatest natural advantage in producing it.[9] Food is needed and grown everywhere. It is expensive to transport because it is heavy and easily rots, and its production is often subsidised. Countries with access to more advanced technology or cheaper energy, or those that can impose their trade on others, will trade more, including buying unfairly cheaply. The places that trade the most are not always, or even often, the places with some natural comparative advantage.

Those who make the most out of trade are not those who are most efficient but those who are best at manipulating others to buy or sell their goods. Trade rarely benefits everyone involved equally. The information that trade is based on is always incomplete and those with money try to keep it that way, which is why they spend millions on advertising to influence and beguile us. The recent economic successes of Google and Facebook, vehicles for advertising and targeting, is yet more evidence that trade is not conducted freely. When such giant multinational corporations are allowed to operate freely, other freedoms are restricted. Information is manipulated, trade is targeted, and unfair competition – monopolistic behaviours – grow. Trade is never free. Freedom means far more than having the right to trade.

FIGURE 5.1: PRODUCTIVITY GROWTH IN THE UK, 1999–2023, ACTUAL AND FORECASTS

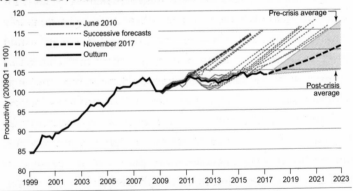

Various forecasts versus the actual (out-turn) of events
– UK productivity when crudely measured.[10]

TRADERS, DRUG DEALERS AND SLAVERS

*In the 1790s 4,000 chests of opium were sold by auction in Calcutta
(by the Company). By the 1830s it had risen to 15,000 ... From the
18th century to the end of British rule in 1947 opium revenues were
the most important source of revenue after land revenue and the salt
tax ... By means of the China trade, opium production allowed the
Company and its agents to siphon off India's wealth.[11]*

– LIZZIE COLLINGHAM, 2017

Lizzie Collingham was writing about the infamous East India
Company when she penned those words. She was explaining
that the way the British company forced Indian peasants to grow
poppies, which produced the opium to be sold to China, makes
the current South American drugs trade look like a love-in. The
British elite amassed their wealth by forcing others to trade, not
by free trade – a fact largely kept out of school history books,
along with a litany of other embarrassing facts, including wealthy
families' personal history of slave-holding. David Cameron appeared shocked when it was revealed that upon the abolition of
slavery his own ancestors had been high up in the lists of the
wealthy families who had received huge reparation payments for
the loss of 'their' slaves. You wonder where he thought the family
fortune had come from. The amount his forebears received would
have been worth millions of pounds in real terms.[12] This legacy
is shared with the families of many children at Eton and it is
surprising that he was so very ignorant of his own family history.

The British traded opium from their colony in India because
the Chinese didn't want anything else the British could produce,
and the British were desperate not to pay for all the goods they
wanted from China – not in silver and gold, at any rate. China
did not originally want opium either, but the British imposed addiction – a public health crisis – upon a sovereign nation for their

own profit. Every Chinese school child knows about the Opium Wars, but they too are told fibs, because their history states that the Daoguang Emperor was a great leader, when in reality he was feckless and corrupt.[13] The British don't have the monopoly in self-aggrandisement; both the USA and China are just as good at that today.

Collingham is among the historians who have suggested that it was Britain's quest for food that gave rise to the British Empire. She found that in 1775 half of all imports into Britain were food stuffs. Much of this importation caused malnutrition in the colonies in which the food was originally grown. Colonial policies for food did little for the nutrition of the colonised and often left populations more vulnerable to food scarcity. This led to hypocritical claims that hunger and poverty were endemic in colonies, thus creating an apparent justification for colonial rule.

Even as recently as the 1970s, in Kenya many farmers stopped growing the beans that had been a staple for local markets and instead began growing French green beans exported by air for a mainly out-of-season European market. As Thomas Sankara, the former President of Burkina Faso, put it, 'Do you not know where imperialism is to be found? Just look at your plate.'[14] Sankara made the humble Renault 5 the official government car of his country to stop officials being too profligate. He was murdered in 1987 by pro-colonial and conservative tribal forces; another legacy of empire.

Part of the story leading Brexiteers told in 2016 and 2017 was that exit from the European Union would allow the British to trade again as they once so magnificently did around the world. It is unlikely that these advocates envisaged sending gunboats to Hong Kong again, demanding that the Chinese buy our amazing manufactures (and our drugs). It is more likely that they were ill informed as to why Britain was involved in so much trade in the past, and did not realise that so much of trade was not free. Most importantly of all, they did not realise that today, as in 1839, Britain makes hardly anything that China needs. The British know relatively little about producing goods efficiently, in comparison with other people. Why should they? They didn't have to.

Other countries that did not have the military might of the British had to rely more on trading things for what they were actually worth, rather than forcing their goods on others. The British were dubbed a nation of shopkeepers by the French in 1794.[15] It was an insult that was quickly received as a compliment. Ever since then, the myth that the British are good at buying and selling things (and are making more money out of such activities than other people) has been propagated. Better to be called a nation of shopkeepers than one of scoundrels, spivs or slavers.

In September 2017, when the government produced a White Paper on future trading after Brexit, all was still remarkably vague. Although the paper noted that around half of Britain's trade and investment was with the EU, it said that UK trading as a last resort could always take place in future under World Trade Organization rules. If there was no deal after Brexit, the EU and UK would charge each other the same tariffs as with trade with the rest of the world. Cars would incur a 10 per cent tariff, which, as car maker Nissan said, would be a disaster for the UK.[16] To date, the consideration of the consequences for trade of leaving the EU continues to be more of a fight between members of the government and their acolytes, rather than a serious public debate. No one seems to have noticed that when you don't make a deal, you keep to the status quo, which would mean staying in the EU, not torching everything built up over decades and ripping it all up in some enormous tantrum.

ECONOMISTS MAKING BRITAIN GREAT AGAIN

The Brexit-supporting group Economists for Free Trade, with members including right-wing economists Patrick Minford and Edgar Miller, argued that trading under WTO rules would work even if the car and similar industries were run down as a result.[17] They have such faith in the magic of free trade that they just know, in their heart of hearts, that something will come good. Another pro-Brexit group, the Institute for Free Trade, founded by Brexiteer and MEP Daniel Hannan, opened in September 2017 with a reception in the Foreign Office where Boris Johnson made those unfortunate remarks about Libya, which distracted journalists from asking these leading Brexiteers why they were so obsessed with free trade.

Another lobby for Brexit, and cheerleader for the magic of ever more free trade, is the Legatum Institute. This is a think tank boasting of its 'unparalleled access to [David] Davis [then Brexit Secretary] and Theresa May'[18] that is central to the Conservative Party's case for a hard Brexit.[19] In 2015, it received over £4 million in funding, naming its major funder as the Legatum Foundation, a company registered in Bermuda, part of a complex network of organisations including ones also registered in the Cayman Islands and Dubai, with the ultimate parent undertaking, Legatum Partnership LLP, registered in Jersey.[20] Perhaps by free trade they mean free from the prying eyes of the tax authorities and regulators? Yet another group, Ulster Evangelicals for Brexit, advocate free trade, though they also quote the Bible suggesting that plague will come as the result of not leaving the EU: 'And I heard another voice from heaven, saying: "Come out of here, my people, that ye be not partakers of her sins, and that ye receive not of her plagues".'[21]

(Baroness) Philippa Stroud, chief executive officer of the 'free trade brings prosperity to all' Legatum Institute, also has a history of evangelical belief with a similar trajectory, although she has not, to our knowledge, mentioned the threat of plagues from being a member of the EU. The founder and funder of Legatum is the Dubai-based, New Zealand-born billionaire Christopher Chandler, who made a fortune in the 'wild capitalism' days in Russia in the 1990s. Both the Trump campaign in the USA and the Brexit campaign in the UK were linked with people who had first-hand experience of the benefits of unrestrained capitalism; benefits primarily for themselves. However, not everyone who is an advocate of ever more free trade is in favour of Brexit, a process likely to restrict trade.

On a more sober note, the former Mayor of New York, billionaire businessman Michael Bloomberg, gave his opinion in October 2017 that 'Brexit is the single stupidest thing any country has ever done, apart from the election of Donald Trump as its President'.[22] The Confederation of British Industry (CBI), the British Chamber of Commerce and the Institute of Directors were all on Bloomberg's side. It is educational to discover that these bodies know what Britain is good at, what it can do, and what it cannot do well alone any more – at least without the gunboats.

By summer 2018, there was great political tension and enormous confusion. Parts of the Remain camp were by then employing the arguments of the pro-globalist right. These included suggestions by the likes of the Blairs and the Clintons that it is only free trade within the EU that keeps the British economy ticking over. Conversely, the Brexiteers appeared to have hijacked arguments put forward by the anti-globalist left, such as suggesting that the 'elite' are out to do down the people and there is a conspiracy of shadowy interests working to deny people a fair destiny. The people of Britain became increasingly confused and bemused, not least because they were constantly being told just how great their country was, which did not concur with the personal experiences of a growing number.

Not surprisingly, some have fallen for the idea of recreating a 'golden age', making Britain great *again*. But the British cannot now repeat their imperial use of military and economic power to impose bad deals on others. The issue of investment has been critical. Because Britain had such a large empire in the very recent past, the dominant financial and hence political interests in Britain do not prioritise domestic investment. The primary source of wealth for Britain has always been the exploitation of other nations, with the British military occasionally acting as bailiff, and the Secret Intelligence Service providing industrial espionage. As MI6's recruiting website says, 'Every role contributes to the security and *prosperity* of the UK'[23] (emphasis added).

The fate of key British industries in the twentieth century – like coal, steel, textiles and shipbuilding – are illustrative of how they were not especially important to British financiers' interests. The latter failed to invest after World War II, hoping to live off the fat of previous capital investment, for instance by exploiting the shrinking of shipbuilding capacity across the globe. When others started to reinvest with state involvement, British shipbuilding yards were at least a generation behind. China, South Korea and Japan went on to dominate the industry. In 2018, it was reported by the statistics portal Statista that most recently China had 34 per cent of the world market, South Korea 22 per cent and Japan 21 per cent. The EU, which included Britain, and to which was added Norway, took only 11 per cent of the market, leaving just 12 per cent for the rest of the world, including what little shipbuilding is still undertaken in the USA.

Today, Brexiteers ignore the impact of the falling pound on inflation and living standards, preferring to suggest that the fall will be 'good for trade'. When doing this, they are also ignoring the investment problem. We know that without investment, cheaper exports have a limited impact for a limited time. As the then Prime Minister Edward Heath told the Institute of Directors in 1973:

> The curse of British industry is that it had never anticipated demand. When we came in, we were told there weren't sufficient inducements to invest. So, we provided the inducements. Then we were told people were scared of balance of payments difficulties leading to stop-go. So, we floated the pound. Then we were told of fears of inflation and now we are dealing with that. And still you aren't investing enough.[24]

The British are no longer strong in manufacturing. Figure 5.2 (a few pages below) shows how Britain continues to slide down the ranks of global manufacturers as the British still don't properly invest and provide their workers with the resources needed to be as productive as the French or Germans – part of the reason for Britons' relatively low pay.[25] However, one thing that the British did excel at, until its 2008 crash, was banking. So, is Brexit going to set banking free?

According to the Governor of the Bank of England, Brexit will start by costing the banking industry 75,000 jobs, some 10,000 on day one, unless there is a deal that makes it appear as if Brexit never happened as far as banking is concerned. Xavier Rolet, chief executive of the London Stock Exchange up until late 2017, even suggested that eventually over 200,000 banking jobs could go.[26] Many other bankers would have to take pay cuts. (Brexit is not all bad news!) They cannot move to New York, as all the banking posts there are already filled, mostly by Americans. As the European banking agency reveals through its audits of very high pay, every other country in the world pays bankers much less than those working in London, so they cannot move elsewhere to prop up their pay. There is, therefore, a little glimpse of hope. At least we should not see UK top-level banking pay rising in the near or distant future. But when those on the left suggest that Brexit should be embraced, not least because they claim that being a member of the EU has had 'a negligible advantage to the UK',[27] they are spouting folly. Economists are not very good at determining what actually leads to economic advantage and what does not, because what really matters is politics, such as controlling an empire or being able to bend others to your will because of the size of your economy and the fleets you have sailing in every ocean. Economists often only know a very small part of the story, hence the frequent jokes:

Economic forecasters assume everything, except responsibility.
– VAUGHAN HIGGINS AND WENDY LARNER

Why was astrology invented? So economics would seem like an accurate science.
– EAMONN FINGLETON

The First Law of Economists: For every economist, there exists an equal and opposite economist. The Second Law of Economists: They're both wrong.

You know, it's said that an economist is a man who, when he finds something that works in practice, wonders if it works in theory.
– WALTER HELLER

We have two classes of forecasters: those who don't know ... and those who don't know they don't know.
– JOHN KENNETH GALBRAITH

Two economists were sitting at a nudist colony. One said, 'Have you read Marx?' The other said, 'It's these wicker chairs.'[28]

BANKERS, DON'T YOU JUST LOVE THEM?

The British are supposedly good at banking (including creating and profiting from debt and gambling with other people's money). There has been a Bank of England since 1694. It was established shortly after the Dutch invaded England in 1688 to sort us out as the new nascent world power, bringing gifts such as David Ricardo's immigrating parents and hence, ultimately, David himself. Britain is a nation of immigrants, and that is just as true in banking as in every other sector. The immigrants who established the British banking industry mostly came from mainland Europe. A few, such as the Morgans, were originally from Wales, with their banking influence (think 'JP') returning to the UK after spending a period of time in the United States.

There are many banking families: the Quaker Barclays family began working in Lombard Street in London in 1690.[29] Around 1809, the Goldsmiths in London were famous gold bullion dealers and, at around the same time, the Rothschild family had pioneered international finance. Elite families like the Morgans, the Rothschilds and the Barclays gained huge influence over the global economy by the early twentieth century. The Rothschilds also had a big hand in making Britain great under the empire, supporting the De Beers Company, which funded Cecil Rhodes, as well as backing the South African Rio Tinto Group and funding the building of the Suez Canal.

As we mentioned at the beginning of this chapter, in 1986 the Thatcher government changed the rules governing the London Stock Exchange. In their project, called Big Bang, the Conservatives deregulated London's financial markets and London became a more dominant global centre for banking and trading in money. As the BBC explained in 2008:

Trading is one of the most coveted jobs in the financial markets.

A good trader can make tens of millions of dollars for his company every year and take home vast bonuses. It is a stressful job. One wrong move and your profits can be wiped out, your reputation destroyed, and your job gone.[30]

With no sense of what might be just around the corner, the BBC ended its report on City traders in January 2008 with the following warning: 'But the system can break down, as in the case of Barings in 1995. There, Nick Leeson was able to hide huge losses, as he was the trader and manager and looked after the back office.' And then, within a few months of the BBC making that statement, the entire banking system of London was in freefall. No longer was one 'rogue trader' the bad apple: it turned out that the whole barrel had gone sour. When British banker turned rogue trader Nick Leeson was jailed for his exploits in 1995, he was unlucky to have been caught out when the trades went sour. In 2008, thousands of trades went sour and no one was jailed, despite such similar circumstances.

The government in power in 2008 saved the banking industry but received little recognition for their actions. The Chancellor at the time, Alistair Darling, blocked the bid of Barclays Bank to take over the failing Lehman Brothers.[31] The government and the banking industry are closely connected. Since 1571, the City of London has had a parliamentary agent (the City Remembrancer) with special powers in the House of Commons to look out for its interests. No other group has such influence. This is because historically (and still today) the City's money mattered so much. But today the City is fearful. British banks may not be awarded full passporting rights to work freely across Europe. At the time of writing, they are spending hundreds of millions to try to work out what they need to do, and how many of their bankers they might need to move out of London. Many younger bankers have already been moved to offices abroad, and the London housing market has fallen at the top as they are no longer there to buy.

London does *not* have some special comparative advantage that means banks have to be based there. The evidence for this is under the Lord Chancellor's backside. The Lord Chancellor is supposed to sit on a wool bale known as the Woolsack, a symbol of the wool trade's importance to the English economy. In 1938, when it was becoming a little uncomfortable to sit on, it was discovered that the Woolsack had most recently been stuffed with horsehair. It was re-stuffed with wool from all over the Commonwealth, apparently 'as a symbol of unity'.[32] It turns out that sheep can live almost anywhere, and wool is gathered in a great many countries. If there was ever a symbol that comparative advantage doesn't work, then the Woolsack has to be it. Just as sheep can live almost anywhere, banking can be done almost anywhere. There is nothing special about the clay soil of London that makes it especially suited to banking.

Of course, some people believe that, if anything, Britain's banks have been held back by EU membership and Britain will become the financial envy of the world after Brexit. The last book to be co-written by Jacob Rees-Mogg's father, William Rees-Mogg, a former editor of *The Times*. *The Sovereign Individual*, published in 1997, spelled out the blueprint. The people who believe in such plans fear that a minimal financial transaction tax will be introduced across the EU, to curtail the free-wheeling of future financiers. Plans for this tax and other regulations on the greedy are progressing in the EU today; it is no coincidence that many are now set to be implemented shortly after Brexit.

In the *Financial Times Global 500* magazine on Saturday 28 October 2017, a whole-page advertisement for the investment house Edmond de Rothschild, a private bank, claimed: 'We don't speculate on the future. We build it ... wealth is what tomorrow can be made of.' Some of those who financed the Leave campaigns and who argued for Leave had a direct financial interest in avoiding future EU legislation. From 1 January 2019, any state that is a member of the EU must start to introduce the EU anti-tax-avoidance directive that was proposed in January 2016.[33] There has been speculation that this was a key part of the impetus for some of the funding of the Leave campaign, but much of that funding was opaque, or in kind through supportive newspapers.

Others wonder whether Brexit might end the City of London's traditional dominance of finance in Europe because there will be so much relocation to so many other cities: Amsterdam, Paris, Munich, Frankfurt and Dublin are all frequently mentioned. We will have to wait and see what transpires, but it seems very likely now that banking will become better spread out around the European continent, less concentrated in one single city in future.

Of course, London is not the only financial centre in Europe willing to turn a blind eye to tax dodging. We know very well that the EU also contains much corruption, but it is seeking to put its house in order, whereas the financiers backing the Brexiteers are seeking to avoid future scrutiny. Since 2014, the President of the European Commission has been Jean-Claude Juncker, who previously served as the Prime Minister of Luxembourg. As Jan Zielonka, Professor of European Politics at Oxford, explained in November 2017:

> Europeans are not in a position to give the UK moral lessons. The EU is led by the man seen as a symbol of the European tax dodging system. In one of the largest European states, the man in charge of Bunga-bunga orgies [Silvio Berlusconi] is likely to return to power after the forthcoming elections.[34]

In fact, the Italian election on 3 June 2018 resulted in a coalition of far-left and far-right parties, with no job for Berlusconi, but disputes over fraud and corruption are still very much in evidence. When it comes to lessons in morality, there may be many Europeans who can still learn from each other. However, the Brexit process appears set to diminish the status of the larger British banks, and possibly to usher in an era of the UK being seen as a centre for unregulated financial privateering in future. A situation not unlike that which existed before the empire grew, when England was best known abroad for its pirates.

ARMS DEALERS, OR, IF SQUEAMISH, AEROSPACE

One trade the British became very good at from the nineteenth century onwards was the arms trade – the only part of British manufacturing not shrinking greatly in size in recent decades. This is another area in which those in favour of Brexit hope that Britain can excel in future. Britain currently supplies many of the world's armies, including or even especially the less scrupulous and less democratic ones. Saudi Arabia is among the best-known examples of these today, with hundreds of thousands of victims in the Yemen and one recent high-profile killing in their embassy in Istanbul, but none of that stops the UK arming the kingdom. Where there is a will, and a lack of morals, there is a way. Criticism of the arms trade is very muted in the mainstream media, which tends to be in favour of the business, but the trade may become more widely seen as reprehensible in the near future as people begin to better realise what it is and what it does.[35] The tobacco industry was once thought to be benign too, but at least people did not originally know how much it was also killing people, as was brutal child labour.

The British don't like to call them instruments of war, weapons, missiles, bombs, drones, bullets and manacles. 'Advanced aerospace industries' is one favoured term. It has replaced 'ordnance'. From 1854, when the government gave a contract for breech-loading rifles – so much more efficient than those old muzzle-loading muskets – to the Elswick Ordnance Company, right through to BAE Systems, which by 2010 topped the list of the world's arms manufacturers with its Eurofighter Typhoon and Trident submarine contracts, the British have poured cash and innovations into the arms trade.[36]

Alphabetically, from the firms Accuracy International Ltd down to Webley and Scott, the British help manufacture weapons that contribute a significant but often semi-secret proportion of the annual $400 billion global industry for killing people (also known as 'defence'). BAE Systems adds some $26.8 billion a year all on its own. And, depending on how you count them, Britain comes well up – possibly as high as second, but certainly at least sixth – in the list of largest exporters of arms in the world (see Chapter 4 above). Major export markets for the British include Saudi Arabia, the United Arab Emirates, China and India. The British have, since 2010, granted export licences to twenty-two of the thirty countries on the UK government's own human rights watch list, including Saudi Arabia, Israel and Bahrain.[37] These, and many other countries trading in armaments with Britain, have frequently been accused of and also found complicit in torture, illegal imprisonment and unlawful killings.

Conflict areas and human-rights-abusing governments create demand that must be supplied, or so the free marketeer argument goes. Often those in favour of Brexit look fondly upon the policies of the USA. The USA is top of the list of weapons makers, and the Trump administration has been working on a nuclear weapons policy that may end the era of post-Cold War disarmament by bolstering the US arsenal. On 27 October 2017, the US Vice-President, visiting an air base in North Dakota, announced that 'history attests that the surest path to peace is through American strength ... There is no greater force for peace in the world than the US nuclear arsenal.'[38] Putin's second in command might well have replied, 'Except perhaps the Russian one.' Maybe the British will have to resurrect those nuclear bunkers, built around the country from the 1950s onwards, together with instructions as to how to keep safe. The very few of those shelters still working are mainly tourist attractions today, but who knows?

Free traders include the arms industry among areas that may grow rapidly if Brexit is achieved, but the question is highly debatable. BAE announced in September 2017 that it had had no new orders for its Typhoon jets for two years and a long-anticipated one from the Royal Saudi Air Force for forty-eight jets had failed to materialise, putting jobs in the industry at risk.[39] Fortunately for BAE (though to the horror of many in the UK), Saudi Arabia escalated its military action and the order was back on in March 2018, as was a business deal to sell twenty-four jets to Qatar. Whether those orders will be followed by enough others to keep BAE's workers in jobs remains to be seen. But perhaps there will be no problems, as, amazingly, half of the private sector employees on secondment to the new Department for International Trade, created in July 2016 and headed by well-known Brexiteer and former Defence Secretary Liam Fox, were (tellingly) from 'defence' industries.

In Orwellian style, 'defence' means 'aerospace', and 'aerospace' means 'weapons'. The companies involved like to pretend that they make 'systems' or even just posh cars and powerful engines. BAE Systems and Rolls-Royce have provided three secondees to Liam Fox each. Both firms have in the past paid bribes to win export orders.[40] As the Nobel Prize-winning President of Costa Rica, Óscar Arias Sánchez, commented in an interview in 2009, 'When a country decides to invest in arms, rather than in education, housing, the environment and health services for its people, it is depriving a whole generation of the right to prosperity and happiness.'[41]

FIGURE 5.2: THE SHARE OF MANUFACTURING IN ELEVEN MAJOR ECONOMIES, 1990–2010

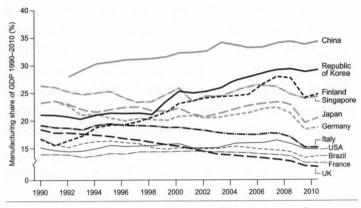

Manufacturing output as a proportion of all gross domestic product.[42]

So, what, apart from arms, is Britain's future in manufacturing? As we mentioned above, in 2013 the UK government produced a series of Foresight reports on the future of manufacturing.[43] Among much else, one report showed that unlike Finland, which recently saw manufacturing grow to 25 per cent of its economy, or Japan, where it was 20 per cent, or Germany, where it was 15 per cent, the UK had seen manufacturing fall to 10 per cent (see Figure 5.2).

THE DECLINE OF MANUFACTURING

Britain was not supposed to be where it is now. Almost seventy years ago, the Festival of Britain on London's South Bank, organised in 1951 under Attlee's Labour government, was intended both to cheer up the population after the war and show what Britain manufactured and sold to the world. It was a pity that Winston Churchill, whose dislike of socialism was stronger than his trading knowledge, claimed that it was all socialist propaganda because it was publicly funded and included celebration of recent achievements, such as the NHS, that had occurred under a Labour government. He ordered the whole site demolished as soon as his government came to power. In the 1950s and 1960s, both the American Marshall Plan to alleviate European poverty by providing economic aid and the new British welfare state helped the working class create an appliance-manufacturing boom. Those sales of British-made washing machines, fridges and motorbikes made life easier for workers. It was a pity that over the years so many companies were later sold by shareholders (the employees and customers got no say) to foreign competitors and hedge funds, who took advantage of globalisation and often moved them abroad for cheaper labour costs, or closed the company down and stripped out the assets, leaving the workers with nothing.

The proportion of GDP coming from manufacturing compared to services fell quickly as a result of 1980s deindustrialisation. In 1970, manufacturing accounted for 33 per cent of the economy (including sectors like mining, quarrying, steel making, gas/electricity and water, plus all the parts that went into cars) while services accounted for 55 per cent. As Figure 5.2 above illustrated, by 2014 manufacturing accounted for only 10 per cent of GDP, while services were up to nearly 80 per cent.[44] And as Figure 5.3 below shows, half of British manufacturing now is cars, food, metals (often a euphemism for arms) and medicinal drugs.

During the 1980s and 1990s, the service sector (meaning anything from financial and legal services to retail, cleaning and care work) expanded dramatically. After Brexit, international financiers and lawyers can threaten to take their business to Paris, Frankfurt or Luxembourg, but many other services cannot move abroad. Very personal services, from hair cutting to undertaking, need to operate in the region where their clientele live and die; if they can't operate there, those services must cease to exist. Disappearing services will be one indicator of reduced prosperity. They disappear when people have so little money they cut their own hair and have to rely on the state to give them a pauper's funeral, the numbers of which rose by 50 per cent in the four years to 2017.[45]

FIGURE 5.3: WHAT DO THE BRITISH MANUFACTURE IN 2015?

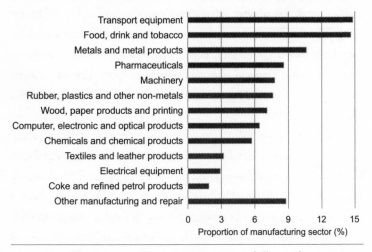

Manufacturing output by sector as a proportion of all manufacturing gross domestic product.[46]

Much of what was left of manufacturing has been sold to foreign owners. Cadbury was sold to US Kraft, who said that they would not close any factories and then did. Nissan, the Japanese car maker, in which Renault owns a large stake, have promised to keep their Sunderland plants open after a government bribe, and Pfizer, the US pharmaceutical company, is trying to take over more British-based companies. Some may welcome the Americans, given their use of the imperial system. As Billy Bragg recently sang, 'Once we ruled over an empire / So it feels like some kind of defeat / To comply with rules drawn up by strangers / And measure in metres not feet.'[47]

Perhaps the British government intended at one point during Brexit that Britain should become a high-tech manufacturing island. In 2017, Theresa May asked Juergen Maier, UK chief of the German engineering firm Siemens, to think about what a fourth industrial revolution would look like. He produced a 246-page review arguing that robotics, artificial intelligence, 3D printing and advanced engineering would be an antidote to post-Brexit challenges.[48] Or maybe, given the low level of skills in Britain as compared to other European countries, the future will be a low-skill, low-wage economy with reduced corporation taxes to persuade more overseas firms to take over more British companies, hoping that they won't then close their UK factories and relocate elsewhere?

By 2017, the Office for National Statistics were releasing manufacturing statistics that showed that since Figure 5.2 was released by the BBC, the absolute amount of pharmaceutical goods being manufactured in Britain had fallen even further. There had been a 7 per cent increase in the manufacturing of food as the pound fell in value and the cost of food imports from abroad rose.[49] Food, as the government may be aware, is not a high-tech industry.

So what else could the British do in future, what else are they good at? What else have they excelled at in the past? Think James Bond 007. Could the post-Brexit future of Britannia involve a beefed-up spying industry? Safe from the oversight of European law, could it send men out, acting on Her Majesty's service, to lay the foundations of Empire 2.0 and make Britain great again?

SPIES, APOSTLES, TROTSKYISTS AND CORBYN

Espionage is the second oldest profession in the world. Moses used spies before taking Canaan, Julius Caesar before landing in England, and the Tudors and Stuarts used spies who were masters of their arts. The British love their spies, and their spy stories. The UK also possibly leads the world in spying, but who knows? It's a secret. MI6, now more properly known as the Secret Intelligence

Service (SIS), was created in 1909, and led by eccentric Captain Mansfield Cumming, who signed his letters with a big green 'C'. There was some rivalry between Six, as it was known, and MI5, the domestic security service; as BBC security correspondent Gordon Corera wrote, MI6 regarded MI5 as glorified policemen, while MI5 thought their foreign counterparts were 'a bunch of cowboys'.[50]

Britain's foreign agents are involved in spying on overseas companies to help Britain's business interests.[51] It is very hard to know whether they are effective at this, but the economic record described above would suggest not. They may have been more effective at working on behalf of financiers in the City of London, at least until the great crash of 2008. Britain still has a romantic notion of its spies, but no idea what they actually do. In 2011/12, the security and intelligence agencies' stated budget was £1.95 billion. By 2019/20, it is estimated to rise to £2.58 billion a year. That is just the part of the budget that is put through some very limited parliamentary scrutiny and signed off by men who all seem to have knighthoods.[52] By definition, we don't know much about any part of the budget that is not put through Parliament and is outside public scrutiny.

Given the British social hierarchies that dictated the tradition of public school education followed by Oxbridge for the elite, it was inevitable that originally spies were recruited mainly from the upper classes – a sort of self-perpetuating gentleman's club, with no (or few) women, of course. Arthur Ransome, author of the *Swallows and Amazons* stories, worked for MI6 (though he was suspected of being a Soviet double agent). On the other side, after the overthrow of the Russian Czar, Francis Meynell from Downside public school was recruited to smuggle in jewels to help the comrades in Britain, at one point hiding pearls in a jar of Danish butter.[53]

Some of the gentlemen in the Cambridge Apostles society in the 1930s really managed to mess up the service when the Cold War was taking off. Trinity College, Cambridge, produced Guy

Francis de Moncy Burgess and his friends Kim Philby, Anthony Blunt and John Cairncross. Together with Donald Maclean they formed the infamous Cambridge Five spy ring of double agents. Their unmasking and the subsequent hunts for 'moles' would prove to be, according to Gordon Corera, British intelligence's darkest hour. But things looked up when the service became a more professional, bureaucratic organisation, and Government Communications Headquarters, or GCHQ, was developed to gather intelligence by technical means, now working in a doughnut-shaped building just outside of Cheltenham.

Not all British intelligence is carried out under the auspices of MI5, MI6 or GCHQ; there are many other organisations who are further back in the shadows than that. For instance, formed in 1968, the Metropolitan Police's Special Demonstration Squad targeted political activists to gain information on activities such as anti-war demonstrations, social justice campaigns, the animal rights movement and environmental justice groups. Possibly as many as 1,000 campaign groups, mostly left-wing, were treated as suspicious. Large-scale spying and surveillance technologies were not as advanced then. Therefore, police spies befriended and betrayed a vast number of organisations, including starting relationships with activists, usually young women, and sleeping with them, occasionally fathering their children, while all the time hiding their true motives and identities. The possible illegality of such behaviour is being tested in the courts at the time of writing.

Stella Rimington, the first female and first publicly named director of MI5, revealed something about the secrets of the service in her autobiography.[54] She detailed the amount of time MI5 spent clocking the activities of Labour Party members, academics, trade union and CND leaders over the years, and even as recently as 2017 she was still worried about the 'Trotskyists' supporting Jeremy Corbyn.[55] She and her fellow spies may be the only people who believe there are many of these particular reds under the beds left who are not using a Zimmer frame! But the question of the legality and morality of MI5's spying on members of legitimate democratic parties should not be overlooked. During the political upheaval of 2019, the word 'traitor' is very likely to be overused, along with the phrase 'enemy of the people'. To coin a very understated British phrase, it would be unfortunate if members of the security services thought they had a role to play in how Brexit and the next general election play out.

Britain's intelligence agencies have made terrible errors, including those that led to Britain taking part in the USA's war with Iraq in 2003, where British spies collaborated with US spies to get it all so very wrong. Currently there are British global listening bases all over the world; technology has largely removed the need for dead letter drops and jars of Danish butter. But how good are they at understanding what they are listening to? Public advertisements are placed to recruit spies from a variety of backgrounds. One such advert asserts that the intelligence service 'works around the globe to control terrorism, reduce international conflict and prevent the spread of nuclear weapons' (except the spread among their friends of course) – but all this is a tough job in these Trumpian times, especially given Trump's close relations with Vladimir Putin.

The future of Britain will not be in dominating others through spying. Although, as Vladimir Lenin once succinctly put it, everything is connected. When, in June 2018, Members of Parliament voted through permission to build a third runway at Heathrow, they may have been partly motivated by the realisation that the UK will desperately need more tourist dollars soon. As the pound falls, tourism into the UK rises in popularity, but those tourists need to be able to get in. Only a few will ever be Russians claiming to have come as tourists to admire lovely Salisbury Cathedral and its 123-metre spire! As one of us wrote, not too tongue-in-cheek, recently, in the build-up to the 2018 royal wedding of Prince Harry to the American

Meghan Markle, that wedding was an almost perfect international advertisement for Heathrow's nearest tourist attraction at Windsor:

> The golden square of English tourism has its corners in London, Stonehenge, Stratford-upon-Avon and Cambridge; at its heart is Oxford, a short train ride from both Windsor and Buckingham Palace. Everyone in the world with money has to travel here once in their lifetime. They are the Meccas and Medinas for unbelievers – the places to go to give thanks for the fact that you own a plastics factory in Changchun or a software firm in Bangalore.[56]

Heathrow lies within that square. One legacy of empire is that it leaves in its wake a great deal of potential tourist attractions: grand universities built mainly on gifts granted through the proceeds of empire; palaces preserved by or even built for empire kings, queens, emperors and one empress; the home town of a bard who might not be so well known worldwide were it not for him putting quill to parchment just as the very first empire steps were being taken, helping English to become the world language. Even Stonehenge might be little known were it not for Rule Britannia and the tourist trade it now brings.

FAIRY-TALE BRITAIN

By late October 2017, the government said that it had produced fifty-eight impact reports on the implications of Brexit for industries. None of the reports, however, could be read by anyone outside of the ministry that produced them, not even the parliamentary Brexit select committee.[57] The government and Parliament were soon at loggerheads over this, and the extent to which the reports were to be redacted. Then, in December 2017, David Davis announced that the reports didn't in fact exist, at least not as actual impact assessments. The UK was beginning to look a little foolish.

Later, during the summer of 2018, some reports were released. Our favourite is the report aimed at those running civil nuclear facilities, which suggests you take 'professional advice' over what to do when the matched UK funding runs out at the end of 2019 in the event of a hard Brexit. Presumably that advice is on the correct concrete to purchase to entomb your facility? The report is not clear.

None of what we have described so far in this book is surprising. How could any nation state have a glorious thousand-year history? Why should we really believe that Britain excels at so much when the evidence that it does not is clear? States, almost by definition, allow power to become concentrated, and over time power always corrupts. With the British Empire, Britain – or, more precisely, a tiny number of upper-class Englishmen (and a few token Scots) – became 'top dogs' and almost all of them then abused their power. Golden ages are usually only golden in a very restricted sense, and then usually just for a few. The patriotic history of Britain is largely a fairy tale; but, like Disneyland, it can make for a good holiday. Like most nations that have been able to exert great power, there is much more to regret about British history than there is to celebrate. And where there has been progress, other nations have made it too, if not earlier.[58] Britain has not had the reality check that losing a war instils. Countries that better understand their own history are those which were not on top for so long or were never placed so very high.

Where Britain has done best, it was often the empire that helped. Empire spread the English language around the world, creating a new international language. English-language radio, films, television and pop music followed, as did much literature and science. Of the fifty-eight industries listed in Table 5.1, think about which of these Britain really excels in now. And to what extent is that pre-eminence in some way connected to the empire? Britain's museums and galleries (no. 38) have an awful lot to show, thanks to the empire; as do its music and performing visual arts (no. 39), higher education (no. 28) and its broadcasting (no. 9). But is tourism and culture enough to underwrite a national economy in future? For a while, at least, this might need to be.

TABLE 5.1: THE FIFTY-EIGHT INDUSTRIES WRITTEN ABOUT IN A SECRET REPORT ON THE EFFECT OF BREXIT

1. Advertising and marketing	16. Crafts	31. Legal services	46. Publishing
2. Aerospace	17. Defence	32. Life sciences	47. Rail, including manufacturing
3. Agriculture, animal health and food and drink manufacturing	18. Design: product, graphic and fashion design	33. Machinery and equipment	48. Real estate
4. Architecture	19. Electricity market, including renewables	34. Maritime/ports, including marine equipment	49. Retail
5. Asset management	20. Electronics	35. Market infrastructure (financial services)	50. Retail and corporate banking
6. Audit and accounting	21. Environmental services: waste	36. Medical devices	51. Road haulage and logistics
7. Automotive	22. Environmental services: water	37. Medical services and social care	52. Space
8. Aviation	23. Film, TV, video, radio and photography	38. Museums, galleries and libraries	53. Steel and other metals/commodities
9. Broadcasting	24. Fintech	39. Music, performing and visual arts	54. Technology (ICT)
10. Bus and coach transport	25. Fisheries	40. Nuclear	55. Telecommunications
11. Business services	26. Gambling	41. Oil and fossil fuel production, including gas	56. Textiles and clothing
12. Catering: retail and wholesale	27. Gas market	42. Payment services and systems	57. Tourism
13. Chemicals	28. Higher education	43. Pharmaceuticals	58. Wholesale markets and investment banking
14. Construction and engineering	29. Insurance and pensions	44. Post	
15. Consumer goods	30. IT, software and computer services, including video games	45. Professional services	

Letter from Rt Hon. David Davis MP, Secretary of State for Exiting the European Union, to Baroness Verma, chair, EU External Affairs Sub-Committee House of Lords, 30 October 2017.[59]

If you think that Britain excelled in any of these areas before empire, think carefully about what you are claiming. There will have been nascent beginnings of everything we have now before empire, but nothing in Britain has been untouched by empire – and much would be far more modest had another European country become the centre of the largest realm the world has ever known. The majority of current university buildings in Britain's oldest university cities of Oxford and Cambridge were built during the empire years. The same is true for Scotland's ancient universities. A very large part of what Britain is good at was established during the time of empire and would not now be here were it not for that empire; an empire that cannot be replaced or rekindled, but has to be recognised, represented fairly in our histories and relinquished, not constantly re-conjured.

CHAPTER 6

HOW NOT TO TREAT IMMIGRANTS

*Leaving the EU was never going to be a straightforward path.
The referendum that led the country to this result was crude and
misleading; the government's approach to talks has been boorish,
illogical and driven by imperial nostalgia. The Tories seem to
think an intricate 44-year-old relationship can be recklessly
dismantled in a matter of years.*

– Maya Goodfellow, *The Guardian*, December 2017[1]

INTRODUCTION

On 2 November 2017, the BBC reported that nurses from the European mainland had been turning their backs on the UK.[2] There had been an 89 per cent drop in the numbers signing up to work in Britain in the year after the Brexit referendum, as compared to the year before. On top of that, there had also been a 67 per cent rise in the number of EU nurses and midwives leaving the register – this was almost certainly because so many more than before were now leaving the UK earlier than they otherwise might. They felt that they were not wanted, even though they knew that they were very badly needed.

The government suggested that they could train and entice

more British people (mainly women) to become nurses and midwives. However, they had also cut bursaries for the training of
nurses within the UK. Since the nursing bursaries were axed in
2016, the total number of students studying nursing has dropped
by 11 per cent, while the number studying for a degree in nursing has fallen by 33 per cent, in just two years.[3] Furthermore, the
places most reliant on nurses from the European mainland were
London and other very expensive southern cities, where rents
were very high. Over 1,000 full-time midwives working in Britain in 2016 at the time of the referendum were EU but not UK
citizens. One in six of all midwives in London (and one in three
of those working in one central London NHS Trust) were EU
but not UK citizens when the vote was held. England as a whole
already had a shortfall of 3,500 midwives. It needed those even
before the referendum vote. But then the UK voted out, and
fewer midwives arrived from abroad as a result.[4]

Across England and Wales, infant mortality rose overall in 2015.
It rose again in 2016. Not since wartime has the rate risen in two
successive years. The rate had been rising for the poorest families
since 2010.[5] Most of those infants who died before their first birthday died in their first few days or weeks of life. In October 2018,
the Royal College of Paediatricians and Child Health warned that
UK infant mortality would be almost 2.5 times higher than com-
parably wealthy states by 2030 if current trends continued, and
still 80 per cent above the average of EU countries by then even if
the trend began to improve again at past improvement rates.[6] In
Britain's southern cities, women only give birth safely because of
skilled European immigrants. And this is just one important group
among the many groups of people whose health now suffers more
due to Brexit. We could have devoted a whole section of this book
to immigrants who are anaesthetists, radiologists,[7] doctors, nurses,
teachers, bus drivers, restaurant workers, fruit pickers, planters,

construction workers, bricklayers and any other area of work where there was already a shortage of labour that had drawn in people from the European mainland to work in the UK. Within months of the Leave vote, newspapers and TV news stations around the world were reporting that migration into Britain had experienced the fastest fall since records began in 1964.[8] Nurses were just one small part of that exodus. Too few were coming; too many going back home early.

In January 2018, the Centre for London think tank reported that demographic data for the final quarter of 2017 had shown a sharp and significant fall in people registering for National Insurance numbers in the UK capital city. The fall was all within the group who were EU nationals; there was no fall in the registration of people from the rest of the world – those normally resident outside of the EU. The fall was sharpest for people aged 25–34. It was young Europeans who were suddenly no longer coming to London just over a year after the Brexit vote.[9] And then in May 2018, the same analysts reported that 'National Insurance Number registrations – by people coming to London from overseas to work – continue to drop in London and the pace appears to be accelerating'.[10]

In this chapter we delve a little deeper into Britannia's more recent uneasy relationship with immigrants. What is it about the British today that makes so many so unwelcoming and so unfriendly?

NOT WELCOME HERE

People stop coming to the UK when they no longer feel welcome. When the economy desperately needs them, this really is a mistake, and one the British are in danger of exacerbating not only after Brexit occurs, but also during the process of trying to leave the EU.

London was most affected by the drop in people coming from Europe because it had previously done so well out of immigration – all to the benefit of its hospitals, its overall health profile, its employment and its educational outcomes. For instance, London schools only do so well because of immigration. The often British-born children of immigrants tend to be poorer than other children in London, but the poorest children in London (measured by qualifying for free school meals) do better at school than the poorest children in every other region of England. Having a good supply of teachers also helps London; many also come from abroad, especially from the EU. But it is this influx of very motivated children that is key in making London what the BBC in 2018 called an educational 'special case'.[11] Worldwide, the children of immigrants tend to progress as their parents project their own aspirations through their children, often while undertaking low-paid work. A year before the BBC reported on London's superior performance, ITV had run the headline: 'Immigrant children improve standards in London schools says Michael Gove'.[12]

The case for London benefiting from immigration is even more obvious when applied to the capital's hospitals. The England-wide summary of hospital-level mortality indicators (SHMI) for the period October 2016 to September 2017 showed that hospitals such as the Royal Free in London, London North West NHS Trust and Imperial College NHS Trust were top of the league tables, followed by St George's University Hospitals Trust (Tooting, London), Chelsea & Westminster and Guys & St Thomas'. Outside London, the best-performing trust was in Cambridge. And then, in great geographical contrast, the worst-performing hospitals in England were in areas where there tended to be the fewest immigrants. These included Brexit-supporting Lincolnshire, Wolverhampton, Blackpool, Southend, Wigan, Great Yarmouth, Southport, Hereford and Newcastle – all places that traditionally found it hard to recruit health staff, even from within England.[13]

Almost enough – often, only just enough – nurses and midwives from mainland Europe had been willing to come when they had equal rights with UK citizens, but often only for a few years. They did this to experience England, working in another country and extending their skills, including speaking English. They had not travelled so far because it was financially worth their while, or because they believed the streets were paved with gold. A nurse in Britain is paid more than in Poland, but the costs of living in Britain are higher, and overseas nurses end up living and working disproportionately in the most expensive areas, where it is hardest to recruit locally. Enoch Powell as Conservative Minister of Health in 1960–63 *encouraged* the migration of nurses from the Caribbean and doctors from the Punjab to fill shortages in the NHS.[14] Without the participation and contributions of these migrant medical professionals, the NHS could have become yet another good idea that didn't succeed. Enoch's invitation to migrate was issued not long before he became well known for his extremely racist anti-immigrant speeches. The claims that are often made about his brilliance seem odd in the face of this intellectual failure. Illogically, he subsequently fostered the idea that immigrants caused the British harm, whereas in fact the contribution of post-war immigration to Britain helped build the country up from a wartime low.

When we characterise the Brexit vote as being about immigration above all else, some of our friends have suggested that we are conflating patriotism with wider concerns about immigration and racism. They say that of course the eighteenth- and nineteenth-century ideals of John Bull (see Figure 4.2) and Britannia still exist, but today there is a healthy cynicism at work, giving 'the powers that be' a reminder that popular support is not to be taken for granted. They mention the Labour government victory in 1945 – when the supposedly 'empire-loving' working classes voted against Churchill. They say that for many, the glories of empire vanished in the trenches of the Great War, in the Great Depression and, more prosaically, when England lost to Hungary at the Empire Stadium on 25 November 1953.

But conflating anti-immigration rhetoric with patriotism is a mistake. Immigrants will continue to be crucial to the economic life of the country. If you care about Britain, you should worry about not receiving enough immigrants. Immigration to Britain rises when the birth rate falls. In 1877, with the birth rate relatively high and immigration low, Annie Besant and Charles Bradlaugh[15] published a pamphlet explaining methods of birth control, complete with 'obscene' illustrations. The pair were tried for violating obscenity laws, but the trial resulted in wonderful publicity. Nine months later, during 1878, the birth rate in Britain fell. Some twenty-eight years on, in 1906, net immigration rates to the UK had significantly increased, because the demand for labour had grown in the face of the lack of British workers. There is a common misconception that immigrants to the UK during these years were mainly refugees fleeing pogroms; in fact, those children who were never born had been replaced by immigrants. Later, the birth rate fell to especially low levels in the 1930s and 1940s due to mass unemployment and so many male deaths in the First World War. By the 1960s, the birth rate had increased, but immigrants were still needed because babies cannot work, and so the immigrants brought in were born to people from elsewhere in the empire in the 1930s and 1940s. Only a very few of these were replacing the workers killed during the Second World War. The vast bulk of immigrants came to replace the babies that the British, by now fully able to put on condoms, had not had a generation earlier.

Sometimes what is seen as racism is about fairness. The case of

Labour MP and putative future Foreign Secretary Patrick Gordon Walker half a century ago wouldn't have seemed out of place in the Brexit vote. Initially leading the polls in his constituency of Smethwick, the incumbent Gordon Walker was defeated by one of the most notoriously racist campaigns in Britain's history, with the Conservatives running the slogan 'If you want a nigger for a neighbour, vote Labour'. To get Gordon Walker back into Parliament, a by-election was contrived in the safe Labour seat of Leyton, with the sitting MP, Reg Sorensen, elevated to the House of Lords to make way for his colleague. Sorensen was widely admired for his fairness. Decades earlier, in 1933, at the Labour Party Congress, he had been a major critic of the harsh means by which the British were striving to maintain their empire in India, telling the congress that 'the operation of Imperialism in India is in essence no different from the operations of Hitlerism ... We are appalled by what is happening to the Jews in Germany, but what is happening in India is just as bad.'[16]

Under Gordon Walker, Sorensen's comfortable majority was overturned, with the 1965 by-election returning the Conservative candidate Ronald Buxton. It is possible that the people of Leyton were supporting the racist Tory policies that had seen Gordon Walker ousted in Smethwick. However, many may have also thought that Reg was an excellent constituency MP and that he had been unfairly treated. For some voters, the two issues may have been inextricably linked, with the prevailing racist attitudes of the time coupled with a sense of unfairness at being taken for granted. Labour won the constituency back in 1966 and has held it ever since then, winning 32,324 votes in 2017, with the Tories in second place with 9,627. The capacity to remind our 'betters' that allegiances are not to be taken for granted played a part in both the Brexit vote and Trump's victory, and perhaps even the emergence of Jeremy Corbyn.

Some lucky ones were taught a more enlightened curriculum at school in the 1960s. For these few, their memory is not one of being taught the glories of the British Empire but of E. P. Thompson, Christopher Hill and Eric Hobsbawm; and later of David Harvey and writings in the journal *Antipode*; of Fanon and of Marcuse (teachings on socialism, Marxism, industrial capitalism, the right to the city, colonisation and critical theory). One, whose parents had watched events unfold in Leyton in the 1960s, told us that despite being tempted by Lexit:

> I still voted Remain and was dismayed rather than shocked by the Leave vote. I wonder how many like-minded people voted to leave what they saw as a monolithic neoliberal construct that was inflicting pain on the most vulnerable. After all, Grexit [the idea that Greece might exit] came before Brexit.[17]

We need to remember that the Eurozone was also inflicting austerity on entire countries such as Greece, and that the EU as a whole, with the laudable later exception of Germany, had an increasingly anti-immigrant policy following the refugee crisis. There were many different reasons for voting Leave.

AFFLUENT IMMIGRANTS AND IMMIGRANTS FOR THE AFFLUENT

The Brexit and Trump victories have resulted in the legitimization of racism and white supremacy to an unprecedented degree. A week prior to the referendum, pro-immigration Labour MP Jo Cox was brutally murdered by a man who shouted 'Britain First' as he killed her, and who gave his name in court on being charged with her murder as 'Death to traitors. Freedom for Britain'. Since the referendum, racist hate crime has increased by 16 per cent across Britain, and peaked at a 58 per cent rise in the week following the vote. Weeks

after the referendum, Arkadiusz Józwik was beaten to death in Essex,
having reportedly been attacked for speaking Polish in the street.
– NADINE EL-ENANY, 2017[18]

British governments and the British public in general are very
good and very well practised at being nasty to immigrants. There
is a long history to this vitriol. When British imperialists went
into other people's countries, they were traders, soldiers, gover-
nors, administrators and missionaries. Even when settled, they
were never (as far as they were concerned) immigrants. It was
just us expats (ex-patriates!), and those that we called the natives.
'Patriate' means 'of the mother country', to which they might one
day repatriate, or 'repair to' (from the Latin *repatriates*).

Anyone coming to Britain from the nineteenth to the twenty-
first centuries was a 'bloody foreigner' or – and it essentially
meant the same thing – an immigrant.[19] The exception to derogatory name-calling came only if the immigrant was rich or
had prospects, in which case they might be termed 'exotic' or
an 'investor'. Britain was often in the past a welcoming place for
the idle rich aristocratic expatriates of other countries. Harder-
working but still extremely rich mill-owner's sons such as Engels
and his occasionally impoverished but essentially posh author
friend Karl Marx were tolerated. Despite not being welcomed,
however, people at the other end of the income scale often did very
well. A young immigrant, Michael Marks, set up a stall in Leeds
market in 1886 selling everything for a penny and later going into
partnership with his friend Thomas Spencer, who gave England
what was, until recently, one of its favourite shopping destinations.

In 2017, all but one of the top twelve people in the Sunday
Times Rich List were immigrants. In April 2018, it was reported
in the *Financial Times* that wealthy Chinese had been given 146
out of the 355 'investor visas' offered to rich overseas people who

invest in Britain. A Tier 1 investor visa allows someone to settle permanently in the UK after two years if they invest £10 million, after three if they invest £5 million, and after five years if they invest £2 million. The investment has to be in government bonds or any actively trading UK-registered business. It doesn't matter what that business does, although the visa can be refused or revoked if the source of funds is found to be illegal or the person is living less than half their time in the UK.[20]

Part of the reason Britain has been so happy to welcome in the super-rich from other countries is that extremely rich people currently bankroll political parties, especially when that is in their direct financial interest – if they can successfully lobby for lowered taxation and regulation, that's money well spent. As the rich have become richer, all political parties have moved steadily to the right, at least until around 2013, when the take of the 1 per cent peaked at 15.9 per cent of all income;[21] within two years Jeremy Corbyn was elected leader of the Labour Party. Until 2015, this rightward movement had occurred almost continuously since the late 1970s, when the richest had their lowest ever share of national income.

Britain is, of course, far from being the only country in the world where the rich have been taking more and more until very recent years. In New Zealand, the wealth (note, not income) share of the richest 0.01 per cent rose from 6 per cent of all GDP in 1996 to 21 per cent in 2015.[22] Globally, it has been estimated that – if current trends continue – the richest 1 per cent will own 64 per cent of the world's wealth by 2030.[23] This estimate shows that such trends clearly cannot continue. Over the past few centuries, the take of the rich has risen and fallen almost cyclically; rarely has it grown as high as this, and when it grows so high it skews our thinking and behaviour.[24] New Zealand, like Britain, welcomes in affluent immigrants who buy up huge amounts of land, while complaining bitterly about poorer immigrants who do so much of the work.

This is a trend set to continue for as long as world wealth and income inequalities rise. Very recently, researchers concluded that if the patterns observed between 2008 and 2017 continue, then globally the wealth of the top 1 per cent will increase by around 6 per cent per year, from around $140 trillion in 2017 to $305 trillion in 2030. By contrast, the wealth of the remaining 99 per cent would increase by only around 3 per cent per year, thereby rising from around $140 trillion in 2017 to $195 trillion in 2030.[25] Such a trend would result in the most affluent having so much power that work in large part becomes, directly or indirectly, serving the rich. The exceedingly rich would be able to afford roughly twice as many servants as they can today. But, as ever, the wealth of the rich depends entirely on the labour or suffering of the poor.

Despite all the depressing statistics, there are still good grounds for hope. In fact, the depressing statistics make hope even more feasible, because they suggest that the continued amassing of wealth by the already wealthy is near impossible without the almost total acquiescence of well over 99 per cent of the rest of the population. In short – just how stupid are we? But we don't just have to rely on the collective intelligence of the 99 per cent to hope things can get better. In recent years, income inequalities have fallen in both a majority of OECD countries and a majority of countries worldwide.[26] Wealth inequalities tend to lag behind income inequalities, so that, although wealth inequalities will continue to rise for a few years to come, unless the current trend for falling income inequality is reversed, we should expect wealth inequalities in future to fall too. The introduction of more wealth taxes would greatly speed up that process, however.

In London in 2018 it was already being reported that the exceedingly rich were having trouble getting servants. This is partly because they were no longer as exceedingly rich, as the pound slumped. And the potential servants from mainland Europe were looking at the UK and thinking to themselves, 'How can I avoid going there?' For instance, within the twelve months to June 2018 there was a 75 per cent drop in the number of young women (and a few young men) willing to come from the European mainland to be au pairs for the rich.[27] The gap could be filled with people from even poorer countries, so soon the British rich will more often have to have non-white au pairs for their children, which many – including many non-white rich people – had been trying to avoid. But this is just the latest twist in a very long story of racism and immigration.

The British could, for instance, ask where their football clubs would be without rich immigrant owners and buyers. The world-famous Arsenal is mainly owned by Stan Kroenke, an American businessman with wide sports ownership including an American football team, the Los Angeles Rams. His wife, who also owns sports teams, is the daughter of Walmart co-founder and owner James Walton. She owns the Denver Nuggets, partly due to American National Football League ownership restrictions on how many teams one person can control. Arsenal's co-owner is Alisher Usmanov, born in Russia and living in Switzerland. His money came from metals and mining investments in Russia, where he has mobile phone and publishing interests.

Chelsea Football Club is owned by Roman Abramovich, who now has Russian–Israeli citizenship after delays in getting his UK visa renewed. He made his money in the oil business and is reputed to be the 140th richest person in the world and a good friend of Vladimir Putin. Manchester City is co-owned by Mansour bin Zayed Al Nahyan, whose money also came from oil. The Chinese government, via Media Capital and CITIC Capital, is the other owner. Another Chinese billionaire bought West Bromwich Albion in 2016.

We could go on. Rich immigrant owners are good for a certain kind of celebrity football, as are the immigrant players who regularly come into the country but are somehow not regarded as immigrants, at least while they are playing on the pitch, especially if they are white. Only five of the England World Cup squad of 2018 were not first- or second-generation immigrants to England. What a strange condition for a patriotic game, supported so fervently by so many Brexiteers.

THE BRITISH UNWELCOMING TRADITION

In Britain, the nineteenth century was generally not a good time to be black or foreign. In 1893, one magazine, ironically called *Truth*, described immigrants and foreigners as 'deceitful, effeminate, irreligious, immoral, unclean and unwholesome. Any one Englishman is a match for any seven of them.'[28] Initially it was the Irish who received the most opprobrium, but later this xenophobia was extended to anyone who did not look or sound English, including the Scots migrating to southern England for work.

In the early twentieth century, anti-Jewish sentiment increased with the flight of Jews from Russia and Eastern European violence; they arrived to find an anti-immigrant lobby in full swing. Even popular novelists H. G. Wells and D. H. Lawrence were predicting seven million immigrants who would 'swamp the shores'. The Aliens Act of 1905, passed by a Conservative government and aimed at restricting Jewish immigration, was the first Act to translate British dislike of the foreigners and immigrants that they relied upon into official policy.

The men who came from the colonies to fight in the First World War were firmly told after the war to go home like good little children. Attitudes changed during the 1920s and 1930s. To accommodate Poles unwilling to return to Poland, Great Britain enacted the Polish Resettlement Act 1947, the UK's first mass immigration law for people not from the empire. It offered citizenship to around 200,000. The Second World War was only won due to the intervention of others: not only the Americans,

Canadians, Australians and New Zealanders, and (especially) the Russians, but also the Poles, people from the Caribbean, those from British colonies in Africa, Indians, and especially the Gurkhas, who were later denied rights of settlement and pensions, until the actor Joanna Lumley took up their case with her cry of '*Ayo Gorkhali!*' (Forward, Gurkhas!).[29] Above all else, however, it was the arrival of troops from the former colonies of the United States of America that swung the war. Nevertheless, British notions of superiority are predicated on being on the winning side.

After World War II, people with a right to enter as British subjects came in significant but far from overwhelming numbers in response to the pleas of the British government to help rebuild the 'mother country'. Then being extremely nasty to black immigrants really began in earnest. While the *Empire Windrush*, bringing Caribbean immigrants, was at sea in 1948, a British Labour government which had accepted the settlement of so many Polish and other displaced Europeans just one year before panicked at the potential arrival of a few hundred 'coloured' workers. The Privy Council sent a memo to the Colonial Office requesting that 'we should not make any special efforts to help these people ... otherwise it might encourage a further influx'.[30] The Conservative Party under Churchill was just as concerned.

As the British Empire began to disappear, as India gained independence, as the sun began to set on imperial flag after imperial flag, the battle to 'keep Britain white' began. Both major political parties were involved in being hostile to those people overseas who were still fighting for their country's independence. Both political parties were caught in the contradiction of needing black and Asian immigrant labour in Britain while denigrating their presence.

The Conservative 1962 Immigration Control Act was matched by Labour's 1968 Commonwealth Immigration Act designed to limit entry of East African Asians, but the clincher was the

Conservative 1971 Immigration Act. This last Act restricted rights to citizenship and contributed to the disgraceful treatment of elderly people of the Windrush generation in 2018 (of which more below). The British public largely remained clueless about empire, apart from a general understanding that it was a 'good thing'. The public knew little about decolonisation and the development, after empire, of a Commonwealth of fifty-three countries. Nor did they have much idea about how the British Empire was linked to the arrival of immigrants from former colonies who, until we recently took their rights away, had always had a right to move to and settle in Britain. The majority of the British public remained bemused and antagonistic to the entry of non-white colonial people whom they had always assumed to be their inferiors, and resented them arriving in 'their' country.

ENTER ENOCH

The man who has gone down in history as the classic nasty remains Enoch Powell (Figure 6.1). The basics of his rise and fall are well known.[31] Originally an academic appointed at age twenty-five to a job at Sydney University, he did war service in India and the Middle East and apparently developed a passion for empire and British imperialism. Powell believed fervently in the sovereignty of nation states as entities of great meaning, and of Britain in particular as a white homogeneous nation. He was less concerned about the sovereignty of those states that were part of the empire. He had once held the ambition to become Viceroy of India but that was thwarted by Indian independence. Entering Parliament in 1950 as MP for Wolverhampton South West in the West Midlands, he served as Minister of Health from 1960 to 1963, encouraging the migration of Caribbean workers into the UK to work in the health service. But then, after a failed bid to become leader of the Conservative Party in 1965, and with the election in a neighbouring town of Conservative MP Peter Griffiths under the slogan 'If you want a nigger for a neighbour, vote Labour' (see above), Powell assumed that electoral success lay in appealing to anti-immigrant sentiment. In a speech in Birmingham on 20 April 1968, he claimed that there would shortly be three and a half million Commonwealth immigrants and their descendants in the country – as if propping up the British state's then faltering economy with migrant labour was a bad thing.

Seeing people with darker skins in England apparently filled Powell with foreboding and, quoting the Latin poet Virgil (wrongly, according to Classics scholars), he 'seemed to see the River Tiber foaming with much blood'. The main river in Wolverhampton is actually the River Tame, thought to be derived from the Celtic word for 'dark'. In 1968, the Tame mainly foamed with industrial waste and the decaying bodies of dead cats and other urban wildlife. However, after this and further speeches, dockers and market traders marched in Powell's support, waving placards stating, 'Back Britain not Black Britain'. Powell regarded this as a patriotic outpouring in defence of a white nation state. In fact, the supposedly spontaneous marches were actually

organised by extreme right-wing activists, according to secret intelligence briefings to the [then] prime minister. An MI5 report to Harold Wilson four days after the Tory frontbencher's inflammatory Birmingham address said the supposedly spontaneous strike and demonstration by 500 workers from the East India dock was actually led by Harry Pearman, a supporter of the anti-communist fundamentalist group Moral Rearmament.[32]

Members of Oswald Mosley's fascist party also ensured porters from Smithfield Market demonstrated in favour of Enoch's claim of the 'menace' of 'charming wide-grinning piccaninnies'. Powell's real supporters were the fascists and Conservatives. By 1969, a majority of Conservative constituency associations, mostly in middle-class areas, had voted to stop all 'coloured immigration'. History repeats itself: 1969 was a dangerously racist farce; 2016, when hundreds of thousands of people from the European mainland were told we wanted them to 'go home', was a tragedy.

**FIGURE 6.1: ENOCH POWELL IN 1987
– THE MAN WHO SPREAD HATE AND FEAR**

By Allan Warren, taken on 1 January 1987, copyright use permitted.[33]

Journalist and writer Sarfraz Manzoor recalled the impact of Powell's speeches forty years later as 'black Britain's darkest hour', which 'remains a toxic cloud floating above all political debate on race relations'.[34] He recalled that after the speech a special Post Office van was provided to carry all the letters in support of

Powell. Manzoor recalled that as a boy of Pakistani origin, Powell frightened him, and 'repatriation was a most terrifying word for a young boy who knew nothing but Britain and who feared what might happen should Powell and his supporters ever gain power'.[35] By the 50th anniversary of the 1968 speech, the Conservative Prime Minister Theresa May had created a deliberately hostile environment for migrants, terrorising so many of the Windrush children who could not produce old documents that they had not previously been required to have. In some cases the Home Office had destroyed their landing cards. Some have lost their jobs, others have been evicted from their homes, still others have been denied treatment by the NHS when ill despite having paid their taxes for years, and a few have been threatened with deportation, or even deported.[36] By mid-May 2018, the Home Office was investigating sixty-three cases in which people were thought to have been wrongly deported. The previous year, the Chief Inspector of Borders and Immigration said that they currently had a list of over 140,000 people in Britain who had been told that they had no right to remain and might be forced to leave. One MP described Theresa May as 'Enoch Powell in a dress'.[37]

Powell would also have been delighted with the vote to leave the European Union. He opposed Britain joining the European Economic Community in the 1970s, claiming it was a surrender of sovereignty, turned his back on the Conservative Party and became an Ulster Unionist MP in Northern Ireland from 1974 to 1987. In retirement he was vehemently against the Maastricht Treaty that created a European Union, and deplored the economic migration of EU workers. His doctrine of 'Powellism' – demanding white national sovereignty, combined with anti-immigration rhetoric and a continued 'stirring of the racial pot', as one biographer put it – made him an icon for white supremacists, and sadly his legacy has lived on long after his death in February 1998.

WHAT THE CHILDREN THOUGHT

Being hostile to immigrants and black people does not come naturally to human beings; it has to be taught from an early age. Governments and politicians who denigrate and agitate against minorities; parents who have been taught an ethnocentric curriculum emphasising British exceptionalism; teachers who have had little training in how to deal with race hate – all contribute to a perpetuation of stereotypes and unpleasantness towards citizens from minority groups, migrant workers and refugees. Of the many examples of race hate in the 1980s, one was the response to a letter published in *The Independent* newspaper after the murder of an Asian boy by a white pupil in Manchester, which suggested that an increasing number of teachers were 'working to disabuse young white people that they have any social, moral or political right to harass or attack their non-white fellow citizen'.[38] This resulted in a collection, if not a van full, of hate mail to the letter's author, including one reply complaining that 'non-white people in this country are not our fellow citizens. They are aliens temporarily living here until the English people come to their senses.' That particular letter was signed off 'Heil Hitler'.

In 1986, a local authority advisor asked 300 Tyneside pupils to write an essay on 'black people' and found 75 per cent held negative views, of whom 25 per cent were very hostile, with a repatriation theme emerging strongly. For example: 'Black people mostly come from Africa. They started taking our jobs and making everybody unemployed. I think anyone who even looks black should be deported'; and 'I think the Pakis steal jobs from the English'; or 'Coloured people from different countries should be chucked out of our country.'[39]

A year earlier, in 1985, the report of the committee headed by Lord Swann on Education for All also told a story of how the authors of that report had sent local authority inspectors to visit

schools with few or no minorities. They found evidence of ignorance and antagonism to immigrants and minorities. One head
of history noted that 'in every class some children would pack
all immigrants off back home' and pupil essays included such
sentiments as 'We take everyone in because we're mugs ... it's our
country and we should come first' and 'There are millions of immigrants from China–Pakistan that speak all different languages
... I think they should be chucked out.'[40]

One of the authors of this book was a schoolboy during these
years, at a school where the proportion of children from ethnic
minorities was slightly above the national average. He can remember being asked to join in kicking the heads of 'coloureds', and to
take part in 'Paki-bashing'. He can remember the National Front
coming into the school without the teachers realising, and beating a
boy up in an alley near a playground within the school grounds. He
can remember the police being extremely racist. He can remember
particular teachers being great, and others finding children who
were not white more of a threat, including head teachers. And this
author is white. Anyone who was a child in Britain in the 1960s,
1970s or 1980s who was not white has a series of stories to tell. They
often choose not to tell them. They are the majority.

It was clear that any attempt to offer a multicultural anti-racist
education from the 1960s to the 1990s was a daunting task. There
had been little political support for teaching something about the
backgrounds and life experiences of former colonial settlers and their
children, and even less for helping white pupils examine their own
beliefs. Nor has there ever been much enthusiasm in schools for re-
assessing the relationship of Britain to her former empire or Britain's
place in relation to the rest of the world. By the 1990s, any moves in
these directions were firmly ruled out, and in 1993 five white youths
could murder a young black citizen with cries of 'What, what nigger',[41] with the authorities taking twenty years to bring just two of

these men to justice. All of this brings us into the twenty-first century and new ways of being unpleasant to immigrants and minorities.

Most recently, immigrant children have been targeted by the Conservative Party in schools, sparking concerns that they were looking for families to deport. In May 2016, the Department for Education announced a new policy of adding nationality and country of birth to the requirements for the compulsory national school census, with this requirement coming into effect in September 2016. Schools had been found demanding to see parents' passports and producing 'foreign children lists'. As one parent put it in 2017 following the Brexit vote, 'Eight years ago we were worried about the BNP. Four years ago we were worried about UKIP. Now it is the Conservatives themselves who are the driving force behind division and fear.'[42] Following pressure from campaigners, ministers dropped plans to introduce ethnicity and nationality data collection for nursery school-age children in late 2016.

FIGURE 6.2: THE BOY AT THE BUS STOP, THE DANGER OF THE SCHOOL CENSUS, MAY 2017

Posters opposing the government's collection of data on pupil nationality and birth country appeared around London over the weekend 13–14 May 2017 and on social media. Twitter: @ewa_jay. Reprinted with kind permission of the photographer, Wasi Daniju.[43]

Campaigners had produced posters and put them up (illegally) in bus stops in London. Figure 6.2 shows a child looking at one near the Elephant and Castle (or at least just a short bus ride away). The poster read: 'I have the right to go to school and not worry about which newspapers or companies know I'm there ... School census: refuse to answer nationality and country of birth questions by May 18th.' We do not know the country of birth or the nationality of the little boy in the picture – and why should we, or his school, or the government?

There is a story about a mirror in the Smithsonian Institute in the United States (and now found in many zoos). Above the mirror was written 'Most dangerous animal in the world'. The idea of the exhibition was to teach children that they, collectively, as human beings were the most dangerous animal on the planet: the animal that could warm its oceans, lead more species to extinction than any other, introduce monocultures and create the circumstances for famine and drought. One day a group of children from a black inner-city school visited and a little boy, looking not unlike the child in the image above, was seen staring into the mirror trying to work out what made him the deadliest creature on earth. The organisers of the exhibition had always imagined that people would realise that it meant all human beings – us collectively. It is comforting to imply that we are all equally culpable, but not true.

REDUCING IMMIGRATION

Tony Blair's Labour Party decided to be cruel and mean-spirited to immigrants with a 1999 Act which created a new system of detention, enforced dispersal of asylum seekers, and vouchers for food. This was in spite of a Human Rights Act passed in 1998 (and opposed by the Conservatives who were later busy dismantling it in 2018). Yarl's Wood concentration, detention and 'immigration removal' centre was opened in 2001. In 2002, as it burnt down, the private security guards are alleged to have locked detainees in the burning building.[44] The site was quickly rebuilt. In 2016, the Home Office refused to say how many women detainees had been raped or sexually assaulted by staff in the centre because such disclosure would 'prejudice the commercial interests of people involved with Yarl's Wood such as Serco, the private company that [now] runs the facility.'[45] When the centre first opened, US President Bush had only recently declared a 'war on terror' after the attack on the Twin Towers in New York, the Iraq War was about to begin, and, amid the fears of gains by the BNP in local elections, Home Secretary David Blunkett was tasked with producing a White Paper on immigration and citizenship. In this document, Blunkett announced that 'the tensions as well as the enrichment which flows from the inward migration of those arriving on our often wet and windy shores'[46] must be examined. The subsequent 2002 Act incorporated an English language and citizenship test for aspiring citizens, although a suggestion for separate schooling for asylum seekers' children was opposed. Alastair Campbell, the Prime Minister's spokesman, recorded in his diary that 'DB is doing his immigration paper which ... was a bit too pitched to the right-wing media'.[47] Conservative Oliver Letwin told his party's conference in 2003 that asylum seekers should be automatically deported to an unspecified island 'far, far away' for processing.[48] Even in 2018 Letwin is still an MP. Not only has he not been voted out, in fact he's both benefiting from and contributing to the climate of intolerance towards immigrants.

An island was probably not required, as the Yarl's Wood immigration removal centre eventually became a place to be feared and a place of harassment just as frightening as any prison hulk or anthrax island. In February and March 2018, 120 people there went on hunger strike in protest at the conditions of their detention.

Over a decade earlier, on 15 September 2005, Manuel Bravo had hanged himself in a stairwell in order to prevent his thirteen-year-old son Antonio from being deported with him to Angola the next day.[49] Between those two events, and before them, the instances of atrocity – including indefinite detention; mistreatment of female detainees who have previously been the victims of rape, torture and trafficking; and so much more – were just too numerous and heart-breaking to document here.

Michael Howard made immigration and asylum an election issue in the 2005 general election, calling for a withdrawal from the UN Convention on the Status of Refugees. The convention gave refugees rights which, although often initially ignored by the British authorities, could later be used in action for redress in the courts. He lost the election. But in a further Immigration Act in 2006, Labour created a UK Border and Immigration Agency, part of a new climate of opposition to immigration, responsible for policing borders, dealing with arrivals and deportations, sponsoring migrant workers and overseas students and preventing illegal migration. Then, in 2011, Labour opposition leader Ed Miliband announced that open EU migration was a mistake. From its inception, the Border Agency was noted for its inefficiency and in some cases unlawful actions. The Home Office took back control of the agency in March 2013, this 'control' subsequently also proving to be chaotic. Even staff in the Border Agency reported suffering exceptionally high levels of discrimination and harassment.

In the spring of 2013, the coalition government, terrified by the gains of the BNP in local elections and the rise of UKIP more widely, decided to step up the nastiness. UKIP had come second to the Liberal Democrat winner in a by-election in Eastleigh in Hampshire. UKIP claimed that at the end of the year, when restrictions on immigration from Bulgaria and Romania were lifted, untold numbers of the 29-million-strong Bulgarian and

Romanian population would enter the country and that there would be 'fewer jobs available, pressure on hospitals, longer queues for care, wages going down, less money to go around and longer waiting lists for council housing'. The Bulgarian Ambassador said UKIP leader Nigel Farage was 'usually very feeble in presenting solid arguments' and preferred to 'engage in propaganda which deviates markedly from the essence of the debate', adding, 'It is very disappointing and very discriminatory.' Nevertheless, the notion that immigration should be reduced to 'tens of thousands' became a Conservative mantra. This was an arbitrary target thought up and defended by people who never justified it as any more than a slogan. They were often indifferent as to whether overseas students staying in Britain for a limited amount of time were included in the figures, unless they thought they could score political points by appearing to be tough. After an agonising reappraisal of immigration policy by all parties, David Cameron promised again to be tough on immigrants, pledging to remove the rights of migrants to social housing. Perhaps he had not been informed that 95 per cent of migrants lived in private rented housing. Or perhaps it was all tokenism and political opportunism, never much thought out. But all this did was spur UKIP to set out its plans for withdrawal from the EU and the removal of benefits from EU workers and foreign citizens, along with a raft of right-wing domestic policies.

At the very same time, private landlords in London were raising rents to new peaks. The average rent for a London home increased from £1,250 a month in 2007 to £1,600 a month by 2017 (higher than UK median income after tax). This was not because they had to, or needed to, but just because they could. The availability of social housing continued to fall, with the right-to-buy policy on council housing continuing uninterrupted and occurring fastest where there was most need for housing. In contrast to London, rents in the north-east, Yorkshire and Humberside and the north-west of England were now three times less a month as compared to those in the capital, actually falling over the course of the decade in the north-east of England. Ironically, it was later shown that where the cost of housing had increased *the least* was where people voted most strongly to leave the EU.[50] Voting for Leave was similarly much higher in areas with low levels of immigration. More contact with migrants and members of ethnic minority communities takes the edge off negative perceptions. When people are prevented from mixing, they remain suspicious. It is not the people you know that worry you.

The then Home Secretary Theresa May took aggression to extreme lengths in March 2013, ordering billboard vans to drive around London bearing the message 'In the UK Illegally? Go Home or Face Arrest; text Home to 78070 for free advice and help with travel documents' (Figure 6.3). This was all part of her 'Operation Vaken' – named after a phrase that also appeared in a poem promoting fascism in Germany in 1992.[51]

FIGURE 6.3: GO HOME OR FACE ARREST – OPERATION VAKEN, JULY 2013, LONDON

Taken by Ian Burt on 27 July 2013, copyright use permitted.[52]

The Go Home campaign sparked much outrage. Bishop Patrick Lynch, responsible for migration in the Bishops Conference of England and Wales, pointed out rather mildly that 'it gives the message that all migrants and foreigners are unwelcome in the UK'. Even the *Daily Mail* reported: 'Home Office vans telling illegal migrants to go home investigated by advertising watchdog'.[53] Of 1,653 enquiries sent to the advice line, over 63 per cent were hoaxes, and apparently the entire exercise resulted in only eleven migrants leaving.

GETTING RID OF THE UNWANTED

Undeterred, Theresa May at the Home Office produced yet another Immigration Act in 2014 intended to 'make it easier to remove those with no right to be here, limit the appeals system, prevent illegal immigrants accessing or abusing public services or the labour market, and end the influence of the European Convention of Human Rights on immigration appeals'. This Act included expectations that private landlords, driving instructors and vicars, as well as hospitals and schools, would check on the legal status of people and report if uncertain. Attempts to deny that there were targets for the deportation, removal or voluntary departure of people from the UK became, by 2018, a source of much confusion, resulting eventually in the resignation of the Home Secretary Amber Rudd, who had only been appointed in 2016.

In spring 2018, Prime Minister May also refused to drop the inclusion of overseas students in immigration numbers, claiming that many of them overstayed their conditions of entry and did not return home. Research eventually demonstrated that 97 per cent of students did return to their home countries after their studies.[54] When the Department for Education sent out instructions that schools should collect the nationality and birthplace of all children and send the information to the department, this caused some parents to fear it could result in them and their children being deported.[55] Curiously, this demand from Big Brother included the instruction to separate out children born in East and West Germany! At the same time, the Home Office had announced plans to make all companies and businesses list their 'foreign workers' (i.e. their international employees). In June 2018, Global Justice Now, which was initially launched as Action for World Development by Oxfam and Christian Aid in 1969, felt it necessary to launch a campaign to make every MP pledge that they would not act as border guards, so that their surgery would be a safe place for everyone who lives in Britain. Since 2012, hundreds of people who have approached MPs for advice have been reported to the Home Office for immigration enforcement.[56]

FIGURE 6.4: THERESA MAY OPENING A CHURCH FÊTE IN 2007, SIX YEARS BEFORE VAKEN

Taken by Andrew Burdett on 2 June 2007; copyright use permitted.[57]

The numbers of people who had been deported or removed from the country were supposedly kept by the Home Office, and also checked by the Oxford University Migration Observatory. The

Home Office helpfully explained that deportation is defined as 'removal, if conducive to the public good'. This should have meant only people who had committed serious crimes and who might reoffend, but appeared to have been extended to any crime, however trivial, and even for having made but subsequently corrected minor errors on a tax return.[58] Removal is defined by the Home Office as 'enforced removal of those who enter the country illegally, overstayers or violators of entry permits', and voluntary departure means simply leaving, although Assisted Voluntary Return Officials are on hand to help with arrangements. Unfortunately, forced and voluntary removals are counted together. So, in 2015, 41,879 were counted as removed, dropping to 39,626 in 2016.

THE WINDRUSH SCANDAL

Back in Britain, the week of 16 April 2018 was perhaps the worst week of all for the government when it came to trying to pretend that they cared. It was during that week that the story of the treatment of elderly Caribbean people and their children – all those arriving before 1973 and unable to provide the documentation to prove their residence – exploded across the national and then international media. It was unfortunate (for the UK government, not for the deportees) that the biennial Commonwealth Heads of Government Meeting was in London that week and they were suitably outraged at the threats of deportation of these British people. The Jamaican Prime Minister and eleven others asked their host, Theresa May, for a meeting to discuss the issue but were refused! This was not a good move. May had just wanted to discuss trade with Commonwealth countries after Brexit. She apologised to the twelve the next day.[59] It was too late.

The Windrush story had been doggedly pursued in *The Guardian* by journalist Amelia Gentleman for months, but only came to media and political attention with the refusal of cancer treatment to Albert Thompson, who had arrived from the Caribbean as a teenager forty-four years earlier to join his mother, lived and worked all his life in Britain but was now told to prove continuous residence or pay £54,000 for treatment.[60] Labour leader Jeremy Corbyn had raised Thompson's plight with May in March 2018 but was told she was not aware of the case. Amelia Gentleman is married to Jo Johnson, brother of Boris, who was Foreign Secretary at the time of Amelia's investigations, while Jo was Minister of State for Universities, Science, Research and Innovation. It is surprising, to say the least, that ministers and the Prime Minister could have been unaware of the issue when one of their spouses knew the cases so well.

On 17 April 2018, in *The Guardian*, Amelia Gentleman began to detail the cruel cases of the people and their children who arrived around the time the *Empire Windrush* liner arrived in Britain, and who many decades later found that the Home Office was demanding impossible documentation if they wanted medical treatment, or to get a passport to travel to another country, or even to keep their job, or rent somewhere to live. The stories included a woman who had lived in the UK for fifty years and worked as a cook in the House of Commons but was threatened with deportation, and a former NHS driver who had arrived in the UK in 1968 as a fourteen-year-old and spent thirty-five years working and paying taxes, but was left jobless, homeless and living in an industrial unit after being told fifty years later that he was now an illegal immigrant. On 20 April 2018, Gary Younge argued in the *The Guardian* that Theresa May saw Windrush migrants as an easy target. On 21 April, in the same newspaper, Robert Booth and Nick Hopkins presented detailed evidence that the then Home Secretary Amber Rudd had boasted to the Prime Minister that she would hunt down even more illegal migrants and accelerate Theresa May's own deportation programme. On 24 April, Suzanne Moore explained that the Windrush scandal was no accident – it was clear and calculated Tory policy. On 27 April, Jessica Elgot and Heather Stewart reported that, having denied that the Home Office had set targets for removing people, Rudd had eventually been forced to admit that there were indeed targets – which would now be ditched. On 30 April, Amber Rudd finally resigned, to be replaced by Sajid Javid. It is worth remembering that back in 2015, before the Conservative Party conference of that year, Sajid Javid, a former banker, had suggested that free movement of people should be linked to a country's GDP. He proposed that only migrants from richer countries in the EU should travel freely, while those from poorer countries should not be allowed in.[61] Theresa May had replaced one Home Secretary deeply enamoured with prejudice against the poor with someone very similar.

In 2018, the independent Chief Inspector of Borders and Immigration reported that some 140,000 British people had been told they faced removal as they had no official legal status in the country. A hostile environment had certainly been created for black and other minorities, settled for years in Britain, who feared themselves liable for deportation.[62]

Between 2002 and June 2018, some 8,000 Caribbean nationals had been removed or deported. Supporters of the deportation pointed out that those who had been recently deported received some help. In Jamaica, a National Organization of Deported Migrants (NODM) had been set up in 2010, funded by the British High Commission to assist involuntarily returned (deported) migrants to prepare for and adjust to life in Jamaica. Because they often had no relatives in the country (a country that they had sometimes never or only briefly lived in), helpful hints were to be found in NODM booklets distributed to them before embarkation. These hints included: 'Try to be "Jamaican" – use local accents and dialect (overseas accents can attract unwanted attention), don't walk after dark in dangerous places, keep your wallet and phone safe, and find lodgings in areas considered safe.'[63]

WHAT ABOUT BREXIT?

The *Daily Telegraph* followed its coverage of the Windrush scandal by noting the 'alarming mess' in all government departments and asked, 'How can a government so callous and chaotic be trusted with Brexit?'[64] On past evidence, it probably would be trusted – at least by the usually loyal 40 per cent of people who say they will vote Conservative and who appear impervious to the Tory government's actions as long as their house prices don't fall. However, thankfully for British politics, for those who care about the Windrush generation, and for those who don't want to see all this bigotry and self-ishness continue unchallenged, their house prices were about to fall.

For a short while, the revelations of the Windrush scandal had appeared to overtake even the Brexit coverage in the media. However, remembering the close links between the Brexit campaign and anti-immigrant policies, it was no surprise that once the scandal coverage died down, normal service resumed, and the government continued its chaotic journey towards Brexit. A YouGov poll published in the week of 23 April 2018 found 'overwhelming support for the hostile environment policy'.[65] Britain is a deeply divided country that is currently torn apart by fear, hate and ignorance. Many people were not supportive of immigrants, no matter how long they had been in the country or how British they might have been. One woman affected by the deliberately inflexible policies introduced by Theresa May noted that 'I grew up with the National Front around my area. I thought these attitudes had been stamped out. The government has stoked it up again … this has ignited the fire of racism again.'[66]

In Parliament, the hostile environment for immigrants and the success of the Leave campaign in 2016 were always inextricably linked. The Leave campaign had specialised in being extra nasty about immigrants, which included anyone who had arrived after World War II, any EU migrant worker, any asylum seeker or refugee, or, as Afua Hirsch described it so well, anyone with a darker skin, who is definitely regarded as 'not British'.[67]

Nigel Farage, that public school-educated Member of the European Parliament, who appeared to combine an appearance of a smirking Toad of Toad Hall with Powellite unpleasantness and Del Boy dodginess, managed to stoke up antagonism towards all the categories of already bullied people in his attempts to appeal to his supporters, whipping up yet more hatred. Nigel has form. As one newspaper headline put it, 'Farage's fascist past? Nigel boasted about his NF initials and sang "gas them all", claims schoolfriend'.[68] Whether or not Nigel had any genuine friends at school, he made lots of friends later. His party, UKIP, collected 4 million votes in the 2015 general election. The Leave.EU campaign, of which Farage was a figurehead, embraced a curious mix of long-time Eurosceptics, anti-immigrant agitators and self-interested political climbers. It was funded by the multi-millionaire donor Arron Banks and claimed success for, as Farage put it, 'a victory for real people, a victory for ordinary people, a victory for decent people'.[69] Later it emerged that some of the 'real people' Banks socialised and drank vodka with were Russian businessmen, who were apparently wanting to sell him a goldmine.

It is worth speculating whether some of Farage's ordinary people included the 75 per cent who had held negative views of ethnic minorities in the 1980s, now in their fifties, and those older Tory voters still imbued with imperial nostalgia. The outpouring of racist, xenophobic and anti-Semitic attacks on minority groups was documented before and after the Brexit vote, especially by the government-supported organisation Tell MAMA, which from 2012 has been documenting race hate, antisemitism and Islamophobia. When claims were made that leaving the EU would result in less immigration, there was a spike in overt and covert hate crime, with long-settled immigrants, EU workers, refugees and asylum seekers, Muslims, Sikhs, Jews and anyone 'looking foreign' all finding themselves targeted. Most shocking was the murder, the week before the Brexit vote, of MP Jo Cox, by a man shouting 'Britain First' – the name of a far-right, fascist group formed in 2011 by former members of the British National Party. The police recorded a 57 per cent rise in reported hate crime in the four days after the vote. The Muslim Council of Britain reported eighty-five hate incidents in three days. A Polish social club in Hammersmith was vandalised with slogans of 'no more Polish vermin', Polish school children were given cards calling them vermin, and the Polish Ambassador expressed shock at the rise in anti-EU xenophobia when a Polish man was killed in Essex.[70]

FIGURE 6.5: STOP IMMIGRATION START REPATRIATION – NATIONAL FRONT BANNER 2016

Photograph taken in Newcastle upon Tyne and published on 26 June 2016 by the Daily Mail, *who did not credit the photographer, Emma Foster. Reproduced here with her permission.*

The *Daily Mail* called the complaints of the Muslim Council of Britain propaganda. An article in September 2016 headlined 'The Great Brexit hate crime myth' claimed to show 'how claims of an epidemic of race crimes since the referendum are simply false'.[71] The figure of a 57 per cent rise in hate crime released by the National Police Chiefs Council was branded questionable, with the paper asserting that complaining about hate crime is a lucrative industry and left-wing dogma. The message was clear: to those people being spat at in the street, having racist slogans painted on their homes, receiving hate mail, seeing their children frightened in the streets by racist comments – we don't believe you.

The issue of the three million EU nationals living and working in Britain was still to be faced, although there are already reports of EU nationals being told by the Home Office, usually incorrectly, to remove themselves and their families from the country. The German paper *Der Spiegel* noted in December 2017 that 'Britain grows more hostile to EU citizens'[72] and the problem of what will happen to EU people living and working in Britain was, by mid-2018, still largely ignored. Even as we write, in late November 2018, the question remains unresolved, with Sajid Javid now resorting to promises that a simple smartphone app might solve the problem. Why would anyone believe that a government as incompetent as this one could arrange that? Particularly given that the party's official conference app suffered a major security breach in September 2018, revealing personal details of senior Cabinet ministers, MPs and journalists. This suggestion originally came out of Amber Rudd's tenancy at the Home Office but we have still seen no sign even of a prototype version of the mobile app, through which EU nationals resident in the UK could complete a registration form to stay in the UK. Rudd claimed it would be as easy as setting up an account at the clothes shop LK Bennett (which sells dresses for £300 and over). The Post Office said that registration by phone would not work.

The Home Office said they had not yet begun hiring 1,000 workers for a customer service hotline for EU registration.[73]

With every week that passed in 2018, 1.2 million British citizens living and working in the EU were still wondering and then worrying more and more about their post-Brexit status. In January 2018, a group of Britons and the Anglo-Dutch Society won a legal ruling in a case contending that EU citizenship exists in parallel to national citizenship, and that leaving the EU does not therefore automatically lead to British citizens losing their European citizenship. The case was referred to the European Court of Justice.[74] During those same quickly passing weeks of 2018, thousands of young adults from the European mainland stopped coming to the UK and growing numbers of UK citizens began to emigrate to the mainland. Most will go quietly, thinking it will be temporary, but often never to return. In October 2018, one recent British graduate, who had mastered fifteen languages and written two books, bought a one-way ticket to Barcelona explaining, 'I don't want to live in an environment where I have to apologise for believing in European unity.'[75]

In recent years, hostility to immigrants has become as bad as the examples we gave from the nineteenth and early twentieth centuries earlier in this book. Widening the definition of an immigrant to include everyone with one drop of 'impure blood', or an affiliation to any religion other than the Church of England, or having a 'funny-sounding' name or accent, should include about 20 per cent to 25 per cent of the UK population. Contrast the general treatment of immigrants to Britain with the reception given to Meghan Markle, which offers non-republican liberals at least a little joy, especially since news broke of her royal pregnancy; the baby is due in April, the month after Brexit. Although as one US commentator recently put it:

It is possible that some of the Windsors, whose high-colonial racism appears as regularly as the Queen's midday gin-and-Dubonnet, are privately aghast at the prospect of a woman of color joining their ranks. But Markle's arrival has not created the sort of crisis that arose in 1936, after Edward VIII fell in love with the twice-divorced Wallis Simpson – 'a pretty kettle of fish', the Queen Mother said...[76]

IMMIGRANTS ARE THINNER AND OFTEN HAVE UNUSUAL NAMES

Shortly after the Brexit vote, a senior lecturer who specialised in competition economics at the Norwich Business School, Peter Ormosi, wrote a somewhat tongue-in-cheek article about the correlation between obesity and voting Leave.[77] Unsurprisingly, newspapers such as the *Daily Mail* were not amused. Peter published a table of figures (see Table 6.1) showing that while just 13 per cent of people in Oxford were obese and only 30 per cent there voted Leave, more than twice as many were fat in towns such as Great Yarmouth, where more than twice as many voted Leave.

TABLE 6.1: DISTRICTS IN ENGLAND AT THE BREXIT EXTREMES AND RATES OF OBESITY, 2016

Top 10 districts with largest % of Leave votes			Top 10 districts with smallest % of Leave votes		
District	% Leave	% Obese	District	% Leave	% Obese
Boston	76	31	Lambeth	21	16
South Holland	74	31	Hackney	22	18
Castle Point	73	28	Haringey	24	18
Thurrock	72	30	City of London	25	18
Great Yarmouth	72	31	Islington	25	17
Fenland	71	31	Wandsworth	25	15
Mansfield	71	32	Camden	25	14
Bolsover	71	32	Cambridge	26	15
East Lindsey	71	30	Southwark	27	21
North East Lincs	70	29	Oxford	30	13

Local authority areas, the highest and lowest percentage voting Leave and adult obesity rate estimates.[78]

Could it be that disgruntled fatties voted out? Or might something more interesting be at play? Age and class are part of the story of the geography of body size in Britain, but there is more to it than that.

The graphs below (Figure 6.6) show the correlation between obesity and voting Leave. Where the majority of people were of healthy weight, fewer than one in five voted out.

FIGURE 6.6: REFERENDUM OUTCOME AND BODY WEIGHT, ENGLAND LOCAL AREA PERCENTAGES

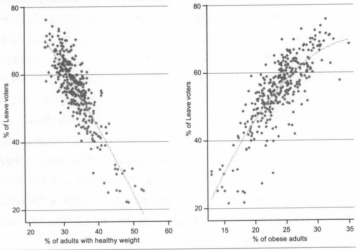

Originally titled 'The weight of Brexit: Obese adults leading the way out of Europe'.[79]

So, what is going on? One predictor of voting Leave that showed up very strongly was the proportion of immigrants in each area, whereby the higher the proportion of immigrants, the less likely people were to vote Leave. Immigrants tend to be thinner and younger and fitter. Furthermore, the presence of thinner people tends to cause others around them to try harder not to get fatter. Being fat in Oxford is not easy because you stand out more, and it is easier to be thin because more people are better off and can afford less-fattening foods. Being fat elsewhere is more normal.

When and where it becomes normal to be overweight, being overweight begins to spread. It has been called the epidemic of obesity. The serious point being made here is that the correlation could well be real, and the reasons for that correlation may be obscure and intermediate, with neither factor directly influencing the other, but both being related to a third factor that is more decisive.

Incidentally, a situation rarely commented on is that the poorer parts of Britain not only have more overweight people, and fewer immigrants, but also more severely underweight children. There has been a rise in underweight children in those local authorities most affected by austerity cuts. This has recently been seen in both school reception classes (when children are aged four and five) and in Year 6 (when aged ten or eleven), despite the overall percentage of underweight children remaining broadly static for England as a whole. Almost 50 per cent more reception-aged children were underweight in the poorest tenth of areas in the UK than in the richest by 2017, and the difference was 15 per cent by Year 6 (when at least they have had school meals). Some 55 per cent and then 69 per cent more children are either obese or overweight at the same ages in the poorest areas compared to the richest.[80] In the rich world, similar statistics are seen only in the USA.

Karl Pearson, the nineteenth-century mathematician credited with being one of the inventors of the Bell Curve, thought (as we noted in Chapter 3) that it was acceptable for the poorest children to be poorly fed. Even today it is apparently acceptable to allow the poorest children to be poorly fed. Do people still think, as so many of the elite did in the nineteenth century, that they are of a degenerate stock and will never amount to much, or do they consider them just unimportant dross? Today, it is still seen as acceptable for children to have to eat inadequate or cheaper unbalanced diets due to poverty. At the very same time, a £24,000-a-year private school held an 'austerity day' with baked potatoes and beans for lunch (hardly an inadequate lunch).[81] It was intended to raise awareness among its pupils of the struggles of poorer children, but was much criticised for being 'tone-deaf'.

All kinds of things correlate well with the relationship between immigration and vote Leave. As early as 18 July 2016, the appropriately named Mario Cortina Borja, Julian Stander and Luciana Dalla Valle wrote a quick paper entitled 'The EU referendum: surname diversity and voting patterns'. In it, they included the graph shown in Figure 6.7. Apparently, areas with more unusual surnames were less likely to vote Leave. Many people with unusual surnames would not have had a vote in the referendum because they would not have been UK citizens, but the presence of immigrants in an area turned out to be a very good predictor that many people would want to stay in the EU (see Chapter 1).

FIGURE 6.7: ASSOCIATION OF LEAVE VOTE WITH PEOPLE WITH UNIQUE SURNAMES, 2016

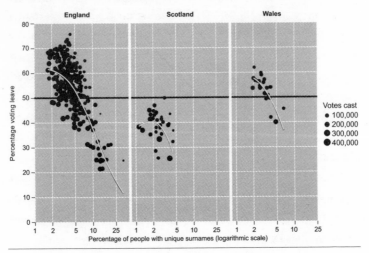

A log scale is used, since very few areas of the UK are hyper-diverse.[82]

For people living in areas where there are many others with unusual surnames, it can be easier to learn that the British were not as great a force for good as they may have been led to believe at school. Brexit might be the only way to make most of the British see what they really are. Afua Hirsch, who grew up in Wimbledon, explains in her recent book *BRIT(ish): On Race Identity and Belonging* that: 'The most persistent reminder of not belonging would be The Question. Where are you from? ... They already know the answer which in their imagination is a mythical "darkie" country.'[83] And this is how we so often speak when talking to children whose parents or grandparents are immigrants. The first generation to arrive almost always had to deal with much worse.

So, why have we been treating immigrants so badly? Events revealed that many of those who most wanted Brexit were prepared to say and do anything to get what they wanted. This included dehumanising immigrants, presenting them as sub-human, and attempting to scare the British about them. As a recent *Guardian* article noted, 'Researchers found immigration to be the most prominent issue in the 10 weeks running up to the vote, leading 99 front pages. Of those, more than three-quarters were from the four most virulently Leave newspapers: the *Sun*, the *Mail*, the *Express* and the *Telegraph*.'[84] The proprietors of those newspapers thought salvation lay in following the divisiveness and economics of the USA, not the solidarity and policies of Europe. They were prepared to treat immigrants as badly as they possibly could to try to get what they wanted.

One great irony is that the USA is hardly to be envied. What bigots like about the USA is that the melting pot never melted. As Matthew Stewart, who has written widely on the origins and future of the USA, explains:

> As of 2016, it took $1.2 million in net worth to make it into the 9.9 per cent; $2.4 million to reach the group's median; and $10 million to get into the top 0.9 per cent. (And if you're not

there yet, relax: Our club is open to people who are on the right track and have the right attitude.) 'We are the 99 per cent' sounds righteous, but it's a slogan, not an analysis. The families at our end of the spectrum wouldn't know what to do with a pitchfork. We are also mostly, but not entirely, white.[85]

Britain has been looking towards the wrong nation for guidance – the USA, a country whose rulers have largely hated immigrants for some time, despite hosting an economy that always required more labour, and despite now being made up almost entirely of the descendants of immigrants. This hatred has existed ever since the first slave was vilified and the second wave of immigrants arrived, but it was covered up by pretending to be a melting pot.[86]

In Britain in 2016, as Will Hutton and Andrew Adonis made clear in their 2018 analysis of the vote, 'it was immigration that decisively swung opinion. On the eve of the referendum, 63 per cent believed that refugees were one of the most important issues facing the country, compared to just 39 per cent saying the same for the NHS, or 33 per cent the economy.'[87] Treat immigrants so badly and eventually you begin to believe your own lies. And then you don't just severely harm them. You begin to damage yourself.

Once you realise how lucky you are to live in a country of immigration, you begin to realise that what actually holds Britain together, especially in its London heart, are the immigrants. Or, as Robbie Shilliam puts it in a very recent book, dedicated to the people of Grenfell: 'This detritus of empire has rarely been considered the material from which to build new publics, and certainly not in the metropolitan core. But the stone which the builders rejected shall become the chief cornerstone.'[88] Today we are all the detritus, the debris of empire, and we have to build a new raft from that.

CHAPTER 7

IMPERIALLY ROOTED EDUCATION AND BIGOTRY

Speaking to us from across the decades, the playwright Tennessee Williams challenges the concrete notion of people as entirely either good or bad, noticing instead only 'right and wrong ways that individuals have taken, not by choice but by certain still-uncomprehended influences in themselves'. And, in lieu of some post-hoc cure, he invokes the 'crying need of a great worldwide human effort to know ourselves a great deal better'. Extraordinary, isn't it, given our impressive reach of knowledge and progress, how we remain so opaque to ourselves?

– Sam Guglani, October 2017[1]

INTRODUCTION

Countries with more equal education systems around the world, including almost all of the rest of Europe, have better-functioning economies and appear to produce a happier, healthier, more able, more productive population.[2] As we noted earlier, among OECD countries, only the (few) affluent citizens of Chile spend relatively more on private education than do the British. In enormous contrast, most other affluent countries have hardly any selective private education. The majority of OECD countries spend most on the education of children who find school more difficult. They do this through higher state education spending for those who need it, not by spending more on private schools with 'charitable status' for those who are already ahead.

The old British myth about the ability and variability of potential in children is a comforting myth that sustains educational and social inequalities. As we pointed out in Chapter 3, the myth existed in the Labour Party's original Clause IV, penned in 1917 by eugenicist Sidney Webb and adopted in 1918: 'To secure for the workers by hand or by brain...' It was still there in Tony Blair's 1995 rewrite, 'for each of us the means to realise our true potential', implying that those potentials greatly varied. It comforts people who might be uneasy with the degree of inequality they see, but who would rather seek to justify it than confront it. The myth of greatly varying inherent potential helps some leading politicians in Britain, from right across the political spectrum, justify to themselves why they are privileged and why they are in their jobs and why they need have so little respect for the majority of the population. Ironically, the 'underprivileged' were often lucky – truth be told – to escape being sent to a boarding school, as Webb and Blair were when young boys.[3]

In this chapter, we provide as much detail as we can bear to recount (and as much as we can squeeze in, given the amount of space allowed in a book of this kind) on the background, predilections and various follies of the members of the Cabinet who were in power as the Brexit negotiations began; those of all the new Cabinet ministers who replaced them, as so many of the June 2016 intake resigned; and those of some of the leading proponents of Brexit, not in government, but willing the process on from the sidelines. They are, of course, not entirely bad, but they had found themselves in a situation that was mostly not of their making – to be in power at the tail end of the decline of the last gasp of empire thinking. And they had all been made by their education, by their schools and their families and the society within which they mixed. In future, we may look back at them more in pity than in anger.

ON GOOD AND BAD

Tennessee Williams's success with *A Streetcar Named Desire* came in 1947. He tried to explain how the places and situations that people find themselves in, and how they deal with these, are not necessarily a result of their own choices but are usually (or at the very least sometimes) much more a product of circumstances not of their making. Britain ended up with a set of politicians who could not comprehend what influenced them to precipitate a referendum on leaving the European Union that achieved a result that most MPs did not want. But a minority of them, and their predecessors, had been arguing about Europe since the 1970s referendum, then quietly throughout the 1980s Thatcher era, then more loudly in the 1990s and then even more seriously within the Conservative Party in the 2000s.

Depleted of imagination by years of post-empire introspection, the British Conservative Party Cabinet in 2015 had become dominated by ex-pupils of Eton – an odd school.[4] In 2005, a junior art teacher won an unfair-dismissal claim against the school, subsequently being awarded £45,000 in damages. It had accepted that Prince Harry had received 'help' in preparing his expressive art project, but the exam board cleared him of cheating (politically, probably a wise decision). At the tribunal, various allegations were made against staff at the school, which were reported in some detail by the media in February 2006.[5] Later, in 2017, there were two episodes in which many Eton pupils became aware of upcoming questions in the pre-U (A-level equivalent) economics and art history papers. The deputy head had to resign.[6] As we say, it is an odd school.

Why did so many pupils from just one school end up at the top of government? Is it because Eton is somehow able to select the brightest and best, those imaginary golden children? Or is it because it selects children that mostly just happen to be from some of the wealthiest families in the country, those who can afford to smooth their progress through life? Obviously, there is now a question mark over how some Eton students got their exam results, but many children can be trained by good teachers with small classes to pass exams. Eton is successful at getting children into Oxford and Cambridge. It is also very successful at giving them a sense of effortless superiority. It is wrong to stereotype but, thinking of the individuals from Eton whom you have heard about (David Cameron and Boris Johnson especially), how appropriate are the following adjectives: hard-working, knowledgeable, honest, modest, compassionate? Why go into politics when you are so wealthy that you hardly need any job? Could it really be just a high sense of public duty and service? Could it be the desire to be a leader, or for power, or to be in the limelight? Or could it be to protect your and your family's and friends' wealth – the one thing most Eton pupils have in common?

The men (and a very few women) who made up David Cameron's 2015 Cabinet were a very odd bunch with very unusual backgrounds. As teenagers, they had all (as far as we know) idolised Mrs Thatcher, who was aged fifty-three when she became Prime Minister. Quite what a set of teenage boys then saw in a woman old enough to be their very strict and domineering grandmother is hard to fathom, but single-sex boarding schools and minimal maternal contact has strange effects.

In 2015, there had to be a general election because of the five-year rule. Because of the lack of a majority, the previous government had been a coalition of two parties. It was widely expected and predicted that no party would gain an overall majority. The Conservative Party thought that they would lose votes to UKIP, and UKIP in the end did secure 13 per cent of the vote, though only one MP.

It was partly because they were hoping to attract some UKIP voters that the Conservatives promised an EU referendum by 2017, after negotiations over the rights of EU migrants. It had been a running sore for decades – Thatcher's demise was partly brought about over Europe, with Michael Heseltine, John Major and Kenneth Clarke all railing against Thatcher's Europhobic drift. Unexpectedly, the Conservatives won the 2015 election outright, with a majority of twelve seats (albeit with only 37 per cent of the vote) – the first Conservative majority since 1992, and only their second since the formation of UKIP in 1991.

A hung parliament and another alliance with the Liberal Democrats had been expected. This surprise win meant that the Conservatives had to fulfil their manifesto commitment, despite the majority of MPs, all other political parties except UKIP (and one previously insignificant Northern Irish party – the DUP) wanting to remain in the EU, and the Conservative Party (now so divided over Europe) officially remaining neutral. Why did wealthy UKIP donors, DUP stalwarts and at least half of all Tories want 'out' so very badly? What did they think was in it for them?

Prime Minister David Cameron and twenty-three of his thirty Cabinet ministers supported Remain. Unexpectedly, the June 2016 referendum was won by the well-funded Leave groups, which outspent Remain, and David Cameron resigned the next day, a political gamble having turned into a personal disaster. He was replaced within two months by Theresa May, whose time as

Home Secretary from 2012 had not been noteworthy apart from her repeated criticism of the European Convention on Human Rights and her uncompromising attitudes towards immigrants, refugees and asylum seekers. The stated purpose of the Immigration Act 2014 was 'to limit ... access to services, facilities and employment by reference to immigration status'. It also prevented some people from renting accommodation, getting driving licences or opening bank accounts. For Theresa May, the purpose was 'to create here in Britain a really hostile environment for illegal migration'. 'Illegal' was interpreted as not having every document the department arbitrarily decided that you needed, even when those documents had been lost by the Home Office itself. Theresa May's mission was to find any pretext to deport any migrant, however blatantly unfair. Her next mission, building on this supposed achievement, was to deliver a 'red, white and blue Brexit'.

As the *Financial Times* put it in late 2017:

Every conversation [on the mainland of Europe] starts with the same question: 'What's happened?' The Germans are not about to rescue Britain from the Brexit mess, but they are genuinely baffled, and not unconcerned, as to how things have reached this sorry pass. Ministerial sackings and lurid tales of sexual harassment at Westminster compound the confusion ... Government and parliament have lost control. A majority of MPs think Brexit is a mistake but feel obliged to pursue it lest they be accused of defying what the tabloids declare to be 'the will of the people'. This is what happens when the subtle checks and balances of representative democracy are subordinated to the crude majoritarianism of referendums. Germans, ever mindful of what happened in the 1930s, understand this.

Brexit represents the biggest upheaval since 1945 in Britain's political and economic life – an enterprise of enormous complexity and consequence. It is all-consuming. Yet the project is being steered, if that is the right word, by an administration drained of political authority by a misjudged election and by a Conservative party at war with itself.[7]

THEN ANOTHER POLITICAL GAMBLE

Theresa May had repeatedly said that she would not hold a general election. However, the Labour Party was in disarray, with the majority of Labour MPs wanting to get rid of their elected leader, Jeremy Corbyn. Opinion polls had consistently shown a Conservative lead over Labour of up to twenty points. So, in April 2017, Theresa May had decided, on a walking holiday in Snowdonia, not in Cabinet, to hold a snap election in June. She anticipated securing a larger majority to strengthen her hand in the forthcoming Brexit negotiations. Many Labour MPs welcomed it, hoping it would precipitate Corbyn's demise. May then lost her majority in the House of Commons, had to do a deal with Northern Ireland's politically and religiously extreme DUP, and then – to turn a terrible week into an even more horrible one for her, two thirds of Conservative voters surveyed by ConservativeHome wanted her to resign by 10 June.[8] But she soldiered on until fire broke out in Grenfell Tower four days later and she was expected to show some compassion. Demonstrating compassion doesn't come easily to Theresa May, but luckily she was surrounded by even more dreadful potential rivals. Come November 2017, Cabinet members were having to resign due to revelations of sex scandals and blatant breaches of the Ministerial Code. By June 2018, a member of her Cabinet had had to resign over a scandal on average every six weeks.

Stephen Crabb, previously Theresa May's potential leadership rival, had resigned as Work and Pensions Secretary in June 2016 after admitting that he had sent 'sexual chatter' to a nineteen-year-old when he was forty.[9] In November 2017, Defence Secretary Michael Fallon resigned after an alleged pattern of sexual harassment over the course of many years.[10] Further allegations of a sexual nature were affecting other members of the Cabinet at this time, as well as some revelations of tax avoidance and evasion in British overseas territories.

As Stephen Crabb had previously explained, 'Most MPs are risk takers to one degree or another. Usually in the areas of money, sex, political opportunism. Add in the adrenalin, the attention you get, and the time away from family ... toxic mix.'[11] Among the Tories, such behaviour seems particularly prevalent. Narcissism can lend itself to less self-control. It is worth remembering that right-wing politicians often accuse the poor of not having enough self-control when it comes to sex and money. It was seen in Ronald Reagan's 1976 trope of the black welfare queen, and in Peter Lilley's 1992 'little list' of 'scroungers' (which included 'young ladies who get pregnant just to jump the housing queue'), and in Esther McVey, in her role as Work and Pensions Secretary, saying that it was 'right' that more people were using foodbanks.[12]

While taking away from others, Conservatives simultaneously celebrate taking so much for themselves. Much of what Cabinet members have been accused of is not specifically illegal, but it is immoral. They are members of a political party that attempts to moralise about the behaviour of others, especially people poorer than they are.

When the official Downing Street photo of the Cabinet was published in 2016 (Figure 7.1), a photoshopped similar photo went viral. The huge 1836 painting of Ada Lovelace behind them had been replaced by Edvard Munch's painting *The Scream*.

Scream-worthy revelations of personal, financial and sexual impropriety engulfed the Cabinet at the time. Historians of the future, even those familiar with the peccadilloes of politicians in the long-distant past, may be amazed at the behaviour of the people in charge of the most important issue for Britain in the early twenty-first century – leaving the EU.

The questionable behaviour may have reached all the way to the top. In November 2017, it became apparent that Capital Group, the private equity business in which the Prime Minister's wealthy husband Philip May is a senior figure,[13] was listed in the Paradise Papers as being involved with Bermuda-registered companies. Theresa May [23 in Figure 7.1, below] refused to commit to a public register of the ownership of offshore companies and trusts, apparently not regarding transparency and accountability as priorities.[14]

And, all the time that they were helping to ensure corruption would be harder to spot, many were being found out for their own misdemeanours. It is no wonder they were so keen on confidentiality. Apparently, Damian Green [12], the then First Secretary (effectively Deputy PM), had made inappropriate advances to a woman thirty years his junior when she met him for advice on becoming involved in Conservative activism. Subsequently, after seeing her photo in a newspaper, it was claimed that he sent her a 'suggestive' text message. Within days, accusations of his having had pornography on his computer in 2008 surfaced.[15] In December 2017, he was sacked by May, though it was confirmed that he would receive a pay-off of £17,000. On the same day, Mark Garnier, Parliamentary Under Secretary of State for International Trade, was cleared of misconduct, as it apparently does not break the Ministerial Code to order your parliamentary assistant to buy a sex toy, despite her being distressed by this.[16]

FIGURE 7.1: THERESA MAY'S 'SCREAM' CABINET OF 2016 – THE WORST EVER CABINET?

Source: Photographed by Zoe Norfolk on September 13th 2016 and reproduced with her permission.

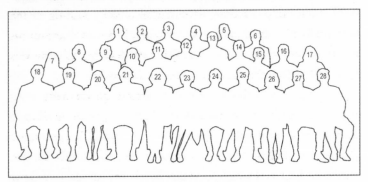

Theresa May's first Cabinet of 2016 – an easy identification list:
1. Jeremy Heywood 2. Gavin Williamson 3. Jeremy Wright 4. Patrick Mcloughlin 5. David Gauke 6. Ben Gummer 7. Priti Patel 8. Andrea Leadsom 9. David Mundell 10. Natalie Evans 11. Sajid Javid 12. Damien Green 13. Chris Grayling 14. David Lidington 15. Alun Cairns 16. James Brokenshire 17. Karen Bradley 18. Greg Clark 19. David Davis 20. Justine Greening 21. Boris Johnson 22. Amber Rudd 23. Theresa May 24. Philip Hammond 25. Michael Fallon 26. Liz Truss 27. Liam Fox 28. Jeremy Hunt

It is called the scream Cabinet as a photoshopped version of the above official portrait with the picture The Scream behind the manspreading men in suits was widely circulated at the time. Photographed by Zoe Norfolk on 13 September 2016 and reproduced with her permission.[17]

In 2016, Amber Rudd [22], Home Office, was asked to come clean over her links to two firms set up in tax havens.¹⁸ She brushed that off, resigned in April 2018 after misleading MPs over what became known as the Windrush affair, but rejoined the Cabinet later that year.

Philip Hammond [24], Chancellor of the Exchequer, also had most interesting financial affairs (on which more below). In 2014, the *Daily Mirror* newspaper suggested that he legally 'avoided thousands of pounds in tax after transferring his share of a £600,000 buy-to-let property to Mrs Hammond almost two years ago'. When questioned about the property, he asked the reporter, 'What has it got to do with you?'¹⁹

Boris Johnson [21], Foreign Secretary until July 2018, had (among so much else) 'fathered a child after a brief adulterous affair (not for the first time)'²⁰ in 2009. Although attempts were made to keep this news secret, a High Court judge ruled that the press was justified in publishing it because the politician's 'recklessness' in conducting extramarital affairs resulting in the conception of a child on two occasions called into question his fitness for public office. Contrast this with how Bill Clinton was pilloried for his brief affair with Monica Lewinsky.

In 2014, Unite the Union investigated government links to private healthcare. It exposed the links to private healthcare interests of seventy-one MPs, but had an appendix specifically dedicated to Jeremy Hunt [28], Health Secretary from 2012 to 2018 (who became Foreign Secretary in July of that year). Andrew Law, chairman and CEO of a global hedge fund with multi-million-pound healthcare investments, had made ten donations totalling £32,920 to Jeremy Hunt's constituency office between 2004 and 2014. He had also donated forty-six times to Conservative Party central office between 2008 and 2014, in total giving more than £1,229,677. Law was a board member and funder of Social Finance Ltd, which could make investors big profits out of the NHS through schemes that the government was just starting to fund.[21]

In between being unable to control their greed and finding new ways to gain financially, ministers, especially male ministers, were also repeatedly revealed as being unable to control their libido. Complaints against Michael Fallon [25], Defence Secretary, included his repeatedly putting his hand on a young journalist's knee. She reported, 'I calmly and politely explained to him that, if he did it again, I would punch him in the face.' The Leader of the House (and May's first Environment Secretary) Andrea Leadsom [8] also objected to lewd suggestions that he had made to her. He was forced to resign in November 2017, replaced by Gavin Williamson [2], former Chief Whip, previously well known only for keeping a live tarantula spider in his desk drawer: 'I've had Cronus since he was a spider-ling, so I have a very paternal sort of approach. It's very much the same sort of love and care that I give to my spider as I give to all MPs.'[22]

David Lidington [14], Justice Secretary from June 2017, opposed gay rights and wanted to scrap the Human Rights Act.[23] Justice for whom, you might well ask. He was moved out of Justice in January 2018 to undertake some of Damian Green's duties. He in turn was replaced by David Gauke [5], May's first Chief Secretary to the Treasury, as the merry-go-round sped up.

Justine Greening [20], Minister for Education, Women and Equalities, is said to have shouted at David Cameron, 'I didn't come into politics to distribute money to people in the Third World!' when he put her in charge of overseas aid.[24] Among much else on her parliamentary record, she has voted to end financial support to help poorer children stay on at school to increase social mobility; voted against schemes to help young people who have been out of work for many months to find employment; and voted to reduce the benefits of people in social housing. She resigned in January 2018, replaced by Damian Hinds who began his tenure by making simple mistakes, claiming for instance that school spending was rising, when – in fact – funding had been frozen, representing a real-terms cut to school budgets.[25]

Liam Fox [27], Secretary for International Trade, used public money via his expenses claims as an MP to pay his long-standing friend Adam Werritty to accompany him on official trips in his previous role as Defence Secretary. With Werritty, he shared both private healthcare interests and interests in the now defunct Atlantic Bridge Charity. This charity forged links to radical right-wing neocons in the US.[26] Werritty joined Fox on numerous official visits and attended meetings with foreign dignitaries despite having no government post or security clearance. Fox admitted errors of judgement in mixing his professional and personal loyalties. Investigations into this lapse had resulted in his resigning from his Cabinet post in 2011.[27] Theresa May considered it appropriate to make him Secretary of State for International Trade nonetheless.

David Davis [19] was made Secretary for Exiting the EU in 2017. For more on him, see the start of Chapter 9 below. On 8 July 2018, Davis resigned and was replaced the next day by Dominic Raab, best known previously for calling feminists 'obnoxious bigots' and doubting whether those who used foodbanks were poor.[28] In turn, Dominic appointed as his deputy Chris Heaton-Harris, former MEP and one-time chair of the European Research Group. You'll remember Heaton-Harris as the one who wrote to all Vice-Chancellors asking for the names of academics lecturing on Brexit. His request was described by Lord Patten, Vice-Chancellor of Oxford University, as 'idiotic and offensive Leninism'.[29] Dominic did not last long. Having helped negotiate a Brexit agreement in November 2018, he then resigned over it, to be replaced by a third Brexit Secretary, Stephen Barclay.

Other bit parts were played by the author of the disastrous 2017 Conservative manifesto Ben Gummer [6], who had one of the shortest Cabinet careers in history when he was voted out of office in 2017. That manifesto had promised to means-test the winter fuel allowance and make drastic changes to social care funding. Jeremy Heywood [1] was not a politician but made it into the photograph as the then Cabinet Secretary. Heywood died of cancer in November 2018, Mark Sedwill taking his place. He did keep a low profile, but as commenter Peter Oborne noted: 'Heywood is a perfect manifestation of everything that has gone so very wrong with the British civil service over the past 15 years'.[30] Among much else to criticise in his record, when he was the senior executive at Morgan Stanley and boss of the team involved in the botched flotation of a care homes provider, he had some responsibility for a 'disaster which saw 31,000 elderly people put at risk of being made homeless'. And that was just when he was briefly working outside of government.

Greg Clark [18], Secretary of State for Business, Energy and Industry, had been the president of Cambridge University Social Democrats, but became a Conservative MP in 2005. His views on the state's responsibilities were revealed in an article that he, as the newly created Minister for Decentralisation, wrote for the *Catholic Herald* in 2010 entitled 'It's time for Government to stop getting in your way: the Coalition wants to release the philanthropic energies of believers'.[31] He has never rebelled against his party in the current government, even at the very extremes, when they cut the most important of the rights of the poorest and most vulnerable in Britain while passing laws to reduce the taxation of the wealthy.

Michael Gove, Secretary of State for Environment, is widely regarded as excessively polite. However, as Secretary of State for Education from 2010, he was described in 2013 by Ralph Manning, lecturer in primary education, University of East Anglia, as having a 'blinkered, almost messianic, self-belief, which appears to have continually ignored the expertise and wisdom of teachers, head-teachers, advisers and academics, whom he often claims to have consulted'. Gove's reforms to the primary-level national curriculum were described as 'neo Victorian'. The 2013 conference of the National Union of Teachers (NUT) unanimously passed a vote of no confidence in Gove, the first time in its history that it had performed such an action, and then called for his resignation.

In 2014, Gove was demoted to Chief Whip. In 2016, he was asked why he supported Vote Leave, considering the amount of expert opinion advising against it. In his reply, he said, 'The people of this country have had enough of experts from organisations with acronyms saying they know what is best and getting it consistently wrong.' This was interesting, as in a Green Paper on special educational needs in 2011 he had promised to 'strip away unnecessary bureaucracy so that professionals can innovate and use their judgement'.[32] He became a candidate in the 2016 Conservative Party leadership contest at the very last minute, scuppering the chances of Boris Johnson, whom he had previously supported. This was described in the *Daily Telegraph* as 'the most spectacular political assassination in a generation'. In June 2018, when Secretary of State for Environment, Food and Rural Affairs, he is said to have 'physically ripped up a report on Theresa May's preferred option for a new customs partnership with the EU'.[33] By late November 2018, Gove was back to supporting May's latest withdrawal agreement but taking part in a 'Gang of Five' demanding changes to it at the same time.

Chris Grayling [13] was the Transport Secretary between 2016 and 2018. Eight of his reforms as Justice Secretary (2012 to 2015) have either been scrapped or overturned by a court.[34] He has been nicknamed 'Failing Grayling' because of his poor performance in government. Error prone, he even managed to open his ministerial car door on a cyclist in 2016 and then failed to give his details after causing this crash.[35] His Minister of State for Transport was Jo Johnson, who resigned on 9 November 2018 over Brexit.

Sajid Javid [11], formerly a banker, became an MP in 2009 and

Home Secretary in April 2018, having been Secretary of State for Communities and Local Government since 2016. He admits to an obsession with Ayn Rand, the poster girl of a particularly hardcore brand of free-market fundamentalism – the advocate of a philosophy she called 'the virtue of selfishness'.[36] It is widely reported that Javid earnt up to £3 million a year as a banker, owning property in London worth in excess of £6 million, though he has never confirmed these claims.[37] He regularly attends secretive neocon conferences in the USA.[38]

Natalie Evans [10], life peer and currently Lord Privy Seal and Leader of the House of Lords, became the director of the charity New Schools Network in 2013.[39] The organisation encouraged the establishment of free schools outside the normal local authority provision, using state funds. In 2010, the Charity Commission had to remind the trustees of their responsibility to remain politically impartial. This might now be tricky considering Evans is a government appointee in the Lords, and her husband a Conservative special advisor.[40] In 2015, amid much criticism of free schools, Labour Party policy-makers agreed not to fund any new free schools. It doesn't take a genius to work out what mayhem is caused by funding a small group of parents or a religious group to establish their own school, unplanned by the local authority and without regard for neighbouring schools. Of course, if the object is to create such mayhem, and do down well-planned state schooling, then the logic is clearer. But often Tory policy is as much the product of un-thought-through cock-up as overt conspiracy.

David Mundell [9], Secretary of State for Scotland, was perhaps treated unfairly when he tried to open a foodbank and had to flee the protestors who saw his party as the root cause of a need for foodbanks. Was he just naive, or has he accidentally found himself in the wrong political party? He has not been involved in any known scandal to date other than buying at tax-payers' expense 'photo-editing computer software to take hundreds of pictures of himself'.[41]

Alun Cairns [15] is Secretary of State for Wales. In 2008, as a Welsh Assembly member, he referred to Italians as 'greasy wops' on a radio programme.[42] Unusually for a politician, he immediately apologised.

Priti Patel [7] had been the Secretary of State for International Development for over a year when she 'went on a family holiday to Israel'. That turned out not to be the whole truth. She was either economical with the truth or actually lied about the trip to the Prime Minister and was forced to resign after it emerged that she had held a series of unofficial meetings with Israeli ministers, business figures and a lobbyist. Having previously worked in the tobacco and alcohol industries, she voted for the ban on smoking in public places to be overturned and was in favour of ending the alcohol duty escalator. Patel was replaced by Penny Mordaunt in November 2017.[43]

James Brokenshire [16], Northern Ireland Secretary, was a partner in an international law firm advising on company law and corporate finance transactions (an area associated with tax avoidance schemes) before becoming an MP in 2005. Having failed to get the political parties to agree to meet again at Stormont, or achieve anything else of note, he resigned due to ill health in January 2018, to be replaced by Karen Bradley [17]. Bradley made headlines in September 2018 by admitting that when she was appointed Secretary of State for Northern Ireland, she had had no idea that Northern Irish people tended to vote on sectarian lines – a fairly elementary fact and perhaps something that the Cabinet minister responsible for the region should be aware of. Bradley had moved from the Department for Culture, Media and Sport, where she was known for vetoing the appointment of a black woman to the board of Channel 4.[44] The other four candidates, all white men, were approved, while the reasons for Althea Efunshile's rejection were questioned, as she appeared to be well qualified for the post. Bradley in turn was replaced by Matt Hancock. In July 2018, Hancock became Secretary of State for Health. By October, he was being described as 'a hyperactive man-boy whose enthusiasm and bumptiousness – combined with a gift for telling people what he thinks they want to hear – far exceed his natural talents'.[45]

David Gauke [5] was appointed Secretary of State for Work and Pensions in June 2017. In September 2017, he decided to accelerate the rollout of the increasingly criticised Universal Credit, which sought to replace multiple benefits with a single system, but which reduced the income of some of the country's poorest families. The following month he wrote to the parliamentary Work and Pensions Committee to say he saw no grounds for pausing that rollout despite a mountain of evidence suggesting that it was driving thousands into debt, eviction, destitution and mental distress.[46] Frank Field, chair of the committee, said: 'I don't know if the Department for Work and Pensions is deliberately concealing information about Universal Credit or is simply incompetent. Either way, it is not good enough.' A week later, Gauke failed to turn up to an emergency House of Commons debate on Universal Credit and ignored the vote (299 for, 0 against) to pause its rollout.[47] In June 2018, the National Audit Office released a highly critical report, pointing out that, already, four in ten claimants of Universal Credit were experiencing financial difficulties, and in areas where it had been rolled out there was evidence of increased hardship, greater use of foodbanks and increased levels of rent arrears. The report concluded that the project is not value for money now (compared to the previous benefits system) and that its future value for money is unproven.

Both the benefits system and the immigration system had become hostile environments, but Conservative politicians denied that they were causing unnecessary hardship and distress, while insisting that people must stick to the rules – rules increasingly designed to trip people up. The message from the top was that there were battles to be won (against people who needed benefits, or just wanted, for good reason, to live in Britain). The needy became the enemy.

Increasingly, people had to resort to the Human Rights Acts to defend themselves. In October 2018, it was admitted by the Department for Work and Pensions that sick and disabled people had been denied their rightful benefits for over seven years. Over 180,000 people were owed arrears payments, estimated at £1.67 billion.[48]

Patrick McLoughlin [4], most unusually for Conservative MPs, had previously been a manual worker (a farm worker and a coalminer) before becoming an MP in 1986. When Theresa May became Prime Minister, he became chairman of the Conservative Party. However, following both the disastrous general election result in June 2017 and the shambolic party conference in October, there were calls for his resignation from within his own party, as he was thought to have played a key role in both events. He resigned on 8 January 2018.

Andrea Leadsom [8], the Leader of the House who had accused Fallon of making lewd remarks, had made unfortunate comments after David Cameron's resignation suggesting that being a mother would make her a better PM, which opened the way for Theresa May to become leader. Leadsom was the television star of Vote Leave. When questioned about the slow Brexit progress on *Newsnight*, she said, in a line noted for its intellectual paucity, that broadcasters should be 'a bit more patriotic'. She is married to a hedge fund manager. Leadsom was presumably still being patriotic when she joined the 'Gang of Five' who in November 2018 were demanding changes to May's 'final' withdrawal agreement.

Liz Truss [26] was appointed as Secretary of State for Justice and Lord Chancellor in 2016. She was highly criticised by the Lord Chief Justice for her (anticipated) failure to visibly support the judiciary after tabloid newspapers referred to the High Court of Justice with headlines like 'Enemies of the People'.[49] In 2017, she became Chief Secretary to the Treasury. She voted Remain and then switched to Brexit.[50]

Julian Smith, an MP since 2010, was little known before being promoted from Deputy to Chief Whip in November 2017. In 2013, he was accused of authoritarianism when he called for *The Guardian* newspaper to be prosecuted for publishing stories about the extent of state surveillance based on leaks from the US whistleblower Edward Snowden. His remarks were condemned as McCarthyism and 'absolute scaremongering' by Labour MPs.[51]

Jeremy Wright [3] became Attorney General in 2014, breaking the usual tradition of appointing a QC. Under Wright's aegis, the government was repeatedly taken to court and lost, appealed and lost again. After failing to overturn a court case insisting that Parliament had a right to vote on Brexit, a Conservative MP simply said, 'It would be better to have a more senior lawyer around the table.'[52] Jeremy Wright became Culture Secretary on 9 July 2018. His replacement as Attorney General was Geoffrey Cox, who was said to have outside interests that made him the highest-paid MP at the time he claimed £1 back for the cost of a bin bag.[53] In 2015, his work as a QC earnt him more than £520,000, on top of his MP's salary of £74,000, but his claim for a 49p bottle of milk was ruled out of order by the parliamentary authority.[54]

Brandon Lewis, Minister of State for Immigration (a role that, as of June 2017, entitled the holder to attend Cabinet despite not being a member) was educated at the private University of Buckingham, and entered Parliament in 2010 on a 'clean expenses pledge'. Since then he has had his claims for £37,000 for a political campaign group and for £31,000 for hotel expenses questioned. His three homes are worth at least £3.5 million.[55] In January 2018, he became chairman of the Conservative Party.

Damian Hinds was Minister of State for Employment (likewise, an attendee of Cabinet meetings, though not a member) in 2017, famous on Twitter because, as journalist Ian Dunt put it, 'Even the tiniest event is diligently catalogued, as Hinds recounts his uninspiring day. For all its tedium, it has its benefits: Not only does it make you feel good about your own life, it also discourages future generations from becoming MPs.'[56] In January 2018, Hinds became Secretary of State for Education.

Of course, a list of shame can be produced for any Cabinet or shadow Cabinet – but never as easily as the above was compiled.

Jacob Rees-Mogg has never been in Cabinet. However, he is chairman of the European Research Group, which supported Brexit. Its twenty-one Conservative MPs currently pay £2,000 a year membership fees, which they claim back as legitimate parliamentary expenses. An article in the *New Statesman* reported:

> The ERG is more of a 'party within a party' than Momentum. It runs its own whipping operation and tells members what they should and shouldn't say. It co-ordinates attacks on Remain-leaning ministers such as Philip Hammond and top officials at the Treasury, the Bank of England and the Office for Budget Responsibility. In a rare example of a newspaper shedding light on the group, *The Times* described it as 'the most aggressive and successful political cadre in Britain today'.[57]

Rees-Mogg's name was one that featured prominently in among the reporting of the Paradise Papers. He was the first in line to try to oust Mrs May from her job in November 2018, very publicly submitting a letter of no confidence in her, hoping to trigger a leadership contest.

One very understandable reason for some of these MPs to want to leave the EU is to stop the new EU Anti-Tax Avoidance Directive from becoming UK law, which it must do in 2019/20 if the UK were to remain in the EU. It is often not so much for themselves that they wish to avoid this tax, but for their rich sponsors. The Conservative Party is almost entirely funded by a few people who are at some risk of being affected personally by these new EU directives.

It is curious that leaving the EU moved from being seen as a battle in the first year after the vote, to being a war in the second, at least as the *Sunday Times* reported it by the end of 2017.[58] The Brexit War Cabinet by late 2017 included Theresa May, David Davis, Liam Fox, Boris Johnson, Philip Hammond, Jeremy Hunt, Michael Gove and the new Defence Secretary Gavin Williamson.

By December 2017, Brexiteers formed a majority on the body deciding Britain's future, even though some of them previously voted to Remain. While there are not so many Old Etonians in May's Cabinet as there were in Cameron's, almost all the Cabinet members and the Brexiteers were educated at private schools and mostly at Oxford, PPE (Philosophy, Politics and Economics) being favoured as their degree subject.

As there is little evidence that the curriculum in their schools, in turn reflecting exam boards of varying vintages, has changed much over the years from that which we described in Chapter 1, it is likely that they were taught both an imperially oriented curriculum and one which gave them that sense of superiority and, more importantly, the opportunity for networking among rich and like-minded friends.

NOT JUST SEX BUT ALSO MONEY

In May 2012, the *Daily Telegraph* revealed that, of the twenty-nine members of Cabinet at that time, some eighteen were millionaires or multi-millionaires.[59] The Prime Minister, David Cameron, aged forty-four, was valued at £3.8 million. By 2016, the Cameron family's combined wealth was estimated to be $50 million (wealthy people count their money in dollars, not pounds). His wife's worth, like his, had come from property bought with monies they inherited from wealthy parents, who in turn had benefited from relatives, who had, for example, made great gains from slavery within the British Empire.[60]

In 2012, the *Telegraph* newspaper reported that the property holdings of the Cameron family meant that 'the analysis also forecast that the combined wealth of Mr and Mrs Cameron was likely to rise sharply in coming years because they would inherit an estimated £25.3 million'. David was educated at Heatherdown, a private preparatory school where Prince Andrew (the Duke of York) and Prince Edward (the Earl of Wessex) were also pupils. From there, David went to Eton and then on to Brasenose College, Oxford. There, he studied PPE, but also belonged to the Bullingdon Club (Figure 7.2), which was supposedly founded as a sporting club for wealthy men in 1780. The club is now known for ostentatious spending, boisterous rituals and trashing restaurants – getting away with it by paying off the owners not to involve the police. Lord Ashcroft (of whom more later) co-wrote a book repeating rumours that David reportedly placed a portion of his anatomy in a dead pig's head on one particularly rumbustious evening at the equally notorious Piers Gaveston dining society. This is just one of many rumours that are almost certainly false. What is remarkable is that they can be made and spread so easily and appear partly credible because of all else these MPs are known to have done.

FIGURE 7.2: THE BULLINGDON BOYS – WHO HAVE NEVER USED A CO-OP!

This cartoon reflects the various allegations of inappropriate behaviour made against them. Reproduced with kind permission of Steve Bell.[61]

The wealthiest of all of David Cameron's ministers had been Thomas Galloway Dunlop du Roy de Blicquy Galbraith, 2nd Baron Strathclyde, said to be worth £9.5 million in 2012, achieved mainly 'from inherited wealth and a stake in his family's estate management company'. Having been Leader of the House of Lords and Chancellor of the Duchy of Lancaster with a seat in the Cabinet since 2010, Lord Strathclyde left government in 2013 to pursue a business career, but what does that mean when someone is already so wealthy? He remains in the House of Lords, and occasionally says unhelpful things such as, 'Brexit is complex enough without Labour carping from the sidelines'.[62]

Philip Hammond, who was the Defence Secretary in 2012 and became Chancellor in 2016, had his wealth estimated in 2012 at around £8.2 million. This had been built up from what Christopher Hope, writing in the *Telegraph* in 2012, described as stakes in a healthcare and nursing home development and consultancy work.[63] The main way in which someone makes that kind of a profit from care homes and nursing homes is by paying care workers low wages and charging residents high fees. Hammond studied PPE at University College, Oxford. In 2017, it was reported that 120,000 elderly people had died prematurely between 2010 and 2017 due to cutbacks, including in social care and private care home funding.[64]

Jeremy Hunt was the Culture Secretary in 2012, but was soon elevated to Secretary of State for Health, before becoming Foreign Secretary in July 2018. In 2017, it was suggested that he might make £17 million from selling Hotcourses Ltd, the educational guidance company he had co-founded in 1996. Looking at the website for Hotcourses, it is not easy to see where its income comes from, because it just locates, for free, courses for students to apply to. Presumably it receives money from the educational bodies that it promotes, either just for inclusion in the database or by commission (but if so, it does not look as if the students are told how much that might be). Hunt was educated at Charterhouse public school, current fees £38,000 a year, where he was head boy. He went to Magdalen College, Oxford, studying PPE alongside contemporaries Cameron and Boris Johnson. Hunt was keen to privatise areas of the NHS, inevitably allowing a few people to make a financial killing out of the health service. He has in the past said that he thinks homeopathy works, and that traditional Chinese medicine should be available on the NHS, resulting in the nickname 'Minister for Magic'.[65] In April 2018, it was announced that the parliamentary authorities were investigating his failure to declare his recent purchase of many luxury flats.[66]

A younger contemporary of Cameron's was George Gideon Osborne, son of wallpaper magnate Sir Peter Osborne and inheritor of much private wealth. He was educated (as Gideon Osborne) at private schools in London – Norton Place, Colet Court (now St Paul's juniors) and St Paul's School, where he was known as George. Osborne entered Parliament in 2001 at the age of thirty. He was made Chancellor of the Exchequer in 2010. Despite demonstrating that personally he was out for anything he could get – avariciously claiming £47 for DVDs of his own speeches as parliamentary expenses, and later securing a series of very well-remunerated posts almost immediately after leaving the Cabinet (while remaining an MP) – Osborne imposed severe austerity on the country, massively cutting benefits to poor working-age people and freezing pay to public sector workers. However, he cut taxes for richer people and also claimed expenses for his own houses and paddocks. There appear to be none so mean as the wealthy.

While we are mentioning the wealthy, we must remember that the richest MP influencing politics in the country (but never making it to Cabinet) is, as revealed in the *Telegraph* in 2012, Zac Goldsmith, who inherited a £284 million fortune from his financier father, James Goldsmith. In 1995, James set up the Referendum

Party, demanding a referendum on EU membership. He financed it heavily and put up hundreds of candidates in the 1997 general election. They did very badly, but it was, in effect, the beginnings of UKIP's success. Zac portrays his father's 'rebel army' of Brexiteers as valiant victors who saved Britain.[67] He doesn't appear to realise that without cash, James would have been nothing, and that what James did was help to propel the UK to a potentially disastrous Brexit, for which Zac is currently no doubt proud.

And while we are on the subject of the richest MPs, we should not forget Jacob Rees-Mogg: what kind of boy has his portrait painted at age eighteen when he leaves school (Eton) to be placed in the Eton College Portrait Collection, and later calls the £250,000 the House of Commons spent on MPs' portraits 'chicken-feed'?[68] A millionaire by the age of sixteen, he is extraordinarily wealthy; he 'invested' well.[69]

A COTERIE OF SHAME

Many politicians are appalling, a self-interested coterie of shame. Chief among these must be Boris Johnson, whose career is breathtakingly shameless. Cultivating a humorous shambolic personality, Alexander Boris de Pfeffel Johnson was born in New York and educated at Ashdown preparatory school in Sussex, then at Eton and next at Balliol College, Oxford. There, he was elected president of the Oxford Union and took part in Bullingdon Club hijinks. Following a career in journalism, he was sacked by *The Times* for deception, having invented a quote, and then gained employment as the *Telegraph* correspondent who wrote untrue stories about straight bananas and cucumbers being an EU legal necessity. An MP from 2001 to 2007, he was twice Mayor of London (2008–16) but returned to Parliament as an MP in 2015, making light of his widely suspected ambitions to be Prime Minister.

Continuing a long-held and cherished legacy of public

deception, he announced himself a supporter of the Leave campaign and he fronted the red bus with the lie that £350 million a week would be returned to the UK for the NHS, if the country left the EU – a claim he repeated in September 2017. It is extraordinary that someone who initially appeared unsure about which side to take – until, presumably, he had weighed up what was in his political self-interest – should have had such a profound effect on people's decision to vote for Brexit.

During the campaign, Johnson made incendiary claims, including that the 'part-Kenyan' President Obama had encouraged Britain to stay in the EU out of an 'ancestral dislike of the British Empire'. It is hard to decide if Johnson really is a fool or just insensitive and arrogant, liking to shock on the basis that all publicity is good publicity. His antics and buffoonery have probably made him the most recognisable UK politician. When Johnson was made Foreign Secretary by Theresa May in 2016, Carl Bildt, a former Swedish Prime Minister and Foreign Minister, said, 'I wish this was a joke but I fear it isn't.'[70] It became anything but a joke as Johnson variously insulted other countries and world leaders. In November 2017, he endangered a British woman held in an Iranian jail by falsely claiming in Parliament[71] that she was 'teaching journalism', which could give the Iranian government cause to increase her imprisonment. He had become a menace. Thankfully, he resigned as Foreign Secretary in July 2018.

By January 2018, it had become clear that May's Cabinet had more members from affluent constituencies than any previous Cabinet this century. A majority of Cabinet ministers held seats that were among the 100 (out of 650) most affluent in the country, nine from the most affluent fifty. There were only two Cabinet ministers representing people from some of the deprived constituencies and they were mostly elected by the better-off residents of each area. These were Amber Rudd, who holds the highly marginal Hastings and Rye and is no longer in the Cabinet as we write in November 2018, and Brandon Lewis (educated at the privately funded University of Buckingham), who is now Minister without Portfolio and MP for Great Yarmouth. These were the only two representing seats among the 100 most deprived.[72] When Amber (educated at Cheltenham Ladies' College) was no longer a minister, that count briefly fell to one.

VOTE LEAVE

Those advocating a more distant relationship with Europe had strong support even before Britain joined the European Economic Community. Joining was a decision taken in 1972 under Tory PM Edward Heath, then carried out in 1973, with a referendum being held in early 1975 under Labour's Harold Wilson. Two thirds of the British public voted to stay in what was then called the European Economic Community (EEC), which was the forerunner of the European Union, created in 1993.

One prominent opponent of the EEC was MP Enoch Powell, who in the 1970s turned his attention from vilifying immigrants to opposing any form of union with Europe. He gave speeches claiming it was a surrender of sovereignty and that Britain could have influence in the world without Europe. He was joined in his campaigns by the future short-lived Labour leader Michael Foot. As Tony Benn put it in the run-up to the 1975 referendum:

> We are at the moment on a federal escalator, moving as we talk, going towards a federal objective we do not wish to reach. In practice, Britain will be governed by a European coalition government that we cannot change, dedicated to a capitalist or market economy theology. This policy is to be sold to us by projecting an unjustified optimism about the Community, and an unjustified pessimism about the United Kingdom, designed to frighten us in.[73]

What Benn could not have known then was who would actually run Britain from 1979 through to 1997, or that Margaret Thatcher would be followed by a Labour Party newly transformed into New Labour, which would continue to enact policies Benn was opposed to, or that these would be continued by the coalition government up until Benn died in 2014. In the event, what Tony Benn had worried about thirty-nine years earlier – a great growth in economic inequality and rise of social class division – came to pass, but due to politics at home, not in Europe.

As noted earlier, when unsuccessful in keeping Britain out of Europe, Enoch Powell took himself off to Northern Ireland as an Ulster Unionist MP from 1974 to 1987. Veteran MP Kenneth Clarke believed Powell's Euroscepticism was kept alive over the years by 'a constant backdrop of right-wing nationalist Conservative MPs agitating on Eurosceptic causes'.[74] Clarke also suggested that David Cameron's decision to call a referendum was partly to placate this group, as well as to avoid votes going to UKIP.

The Vote Leave campaign, which would later be designated the official Leave campaign, was founded in 2015 by Dominic Mckenzie Cummings, who became the campaign director (Figure 7.3). Born in 1971, he was educated at a private boarding school in the north of England, Durham School, founded in 1414, where the fees for full boarding are now around £30,000 a year. Cummings got a first-class degree in ancient and modern history at Exeter College, Oxford, in 1994. He then spent three years in post-Communist Russia. In common with Enoch Powell and Boris Johnson, he has a penchant for quoting Greek and Roman writers and generals, his favourite being Thucydides, Athenian historian and general. He did this liberally in a 237-page paper produced in 2013 for the then Education Minister Michael Gove, for whom he worked as an advisor. This paper supported claims that the educational performance of a child is largely accounted for by their genes. He has been called a 'career psychopath' by none other than David Cameron.[75] He had a great influence on the vote to leave the EU, being credited with the slogan 'Take Back Control'. In late spring 2018 he was professing that there would be revolution and SW1 (Westminster) would become a 'smoking ruin' if the Brexiteers of his ilk did not get their way.[76]

FIGURE 7.3: DOMINIC CUMMINGS IN 'AWE AT HIS OWN STRATEGIC BRILLIANCE'

Quotation about Dominic Cummings's brilliance courtesy of: Elledge, J. (2018) 'If only we could all be as clever as Dominic Cummings', New Statesman, 24 May.[77]

A second influential figure in the Vote Leave campaign – indeed, credited along with Cummings as being a major agent in their victory – is Matthew Elliott (Figure 7.4). Elliott was educated at the private Leeds Grammar School and then the London School of Economics, going on to work as a political secretary to MEP Timothy Kirkhope in 2001. In 2004, he co-founded the TaxPayers' Alliance, dedicated to explaining the benefits of a low-tax economy and to gaining influence in 'the corridors of power'. In 2011, he helped defeat the attempt to create a slightly fairer voting system, acting as the campaign director of NotoAV. He was regarded as a clever political strategist and, in 2015, became chief executive of Vote Leave. He claims to have recruited Boris Johnson and Michael Gove into the campaign.

Matthew is also a senior fellow at the Legatum Institute. This, as noted earlier in this book, is a right-wing organisation aiming to 'pass on to the next generation [a world] of increasing prosperity and human flourishing'.[78] The Legatum Institute mainly produces reports with content such as:

> The alternative now awaits. A century ago, Britain was the 'free trade nation', a cause that brought crowds of tens of thousands to the streets in its defence, being vital both to the livelihoods of Britons and to the economic miracle Britain gave the world in the century to 1914. But in the century since, our trade – and the world's – has been subsumed into a restrictive system that creates poverty. The global economy is essentially stuck.[79]

A second organisation that claimed it had an enormous impact on the EU referendum was Leave.EU, a group co-founded by businessman Arron Banks and property developer Richard Tice. Arron went to school first in South Africa, then at Crookham Court Manor private boarding school[80] in Berkshire, from where he was expelled for stealing lead from roofs and other bad behaviour, before going on to state schools, but not to university. He had a career in business, mainly insurance, apparently setting up thirty-seven companies all in slightly different variations of his own name. His business interests have included mining in South Africa and Lesotho, and his wealth is estimated at around £250 million, although that figure is questioned by some reporters.[81] He was an enthusiastic supporter of UKIP and a friend of Nigel Farage, donating £1 million to UKIP before being expelled from the party in March 2017. In November 2017, the Electoral

Commission launched an investigation into his donations to the Brexit campaign, as it is not clear from where and how his donations were made. On 1 November 2018, it was reported that the National Crime Agency would open a criminal investigation into Banks's alleged offences.

As reporter Adam Ramsay put it:

> The thing which always struck me as odd about Arron Banks' donations to Brexit was not the scale of them. It wasn't even that he may have given a bigger portion of his wealth than he let on. After all, rich people sometimes care about things. Sometimes they care a lot. What struck me as odd is, as I asked his sidekick Andy Wigmore on Twitter the other day, why use a front company?[82]

Banks walked out of a select committee hearing asking about his connections with Russia on 12 June 2018, apparently claiming he was late for lunch with Ian Paisley Jr, a DUP Member of Parliament.[83]

There were other Leave groups such as Grassroots Out (GO), although this was little more than another UKIP front, with Farage at its launch and UKIP financier Arron Banks providing the cash. The group was formed in January 2016 with Tory MP supporters Liam Fox, Peter Bone and Tom Pursglove, Labour's Kate Hoey and Nigel Farage from UKIP. The campaign claimed to have plans in all constituencies to knock on doors and persuade the public to 'GO'. In total, Arron Banks is thought to have paid £8.1 million for Brexit; Peter Hargreaves (who runs a finance company) paid £3.2 million; James Hosking (another financier) £1.7 million; Lord Edmiston (involved in cars) £1 million; and Crispin Odey, an asset manager, £0.9 million. Between them, these five businessmen funded 61 per cent of the Leave campaign bill.[84] In

2018, Banks announced that he would back Nigel Farage, if he decided to join the DUP to win a seat in Parliament.[85] Were this to happen, it might appear to be a repeat of Enoch Powell's career.

FIGURE 7.4: MATTHEW ELLIOTT – CHIEF EXECUTIVE OF VOTE LEAVE 2015–2017

Matthew Elliott was chief executive officer of the TaxPayers' Alliance from 2004 to 2014. It is not known how much tax the people who funded the alliance paid, as it is never revealed whether or not they are domiciled in the UK, or in most cases even who they are. Reproduced with kind permission of Matthew Elliott.

WHAT HAPPENED?

So, what are the results of having such a sorry bunch of politicians, their advisors and rich backers in charge during a period of momentous change for the four nations of the UK? The major result is that people in the UK, especially those on low wages and benefits, have suffered under so-called austerity measures that now affect their housing, food, health, life expectancy and poverty levels to a degree not seen since the 1930s. A report produced in November 2017 by the Child Poverty Action Group and the Institute for Public Policy Research documents the huge numbers of families with children who will be further pushed into poverty due to cuts in wages and benefits. The report estimated that money lost due to the Universal Credit rollout will average £1,200 a year per family affected.[86] This sum is, of course, peanuts to our rich politicians and their backers.

We are always catching up with what has just happened. It was not until May 2018 that researchers worked out that a million extra children whose parents were in work had been plunged into poverty after 2010, and that by 2018 some 3.1 million children with working parents were living below the official breadline in the UK. Of these children, the majority (600,000) had 'been pushed into poverty as a result of the government's in-work benefit cuts and public sector pay restrictions'.[87]

The majority of the poorest tenth of children in the UK have no annual holiday (defined as time away from home not staying with relatives and friends). The average spend of the poorest tenth of families on holidays per year is £312 – for the whole family, not per person. For those families in the best-off tenth of the population it is £3,791 per family, and that will be modest compared to the spending of the best-off 1 per cent who would think that under £4,000 spent per family per year on holidays was risibly austere.[88]

There are no signs so far that voting to leave the EU has improved or will improve the lives of most people in the UK. The ineptitude of those supposedly in charge of negotiations to leave the EU, its single market and customs union and all the other legal, crime, aviation and other implications for life in Britain is a matter for amazement for many other EU politicians and most of the world. Being pro-EU is not universal in mainland Europe. Austria has three anti-EU MEPs out of nineteen. Switzerland and Norway have no wish to fully join the EU. Hungary and Poland have politicians who often talk against the EU. However, among Western European countries, only the UK has had a party as powerful as UKIP turned out briefly to be, and a Conservative Party so far to the right that half of it sees the EU as being some kind of socialist conspiracy.

In Hungary, the sentiments have at times been very similar to those of Brexiteers in the UK, but others have said:

> Orbán's Hungary is not the future of Europe, it is its declining, nationalist past. It is a country with an ageing and ever decreasing population, turned in on itself, scared of everything outside, and increasingly inside, its borders. Ironically, it mainly survives because of the very future it rejects, subsidies by the much-maligned European Union.[89]

So how did the Brexit vote happen and what are the consequences? This is too big a question for just one book to answer and, as yet, we do not know the full consequences, but we do know more and more about the 2016 voters. Analysis of Brexit to date has tried to suggest that it is possible to model individual voters' behaviour and achieve predictions that are correct in over nine out of ten cases. That percentage seems relatively impressive; however, it is reached by including in the models yes/no/don't know answers to questions such as 'Is immigration/terrorism a problem?', 'Does the EU erode UK sovereignty?' and 'Will the UK be better outside of the EU?' This is not far from asking if you agree or disagree with each campaign slogan and, hey presto, you can state: 'Over 93 per cent of voters are correctly classified by the analysis – this represents an 86.2 per cent reduction in prediction error.'[90] Asking if someone likes a political party and then claiming from that how good you are at predicting whether they will vote for that party is not impressive.

A better way of understanding the Brexit vote is to consider why and how so much money was spent on trying to get people to vote Leave. That money changed the minds of millions of people who had for months been saying that they would vote to stay. In the end, the official ratio of spending on Leave versus spending on Remain was, to the nearest 1 per cent, 52:48, identical to the final voting ratio.[91] However, that only covers spending between 15 April and the close of polling on 23 June 2016. In reality, there had been campaign spending for Brexit ever since the rise of UKIP in 2014. The Remain campaign could not start until there was a realistic prospect of Britain leaving the EU, which only occurred after Cameron's unexpected election victory in May 2015 at the very earliest. The Leave campaign also had the uncosted support of Rupert Murdoch and most of Britain's tabloid newspapers, as well as the *Telegraph* and *Sunday Telegraph*.[92]

Over the years to come, we will learn more about undisclosed amounts spent on the multiple Brexit campaigns, successfully hidden from sight at the time. The DUP spent £282,000 (almost five times its 2015 general election expenditure) on a Brexit advertisement that did not run in Northern Ireland but in a London commuter paper. The Electoral Commission is currently investigating the spending of Vote Leave, BeLeave, Veterans for Britain, Leave.EU and Better for the Country Ltd.[93] The founder of the Good Law Project had threatened the Electoral Commission with judicial review, if it did not reopen investigation of facts that he said raised 'obvious and serious questions about the Electoral Commission and the referendum. Was our watchdog asleep on the job?' In the next chapter, we look a little further at who actually voted the UK out and why and how they were persuaded to do so.

We started this chapter by looking at the record of Cabinet MPs, revealing their attitudes and approach to other people, to what they saw as 'fair game'. This was just the tip of an iceberg of disrespect for people less powerful than themselves, for women, for the poorest in society and for the multitude of people they felt didn't count, losers in a system rigged to create losers. We could have focused on the earlier 2009 MPs' expenses scandal and the revelation that many of them were out for whatever they could get by fair means or foul. We could have looked at individual areas of policy, at how housing policy, ostensibly aimed at increasing home ownership (but having the opposite effect), was rigged to support huge profits for private landlords, property speculation that massively inflated house prices, and a dearth of new housing for ordinary people. Or at moves to increase privatisation within the health service by people with vested interests in private health provision. Or at moves destabilising the education system by labelling schools as good or bad, and ensuring that politicians' children and their friends' children got unfair advantage. Incidentally, Brexit may well have brought forward the moment that the London housing bubble truly burst, with London house prices falling by 4.1 per cent in the year to November 2017 (the largest fall since the crash of 2008/09), and flats falling in price by 6.7 per cent in that same year. By October 2018, prime central London prices had fallen by 18.4 per cent from their 2014 peak, or much more if the fall in the pound is included.[94] It is beginning to look like 'game over', but those who want to make London a Mecca of private provision for the global rich continue to strive for their goal.

You do not have to be a genius to realise that the easiest way to make private healthcare and private schools appear better than they are is to impoverish the state sector. We could have looked at tobacco, long since proven to cause incredible harm to users and anyone in their environment, without any social benefits, and the uphill battle against those who financially benefited from it to reduce its promotion and sale. Or at which politicians most support high-speed, high-stakes gambling, despite the misery that addiction causes to people and their families. In 2016, the founder of an online bookmaker paid herself £217 million, momentarily making her the most highly valued Briton ever[95] – just one example of individiuals growing wealthy from the promotion of private debt.

SO, ARE ALL POLITICIANS USELESS?

Eden lied about Suez and his government concealed its purpose; but he believed in that purpose and believed it to be in the national interest. Blair dissimulated about Iraq and his government used dark arts to clear its path. But he believed in the adventure and believed it to be in the national interest.

Brexit is worse. The means are the same as with Suez and Iraq but half the cabinet and most of the parliamentary party don't even believe in the ends. I seriously doubt whether Boris Johnson does. A terrified, paralysed prime minister leads a seasick party and doubting government towards she knows not what.

Wickedness may not always lie in the carrying forward of bad projects. It may also lie in allowing oneself to be carried forward by them, knowing their wrongfulness. Perhaps that is the more culpable, for zealots at least believe their madness. A special kind of guilt attaches to the sane majority of the Conservative Party today. It is written across their faces.

– Matthew Parris, former Conservative MP, 3 February 2018[96]

As Christmas 2017 approached, Frankie Boyle memorably described the three main politicians in charge of Brexit as including:

Liam Fox, a man who looks like he could finish a steak while looking at footage from Hiroshima; Boris Johnson, who for the first time finds himself in a cabinet without it involving someone saying: 'Quick! My husband's home early!'; and David Davis, Sid James after a *This Morning* makeover and a half-hearted tilt at therapy.[97]

It is sometimes very hard for many people to understand why the British public was so easily fooled into voting for men like these. Part of the answer is that millions of British people actually agree with Fox, Johnson and Davis when they hear them talk and (with due deference) trust them. If you don't understand why, you need to get out more and mix with people not like you.

In contrast to these reprobates, the majority of Labour MPs might appear to be almost saint-like, which of course they cannot be. Currently ranking top in the saint stakes is Jeremy Corbyn, the MP who has claimed the least in parliamentary expenses despite being an MP since 1983. Criticised during the referendum campaign for giving the European Union only a seven out of ten for performance, Corbyn has often got into trouble for his honesty. He once explained that he would never use nuclear weapons if he were Prime Minister.[98] However, his straightforward and honest approach has also won him friends in unusual places. In late 2017, the *Financial Times* reported one London banker explaining, 'City people looked at the Labour manifesto and saw a traditional social democratic offering, it wasn't radical in a negative sense, whereas the Tories now seem closed-doors and nativist.'[99]

Previous Labour leaders have found that it takes courage and determination to be a party leader and potential Prime Minister. Enemies, before and behind you, will disparage your appearance, sneer at your policies, patronise you and say that you have no talent, are too ordinary – but also too odd. The same was said about Clement Attlee, Labour Party leader for twenty years, Prime Minister or Deputy Prime Minister for half that time, whose leadership gave the country a welfare state and its first proper taste of social and economic equality.

Citizen Clem (who studied at Haileybury College followed by a history degree at University College, Oxford) learnt about poverty and inequality via the Haileybury club in the East End of London. He acquainted himself with the early varieties of socialism, and also worked a stint for the economists and social reformers Beatrice and Sidney Webb, on the 1909 Royal Commission on the Poor Laws minority report. Beatrice Webb, an early disparager, told him that to be a first-rate organiser he had to have more 'push', and later commented that, though gifted with intellect and goodwill, 'he had, alas, no personality'. Similar things were said about Jeremy Corbyn.

London's East Enders thought differently to Beatrice, just as the mass of new Labour Party members – drawn from far less socially exclusive backgrounds than the other members of the other major political parties – feel differently about Corbyn. Attlee was co-opted as Mayor of Stepney at the end of the First World War. He was first elected as MP for Limehouse in the 1922 election (when nationally Labour won only 30 per cent of votes cast). Insults from his own side rapidly followed, Emmanuel Shinwell suggesting that he was 'just an ordinary person … not going very far', and Ramsay MacDonald, leading the first Labour (minority) government, announcing that 'he was a competent colleague … not the talent to be at the top table'. Despite that, MacDonald appointed him Under Secretary for War.

Having been wounded at Gallipoli and then in Mesopotamia (now Iraq), Attlee had ended the First World War as a major, so he was more qualified than many for that job. As it turned out, he was just as suited to being at the top table as any of them, but that was not considered imaginable at the time. No one without the declared push, proper personality or talent to lead could, apparently, make it. The analogy is clear, although the squabbles within Labour in the 1930s make the party's current nastiness seem mild, and there was no let-up on Attlee. The Conservatives mocked his suburban lifestyle, with an American journalist describing him as 'the epitome of the English suburban man', with a wife and four children, golf clubs, pipes and garden tools, small and bald. Think of the jibes levelled at Corbyn over his allotment and beard. George Orwell called Attlee a 'dead fish', and Labour journals were no help, with the *Tribune* openly deriding him. Kingsley Martin, editor of the *New Statesman*, compared him to an ineffective schoolmaster; later, 'like a geography teacher' became a common insult, and remains so.

Attlee's speaking voice constantly came in for derision. Aneurin Bevan (Ty-Trist Colliery and Central Labour College, London) wrote that 'he was determined to make a trumpet sound like a tin whistle'. After the 1934 party conference in Southport, and just before his election as Labour leader, Attlee wrote, 'I wish people would not always be strangling their friends instead of their enemies.' Churchill should have regretted underestimating Attlee as 'a modest man with much to be modest about'. Compare Churchill's slight to what Conservative leaders said about Corbyn before the huge June 2017 general election swing of support that Labour racked up. Attlee joined the Second World War national government as Churchill's deputy in the War Cabinet, and Churchill came to depend on Attlee's sensible advice and actions. Attlee's only criticism of Churchill, one biographer noted, was: 'The trouble with Winston is that he nails his trousers to the mast, and then can't climb down.' It is, admittedly, hard to imagine a government of national unity forming in the aftermath of a disastrous hard Brexit, but anything is possible.

In May 1944, Churchill and the Conservatives did not imagine a forthcoming election defeat. Despite attempts in 1945 to portray

Labour as a party that 'sends round socialists to take all your savings', Labour won a huge majority of seats in Parliament in July 1945. What followed was a national insurance system, new welfare and healthcare, trade union rights, freedom for the colonies from imperial rule, and the implementation of an Education Act that gave free education to all children up to age fifteen. With that in mind, try to imagine what a future Labour government could achieve, given that current government debt is not unlike that in 1945.

We have been here before. Both the fractious Labour Party of the 1930s and that post-2015 have appeared determined to self-destruct. Both periods were the aftermath of great financial crashes, in 1929 and 2008. Both periods saw the leader of Labour derided. Attlee was sixty-two when he became Prime Minister. Corbyn turned sixty-nine in May 2018. Few people will make any comparisons between them, as to how they were treated and how they reacted similarly to all-too-familiar insults. But it takes courage to carry on in the way that Attlee did and Corbyn continues to do. At the time, when from all directions they are derided, it is easy to imagine that what they stand for is being lost. But the weight of insults is always heaviest when a Labour leader campaigns for real change, as Attlee did and as Corbyn is doing. Attlee was lucky. He survived at the top of his party long enough to enjoy the victory he fought for. He became Labour leader at the age of fifty-two, fourteen years younger than Corbyn was in 2015. Corbyn may not lead Labour into government or coalition, but he has moved the Labour Party back to the path that Attlee first trod and away from warmongering. By those criteria, and given his historic mandate in two leadership elections, Corbyn has had more success than any Labour leader for almost half a century.

It was when Britain was last as economically unequal as it is now, in the 1930s, that Labour was in such disarray and the stakes were so high. Economic inequalities rose under every post-1970s

government in the UK, including under all the Labour governments. Perhaps we should not be surprised that in such turbulent
times the Labour Party is again at war within itself. The brief
ceasefires in the Conservative civil war are unlikely to hold for
long. That civil war resulted in Brexit and is far from settled despite the referendum.

At the time of writing, the countries of the UK are in economic
peril as the pound weakens, food prices start to climb and the
housing crisis approaches a crescendo. Absolute poverty rates are
rising, and life expectancy is now falling. You have to look back as
far as the 1930s to find so much going wrong so quickly. Today is
different, but the echo is uncanny, and the ideas of the one leader
calling for social progress at a time of economic disaster are again
widely ridiculed, ignored or dismissed. The country deserved
better than that sorry bunch of politicians who were in charge in
2018, containing so many bent on achieving a hard Brexit in 2019.

Then, in May 2018, in the local elections, as commentator Ian
Warren explained, 'Labour saw its vote share increase by over
10 per cent in the south-east and east of England, coming close
to winning seats in Milton Keynes, Norwich and Southampton
while also improving its performance across the region in seat
after seat.'[100] But still the vast majority of political commentators
could not bring themselves to admit to what was happening. Perhaps it is finally true, partly because things are now so bad, that in
future they can only get better.

As of November 2018, there was little optimism. Theresa May's
585-page Brexit withdrawal plan was greeted, as noted above, with
resignations from her Cabinet, including her second Brexit Secretary, Dominic Raab. A third was speedily appointed, but the Tory
blood-letting continued. There were attempts to oust her by insti-
gating a vote of confidence. Esther McVey, her fourth Secretary of
State for Work and Pensions in just over two years, also resigned

along with a slew of largely unknown junior ministers. Despite having left the Cabinet in disgrace just a few months earlier over Windrush, Amber Rudd was brought back into government to take McVey's role. Puzzled mainland Europeans watched in bemusement. On 18 November, *The Observer* newspaper reported that in Paris, Berlin and Rome it was said that 'Britain has gone into Brexit meltdown'. On the same day, the *Sunday Times* noted that 'those trying to unseat Mrs May have failed to agree on an alternative Brexit plan or an alternative leader'.

If Brexit is to be the end of empire, the British public will need to understand all that was wrong with empire, and it will take a major political party to lead this change. It would help greatly if that party were led by someone who had spent a large part of their life campaigning on behalf of those the British had wronged abroad. That leader would have to hold fast, when all around them there was chaos and derision, and when their enemies tried repeatedly to slur them in every way possible, with little regard for the credibility of their insults. It would take the largest political movement in Europe to achieve such a sea-change in our thinking. If such a movement had been predicted in 2015, it would have been seen as utterly fanciful, and yet the Labour Party is now the largest political party by membership in Europe. We English may still be harking after a return to empire, but that need not be the case. The circumstances we now find ourselves in are fortuitous. Britain could yet become a land of real hope and respectable glory.

CHAPTER 8

A LAND OF HOPE AND GLORY?

*I have witnessed and been part of many attempts to construct
a post-imperial story, one that gave definition and purpose to a
Britain rediscovering itself after two centuries of global hegemony.*
— Gordon Brown, November 2017[1]

INTRODUCTION

Brexit has been a disaster with silver linings. The process of
trying to leave the EU and the end result could finally jolt
the British elite out of their superior complacency, and thereby
make the country a fairer and more humane place. We easily
forget that on 14 November 2011, David Cameron told the guests
at the annual Lord Mayor's Banquet in London that he had 'an
opportunity to begin to refashion the EU so it better serves this
nation's interests…'[2] Such arrogance and ignorance!

Things fall apart when empires crumble – most severely at the
heart of that former empire, in the imperial capital city, and then
across the home country. Rediscovery is attempted again and
again, until eventually the former heart of the empire becomes
reconciled with its new fate. It has always been this way and yet we
rarely try to learn much from the fate of past empires. This time,

we think, things are different. They are not. This time we are told that we will rebuild the empire. We will not. Things fall apart. It's just a stage that the British are going to have to get through.

British failings are understandable, because the British have recently ruled over the majority of the known world. Every group of people that has ever done this has taken time to adapt to no longer being superior. And Britain's leaders are mostly – intellectually or literally – descended from some of the most effective despots the world has ever known. They know how to pull the wool over people's eyes, lie and hold on to power for as long as they can.[3] The national narcissism required to rule an empire does not dissipate overnight. But the benefit of not growing up under the weight of such sad misconceptions is that we finally see through the men (and they are almost all men) who have so recently been trying so hard to lead us out of Europe.

We will make a prophecy here. They do not yet know it, but what the Brexiteers have actually sped us towards is the final whimper of the old ideal of the British Empire. Before Brexit, they could harbour their fantasies of national superiority – unshackled from the EU, where Britain (or at least they) would be both richer and freer. Now they have called their own bluff and are about to be found out.

The future is bright and the geography is clear. Partly as a result of Brexit, the next generation will soon have a far better idea of the sins, misconceptions and ignorance of their fathers, and hence will be relieved when the UK ceases to be a significant military power. It is for the next generation to make Britain decent, to make Britannia humane, and to consign the empire's triumphant songs to history. The rest of the world knows what the British are going through and why Britain has an identity crisis. It is just the British, mainly older white people in Britain, who so often still don't understand it.

AN IMPERIAL MINDSET

Brexit is a disaster for many reasons. One we have not yet mentioned is the environmental threat of Brexit. The UK government has frequently been reluctant to take on board EU environmental legislation. In January 2018, all of the UK's main environmental groups joined forces to explain that the European Union (Withdrawal) Bill threatened the most important UK controls on air pollution, waste and dangerous chemicals; and severely weakened what flimsy controls and commitments the British had made both on environmental protection and on mitigating climate change. This included the planned future reduction, or at least better control of, UK energy use and environmental legislation from farming through to fisheries – especially that required to protect dwindling North Sea fish stocks. The overall protection of nature and of water quality in particular appeared to be no cause for immediate concern for the UK government, other than being useful things that the new Environment Secretary Michael Gove could mention occasionally, as he prepared himself for his second leadership bid. Unlike David Davis and Boris Johnson, Environment Secretary Michael Gove did not resign on 8 or 9 July 2018 after the Chequers fiasco, when everything was supposedly agreed within Cabinet – and in truth wasn't. It seems that Gove stayed in the Cabinet to try to appear loyal, and thus suitable as a future Prime Minister.

All the key non-governmental environmental protection groups in the UK explored the environmental risks of Brexit; they found no areas where those risks were low. Of particular concern were those areas relating to the imminent loss of EU environmental legislation. The thirteen environmental organisations that produced the January 2018 report included the Royal Society for the Protection of Birds, the National Trust and the World Wide Fund for Nature (WWF). These organisations are hardly a collection of rabble-rousers.[4] At the age of ninety-seven, Prince Philip, the Duke of Edinburgh, remained patron of WWF despite having dropped almost all his other official commitments. Even the favourite charity of the consort to Her Majesty objects to Brexit!

Britain is no longer a land of hope and glory when it comes to environmental management. It has been estimated that, given successive governments' ecological mismanagement, one in five of the few remaining mammal species in Britain will be virtually extinct within a decade from now. Beavers, water voles and hazel (common) dormice may have had it. Many species of bats, wildcats and red squirrels are only just holding on.[5] Someone re-writing *The Wind in the Willows* today would have to tell a story in which old Badger could easily find himself shot as part of an unnecessary, unscientific cull, while Ratty is homeless and living in fear of being hunted by mink (his riverbank home having been eroded due to the spread of Himalayan Balsam), while Mole is killed in a trap set by a groundsman to keep a riverside lawn pristine. Even mole populations are falling. And Toad may no longer live in Toad Hall, it having been requisitioned for translocated great crested newts.

Despite European environmental legislation having been in place and continuously improved for the past thirty years, the estimated population of common British toads has fallen by 70 per cent and the species is now on the verge of being endangered itself.[6] But how can this be? Well, apart from everything else, their food source is under severe threat. As an *Observer* article noted in June 2018, 'An insect Armageddon is under way, say many entomologists, the result of a multiple whammy of environmental impacts: pollution, habitat changes, overuse of pesticides, and global warming.'[7]

All the fault of Europe, you might cry; another reason for a hard Brexit now, you might think. Being part of the EU has not saved the 'British' toad! Well, we know you're unlikely to have got this far through this book if you are of that opinion, but you might have turned to this chapter first! If so, read on, as all is not lost. The future of wildlife on the British Isles will be as much affected by what happens next as will the future of the people of Britain. This can still be a land of real hope and actual glory, but the artificial merging of a now much-diminished part of Ireland with Wales, with England and with Scotland has at some point to come to an end. Brexit could be a large part of this inevitable untangling of the remnants of the empire's core from each other. The marriage of Scotland and England was only ever for convenience and they have stayed together only while the economic going was good. Wales and Ireland were never given a choice. Most of Ireland took back control a century ago.

The Brexit vote has often been painted as a contest between 'life's winners' in London and a few other affluent or more cosmopolitan cities, and the economically losing-out majority of the land. However, there is no correlation between the Leave vote and deprivation (see Figures 8.1, 8.2 and 8.3 below). Nevertheless, within England there has been internal colonialism. It is not a 'united' kingdom. The north-east region of the UK is as poor as many parts of Eastern Europe. Inner London is now one of the richest parts of both the UK and Europe. But this is due to the short-term effects of the 1990s financial boom, which ushered in gentrification that, in practice, brought about social cleansing – as there was no longer space for new middle-income English hopefuls to arrive, apart from those prepared to accept Rachman-type rented housing.[8]

BRITISH FAILINGS AND HOPE

If you think the UK is united, think of the blazing image of Grenfell Tower, in the heart of London, and whether there is anywhere else in Europe where the people who make the city work – the cleaners and traders, electricians and bus drivers, the bulk of those who live in social housing (and their families) – are held in such disdain by those in power.[9] The disdain may not be obvious to you, if you are easily fooled by upper-class 'charm' and 'civility'. The local council's 'arms-length' management body was cladding the building for the sake of those who looked at it from elsewhere in the borough, not for the well-being of the residents. The council had neglected the towers and flats around Grenfell for decades and huge sums of money from local taxation could have been used beforehand but was deliberately not raised by the local Conservative borough council, which repeatedly chose not to raise local council taxes when it could have.

Where else in Europe would 4,600 new basements be carved into the ground beneath the city's grandest homes in the space of just a decade, to make so many extra empty rooms for the rich? In aggregate, just the first level of these new luxury subterranean chambers reaches down under the streets of London to the depth of more than fifty new Grenfell Towers. The rich of Kensington were not taxed and instead spent their money building rooms for themselves that they would hardly make good use of.

But there is still cause for great hope. The good news is that London is full of enough housing for all. There are more empty bedrooms in London than there are people who need housing – but almost all of those bedrooms are in under-occupied privately owned property. We do not need to build much new housing in the capital to live better lives. We just need to reorganise how we have chosen to live. The super-rich have done their bit now, by building so many luxury skyscrapers in recent years, and – like those basements – they are mostly still empty. It was as if they knew there would be the need for this housing in future. There is, but the need is not most acute among those who can pay the most.[10] So, at some point, underused buildings in London will have to be requisitioned, starting with providing hostels to help keep the homeless off the streets. If footballers Ryan Giggs and Gary Neville's boutique hotel building can be used to temporarily house the homeless in Manchester, think what a determined government could achieve in London.

A future beyond empire will be very different and created in response to the final mistakes of the old colonial thinkers. This has to occur whether the country is in or out of the EU. The British don't have to fail, but they do need to stop claiming that they are so 'Great' and insisting that they have a right to be considered a top dog, a 'Tier 1' military power that can boss and bully 'lesser nations' with nuclear weapons to supposedly prove their status. And property can no longer be sacrosanct. British property law can be changed. That alone would frighten off overseas investors who buy homes to leave empty in the belief that they will never be seized for the general good. Just talking about the need for requisition will help.

There are still many things the four nations of the UK can offer to the world, even if some of them are very different from the imperial ideas of dominating foreign countries, asserting the pre-eminence of property rights over human rights, and exploiting the labour of others. One thing is certain: it will not make Britain great to become even more of a tax haven, a small offshore island where rich men and women, global corporations and dodgy businesses are encouraged to park their money. Neither is it in the interests of the rest of the world, and especially the rest of Europe, to allow this to happen. Fortunately, it is also not in the interest of 99.9 per cent of UK residents. Why should commuters on Virgin trains pay exorbitant fares to travel to work, while Richard Branson puts his share of the proceeds into overseas tax havens and doesn't even volunteer his riches to help rebuild hurricane-destroyed houses on the Caribbean island where he so often lives?[11]

Britain is impoverished by many who will do anything possible to avoid paying tax, seeing it as a great evil when in fact it is a massive public good. The current tax system is deliberately full of loopholes, and there are armies of largely unaccountable accountants to help the wealthy exploit those loopholes. It would be great if the people of Britain could be decently fed, from local farmers and fishermen rewarded for expanding their efforts and overseas food trade, properly regulated. Instead, we have the shameful spectacle of hungry people in a rich country collecting from foodbanks.

Often, apologists for the state of the UK say, 'But we have such good charities!' That is not something that makes for a Great Britain, let alone a United Kingdom. With Brexit, whether soft, medium or hard, this can all end. Even a much poorer state than the UK need have no recourse to foodbanks and there are many poorer countries that have managed this. The British elite could have ended the shame of having to beg for food without resorting to Brexit, but perhaps they needed the shock to shake them out of their fitful slumber? As the *New York Times* recently explained:

> Britain is undergoing a full-blown identity crisis. It is a 'hollowed-out country,' 'ill at ease with itself,' 'deeply provincial,' engaged in a 'controlled suicide,' say puzzled experts. And these are Britain's friends ... The 19th-century myth of Britain as the 'workshop of the world,' a doughty Protestant nation surrounded by Catholics with an empire on which the sun never set, confronted a post-World War II reality, when a lot of these tales stopped being true ... Confused and divided, Britain no longer has an agreed-upon national narrative, said Charles Grant ... 'Everywhere I go ... people are asking "What's wrong with your country?"'
> – *New York Times*, 4 November 2017[12]

Charles Grant is no outsider; he is thoroughly of the establishment. He helped found the Centre for European Reform in 1996 and has been its director since 1998.[13] He was a director and trustee of the British Council from 2002 to 2008. In 2013, the Queen anointed him a Companion of St Michael and St George 'for services to European and wider international policy-making'. In 2014 he was in Bloomberg Markets' fifty most influential list, one of their ten key 'Thinkers'.[14] But by 2017, everywhere he went people were asking him what was wrong with his country. Given so much thinking, he should have been able to explain what was happening, but he couldn't. He was one of the numerous 'puzzled experts' that the *New York Times* quoted above in November 2017 when its journalists tried to explain to Americans why everything was going so badly in little old England. The Americans knew that the empire was well and truly over – but they could not get the English they asked to say it out loud.

Charles studied modern history at Cambridge University, followed by French politics in Grenoble. He became a reporter for a financial magazine in 1981, then in 1986 he joined *The Economist* (initially reporting on the City of London), and worked there until taking up his present position in 1998. He thought he knew what was going on and how Britain worked. However, he – and many like him – have just begun to realise that there is (and was) something very amiss within Britain. They did not expect Brexit. They knew it was not in Britain's financial interest, but they were also proud to be British. Some might even have started to wonder if Brexit was their fault, including those who supported staying in the EU. Was there a flip-side to being so very proud to be British, of being so gung-ho? Charles now lists his 'Areas of expertise' as beginning with 'Britain's EU referendum'.[15] But he did not see its results coming.

Everyone is an expert after the event. Gordon Brown, British

Chancellor of the Exchequer for ten years and Prime Minister for three, described how in his view the 'fallout from the end of empire' has led to a position where the actual survival of the United Kingdom is at risk. As he bluntly put it, 'In the Britain of the 1950s we managed decline, in the 1960s we mismanaged decline and in the 1970s we declined to manage.' Brown goes on to blame the rise of Thatcherism, neoliberalism and globalisation for the failure of politics, both back then and more recently, to tackle selfish vested interests. Recently he has singled out 'in an age of mega-wealth, individuals who abuse their financial might, to manipulate government to their own advantage'.[16] Had he been manipulated as Chancellor and Prime Minister by some influences from the City? It can be refreshing when people begin to admit their fallibilities. Few former British Prime Ministers ever do – stiff upper lip and all that. You don't conquer large parts of the globe by stopping to consider exactly what you are doing, why you are doing it, and the long-term consequences of your actions.

WHAT WENT SO VERY WRONG?

A notable feature of Britain pre-Brexit was how selfishness was not just widely accepted but often celebrated. As we demonstrated in the chapters above, many still incorrectly extrapolate Darwinian ideas and use them to argue that the world is a place of rampant competition in which Britain has to fight to survive, that it will either sink or swim, and that this is entirely the natural way of things. They suggest that to deny that is to deny reality,[17] implying that the poverty created in Britain (by not properly taxing accumulators, also known as 'wealth creators') is unavoidable. In Britain, the poor, they say, will always be with us, casualties of a law of nature.

While not naming names, Brown's comments above might have been referring to Lord Ashcroft, who supported voting to leave the EU and wrote a short book giving his views on why Leave happened.[18] Earlier, when writing about himself, Lord Ashcroft explained, 'When my parents first learned that they were going to British Honduras, they had to study an atlas to discover its precise location in Central America.'[19] Ashcroft's father was an 'administrator in the Colonial Service', a British civil servant who worked for the empire.

Lord Ashcroft has more than a bit part in the story that this book recounts. For a start, without the exit poll he commissioned, we would not have known that it was Middle England socially (as well as geographically) that most strongly and in such great numbers voted to leave. Born in 1946, he spent some of his early years in what was British Honduras (Belize from 1982) and Nyasaland (Malawi from 1964). He thus had experience at first hand of the servants, of the plumed hats and the officialdom of the last throes of the British Empire. He was schooled at St Catherine's Academy in Belize and then sent to boarding school in England when his parents were stationed in Nigeria. He did not enjoy that school, where, as he says, he received the odd caning before being transferred to the Royal Grammar School in High Wycombe and, from there, went on to what was at the time called Essex Technical College, later becoming Anglia Ruskin University, where he gained a diploma in business studies. He said that boarding school 'taught me resilience'.[20] In 2013, a business magazine summarised 'the secret of his success' as being 'ruthless deal-making. And keeping friends in high(ish) places: as well as bankrolling the Tories.'[21]

Starting with a cleaning company, Ashcroft's business interests have encompassed packaging, car sales, janitor services, security and crime control. By 2010, he was 37th (out of 1,000) in the Sunday Times Rich List. His position had fallen to 95th by 2017, although he was still then worth £1.34 billion.[22] A year later, in

2018, his wealth had shrunk to £1.28 billion and his rank to 107th. The Rich List is important. We included a section from it at the very start of this book, in Figure 0.1, showing donations to the political parties. In 2017, some seventy-one people on the Rich List donated £5.5 million to the Conservative Party (£0.5 million from Ashcroft alone), compared to twelve Rich List members known to have donated to any other UK political party.[23] In 2018, all but one of the top fifty political donors gave to the Conservative Party, the other one giving to the Scottish Nationalists. Ashcroft is honoured with a bust in the Business School in Anglia Ruskin University, where he was made Chancellor in 2000, and buildings in Cambridge and Colchester carry his name on their façades. The reason he is associated with these establishments is because he gave all of them money. But now, in common with many other rich people, as the world is finding out via the Panama and Paradise Papers, questions have arisen about the tax he pays.[24]

From 1998 to 2000, Ashcroft was the Belizean[25] Ambassador to the United Nations. At the same time, he was the UK Tory Party treasurer. Following this and those substantial donations to the Conservative Party, he was knighted, and then, in 2000, made a peer. It was later suggested that he had been proposed for the peerage on the understanding that he would become a UK taxpayer. Years later it transpired that he was non-domiciled in the UK. Nevertheless, he became deputy chairman of the Conservative Party from 2005 to 2010, when the issue was again raised as to where he was domiciled for tax purposes.

Queries as to Michael Ashcroft's tax affairs have led to some farcical situations, such as at the Conservative Party conference in 2017 when he sought refuge in the toilet from a BBC reporter attempting to interview him about his tax status.[26] The Labour Party has called for HMRC to investigate.

Ashcroft resigned from the House of Lords three weeks after

the May 2015 general election, having fallen out with the Prime Minister, possibly because Cameron failed to honour a promise to give Ashcroft an influential job.[27] He reportedly paid Isabel Oakeshott £500,000 to co-write an unauthorised biography of David Cameron, extracts of which were serialised in the *Daily Mail* and published in October 2015.[28] Described as a 'Jacobean revenge biography', it included an uncorroborated lewd anecdote about Cameron that has become referred to as Piggate.[29] Oakeshott subsequently said, 'The thing to point out about that story is that there is no need for burden of proof on a colourful anecdote where we're quite upfront about our own reservations about whether to take it seriously.'[30] The colourful anecdote resulted in the new word necrobestiality entering the language, although it hasn't yet made it into the *Oxford English Dictionary*.

When historians in future look back on Brexit, they may well link the farce of Piggate, and the roles played by those with an interest in promoting Brexit, to the growth of division that led to the Prime Minister calling a referendum he thought he would win, with little thought of what might happen if he lost.

This is a book that essentially is about what went wrong for those who thought they were in charge, why it went wrong, how the (unquestionable) 'will of the people' appears to have been manipulated, and just how hard it has been since then to come to terms with the problems surrounding the United Kingdom's attempts to exit the European Union. You may believe that 48 per cent of those who voted were manipulated into supporting Remain, and that they could not see the light. Or you may believe that not all Leave voters had spent long thinking about what would happen. You are unlikely to believe that everyone came to their own decision without being influenced by any funded lobbying group or media campaign. (In fact, long before the Cambridge Analytica scandal broke, it was revealed in May 2017 how the Leave campaign devoted most of its resources: 'Vote Leave sent, Dominic Cummings wrote, "nearly a billion targeted digital adverts" and spent approximately 98% of their money on digital campaigning.'[31])

But the good news is that it really was not the Russians who arranged all this, or some wonks working in an outfit called Cambridge Analytica. Brexit was a home-grown enterprise. Mostly it was paid for in Britain, although the money was often routed through tax havens. Brexit was 'made in Britain'. And it was made in the school classrooms of England over the past half a century just as much as through the pages of the tabloids in the past few years.

Voters' age, turnout, and former education were key to the outcome. Those educated to degree level behaved as if they had been born a few years later, voting alongside those younger than them. Had we weighted people's votes by the number of years they could still expect to live then, yes, Remain would have won – but only by a 2 per cent margin – and what use is a 2 per cent margin?[32] As we explained at the very start of this book, among those who voted, 71 per cent of those aged under 25 voted Remain according to one poll, but only 54 per cent of those aged 25–49, while 60 per cent of voters aged 50–64 and 64 per cent of those aged over 64 were Leavers.[33] Age, turnout and former education were key to the outcome. But in hindsight the outcome was much more useful to those who would like to see Britain change than a narrow Remain victory would have been, even if you don't support Brexit. A Remain win would simply have resulted in more uncertainty and eventually another referendum and bid to leave; and perhaps by then we would have seen a Leave campaign team with some plan of what to do if they won. Clearly, in hindsight, we can all now see that they did not expect to win at the first attempt. The Leavers had no plan. Or rather, they had a plan – it was to say that they were robbed of their win by the BBC and the establishment and then to battle on. They made the mistake of winning too early.

What went wrong was, in hindsight, only partly a product of people who did not want to contribute to the general good of society (to put it bluntly, tax dodgers trying to avoid EU regulation). Some promoting Brexit were driven by their own self-interest, others by nostalgia or even the remnants of the beliefs that there was a British race and it was special and that, once untethered, it would be great again. Others just saw it as an opportunity to become Prime Minister. The people funding the Leave vote very successfully tapped into an understandable urge to stick two fingers up at the establishment and 'give it to the man' (as they say in the USA). Treat people badly enough for long enough, give them a semi-plausible patriotic option, and they will vote for any extreme that appears to offer a way out where 'tomorrow belongs to me'.[34]

Across much of the Western world, it is the areas with the fewest immigrants in which anti-immigration sentiment has been most easily stoked up by those with motives far beyond trying to reduce immigration. In the USA, it was in West Virginia, an area largely devoid of great in-migration (including inward migration from other states of the USA, not just immigration), where Trump's anti-immigration message received most vocal support.[35] In Germany, the far-right Alternative for Germany (AfD) won most support in the peripheral east of the country where fewer Syrians are to be found. And, of course, in the UK the pattern was the same. People only learn to hate immigrants in areas without immigrants; they need to be directed to hate by people trained and brought up to look down on others – people who know how to hate and disrespect others for a living.[36]

At many points in this book we have provided examples to

suggest that a large part of the problem has been due to the privatised or otherwise separated schooling of many in government (and others holding great power due to their great wealth) over the years, including many leading Brexiteers who were educated in boarding schools or in elite establishments in former colonies. Even Gordon Brown, state educated, was separated from his fellow pupils when he was at school by being placed in a special unit for supposedly gifted children. Britain has yet to be governed by a Prime Minister who went to an ordinary school with everyone else. Private and grammar school boys and girls have dominated – without a single exception.

BREXIT AND BRITISH EDUCATION

One of us has written in detail and at length about education in Britain from imperial times to the Brexit vote – see Sally Tomlinson's *Education and Race from Empire to Brexit* (Bristol: Policy Press, to be published spring 2019). When recounting the history of later nineteenth-century schooling, it was very clear, as we noted earlier in this book, that the most elite of Britain's private schools, the so-called public schools, were often deliberately designed or adapted to produce men who could run a great empire. They were taught to be 'proud to be British' and to have particular British values, including lording it over other people. This is not like patriotism in France or China. Behind British values lies the unspoken assumption that the British are special because they once, still just within living memory, owned an empire made up of countries that now include almost half of the world's population (Figure 3.2).

Social progress has often been a fight against British values. Abolishing slavery, ending child labour, extending voting rights, winning equal rights for women – all went against the British values of their time. Those who say immigrants must accept

British values are ignorant of their own history. The British Empire was partly built on slavery and indentured labour. Empire apologists write versions of history to try to imply the opposite. Recently it has been obvious that British values do not apply to refugees, and that the British are very reluctant to encompass in their own law all the basic rights in the European Convention on Human Rights – that declaration of values which so annoyed Theresa May when she was Home Secretary.

As they developed, British values at first valued people mostly on the basis of their background, their class, their wealth and their land ownership. Britain's attitude to the rest of the world was militaristic: send in the gunboats to teach the insubordinate natives a lesson; engage in war repeatedly and often remarkably thoughtlessly, right up to the present day (think Afghanistan, Iraq, Libya); and export weapons to conflict areas regardless of human rights violations. It is all 'good for business'.

Until recently, British values were instilled, particularly in boys, with help from corporal punishment, fagging and many other innovations in bullying. In other types of school, those for other children – the ones not selected for greatness – the British were taught to know their place, but they too were also taught a largely mythical history of their past. It was many years after corporal punishment was outlawed in British state schools – in 1986 – that it was banned in private schools, in 1999. Why such a gap? And why was Mrs Thatcher such an advocate of birching, voting in favour of it with a handful of much older Members of Parliament when she was a young MP?

Britain is often bizarre. In Poland, corporal punishment in schools was banned in 1783. The ban is enshrined in the country's constitution. Finland introduced a ban in the late 1800s. The Soviet Union outlawed such cruelty to children in 1917.[37] Today, the countries of the UK are among only a tiny minority of places in Europe where it is not a criminal offence for parents to beat or smack their children – although at least in Wales and Scotland that is soon to end.[38] The British are unusually violent to children, and it is their British Empire history that is to blame. UNICEF surveys of recent years have found that children in the UK report higher levels of violence directed towards them than in any other comparable country.[39] The British should be shocked, but to be tough and 'good in a fight' is still very much a British value: 'Are you looking at me the wrong way?', 'Want to take that outside?' Where do such ideas come from?

Those who ran the empire had to be made to feel effortlessly superior so that when they were sent abroad, even when only in small numbers, they could take charge of countries and their populations and not think that there was anything strange or possibly wrong with that. Men in their early twenties were running the affairs of Indian provinces larger than European nations with little other than 'the values' that had been instilled in them at school and, occasionally, Oxbridge.

Today, Britain presides over a series of territories in the world (through Privy Council oversight) where corporal punishment is often still legal, and education is often especially imperialistic. Even after almost all the empire had disappeared, some small countries (mainly islands such as the Isle of Man) remained under the control and sovereignty of Britain. As of 2018, there are fourteen British Overseas Territories and three Crown Dependencies (Figure 2.3) where rich UK residents can avoid paying normal taxes, while those at home have been suffering under a government imposing austerity measures, that were mainly about making poor people deliberately poorer, while dramatically reducing taxation of corporations and the not quite so very rich. Those islands come under the umbrella of the EU as Special Member State Territories. Did some of those rich backers of Brexit fear that if the UK stayed in, then the other EU member states would eventually insist that those islands started playing by the same rules as everyone else?[40] Would they have had to pay their fair share in taxes without Brexit? No wonder they funded the Leave campaign! If Britain accepted higher taxes in its remaining small colonies, the next thing would be higher taxes at home, and then an end to the austerity policies that have helped some of the rich become so much richer at the expense of others.

Austerity was recently linked to colonialism by a doctor working in Liverpool. Dr Simon Bowers explained to a *New York Times* reporter that public sector cuts are connected to 'colonial barbarity'. Bowers went on: 'Austerity isn't a necessity, it's a political choice, to move Britain in a different way. I can't see a rationale beyond further enriching the rich while making the lives of the poor more miserable.'[41] It takes a particular colonial mindset to see the misery of others as a necessary but largely insignificant piece of collateral damage.

People like Lord Ashcroft are very unlikely to ever accept the arguments made in these pages or by doctors like Simon Bowers. Other countries keep their potential Lord Ashcrofts under control and have fewer of them. But he, and the politicians we documented in detail in Chapter 7, believe in their right to be in their positions of power and privilege. Others believe that no one person should be in a position of such power to pursue their own interests so effectively with such huge amounts of money held in so few hands. Often, those who funded the Leave campaign were led to believe in their right to power by their colonial parents or at their private or grammar schools and often Oxbridge, or sometimes when attending military academies.[42] And, above all, they are taught to act as a pack, although at times it has been a very badly co-ordinated pack. Ashcroft suggested in his unauthorised biography that 'it is testament to Cameron that few Old

Etonians have anything seriously disobliging to say about their old classmate'. People who are rich and privileged are unlikely to criticise their friends. Coming from such a tiny section of society, they need and demand group loyalty.

MIDDLE ENGLAND AND A BAD DEAL

A no-deal outcome would lead to economic chaos. The UK would adopt, overnight, third-country status in the eyes of the European Union. Planes would not take off, nuclear fuel would not be imported and haulage traffic to the Continent would grind to a halt.
– PAUL DALY, FELLOW IN LAW, CAMBRIDGE, OCTOBER 2017[43]

Bad news on Brexit will be better for business than no news at all.
– RACHEL REEVES, CHAIR OF THE HOUSE OF COMMONS BUSINESS, ENERGY AND INDUSTRIAL STRATEGY SELECT COMMITTEE, *THE TIMES*, OCTOBER 2017[44]

For the EU27, no deal is clearly better than a bad deal. A bad deal is one that says countries can opt out of being in the EU, opt out of paying their way in future, but still receive some key benefits for free. For the UK and especially Middle England, the group that has more to lose than average, a large number of potentially very bad deals are all preferable to no deal.

Prior to Brexit, the UK had the best financial deal of all member states. Margaret Thatcher's opt-out meant that the UK did not pay its fair share of the costs of membership. More importantly, Britain imported highly skilled but still cheap labour from other member states – labour it had not paid to educate. At the same time, it was a net exporter of its elderly people, who then relied on other states' healthcare systems. Many people suspect that the unravelling of all this will play out badly. People living within Britain will become very confused because they were not made aware of how good the deal had become. They will keep on asking, 'How did we get into this mess?' So, we turn for one last time to the pattern of voting. Figure 8.1 tells you the most important thing you need to know.

Figure 8.1 shows that the greatest support for Remain was in the poshest areas of England (decile ten), but after that the greatest support for Leave was in deciles four to seven, literally 'Middle England', within which only forty-two constituencies out of 212 saw a majority voting Remain – some 80 per cent of constituencies had a majority for Leave in those four decile groups. In the three most deprived sets of constituencies in England, people were considerably (but not in a majority) more likely to vote Remain than in the next four deciles. It was Middle England that voted out most, not the poorest.

FIGURE 8.1: DEPRIVATION LEVELS BY CONSTITUENCY AND VOTING LEAVE, 2016

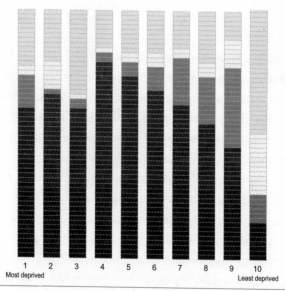

Every English parliamentary constituency is shown, grouped into deciles (tenths) by their level of deprivation and shaded by whether the majority voted Leave (lower, darker bars) or Remain (upper, lighter bars), and how strongly so.[45]

Immediately after the Brexit vote, one of us published an article in the *British Medical Journal*[46] that showed that just over half of Leave voters across the UK lived in the south of England. Also, a narrow majority of Leave voters were posher than average – being from social classes A, B or C1. The article explained that this was partly 'because of differential turnout and the size of the denominator population'.[47] In other words, what turned out to be incredibly important in hindsight was how many people chose not to vote. In what are now more middle-class counties like Essex (62 per cent Leave), Kent (59 per cent), Dorset (57 per cent), Cornwall (56 per cent), Devon (55 per cent) and Hampshire (54 per cent), large majorities voted Leave. These were areas whose populations had grown greatly in recent decades and where turnout was always much higher than in northern areas with larger electorates, which all produced fewer Leave votes.[48] The result of that analysis was repeatedly attacked because many Brexiteers desperately perceived themselves as being on the side of the more impoverished underdogs. That was not true.

The exit poll only told us about voters. Other sources of data[49] showed that only 66 per cent of the population had voted – that is, 72 per cent of all those registered to vote. Men were slightly more likely to vote than women, with people aged 55–74 being most likely to vote. Turnout rates were highest among UKIP supporters and then Conservative supporters, people with degrees, and those living in the south-west of England – where 77 per cent of registered voters there voted. In contrast, in London only 70 per cent of people who were on the electoral roll managed to vote. This was just 56 per cent of London's eligible adult population, as so many people in London were (and still are) not registered to vote.

In the months leading up to the 2016 referendum, it had become harder to register to vote because the Conservative government had changed the rules on how people registered. These changes disproportionately influenced Londoners, who move home more often, are more often students or sharing a home, more often live in overcrowded homes, and more often worry about the negative implications of registering (e.g. debt collection). Had the registration rules not been changed (judging from previous levels of voter registration and turnout in London, and by how the Londoners who did vote voted), the EU referendum in 2016 would have probably had the opposite outcome. But, of course, it would still have been a marginal result.

FIGURE 8.2: DEPRIVATION VERSUS VOTING BY POLITICAL PARTY IN ENGLAND, 2017

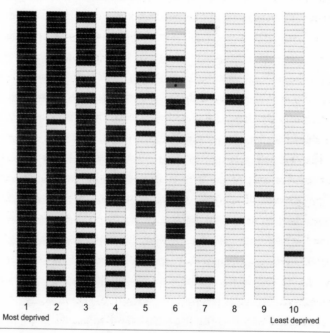

The party winning each seat is shown, from the poorest tenth of constituencies to the richest. Black = Labour; dot = Green; grey = Liberal Democrat; light grey = Conservative. Reproduced by kind permission of Alasdair Rae.[50]

The 2016 Brexit vote was the result of an advisory referendum that was then interpreted as binding by the representatives in

Parliament. The British didn't create the world's largest ever empire by respecting others or by promoting real democracy around the world. In 2016, across the UK, sixteen- and seventeen-year-olds were excluded, in contrast to the 2014 independence referendum in Scotland, where this group was given the vote. And British citizens who were deemed to have lived abroad for too long (more than fifteen years) were also not allowed to vote, which included those who had, for example, retired to Spain, and could be most severely affected by the outcome. Non-British EU citizens living in the UK for decades could not vote. Prisoners also did not get a vote, contrary to European law. But again, had it been a narrow victory for Remain, given what you know now about the Brexiteers – do you really think they would have accepted that, packed up their bags and gone back to their tax havens?

Figure 8.2 shows the general election results for 2017 in a similar way to the EU referendum results in 2016 in Figure 8.1 (above). Figure 8.2 shows that in the decile 4 column of seats, Labour had a majority. However, it also reveals that in the other three out of the four 'Middle England' central decile areas, the Conservatives had a majority, even in the 2017 election when they did so badly. It was in these Middle England constituencies that people were more likely to vote Leave. In short, then, Tory England voted Britain out. These were areas that had often loyally voted Conservative for decades, but economically were not doing anything like as well as other Tory areas, which cannot have seemed right to many people living there. Adults in the least deprived tenth of England areas, all but three being overwhelmingly Tory, had almost all voted to Remain, but people (especially older people, who are more often Tory voters) in less well-off Conservative constituencies overwhelmingly voted Leave. People in much more deprived areas were less likely to vote Leave, much less likely to vote Conservative, but also less likely to vote at all in either elections or referenda.

It would be useful to have the details for much smaller areas than constituencies, but those are not generally available. However, the BBC did manage to obtain figures for over 1,000 wards in England and Wales, about one in nine of the total.[51] These showed that there was a marked correlation between voting Remain and the proportion with university degrees, and a high correlation between voting Leave and the average age of adults. However, when the voting proportions were plotted against the ward deprivation index, there was only a slight positive correlation between deprivation and voting Leave within any town, city or district, and looking just at individual local authority areas often there was no obvious correlation as to whether or not these poorer areas within each district were, overall, voting to Remain or Leave.[52] Older, less well-off, less well-educated Tory Britain was where the most votes for Brexit were. It cannot be said often enough. It was not Sunderland or Stoke that swung it.

Brexit has taught us so much about ourselves that we did not know. Despite all the assertions that it was Labour-voting, poor, northern people who voted most to leave the EU, it was actually poorer Tory voters in poorer Tory areas who most voted out. And many of these were older Tory identifiers. It was not the votes of those at the bottom, the most deprived areas in this so divided, so unequal country, that were responsible for the outcome of the 2016 referendum. Instead, it was the votes of people in areas of England that had most often voted Tory in the past but had not seen much reward for their loyalty. Wales, in case you thought we had forgotten the principality, voted almost exactly along the lines of the UK average voting distribution and did not swing the result one way or the other.

In this book we have tried to explain why we are where we are – and not to be too downbeat about it all. We have tried not always to be too serious and we have tried also to be sympathetic to an understandably bewildered readership living in such a strange place where people refer to their state as 'Great' – the only state in the United Nations to do so. Far more modest states with less pompous names are today rated as enjoying the highest levels of wellbeing, happiness, innovation and productivity in the world. The top six states in the United Nations World Happiness report are either in the European Union or enjoy free movement of labour treaties with the European Union. They include Norway, which has the Norwegian krone as its currency, and Switzerland which has the Swiss franc. Denmark has Danish krone and Iceland, which also enjoys free movement of labour with the EU, has its own króna too. The other two, Finland and the Netherlands, are in the Eurozone.[53] Of these six, only the Dutch ever had a significant empire, although the Danes did at one time control both Iceland and Greenland, and some parts of Britain. The four states in this list not in the Eurozone are all interesting models for Britain with its pound sterling.

If Britain crashed out of the EU with no deal, then the immediate repercussions are predicted to be far worse for Britain than for any other EU country. In the medium and long term, the shock could be something that jars the British out of their current state of complacency. As we say, there is a potential silver lining. But the pound will certainly slip further in value, and there is a high probability of a run on the pound accelerating that drop. The shock of all this might be what is required for the British to stop accepting the anti-social behaviour often demonstrated by those with power and privilege in Britain. It is wrong to not pay your taxes, yet continue to wield enormous influence through the media, and influence legislation disproportionately according to your self-interest. That may be hard for many to see, but in the short term, as prices rise and food becomes more expensive, disproportionately affecting the poorest, and as the immigrants are no longer arriving in enough numbers to be blamed, the attention will increasingly be focused on the rich and greedy.

The young and healthy migrants who came in recent years will increasingly leave and are already leaving. Much more importantly, fewer will come to replace them – most had always been transient. The oldest and most infirm of retired British emigrants are more likely to return from the mainland at a cost to Britain, as they then need to be housed and will become an extra demand on the already struggling health and social care services. Even if they don't require social housing, their return will diminish the available stock overall in the short term, especially as they tend to occupy homes at much lower densities than departing migrants from the UK. Hard Brexit is a perfect storm. It is the most ill, frail and desperate of Britain's expats, from Spain and elsewhere in the mainland, that will have to return first. The current health crisis has already resulted in some UK visa quotas being rescinded for medical staff.[54] As the Leader of the Opposition explained in summer 2018, even before Brexit there was 'mounting evidence austerity is killing people', with consecutive governments underfunding the NHS.[55] Now, the NHS has to plan for a no-deal Brexit and all the immediate harm to health that would lead to as medicines become more expensive, staff leave the country, medical isotopes for cancer treatment become harder to obtain, as well as many types of medical equipment.[56]

The whole of the UK, if it remains united,[57] will suffer. There is much debate about which parts will suffer most. The north-east of England is predicted to lose much of the very last of its remaining manufacturing industry, with headlines in Newcastle upon Tyne's local *Chronicle* newspaper reading 'Vote Leave economist admits Brexit would "mostly eliminate manufacturing"'.[58] That headline was written before the actual referendum took place. Newcastle was the only part of the north-east to vote to Remain, by a 1 per cent margin. The only well-known pro-Leave economist, Patrick Minford, predicted the closure of the Sunderland Nissan car factory prior to the vote, and Sunderland was famously the first area to declare for Leave. Two years later, in February 2018, Sky

News revealed leaked documents showing that far more recently civil servants had concluded that the north-east would suffer even worse, if there was 'no deal', with the size of its economy predicted to be reduced by one sixth (16 per cent), followed by the West Midlands, where the economy was predicted to shrink by 13 per cent.[59] But the Brexit vote was not about deprived areas voting out, as we have explained at length. The correlation between how deprived an area is and voting Leave (shown in Figure 8.3) was only 0.037 – essentially no correlation. It was not people who were poorer who voted Leave in high numbers, but people who found the propaganda that immigrants created problems believable. They tended to live in areas of low immigration. In poorer areas of high immigration, everyone was more likely to vote Remain.

FIGURE 8.3: VOTE LEAVE AND DEPRIVATION BY LOCAL AUTHORITY IN ENGLAND, 2016

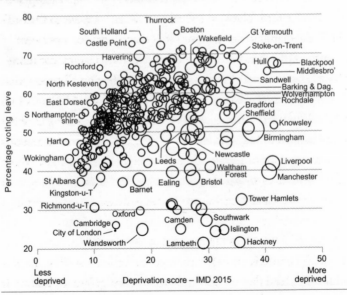

Each area is a local authority drawn in proportion to its population and positioned according to how deprived it is and the proportion voting Leave.[60]

It is well worth asking again: why might levels of overall deprivation have had so little effect on the vote to leave? It is true that
the south-east of England and London depend much more on
labour from the European mainland, but less on trade with the
EU. However, when you look at the places that voted most to
leave, from affluent East Dorset to poorer Blackpool, what the
vast majority of Leave areas had in common was the arrival of
fewer overseas migrants in recent decades. In contrast, from well-
off Cambridge to much poorer Hackney, it was areas of very high
immigration from overseas where the Leave vote was lowest.

The same leaked government report referred to above estimated
that London would see a negligible immediate reduction in the
size of its economy if the UK remained in the European Economic Area, a 5 per cent reduction if the UK left with a free trade
agreement, and an 8 per cent reduction (just less than a twelfth)
following a hard Brexit. However, consider what might happen to
a city like Oxford following a hard exit. What happens to Oxford's
BMW car manufacturing plant, which accounts for 1 per cent of
the entire UK manufacturing industry? Britain's largest car manufacturer, Jaguar Land-Rover, is already transferring all production
of its Land Rover Discovery SUV from the West Midlands to a
plant in Slovakia.[61] In the event of a hard exit from the EU, what
would happen to Oxford's hospitals, which rely so much on labour
from the European mainland, and to its two universities, which
pride themselves in being international but may soon begin to
look very parochial – backwards places in a backwater country?

THE REST OF THE EU AND NO DEAL

Outside of the UK, it has been suggested that it will be the Republic of Ireland that initially suffers the most. However, Dublin is
currently experiencing a building boom as firms quietly relocate to
Europe's only other English-speaking state. One of the three major

credit rating agencies, Standard & Poor's, made the prediction that Ireland would be the worst-hit, based on the current patterns of imports and exports of goods and services across the European Union (see Figure 8.4). If there were to be a hard border or other similar constraints, it is estimated that Ireland's economy would shrink by up to 10 per cent due to lost exports – all else being equal.[62] A total of 14,000 jobs in Ireland's racing industry might be at risk, if horses are not allowed the same free movement they currently have under EU rules. But all else will not be equal. Ireland, and especially Dublin, could pick up a very large number of jobs that will have to move out of London to somewhere nearby, to be within the EU. There is nowhere else in Europe quite so nearby where so many people normally speak English. As of July 2018, a hard border with Ireland is probably off the cards, but if talks stall at the very last moment, then nothing is agreed until everything is agreed.

FIGURE 8.4: COUNTRIES PROJECTED TO BE MOST HARMED BY A UK EXIT FROM THE EU

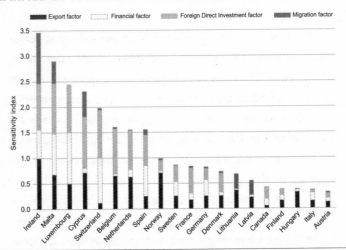

Estimates published on 9 June 2016, just before the Brexit referendum, by Standard & Poor's.[63]

The situation in Ireland is further harmed by commentators who believe that 'it is difficult to disagree with the conclusion ... that the so-called grievances and complaints [of Catholics in Northern Ireland in the 1970s] that have been publicised all over the world have been hugely exaggerated'[64]. This particular commentator currently holds the position of chief economic advisor of the think tank Policy Exchange, writing numerous articles in support of Brexit from a minority unionist perspective.[65] The majority of people in Northern Ireland voted to Remain.

Commenting on the Standard & Poor's findings, Panicos Demetriades, the former governor of the central bank of Cyprus, wrote that, after Ireland, 'Next in line are Malta, Luxembourg and Cyprus – all three of which have significant trading links with the UK. But they are the smallest countries in Europe with hardly a voice in Brexit negotiations.'[66] Cyprus came close to leaving the EU, or at least the euro, but at the last moment it chose not to crash out. People there remain very thankful.

Demetriades concluded:

In March 2013, Cyprus' political leaders realised – just before time was about to run out – that it was much safer taking what was on the table than engaging in a game of chicken where they had much more at stake than the other side. Four years later, the government is taking the credit for a recovery aided by an EU–IMF bailout, all the while criticising Europe for its treatment of Cyprus during those negotiations. By declaring that she is getting ready for a no-deal Brexit, Theresa May probably thinks she is making a well-calculated gamble that will help her own political survival. But I wonder if she or her advisers have contemplated how they will escape from the avalanche of economic and political repercussions as we get closer to March 2019 without a deal. Studying cases where other countries came close to leaving the EU could be a good starting point.

He has a point, but does he know how stubborn and pig-headed the British can be?

Cypriots might have thought that they were supremely able when it comes to digging their heads in the sand and prolonging an argument for some time, but they are mere amateurs at being obstinate in comparison to the mother country of their one-time colonial overlords. Britain ruled Cyprus from 1878 to 1960. Still, look on the bright side – the Cypriots as well as almost all the rest of the world will be able to tell the erstwhile mother country, 'We told you it wouldn't work.' Former colonies know they are truly free when they look back at the motherland and offer it help, guidance and perhaps some aid if things go really badly wrong. There is always hope. And most people, especially in more equitable countries, are pro-social. Now is the time for the pro-social majority to take back control over the egotistical and narcissistic few who have dominated the UK, and especially England, for too long.

Had the UK not voted for Brexit in 2016, the debate would simply have rumbled on. The Brexiteers would have called for, and eventually won, the right to hold a second referendum. At some point they might well have won that, or even a third one. All the time, the level of hatred and fear of immigrants would have been stoked up. And, all the time, everything that went wrong in the UK would have been blamed on 'the elite' having interfered in the 2016 referendum and having prevented a Leave victory. The Conservative government would have had the time they needed to have privatised the National Health service more fully; they would have converted thousands of secondary schools to become secondary moderns again, and a few to become grammars, as they had promised. And a fire in a block of flats in Kensington would just have been treated as a one-off unfortunate event, not a portent of our times. There were fires in tower blocks in London in the years immediately before Grenfell from which not only were lessons not learnt, but the fires themselves were increasingly being accepted as unfortunate but inevitable and hardly newsworthy events even when people died. Housing would have been left even more to the mercy of the market, rather than being seen as the responsibility of the state to solve. Without even having left, so much is already so different because of Brexit. So many bad things have not happened because the government has not had the parliamentary time to make them happen – because it has had to spend almost all its time arguing about Brexit. Britain does and did not need to leave; but it does and did need to change.

CHAPTER 9

WHY NOT BREXIT?

I was in this studio on referendum night … and the polls at that point were telling us there was going to be a 10-point advantage to Remain. So I put some money on. And it's still paying my office drinks bill.

– [Now former] Brexit Secretary David Davis tells LBC radio that he made £1,000 betting Britain would vote Leave, January 2017.[1]

INTRODUCTION

There have been many suggestions as to what lay behind the UK's vote to leave the EU. It was partly British politicians incorrectly blaming the EU and immigration for the state of the economy, rather than looking to their own tolerance of gross economic inequality. But how much of the vote, especially the older vote, also concerned racism regarding immigration, or giving the governing elites a poke in the eye?[2] There have been a great many untruths told about Brexit. David Davis, the first Brexit Secretary, was speaking to LBC radio in January 2017. He is against minimum alcohol pricing. His former chief of staff described him as being 'drunk, bullying and inappropriate'.[3] Did he really spend less than £5 a day on his office drinks bill?[4]

Davis was replaced by Dominic Raab as the second Brexit

Secretary. In 2017, Raab, then Justice Secretary, was criticised for describing the concerns of a disabled woman and her demands for action as a 'childish wish list'.[5] In April 2018, his diary secretary was reported to have said, 'He finds it difficult dealing with women. He's very dismissive.'[6] On 24 July, within just a couple of weeks of being appointed Brexit Secretary, Theresa May took personal charge of his key role in that job.[7] Raab was a vocal Leave supporter, wanting an end to the humiliation – as he saw it – of having to work collectively with other European countries. For Raab, the full humiliation was only just beginning.

Former BBC business correspondent, later ITV political editor, Robert Peston had written a year earlier, in October 2017:

> Victorious Leave was a coalition of those who feared they had lost control of their country and those who feared they had lost control of their livelihoods. They wanted an end to the humiliation of kowtowing to foreigners and an easing of the never-ending struggle to make ends meet. Boris, Gove and the leaders of Vote Leave promised all that. Whereas from the other side, the Stronger In camp, it was all dire warnings from David Cameron and George Osborne that things would only get sh***** if we left the EU. It was hope versus fear. And for millions who didn't think their lives could get much worse – and who quite liked the idea of giving a bloody nose to the posh boys, Cameron and Osborne – hope inevitably won.'[8]

Hope won in 2016; hope over fear. Hope was originally in the subtitle of this book, and even though the publisher quite rightly deleted the phrase as it did not describe most of what you have just read, it is now time to try to end with a little more hope. In 2017 and 2018, the situation looked dire. By the summer of 2018, the British side of the negotiations to leave were in the hands of a man who had, in effect, been told at the very start of those summer negotiations that he could not be trusted by his own Prime Minister. If ever there was a need for hope, it is now.

THE UK WAS ALONE

The United Kingdom was already on its own in Europe long before it was even announced that there would be a referendum. Most people were becoming poorer, despite the country as a whole becoming richer, as Figure 9.1 shows.

In March 2017, the *Financial Times* statistical journalist Valentina Romei explained:

Between 2007 and 2015, the UK was the only big advanced economy in which wages contracted while the economy expanded. In most other countries, including France and Germany, both the economy and wages have grown. Italy and Portugal are yet to reach their pre-crisis levels on both measures, while in Finland and Spain real wages grew in periods of economic contraction. The UK sits on its own as a rich economy that experienced a strong economic performance while the real wages of its workers dropped.[9]

Figure 9.1 shows very clearly what she was describing in words, in just one simple picture. The UK with its recessional mindset, its growth of poorly paid zero-hours contracts, and much else besides, stood out like a sore thumb.

Britain had become the only large country in Europe that had seen unemployment fall, only to be replaced by an increase in numbers of people working in ever more precarious lower-paid jobs. This was the longest period of earnings stagnation in 150 years: stagnation that still continues for the majority today.[10] However, the data used to draw Figure 9.1 was not revealed until 2017, a year after the 2016 vote. It applied to the change in living standards before the vote, to the economic change between 2007 and 2015. It showed the UK sitting all alone.

FIGURE 9.1: THE UK WAS ALONE AMONG ADVANCED COUNTRIES IN THE WORLD IN 2015

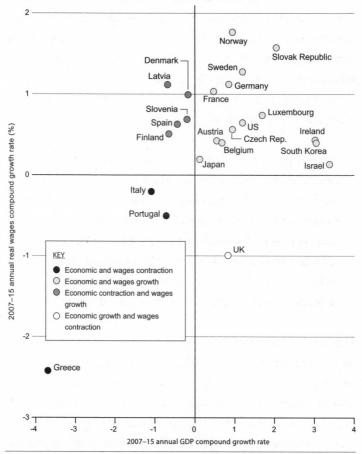

How the UK differed from all other affluent countries in 2015: economic growth but falling wages.[11]

At least in Greece, when the country became richer, everyone benefited. In Britain, as soon as any economic recovery began, the rich pocketed all the proceeds – at the expense of the large majority. Such a scenario is only achievable with uncontrolled greed at the very top and a prevailing spirit of meanness. UK government policy at the time was to reduce taxation for the best-off individuals and for corporations, to have an extremely lax attitude to tax avoidance, coupled with draconian austerity for the least well-off, including brutally sanctioning millions of people for the slightest welfare benefit rule infringements. The result was revealed in 2018 as being a far bigger squeeze on living standards than had ever been realised before.[12]

WHAT MAY HAPPEN NOW?

In January 2018, Theresa May gave a speech in Davos. It was not well attended. She began to conclude by telling the small audience listening to her that 'the United Kingdom has a proud history of stepping up and seizing the opportunities of our time. We stand ready to do so again.'[13] But, as the *New York Times* reported it, 'By that point, several [of the very few] people attending the speech were standing and walking toward the exits.' The Americans could not help but express pity. Theresa and Britain were, again, alone in the room. Sometimes the search for hope looks hopeless.

Today, as a number of people, including many senior civil servants, have suggested, the British are in a very bad place. The British have already lost what little economic growth had occurred before the referendum took place[14] and seen their wages go down in real terms, with the highest rates of decline recorded since the 1860s.[15] Even when there was a rise in pay in late 2018, it was still barely keeping up with inflation.[16] At the very same time, there has been rapidly rising inequality in school education since 2010 as a direct result of a government policy of cutting funding for state education.[17] Almost everyone has been badly affected: children, working-age adults and especially the elderly.

Death rates have risen, with about 120,000 excess deaths being recorded between 2010 and 2017.[18] The year 2018 was even worse.[19] Rising life expectancy in the UK has stalled in a way that has not been seen since the 1860s. So many people would still be alive now were it not for the appalling record of the government on health and social care since 2010, and an anticipated extra one million previously expected years of life are now projected to be lost by 2057 if these trends are not altered.[20] By late October 2018, it had become clear that life expectancy in the UK was still below its 2014 peak and infant mortality was now steadily rising.[21] Nowhere else in Europe had such a bad recent record.

Those in charge of Brexit tried to suggest that the EU would suffer when the UK left, and other countries might try to leave. In fact, by November 2017 the EU Commissioner for economic and financial affairs recorded that 'we [meaning the EU27] have entered a new phase of economic recovery, with stronger growth driven by resilient consumption'.[22] Even if the British tried to revoke Article 50 at the last hour and remain in the EU as they were, they would never recover fully from the damage that voting for Brexit has already done. Britain, if it cannot swallow an enormous amount of humble pie, will almost certainly have to leave on economically poorer terms, regardless of events. No one is sure, because this has never been done before. But we do know that the British are not good at eating humble pie and being able to say sorry – it is not a 'British value'.

When Greenland left what was then the European Economic Community in 1985, it followed three years of negotiations, not the two that Britain has. There was no Article 50 process as regards Greenland's exit because the treaty of which that article is a part did not then exist. The population of Greenland, at 56,000, was more than 1,000 times smaller than the UK and still they spent three years sorting things out.

As one of the negotiators then put it, 'If it took Greenland more than two years to negotiate mainly on fisheries, in my eyes it will be an immense job for the UK and it will take many more years before they find a valid solution.'[23] On top of that, anyone in Greenland who keeps Danish citizenship is still an EU citizen. Greenland never really left, even though 52 per cent of people there voted to leave. But it had fish, a lot of fish. It had something worth hanging on to and talking about, so the EU negotiated over that. And the EU kept hold of a great deal of those fishing rights and gave the Greenlanders some useful rights in return. Greenland is currently one of the EU's overseas countries and territories (see Figure 2.3 in Chapter 2 above) and receives EU funding for sustainable development, with a focus on education, currently equivalent to a significant €550 per person per year. In 2015, a joint declaration about closer relations between the EU and Greenland was signed by Denmark, Greenland and the EU.[24] Greenland had once been a Danish colony; now it was a sovereign country very closely entwined in the European Union.

The European Union is also greatly strengthened by the UK trying to leave. It is now very clear to other countries what the repercussions for them of toying with the idea of leaving would be. After many decades of cross-border trade and movement of people, leaving is now unimaginable for almost every member of the EU27, especially for all countries with a substantial land border with another EU country. The migrant crisis of 2015/16, which caused the closure of some borders and weakened Angela Merkel's leadership in Germany because she welcomed in so many refugees, will be solved eventually without the EU breaking up.

Having no land borders or just short ones (like the Irish border) is partly why it was Greenland that left first and the UK that tried second. It is why the citizens of Gibraltar voted so desperately in such large numbers to Remain, because of a land border with Spain. The UK is helping to demonstrate the problems of leaving for everyone else to see. As a result, Greece (which has a land border with Bulgaria) is currently being welcomed back into the heart of the EU, and talk of leaving in Greece is rapidly subsiding. The core of the EU is strengthening. Ever-closer union will mean ever-closer union from now onwards. And, for a time, the UK will almost certainly not be a part of that, unless it decides at the very last minute that it cannot afford to leave. Because the British elite so very much hate embarrassment, they would rather suffer greatly than admit to having made a mistake – that is not the British way. Stiff upper lip, walk tall, never apologise. The worst fear of Britain's Conservative leader is asking the other twenty-seven members of the EU if the UK could change its mind and not leave, and then being told it must go – imagine the humiliation.

As of December 2017, a soft Brexit appeared to be on the cards. At that time, it was realised that a hard Brexit would be a disaster with no sensible agreement on trade and borders. Most of the British government and many of their supporters knew that. There were, however, a few in the Conservative Party such as Boris Johnson, Andrea Leadsom and Liam Fox, who all stood for the Tory leadership in 2016, who in the run-up to that Christmas were portraying themselves as amazingly staunch supporters of a hard Brexit. They appeared not to realise just how disastrous a hard exit would be and, because of such poor thinking, it appeared at that time that such a thing could happen. Later, a day after he resigned as Foreign Secretary, Boris Johnson commented on Theresa May's chosen path (the 'Chequers plan', as it was called in July 2018) that, if it were followed, 'we are truly headed for the status of colony – and many will struggle to see the economic or political advantages of that particular arrangement'.[25] This led many to ask, if Boris thinks the former British Empire was such a great thing, what is so wrong with being a colony for a time?

To the Brexiteers, a soft exit would be an expression of national failure. A soft Brexit would probably not be great. The British would lose the right to vote in the European Parliament. But at least free movement of labour and goods and science funding would remain. It would lessen the blow to Britain's economic and education systems. In late 2017, there was even speculation that it was possible that Boris Johnson wanted a soft Brexit, but wanted to be able in the future to claim (falsely) that it would have been so much better if there had been a hard Brexit. What everyone did know was that Boris very badly wanted to be Prime Minister. There had been so much 'playing politics' for anticipated personal benefit. Trust in Tory politicians was at an all-time low by this point.

After any kind of Brexit, Britain would have no MEPs, so Nigel Farage would be out of a job in that Parliament. Ironically, he said he didn't intend to give up his £73,000-a-year EU pension, which would be part-funded by the EU 'divorce bill'.[26] After Brexit, Britain will have no representatives in the Council of Ministers. So the rest of the EU could be left to get on with their necessary reforms. They would also no longer have to put up with the British Conservative Party and UKIP MEPs allying themselves with the far-right Polish Law and Justice Party, Alternative for Deutschland, and other new neo-Nazi groups that may arise on the mainland. The great bulk of the largest far-right bloc in the European Parliament, right of mainstream European Conservatives, comes from Britain.

AGAIN, HOW DID WE GET HERE?

European elections are held every five years. There has been a slow creep in the UK towards greater acceptance of the far-right perspective over the past few decades, from the BNP to UKIP. This has gradually normalised and desensitised the British to the bigotries of individuals in more moderate political parties, with detrimental effects to both the wider UK economy and society. In the 1979 and 1984 European elections in the UK, no far-right candidates stood, or if they did they gained almost no votes. In 1989, the National Front secured less than 1 in 1,000 votes. In 1994, UKIP won 1 in 100 votes. In 1999, UKIP and the BNP together won 7.5 per cent of all the votes, with their combined share rising to 20.4 per cent in 2004. And then, in 2009, the position of the Conservatives became ambiguous.

In 2009, the British Conservative Party was moving towards the European far-right, but UKIP, the BNP and English Democrats still secured 23.8 per cent – almost a quarter of all the votes in the European elections of that year. If we then add half the Tory 2009 vote to that (as no one knew where the Tories really stood in 2009), far-right parties gained 37.6 per cent of the EU parliamentary vote in 2009. The Conservatives had stopped being a centre-right party in Europe in 2009 and were moving to become a far-right party in the run-up to the EU referendum. Adding half their vote to the far-right bloc may be underestimating just how far to the right the party had moved.

A normal European Conservative Party would never support, let alone introduce, a referendum on EU membership. The British Conservatives left the mainstream in 2014 and joined the misleadingly titled European Conservatives and Reformists group of seventy-four MEPs. Its title is misleading because it does not include other European Conservatives! But it does include AfD, said by the BBC to be 'tinged with Nazi overtones'.[27]

In 2014, and with the British Conservatives now well and truly aligned to an odd collection of other far-right groups in Europe with their new European parliamentary grouping, their entire share of 23.1 per cent can be added to UKIP's 26.6 per cent and the Ulster Unionists' 0.51 per cent, to conclude (in hindsight) that some 50.2 per cent of all those who voted in the 2014 European elections in the UK voted for parties to the right of mainstream European conservatives (51.9 per cent when other, even more minor far-right parties are added). That is quite a journey in a very short time (Table 9.1).[28] The British do not see their Conservatives as far-right because, for the most recent four decades, the entire British state was moving towards the political right. Governments of every political label were introducing more free, rather than fair, market policies, privatising public goods, introducing student loans, and all the time telling the general public that this was good for them.

In many ways, what has happened (so far) had to happen. The British could no longer adapt and evolve. They had hit a brick wall. The issue of Europe had been splitting the Tory Party apart since at least the days of John Major's premiership. As soon as Margaret Thatcher resigned, the in-fighting in the Tory Party became very visible – because only she could control 'the vegetables', as *Spitting Image* suggested she called them. That was 1990. Since then, it has been twenty-eight years of Tory civil war. Brexit is the endgame of that squabbling. By July 2018, the fighting was beginning to get very nasty. The Conservative Party was on the verge of tearing itself apart. So, who said there isn't hope? As (leading Eurosceptic Tory) Jacob Rees-Mogg has repeatedly threatened, the chances of a Tory split have not been this good since 1846, with the repeal of the Corn Laws. After that event, the Tories did not secure a majority in Parliament for twenty-eight years. When they did make it back into power, they were much transformed and under the leadership of Disraeli. Back then, their party survived, but no political party survives for ever.

TABLE 9.1: SHARE OF THE VOTE TO PARTIES TO THE RIGHT OF MAINSTREAM CONSERVATIVES, UK IN ALL EUROPEAN ELECTIONS 1979–2014

1979:	0.0 per cent
1984:	0.0 per cent
1989:	0.1 per cent
1994:	1.1 per cent
1999:	7.5 per cent
2004:	20.4 per cent
2009:	37.6 per cent
2014:	51.9 per cent

Half of Conservative votes are assigned to the right of European Conservatives in 2009 because their position at that point was ambiguous. By 2014, the UK Conservatives were formally allied with far-right parties in Europe and no longer at all associated with the main EPP block. In 2004, the Conservatives were in EPP-ED, UKIP got 15.6 per cent of the vote, BNP 4.8 per cent. In 1999, UKIP got 6.5 per cent, BNP 1 per cent. In 1994, UKIP got 1.0 per cent, National Front 0.1 per cent. In 1989, the National Front won less than 0.1 per cent.[29]

What is good about the Brexit process is the unravelling of unfairness. Because of unfair deals made by Mrs Thatcher, the British did not pay their fair share into the European Union. That now ends.

The dominant Leave position was that foreigners in some shape or form were to blame for the country's social and economic ills. That was a very unfair conclusion. That now ends as a credible idea. In the months and years to come, no matter how we leave (and especially if we don't), the Brexiteers will undoubtedly claim that the reason Britain is still failing is that the EU gave it unfair terms. Notwithstanding their excuses, outside the EU, Britain will be responsible for its own situation. Indeed, even inside the EU, its misfortunes were largely of its elite's own making.

Remain was led by Prime Minister David Cameron who, for self-serving ends, had also often claimed that foreigners were mainly to blame for people's poor wages, lack of housing and an 'unaffordable' benefits bill. He moderated his spoken views at the last minute to try to prevent Brexit, but the Conservative Party's racist and xenophobic opportunism of the recent past had already rotted much of the political fabric. The Leave campaign were able to use these oft-repeated lies to make a shabby patchwork quilt of new lies and so avoid the big economic questions and consequences of Brexit being scrutinised. Thankfully, today that shoddy scapegoating and patriotic baloney is unravelling under the glare of reality. Not that that will stop Nigel Farage and his friends spouting it until well after everyone else has become bored stiff of hearing it. But the hope is that most people will now see through the lies. There is no gold at the end of the Brexit rainbow.

The British in 2018 were starting to hear much more about how they were benefiting from the EU. For example, the UK had been taking a larger share of EU science budgets than any other country. That now ends. The researchers have begun to leave. The money they spent while living in the UK leaves, new students do not come, facilities are not built, builders are not employed, discoveries are not made, or at least not in the UK; innovation atrophies. So, what were Labour doing about it and why were they not following the lead of the few Liberals in Parliament in calling for the cancellation of Article 50?

Under Corbyn, Labour was playing a canny game. Brexit won the vote. People couldn't just be asked to vote again to get the 'right' result. The key issues had not been debated. Corbyn's position of remain and reform was hardly covered in the referendum campaign by the media, probably because so many in the conforming mainstream so distrusted his more radical stance in other areas. His reforms were often not reforms that the wealthy really wanted. These reforms were hardly ever mentioned. However, his reservations about the EU were covered in great detail.[30]

Most people cannot be persuaded by abstract discussions about institutions. They make judgements on concrete issues, notably those that affect living standards. So Labour say they will be led by what is best for the overwhelming majority of people in Britain, not by abstract ideas of sovereignty. It is, for example, in the interest of the majority that Britain continues to receive high science funding from the Continental mainland. Those monies spread out of the research institutes and universities in a way that the wealth of the super-rich never trickles down.

Labour was in favour of staying in a customs union as well, so the BMW plant in Oxford could continue operating, as well as the Nissan factory in Sunderland. In June 2018, most Labour MPs abstained on an amendment on whether Britain should try to remain in the European Economic Area also. They didn't vote against it, as the Conservatives did. They were playing the long game.

With thirty-five seats in the Westminster Parliament, the Scottish National Party was the third most important contender, and the Parliament they controlled in Scotland was vehemently opposed to Brexit. They would not help the Conservatives. In contrast, it was the Liberal Democrats that kept the Conservatives in office until 2015 and thereby made the run-up to Brexit possible. With just twelve MPs in Parliament in 2018, they were largely an irrelevance. The one Green Party MP was more effective in her contributions, as were the four Plaid Cymru MPs. But it was the ten Democratic Unionist MPs who were keeping the government in power, all the way through the political turbulence in the autumn of 2018. They appeared not to realise that by supporting the Conservative attempts to achieve Brexit for Britain they may well have hastened the day that Ireland as a whole is politically reunited.

The Labour Party position of not accepting a deal which makes people worse off than the current relationship with the EU is a great rule of thumb for the vast majority of people. It allowed Labour to make judgements at each twist and turn of events, not driven by a rigid ideology, and it might also be a means of gradually persuading people to reject hard Brexit. The debate that should have taken place about Brexit before the referendum only started to take place in the last few months of 2017. Necessity is the mother of invention.

A PLACE IN THE SUN?

Many British people retired to Spain, where they enjoyed a warmer climate and good healthcare at the expense of others. That now ends. The British imported and exploited young Europeans to do everything from picking fruit in their farms, to changing sheets in their hotels, to delivering their babies, to inventing in their multi-cultural science laboratories. That largely now ends. More than half of the skilled workers from the EU living in Britain in 2017 said that they were considering leaving or had already decided to leave.[31] The unskilled workers from Poland were already leaving in great numbers because the fall in the value of the pound meant it was not worth staying in Britain compared with going elsewhere in Europe. You can tell when something is about to fail when large numbers of people begin to leave. So much for being able to control migration.

The marriage of the UK and Europe was exploitative and one-sided – the UK's most affluent benefited; the rest of the EU and poorer people in the UK less so. Britain could no longer enjoy hosting all that highly enthusiastic and highly skilled labour so cheaply, and, subsequently, most of those workers, consumers, citizens and thinkers returned to mainland Europe when they were no longer needed because, in so many ways, Britain was never – really – that welcoming. But the British were good at appearing to be polite hosts. Now that the true feelings of so many have been revealed, Britain has an image problem.

If Britain does leave, then one day part of Britain may well re-join. Perhaps only Scotland at first, or Northern Ireland. Then even possibly London. The City of London is already a law unto itself. The UK need not all re-join at once; just as Slovenia joined the EU in 2004, Croatia in 2017, but Bosnia and Serbia remain outside for now.

What originally brought Great Britain together in that Act of Union of 1707 has long gone. With no empire, what is there to stay together for? The children of the empire, the home nations and the Commonwealth, all have their own futures. A shared interest between them can no longer be exploited. As we get nearer and nearer to 29 March 2019, it becomes time for more home truths to be spoken. The rest of the so-called Commonwealth care so little about the future of that loose affiliation that in the spring of 2018 they agreed to Prince Charles being its next head. If they had cared, the next leader of the Commonwealth would have been from India.

Britain leaving the EU is often talked about as a divorce, especially when what has to be determined includes a financial settlement – what the UK owes the EU. But the divorce could just as easily be within the UK. Scotland can still leave the rest of the UK. If it leaves, what is it owed for all the Scottish oil revenues England squandered? Thatcher cut taxes for the rich (i.e. mainly the English) on the back of North Sea oil revenues in the 1980s. The great arguments for reparation may have only just begun. England may find out that it has a great many debts. Should not the former colonies, the Commonwealth, be asking Prince Charles for reparations for slavery when he is king? Perhaps there is a reason for not opposing his anointment as the future head of the Commonwealth. Can you imagine his mumbled reply to such a request?

What too of Gibraltar: is it now better off with Spain? Some 98 per cent support remaining British, but 96 per cent voted to remain in the EU. What if they have to make a choice in future between those two options? What of the Channel Islands, the Bailiwicks of Jersey and Guernsey, including Brecqhou, where the Barclay brothers reside? What if the UK leaves the EU, and Britain technically gets the same status – as far as the European mainland is concerned – as small North African islands in the

Mediterranean? No one tries to put their money there. Why would Britain, outside of the EU, be seen as safe?

What of the future of the Isle of Man, another hideout for the cash of the very wealthy? What of all the other British Overseas Territories,[32] which, when Britain was powerful, each had some interest in not joining its nearest neighbour or going it alone? After all, the islands themselves do not benefit that much from being tax havens. They cannot when they hardly collect any taxes.

All the woes of the treasure islands provide further evidence that change is inevitable. Brexit is a disaster, but it is a disaster with many silver linings – most of which none of us saw coming. The Tory Party, that relic of a bygone era of bigotry, snobbery and nastiness, is finally on the ropes. The artificial merging of what is left of Ireland with Wales, England and Scotland may even at some point come to an end and, short of invasion by a foreign power, it is hard to see anything that could have brought the day of reckoning forward faster than this. Brexit could be a major staging post in the transformation of devolution into dissolution. And, as we explained above, England itself is divided. Nowhere else in Europe, not even Germany shortly after its reunification, is (or ever was) as divided as England has become. The variation in life chances between the regions of England is greater than anywhere else in Europe and it has been that way for several decades.[33] Within England there has been internal colonialism. It is not a 'united' kingdom. It is well worth repeating: the north-east region is now as poor as many poorer parts of Eastern Europe. When one of us lived in Newcastle, the Jesmond and Gosforth area of that city where the (mostly southern English-born) elite lived was referred to as the 'white highlands', a colonial term.

States that lose their empires, their status and their self-belief, and finally their reason to be, are prime candidates for internal fracture. In the late 1980s, that is what happened to the USSR, with Russia left as a weakened country, dominated by Moscow.

The Ottoman Empire disintegrated after the First World War, with a little help from Western imperialists splitting its dominions up between them. Istanbul is today one of the three mega-cities on the edge of Europe because of that legacy, the other two being Moscow and London. There is no oversized city within Europe in between these three. They are the three most populous cities of Europe because they are each the former heart of a bygone empire.

Britain has the opportunity to buck the trend if it accepts that its empire status and pretensions are truly over, but the portents are not good. When empires fall, individuals may then try to revive them and try to revive the Spirit of Empire. President Erdoğan in Turkey is now attempting a version of Ottoman Empire 2.0 and trying to take control of more territory. But he is hampered by a society with a strong split between secularists and supporters of Islam, and a Kurdish population that wants its own country. Russia under President Putin is eyeing up possible expansion of territory again, and 'took back' Crimea recently. The USA is another empire slowly losing its power and now either contemplating some desperate actions abroad in North Korea, or pretending to be friends with its dodgy leader, while also supporting proxy wars in Syria and the Yemen. In contrast, confident China only worries about its local South China Sea. But even the most patriotic in China are not planning to claim that China is 'Great', as some in Britain are so frequently tempted to do. Many people in China have been quietly watching and learning from the follies of Western powers. They have had long enough to do so.

HEINEKEN REACHES THE PARTS OTHER MAPS CANNOT REACH

In 1992, Freddy Heineken, the Dutch beer magnate, proposed a new map of Europe, a Europe of the regions. National borders were to be broken up in the case of the largest countries so that Europe would become a set of seventy-five regions. No small group of coun-tries would dominate as the UK, Germany, France, Spain and Italy currently do. All would be relatively equal. His suggestions were ridiculed as utopian at the time, not least because he gave it the title Eurotopia. Later it was realised that he had predicted the breakup of Yugoslavia and Czechoslovakia with remarkable accuracy.[34] He also proposed a united Ireland and a separate Scotland – which in 1992 appeared ridiculous, but today looks less silly.

FIGURE 9.2: HOW THE UK COULD BREAK UP – AS PREDICTED IN 1992

Part of a much larger pan-European suggestion for better borders in Europe.[35]

The borders Heineken suggested were not arbitrary. He worked with two historians to produce his booklet, provocatively titled *The United States of Europe, A Eurotopia?* At the time, in the early 1990s, Eastern Europe was in turmoil and the Maastricht Treaty of that year was turning the European alliance into a political union, not just an economic one.

In the future Europe that Heineken envisaged, each of the seventy-five states would have a population of between 5 and 10 million people. States of the USA average 6 million people. He suggested a capital city for each new state. In some cases, his historians were very clever. They did not suggest a state called Yorkshire, for example, but did suggest that the capital of what would be Northumbria should be York. See Figure 9.2 for the proposed new British Isles regions, and then imagine which might vote first in a referendum to re-join the EU in future? And which region would be last?

Eurotopia may never happen in the UK, but it is more likely now than it has been at any time since 1707, with that rise in probability being largely thanks to the outcome of the Brexit vote. The British need to finally understand that the empire won't return, that it was not a wonderful creation and that they are not for ever destined to sing 'Rule Britannia' at the Last Night of the Proms year after year after year. The British were never happy and glorious; they were ruthless despots.

RACISM MAKES YOU POORER

None of this should blind us to the bigger picture. In reality, there is probably less reason to be optimistic about the longer term economic impacts of Brexit than there was before the referendum. Then, many analysts, assuming that politicians will behave at least somewhat rationally, predicted that even if we voted for Brexit we would still end up remaining in the single market or something very similar.

– JONATHAN PORTES, 2018[36]

So, what will Brexit, even a soft, well-ordered Brexit, cost? By May 2018, the Governor of the Bank of England, Mark Carney, was saying it was near 2 per cent of all national income, or £900 less a year for every household. Boris Johnson vehemently disagreed, saying it was 'absolutely not the case'[37] but offering no evidence as to why it was not. Instead, he pointed out on the very same day that he thought he should have his own private plane to 'help him travel the world and promote the UK's interests', as the BBC politely put it;[38] one that was not grey like that shared by the Prime Minister and the Queen. This follows his suggestion of a new royal yacht and his support for a series of commemorative Brexit stamps. Perhaps next he'll suggest that a new Action Man is modelled on his own body, his physique, his hair style and his facial features. Except, given that he is no longer Foreign Secretary, he will need a new job first if he is to regain any credibility.

By the middle of the long hot summer of 2018, more and more commentators were beginning to realise just how weak the position of the UK had become. As Patrick Cockburn wrote in *The Independent*:

> Johnson's puerile bombast and jingoism has its uses because it neatly sums up what is not likely to happen: 'A great Brexit' he claimed 'will unite this party, unite this House and unite this nation.' But nothing is less likely to happen. Brexit is exacerbating all other grievances and divisions. These will be worse after Brexit than before. Britain is already weaker than at any time since the end of the Stuart monarchy.[39]

The debate over national sovereignty, and whether a national identity can include racial and ethnic minorities, European migrants and others, has to move beyond the pointless rhetoric of 'taking back control' and 'stopping immigration'. The economy in

Britain, as is becoming clearer, will be sadly diminished, if EU nationals are forced out of the country or simply decide to leave because so much of the mainstream media currently portrays them as unwanted in Britain. Despite such xenophobia and racism in our press, the four countries that make up the UK had in fact become relatively accepting of the multi-racial and multicultural nature of their local communities – but that ethos is not being strengthened by our present position, just as the four countries' reason to hold together with each other is now weakening year by year.

Younger people appear to be learning to live together better than their elders and are turning to a political party which does not appear so ethnocentric. A YouGov poll in June 2018 showed that 66 per cent of 18–24 year-olds would vote for a Corbyn-led Labour Party, while only 16 per cent of those aged 65 or above would.[40] Labour enjoys support from a far wider range of people from ethnic minorities than all other political parties combined. The Conservatives are now finally willing to put the spotlight on their few stars who are not white, but observing their party conference still requires looking at a sea of white faces. With every year that passes, Labour gains in strength. The more people are forced to rent, the more money they are made to borrow to study, the more that they see the health crisis for what it is, the more likely it is that they will vote Labour.[41]

The Conservatives no longer even benefit from population ageing, as life expectancy no longer rises under Conservative rule in 2018. And all these pro-Corbyn youngsters will be staying to vote in the UK as they can no longer easily move to the European mainland to find work or study in the future if Brexit goes badly. They will more often have to stay at home and vote. And then they can change everything – how people are housed, how well their health service is funded and how they are educated. They can do this because they both have hope and can see just how mistaken the Conservatives have been – not just on Brexit, but in their general incompetence. Brexit was the tip of the iceberg of Tory ineptitude. Brexit going so wrong leaves the party of stability wearing no clothes.

In July 2018, shortly before both the Brexit Secretary and the Foreign Secretary resigned, a key result of yet another opinion poll was released.[42] When asked between 6 and 8 July, 'Do you agree or disagree with: "Having greater control over immigration is more important than having access to free trade with the EU"', some 48 per cent (up 4 per cent in the space of a few weeks) favoured free trade with the EU, over the 38 per cent (down 5 per cent) who preferred to control immigration instead. Only around one seventh were undecided. Some peoples' views on Brexit in the UK are changing quickly; others are unbending and strongly felt. 'Don't knows' start having opinions, 'don't cares' start caring. The old die, the young become old enough to vote. Much is possible.

In the aftermath of great national disasters, such as having to fight a world war for a second time, great social changes were made: for instance, providing free secondary education to all children in 1944. As yet, there are few signs that those currently in charge of education at all levels are able or willing to think through what an education system for a globally oriented, sustainable and socially just state would look like. It would not include British history as it is currently taught. If our young people have to live in a post-Brexit disunited kingdom, they will need to rewrite the curriculum.

A day or so before Christmas 2017, it was suggested that foreigners should have to pay £10 to enter the UK after Brexit.[43] However, someone might well suggest that were this to happen, the EU should retaliate with a progressive entry fee: £0 for the large number of British people who live in households below the mean household income, but rising to £10,000 (per visit) for those with an income of more than £1 million. Why make the poor pay for the stupidity of the British elite? In fact, the EU27 could even give £10 (or €10) to poorer British people on entry if they taxed the richest British tourists enough to pay for it!

In June 2018, Parliament voted its approval for a third runway at Heathrow, perhaps in a bid to cope with the rising demand for wealthy people in Britain to have foreign holidays and spend their money abroad, as well as the demand for yet more business travel. However, the number of business trips is in fact falling. As the pound falls, the number of incoming tourist arrivals at Heathrow grows and the demand to visit Britain's museum attractions will rise. More foreigners may well pay to stand outside and gawp at Britain's relic and largely undemocratic Westminster Parliament with its separate 'houses' for commoners and lords; more may soon come to view the somewhat dowdy palaces of its extensive royal family, where even minor second cousins appear to get some handout; to walk around the outer walls of its old universities and be able to tick off the assumed birthplace of the bard from their bucket list with a trip to Stratford-upon-Avon. The planet will suffer greatly from the increased flights as more and more tourists land and depart each year at Heathrow, but in the short term, and while we are still working out what it is we can be good at in future, those tourist dollars will be vital.

HOPE AND WHAT CAN THE BRITISH BE GREAT AT?

For some, perhaps for a great many, until the very last hour there will remain a hope (which will be anathema to Leave supporters and the Brexit Club) that the letter Theresa May sent to the EU was only a notification of the UK's 'intention' to withdraw. Intentions can change, and Britain still has the right as a member state to change its mind, as other member states have done with their referendums. Article 50 is about voluntary withdrawal, not expulsion. Thus, the die is not cast, and the letter can be taken back. Or at least Lord Kerr, who wrote Article 50, thinks so.[44] This has been confirmed by other legal experts. Jean-Claude Piris, former legal counsel of the Council of Europe, suggested that it is clear that 'even after triggering Article 50 and notifying the EU of intention to leave, there is no legal obstacle to the UK changing its mind'. Sir David Edwards, UK judge in the European Court of Justice, agrees with this view.[45]

In November 2017, the government tried to give the impression that triggering Article 50 was irrevocable and refused to publish their own law officers' opinions. During the court case when Gina Miller made it clear that Parliament should have scrutiny of any leaving legislation, a government spokesman would only say 'it is a matter of firm policy' that the letter will not be taken back from Brussels. (Remember Attlee's criticism of Churchill: 'The trouble with Winston is that he nails his trousers to the mast, and then can't climb down.') By December 2017, the government had agreed to regulatory alignment: 'single market membership in all but name', according to staunch Brexiteer Gisela Stuart.[46] By July 2018, all was up in the air again and Parliament was about to stop sitting for the long summer recess. There was much talk of a transition arrangement being preferable, but, as we write, that is all still talk – nothing is agreed until everything is agreed.

Cosying up to the USA is also not a viable option for the UK any more. The UK is no longer conveniently located to be 'Airstrip One', as Orwell once put it. It is still the place that has 'lost an empire and has not yet found a role' as former US Secretary of State Dean Acheson explained on 5 December 1962.[47] In fact, Americans recognise that the only interest Trump has in the UK is to try to make himself look like the big man: 'Trump delights in embarrassing European leaders; their squirming is his triumph,'[48] wrote Jeffrey Sachs in 2018. He suggested that Europe should gang up with China to prevent the USA from getting away with breaking international law and bullying Iran. In this game, you don't want to end up being the mostly forgotten sidekick to the bully. The 'special relationship' is over.

It would be both highly ironic and extremely welcome if Brexit resulted in us standing less in awe of the US, and becoming more European; becoming more equal, ceasing to admire wealth and greed unquestionably, and not believing the market should always be king. Currently, we often look to the US to find solutions in education (hence introducing university fees), health and social care, and welfare. We would do better by looking to Europe first instead. Mainland Europeans have no or low educational fees for almost every school and university. As with wars, the final outcome can be the antithesis of what the 'winners' were intending.

The English language, although it now works more to an American advantage, is still a winner, despite President Trump's granddaughter singing in Mandarin to the Chinese President on a recent visit. Even Britain's universities, despite staff being increasingly overloaded by administration and stressed by the temporary nature of most contracts, can be marketed as international magnets for liberal, free and imaginative thinking, at least if they could only resist the urge to become so commercial and point-scoring, concerned mainly with league tables. Globally, people – often but not always (and perhaps a little less each year) – still trust British universities to be unbiased, fair and not corrupt. But Brexit does not enhance the reputation of UK universities abroad.

Despite all the woes laid out in these pages, there is still much hope. The situation in the UK could be so much worse than it is. For instance, YouTube is full of videos with titles such as 'Corruption is Legal in America'[49] based on serious academic papers that 'provide substantial support for theories of Economic-Elite

Domination' – in other words, showing that politicians in the United States almost exclusively do only what the rich want them to do.[50]

Primary and secondary education could be great if the British incorporated more private schools into the state system through nationalisation. Many once affluent families in our non-Empire-2.0 future will no longer be able to afford the private fees. That education also needs to incorporate more truths about imperialism and the actual current world position of the UK into the curriculum, rather than teaching jingoism. We cannot continue teaching the story of industrialisation as if it involved no African slaves, no destruction of the Indian textile industry, no forced sales of opium to China – among so much else that we do not mention to our children. As the countries of Britain become poorer, they simply cannot afford private education on the scale at which they have supported it up to now, particularly when it is deeply uninformative. Nowhere else in Europe comes close to Britain on school segregation based on parents' ability to pay for their children's education, nor do they present their children with a curriculum that tells such a selective story about the past.

Incorporation of private schools need not be compulsory. Currently, private schools have charitable status and other tax avoidance schemes allowing them and their pupils' parents' significant tax breaks.[51] Parents put money in tax-free schemes to pay for future fees, or grandparents donate school fees to avoid later inheritance tax, and VAT is not paid by the schools. This results in the government effectively paying as much as half of the costs of private school tuition and boarding by way of uncollected taxes, and hence spending dramatically more per child than they spend on state school children. This is part of what the case to properly tax private schools is about. Such schools can hardly claim to be 'helping the poor'.

Of course, the UK government subsidises private schools. How else could the parents of 7 per cent of children possibly afford it? Only a fraction (less than one seventh) will be in the top 1 per cent. If the government were to put that money into state schools, they could be radically improved. Private schools could gradually, but not completely, disappear as they become, in fact as well as in theory, a commercial nonsense. A few might survive, largely as a curiosity for the world's richest and their unfortunate children. In other affluent countries, private schools are very rare and only for the least able children of the richest – hence they are so often pitied, if they go to one in Germany, or Finland, or Greece. Prince Philip went to the Schule Schloss Salem in Germany, which today charges fees of €30,000 (£26,000) a year for the youngest children who board there, and more for the older ones.[52] He subsequently attended its twinned school, Gordonstoun in Scotland, which Prince Charles is reported to have hated as a pupil there himself in later years. In Germany, private schools are seen as a place for children who cannot keep up in the state system. In Britain, Gordonstoun has a reputation for brutality, as revealed most recently in an American-made royal TV history. When he first attended, aged thirteen, Prince Charles is said to have been caged naked in a basket and left under a cold shower.[53]

Currently, the British are trying to grow an export market where they provide very poor-quality education to hundreds of thousands of overseas students from affluent backgrounds. The most lucrative nation of all to target is China. As one academic who used to run the Institute for Media and Creative Industries at Loughborough University London (yes, that is in London, not in Loughborough) explained in 2018, his institute could charge £17,500 ($25,000) a year to overseas students from China to take a master's degree in London and they 'don't need a relevant first degree … The result? Extremely pleasant and interesting grad students arrive, virtually none of whom can write English using conventional syntax or grammar.'[54] The British university makes a profit from them, just enough to underwrite its losses elsewhere, but this is not a 'long-term economic plan', as will eventually be discovered.

One suggestion for the economic future of Britain is not to try to attract overseas school children to private schools here, but instead to open up new private schools catering for the offspring of City bankers. This is for the international financial elite who, as Frederick Studemann put it in the *Financial Times*, routinely 'plug their kids into transferable international exam systems'[55] but today are put off sending them away 'to board' – in the old empire way. Studemann went on to suggest that the decisive factor that will determine which European cities take the most bankers will be their school opportunities: 'Forget all the talk of regulatory equivalence, passporting, office space, transport connections, one minister's red lines, another's implementation phase. The secret to wooing refugees from the City is likely to be found in the classroom.'

We have mentioned tourism several times before and it is worth repeating it again. Tourism will continue to be a winner, provided that enough people are prepared to work in the industry, where jobs are far too low-paid currently. Scottish and Welsh castles and wildernesses, Shakespeare and Stratford, Stonehenge, the Giant's Causeway and countless other attractions can be marketed to the world. In some ways, the whole of the UK can be marketed as a museum, a living history of what happens when an industrial revolution and an empire gives way to a smaller version of itself, but is still of interest and historical value. The public pageantry of the British royal family can continue to be part of the living heritage, their European descent and new American links being stressed, but perhaps living more simply, like other European royal families – with fewer houses and only the immediate family being funded by the state – no more hangers-on, no royal scroungers and gadabouts.

And then there are the almost unimaginable gains that Brexit might bring. Certainly before the Second World War, and for some time after, no one could have imagined Japan becoming one of the most egalitarian countries in the world, or West Germany welcoming in an impoverished East Germany and then again welcoming in a million and a half Syrian refugees. Hope springs eternal, and quite rightly too, because it must be first through our imaginations that we can create a brighter, better, fairer future.

More fairness between the four nations of the UK would be a good start in helping make a better Britain. If the rich started to use the NHS more, it would be considerably improved and the attempt to privatise large parts of it cancelled. Many of the rich would have to use the NHS if they became less rich. That is not hard to arrange, via fair taxation, including of land. The rich know it is not hard to arrange – that is why they donate so much money to the Conservative Party (see Figure 0.1 at the very start of this book). But by keeping themselves so rich, they impoverish others. Just as the health service would be better if the richest had to use it, so too would state schools be better funded if fewer people could afford their own exclusive private schools. We repeat because it needs repeating: nowhere else in Europe is so much spent on private education as in the UK. There is no trickle-down of their wealth to others.

Britain overall, but especially London, currently has the most expensive housing of any large city on the planet and young people from most households can no longer afford to buy property or rent decent homes, and consequently often have to forgo starting a family.[56] The average age of having a first child in Britain continues to rise linearly, with absolutely no sign of a slowdown in that rise as we write in November 2018. If Britain became just a bit less attractive to the super-rich, London house prices would start falling faster. London would be seen as less of a 'safe bet'. Landlords who are simply looking to make a quick buck will try to get out quickly, especially when a government that fully taxes their capital gains appears to become a possibility as Labour rises again in popularity in the polls. Possibly, just possibly, house prices could then begin to fall significantly, towards more afford-able levels, and very many more people will have the freedom to choose whether to rent or buy in the future.

Britain is a state that has fast moved away from the post-war beliefs in more co-operation, in striving to be a liberal demo-cracy where everyone has a right to health, decent housing, good education and employment. The arrival of people from former colonies was handled badly and under poor leadership the coun-try has become more competitive, greedy and xenophobic, with scapegoats sought for economic and social problems. This book has tried to show that much of what we have been taught or be-lieve about ourselves stemmed from historical lies, manufactured myths and great ignorance about the shameful truth of the impe-rial past of the British.

As Doreen Lawrence, mother of murdered black student Ste-phen Lawrence, wrote:

> I hated history at school because it had nothing to do with me … I wanted the Macpherson report [into the death of her son][57] to ensure we opened up our lessons so kids in the class knew where they were from. If kids just hear that these people are over here taking our jobs they will believe it. If they hear that in the past Britain has exploited every single aspect of the places these children came from, then perhaps they will see things differently.[58]

Going through the Brexit process increases the hope that we can see things differently in future.

It was wrong that the school curriculum remained so stale and under Michael Gove as Education Secretary became even more 'traditional' and unrealistic for so many young people. It was wrong that the campaigners for Brexit used their lies and scapegoating tactics about EU migrants and refugees to tell people that their problems could be solved by cutting the country off from a Europe that is more progressive and humane than the UK. Fortunately, the current crop of Brexiteer politicians are losing what little credibility they once had as the reality of Brexit becomes clear. Hope rests in a younger generation, many of whom can see through the lies and myths, are happy to accept that they live in a multicultural multi-racial society, and will work to secure the freedoms that self-interested governments are busy throwing away.

The worst effects of Brexit, the economic consequences, may in the long run deliver the greatest benefit of all. If the UK becomes poorer overall, its people may cease to tolerate the excessive wealth of a tiny minority and demand to become more equal. When you can no longer afford those status symbols that once seemed so important to you, you start to realise that all along they were just for show. A watch on your wrist becomes something that tells the time, not something to advertise your wealth. People begin to realise that they don't have to compete with each other, but are better off co-operating, respecting, and helping each other. The British don't even have to look abroad for the evidence. This has been happening within the NHS since its inception. All large organisations could be like that. Bosses in the private sector could begin to realise that they need to look after their staff first, then their customers and least of all any shareholders who are looking for short-term gains.

In future, the British may well keep fewer people in prison because they can no longer afford to imprison the largest number of people of any country in Europe. They may fight fewer wars, for the same reason. They may choose to ensure that hundreds of thousands of British citizens do not have to rely on foodbanks to survive when times are tough and that tens of thousands are no longer forced to sleep on the streets each year. They may become appalled at the levels of child poverty and pensioner misery they currently choose to tolerate, horrified at the worsening treatment of the disabled, and disgusted at the dismembering of health and social services. The British may become much more tolerant of immigrants when they start to miss them. They might decide to really take back control from the few with the money who currently monopolise power. This short-term folly over Brexit may well, in the longer term, make the chastened British kinder as a people, more worldly wise, more modest, more aware – better citizens of the world.

ABOUT THE AUTHORS

© Royal Geographical Society

Danny Dorling grew up in Oxford during the years when most boys still went to work in the car factory. Two of his three brothers are mixed race. The National Front spray-painted swastikas on the subway walls in the town and, once, on the fence of the house he grew up in. He went to university in Newcastle upon Tyne and stayed there for ten years. The majority of households had no adult in work in the city as the shipyard cranes stood still. Danny moved to Bristol, Leeds, Sheffield and then back to Oxford, spending a few months working in New Zealand in between, where he first saw the word 'Manchester' used in supermarkets to mean cotton goods.

© Brian Tomlinson

Sally Tomlinson was born in Stockport, where her grandfather was a foreman in a textile mill. She went to university in Liverpool, a major slave trading port under empire. Her first primary school job was teaching children from the Caribbean and Asian subcontinent in Wolverhampton in the year Enoch Powell was making his anti-immigrant speeches. She has worked in universities in Warwick, Lancaster, Goldsmiths London and Oxford, and has spent her career teaching, researching and writing in the areas of race and ethnicity, education policy and special education. She was trustee of the Africa Educational Trust for twenty years and worked for the trust in Somaliland, Kenya and South Africa.

ENDNOTES

Introduction

1   Porter, B. (2015) 'Epilogue: After-images of Empire' in Nicolaidis, K., Sebe, B., Maas, G. (eds), *Echoes of Empire*, London: I. B. Tauris, pp. 393–4.

2   For instance, Arkadiusz Jozwik was killed on 27 August 2016: *Daily Telegraph* (2017) 'Boy, 16, "killed Polish man with superman punch after laughing about his English"', 25 July, https://www.telegraph.co.uk/news/2017/07/25/boy-16-killed-polish-man-supermanpunch-laughing-english/

3   Luther King, M. (1968) 'The Other America', speech, Grosse Pointe High School, 14 March, http://www.gphistorical.org/mlk/mlkspeech/

4   Bennett, O. (2016) *The Brexit Club: The Inside Story of the Leave Campaign's Shock Victory*, London: Biteback.

5   MacShane, D. (2017) *Brexit, No Exit: Why (in the End) Britain Won't Leave Europe*, London: I. B. Tauris. A sequel to his 2015 book *Brexit: How Britain Will Leave Europe* and 2016's *Brexit: How Britain Left Europe*.

6   Clegg, N. (2017) *How To Stop Brexit (And Make Britain Great Again)*, London: Bodley Head.

7   Hutton, W. and Adonis, A. (2018*) Saving Britain: How we must change to prosper in Europe*, London: Abacus – a rather late plea for the country to stay in a reformed EU; and Kenny, M. and Pearce, N. (2018) *Shadows of Empire: The Anglosphere in British Politics*, Cambridge: Polity Press – a quick historical and political run through from the Boer War to the present, suggesting that the Anglosphere (empire) has 'paradoxical' history and that it will be no good relying on this for much future trade. Both books are interesting in that they show their authors' views changing with the reality of the Brexit process undermining faith in what was the centre ground of British politics, now largely abandoned by the Labour Party that was quickly becoming a normal European social democrat party again during 2017 and 2018, thus moving far to the left of (old) New Labour.

8   These countries were referred to as 'non-white' and 'developing' in contrast to the pre-1945 Old Commonwealth – countries where the original inhabitants had been completely marginalised, and were now largely occupied by emigrants from Great Britain and their descendants. Eire left the Commonwealth in 1949 and became the Republic of Ireland.

9 Ferguson, N. (2003) *Empire: How Britain made the modern world*, London: Allen Lane.

10 Schindler, C. (2012) *National Service: from Aldershot to Aden: tales of the conscripts from 1946–62*, London: Sphere (Little, Brown).

11 Schindler, C. (2012) ibid., p. 92.

12 Sewage, N. (2017) *The Brexit Cookbook: British Food for British People*, Chichester: Summersdale.

13 Edwards, M. (2018) 'Nigel Farage "could join DUP" amid speculation he could be making another bid for Parliament', *Belfast Telegraph*, 11 May, https://www.belfasttelegraph.co.uk/news/northern-ireland/nigel-farage-could-join-dup-amid-speculation-he-could-be-making-another-bid-for-parliament-36896730.html

14 There are many reports available. The most succinct is this: 'According to Forbes, David Cameron Net Worth is $50 Million', https://www.richestceleb.com/david-cameron-net-worth/

15 Fenton, S. (2016) 'David Cameron "charging £120,000 per hour for speeches on Brexit"', *The Independent*, 15 November, https://www.independent.co.uk/news/uk/politics/david-cameron-charging-120000-per-hour-for-speeches-about-brexit-a7418451.html

16 Hardcastle, E. (2017) Notes, *Daily Mail*, 1 December, p. 23, https://www.pressreader.com/uk/daily-mail/20171201/281883003662785

17 Massie, A. (2016) 'A Day of Infamy', *The Spectator*, 16 June, https://blogs.spectator.co.uk/2016/06/a-day-of-infamy/.

18 The Sunday Times Rich List, 13 May 2018, p. 97.

19 The Sunday Times Rich List 2018, and analysis by the authors of that list.

20 Tomlinson, S. (2019) *Education and Race from Empire to Brexit*, Bristol: Policy Press.

21 Hughes, L., Hope, C., Criso, J., Foster, P., Maidment, J. and Raynor, G. (2017) 'Brexit deal in chaos after DUP backlash over Irish border concessions', *Daily Telegraph*, 5 December, http://www.telegraph.co.uk/news/2017/12/04/brexit-talks-deadline-no-breakthrough-ireland-theresa-may-heads/

22 Boffey, D., Helm, T. and Savage, N. (2018) 'Revealed: leaked emails show DUP ready for no-deal Brexit', *The Observer*, 14 October, https://www.theguardian.com/politics/2018/oct/13/leaked-emails-dup-arlene-foster-no-deal-brexit-most-likely-outcome-eu

23 O'Toole, F. (2017) 'Britain has just discovered it's weaker than Ireland', *The Guardian*, 5 December, https://www.theguardian.com/commentisfree/2017/dec/04/hard-brexiters-britain-weaker-ireland-brexit-talks-irish-border-lesson

24 BBC (2018) 'Holyrood set to reject Westminster Brexit powers bill', BBC News, 15 May, http://www.bbc.co.uk/news/uk-scotland-scotland-politics-44113864

Chapter 1: Why Brexit?

1 Ramsay, A. (2017) 'For Britain to solve its economic problems, it needs to stop lying to itself about its past', Open Democracy, 9 March, https://www.opendemocracy.net/neweconomics/trade-empire-2-0-and-the-lies-we-tell-ourselves/

2 Or so a friend suggested: George Davey Smith.

3 Dorling, D. (2018) *Peak Inequality: Britain's Ticking Time Bomb*, Bristol: Policy Press, p. iv.

4 May, T. (2018) 'Trust me, I'll take back control – but I'll need your help', *Sunday Times*, 13 May, https://www.thetimes.co.uk/article/trust-me-ill-take-back-control-but-ill-need-your-help-6dr6lhwws

5 El-Enany, N. (2017) 'Things Fall Apart: From Empire to Brexit Britain', IPR blogpost, 2 May, http://blogs.bath.ac.uk/iprblog/2017/05/02/things-fall-apart-from-empire-to-brexit-britain/

6   Johnston, R., Pattie, C., Rossiter, D. (2015) 'Ensuring equal representation in Parliament: who counts?', LSE British Policy and Politics blog, 20 July, http://blogs.lse.ac.uk/politicsandpolicy/ensuring-equal-representation-in-parliament-who-counts/

7   Fransham, M. and Dorling, D. (2018) 'Homelessness and public health', *British Medical Journal*, 30 January, http://www.dannydorling.org/?page_id=6364. That crisis continues to worsen. In May 2018, we learnt that the number of families in London who were owed a right to be housed by the council as they were statutory homeless rapidly rose to 54,000 in one quarter, in the biggest rise reported since 2014, and probably the biggest rise in a quarter to ever happen. The main cause of homelessness was the forced ending of a private residential contract. Landlords were starting to evict tenants to try to sell up properties as houses fell in price. See: Colthorpe, T. and Brown, R. (2018) 'Society', in Colthorpe, T. and Brown, R. (eds), *The London Intelligence*, Issue 4, London: Centre for London, http://www.centreforlondon.org/reader/the-london-intelligence-issue-4/society/#attractions-monitor

8   Helm, T. (2016) 'EU referendum: youth turnout almost twice as high as first thought', *The Guardian*, 10 July, https://www.theguardian.com/politics/2016/jul/09/young-people-referendum-turnout-brexit-twice-as-high

9   Lord Ashcroft Polls, with turnout figures as given in Speed, B. (2016) 'How did different demographic groups vote in the EU referendum?', *New Statesman*, 24 June 2016, https://www.newstatesman.com/politics/staggers/2016/06/how-did-different-demographic-groups-vote-eu-referendum

10   Hennig, B. and Dorling, D. (2016) 'In Focus: The EU Referendum', *Political Insight*, September 2016, pp. 20–21, http://journals.sagepub.com/doi/abs/10.1177/2041905816666142

11   Dorling, D. (2016) 'Brexit: the decision of a divided country', *British Medical Journal* 354, 6 July, http://dx.doi.org/10.1136/bmj.i3697 or http://www.dannydorling.org/?page_id=5564

12   Liberini, F., Oswald, A. J., Proto, E. and Redoano, M. (2017) 'Was Brexit caused by the unhappy and the old?', IZA Institute of Labor Economics, https://www.iza.org/publications/dp/11059/was-brexit-caused-by-the-unhappy-and-the-old (referring to version posted in March 2018).

13   This research is well summarised in Wilkinson, R. and Pickett, K. (2018) *The Inner Level: How More Equal Societies Reduce Stress, Restore Sanity and Improve Everyone's Well-Being*, London: Allen Lane.

14   Goodwin, M. and Heath, O. (2016) 'Brexit vote explained: poverty, low skills, and lack of opportunities', York: Joseph Rowntree Foundation, https://www.jrf.org.uk/report/brexit-vote-explained-poverty-low-skills-and-lack-opportunities

15   UK Electoral Commission, originally drawn in colour by Benjamin Hennig.

16   Rae, A. (2016) 'What can explain Brexit?', Stats, Maps n Pix blog, 25 June, http://www.statsmapsnpix.com/2016/06/what-can-explain-brexit.html

17   Ormosi, P. (2016) 'The weight of Brexit: Leave vote is higher in areas of higher obesity', LSE Brexit blog, 30 June, http://blogs.lse.ac.uk/brexit/2016/06/30/the-weight-of-brexit-leave-vote-is-higher-in-areas-of-higher-obesity/

18   Osborne, S. (2016) 'Outrage after academic says Brexit voters were probably FAT' (emphasis as in the original), *Daily Express*, 1 July, https://www.express.co.uk/news/uk/685419/Outrage-academic-Brexit-voters-fat

19   ITV News (2016) 'UEA research claims link between obesity and Brexit voters', 30 June, http://www.itv.com/news/anglia/2016-06-30/uea-research-suggests-link-between-obesity-and-brexit-voters/

20   Osborne, S. (2016) 'Outrage after academic says Brexit voters were probably FAT', op. cit.

21   The data Peter used came from Public Health England and was released in 2014, https://www.gov.uk/government/news/phe-release-local-authority-adult-obesity-data

22   Cortina Borja, M., Stander, J. and Dalla Valle, L. (2016) 'The EU referendum: surname diversity and voting patterns', *Significance*, 18 July, https://www.statslife.org.uk/politics/2943-the-eu-referendum-surname-diversity-and-voting-patterns

23   Moore, M. and Ramsay, G. (2017) 'UK media coverage of the 2016 EU Referendum campaign', King's College London, Centre for the Study of Media, Communication and Power, May, https://www.kcl.ac.uk/sspp/policy-institute/CMCP/UK-media-coverage-of-the-2016-EU-Referendum-campaign.pdf

24   'Researchers found immigration to be the most prominent issue in the 10 weeks running up to the vote, leading 99 front pages. Of those, more than three-quarters were from the four most virulently Leave newspapers: *The Sun*, the *Mail*, the *Express* and the *Telegraph*.' Chakrabortty, A. (2018) 'Immigration has been good for Britain. It's time to bust the myths', *The Guardian*, 17 May, https://www.theguardian.com/commentisfree/2018/may/17/immigration-good-for-britain-bust-myths-austerity

25   Watts, J. (2017) 'Brexit: Britons now back Remain over Leave by 10 points, exclusive poll shows', *The Independent*, 16 December, https://www.independent.co.uk/news/uk/politics/brexit-second-referendum-latest-poll-remain-ten-points-leave-bmg-a8114406.html

26   Jack, I. (2018) 'The sun may never set on British misconceptions about our empire', *The Guardian*, 6 January, https://www.theguardian.com/commentisfree/2018/jan/06/british-misconceptions-empire-guilty-colonialism

27   Ipsos MORI (2016) 'How Britain voted in the 2016 EU referendum', Ipsos MORI news blog, 5 September, https://www.ipsos.com/ipsos-mori/en-uk/how-britain-voted-2016-eu-referendum

28   Moore, M. (2018) 'Cumberbatch to play Vote Leave mastermind Cummings in Brexit TV drama', *The Times*, 16 May, https://www.thetimes.co.uk/article/benedict-cumberbatch-to-play-vote-leave-mastermind-dominic-cummings-in-brexit-tv-drama-b297ckpv8

29   Goodwin, M. (2017) 'Brexit Britain: The Causes and Consequences of the Leave Vote', public lecture, text available here: http://www.matthewjgoodwin.org/uploads/6/4/0/2/64026337/leave_vote_lecture.pdf

Chapter 2: Britain's immigrant origins

1   Modood, T., Dobbernack, J. and Meer, N. (2012) 'Great Britain', Chapter 6 in Zapata-Barrero, R. and Triandafyllidou, A. (eds), *Addressing tolerance and diversity discourses in Europe: A Comparative Overview of 16 European Countries*, Barcelona: Barcelona Centre for International Affairs, https://www.cidob.org/en/publications/publication_series/monographs/monographs/addressing_tolerance_and_diversity_discourses_in_europe_a_comparative_overview_of_16_european_countries

2   This chapter is the development of ideas that first appeared in an essay we published in 2016: Tomlinson, S. and Dorling, D. (2016) 'Brexit has its roots in the British Empire – so how do we explain it to the young?', Staggers, *New Statesman* blog, 9 May, http://www.newstatesman.com/politics/staggers/2016/05/brexit-has-its-roots-british-empire-so-how-do-we-explain-it-young

3   He is now only vaguely remembered for his short-lived liaison with Jo Marney after and during splitting up with his third wife, Russian-born Tatiana Smurova. Mr

Bolton's liaison with Ms Marney was reported a year after his wife gave birth to their second child in a train in St Pancras railway station. See: Proto, L. (2016) 'Woman gives birth on Southeastern train arriving at St Pancras… but calls her daughter Victoria', *London Evening Standard*, 16 May, https://www.standard.co.uk/news/london/woman-gives-birth-on-train-arriving-at-st-pancras-a3249206.html. Note, for those interested, both his third wife and his second, Lidia Gouniakova, also a Russian national, accused him of being unfaithful. His first wife was Danish national Karin Dohn. On 6 March 2018, he announced he was starting a new political party, One Nation. See: BBC (2018) 'Ousted UKIP leader Henry Bolton "to set up new party"', BBC News, 6 March, http://www.bbc.co.uk/news/uk-politics-43301773. He will probably be just a footnote in history, and those footnotes found only in the pages of books such as this.

4   Sayer, D. (2017) 'Why the idea that the English have a common Anglo-Saxon origin is a myth', The Conversation, 15 December, https://theconversation.com/why-the-idea-that-the-english-have-a-common-anglo-saxon-origin-is-a-myth-88272

5   It occurred at a time when there was still debate about whether Britain's true colonial history should be acknowledged at all. See: Hirsh, A. (2017) 'Britain's colonial crimes deserve a lasting memorial. Here's why', *The Guardian*, 22 November, https://www.theguardian.com/commentisfree/2017/nov/22/british-empire-museum-colonial-crimes-memorial

6   Buchan, L. (2017) 'Britain's debt will not fall to 2008 levels until 2060s, IFS says in startling warning', *The Independent*, 23 November, http://www.independent.co.uk/news/uk/politics/british-debt-uk-deficit-not-fall-below-2008-levels-2060-financial-crash-economy-warning-a8071696.html

7   Watts, J. (2017) 'UK facing longest fall in living standards for over 60 years, finds think tank', *The Independent*, 23 November, http://www.independent.co.uk/news/uk/politics/uk-living-standards-fall-longest-60-years-records-began-economy-household-incomes-costs-energy-a8071146.html

8   Wearmouth, R. (2017) 'Budget 2017: Chancellor Blasted For Finding More Additional Money For Brexit Than The NHS', Huffington Post, 22 November, http://www.huffingtonpost.co.uk/entry/brexit-nhs-budget_uk_5a158a00e4b09650540e914c

9   Alexander, A. (2017) 'Britain without a judge on the International Court of Justice for first time since 1946', *Daily Telegraph*, 20 November, http://www.telegraph.co.uk/news/2017/11/20/britain-without-judge-international-court-justice-first-time/. Note: 'The UK had fought hard to secure Sir Christopher [Greenwood QC, incumbent 2008–18]'s approval, reportedly urging the Security Council to resort to the Joint Conference Mechanism which was last used ninety-six years ago, leading Indian sources to accuse the UK of "dirty politics".'

10   Stone, J. (2017) 'Brexit: EU cancels Britain's hosting of European capital of culture', *The Independent*, 23 November, http://www.independent.co.uk/news/uk/politics/brexit-european-capital-of-culture-uk-cancelled-leeds-eu-banned-a8071261.html

11   Dorling, D. and Thomas, B. (2016) *People and Places: A 21st-century atlas of the UK*, Bristol: Policy Press.

12   Note that the Auckland region in New Zealand claims an even more diverse mixing, but that is the result of it including so many small island nations in the Pacific rather than just one or two federacies.

13   There is a workspace installation, though in November 2017 it had funding only up to February 2018. In June 2018 (when we last accessed it), the website said it was holding 'Migrateful – Iranian cookery class' on 24 July. No events were listed after that. See http://www.migrationmuseum.org/about-our-project/

14 Royal Mint (2017) 'Britannia on British Coins', Royal Mint website (undated, accessed November 2017), http://www.royalmint.com/discover/britannia/britannia-on-british-coins

15 http://www.royalmint.com/shop/b/br1750zg

16 Rincon, P. (2018) 'Ancient Britons "replaced" by newcomers', BBC News, 21 February, http://www.bbc.co.uk/news/science-environment-43115485

17 Silverton, P. (2016) 'English national anthem: Is Jerusalem the hymn we've been looking for?', *The Independent*, 9 March, http://www.independent.co.uk/arts-entertainment/music/features/english-national-anthem-is-jerusalem-the-hymn-weve-been-looking-for-a6921961.html

18 Trevor-Roper, H. (1983) 'The Highland tradition of Scotland', in Hobsbawm, E. and Ranger, T. (eds), *The Invention of Tradition*, Cambridge: Cambridge University Press.

19 Clarke, H. (2016) *Norman England 1066–c1100, AQA GCSE History*, Banbury: Hodder Education, p. 22, https://www.hoddereducation.co.uk/media/Documents/History/AQA_GCSE_Norman_England_sample_material.pdf

20 Tovey, D. C. (1911) 'Thomson, James (poet, 1700–1748)', in Chisholm, H. (ed.), *Encyclopedia Britannica*, Cambridge: Cambridge University Press.

21 Innes, A. D. (1912) *A History of the British Nation*, London: T. C. & E. C. Jack. Reproduced from an open access source. The whole of the book is available here: https://archive.org/stream/historyofbritishooinneuoft#page/n7/mode/2up

22 The height of such telling was around a century ago. See: Innes, A. D. (1912) ibid.

23 *Who Do You Think You Are* magazine (2016) 'Matthew Pinsent', http://www.whodoyouthinkyouaremagazine.com/episode/matthew-pinsent

24 Easton, M. (2018) 'The English question: What is the nation's identity?', BBC News, 3 June, https://www.bbc.co.uk/news/uk-44306737. YouGov/BBC Survey Results: sample size: 20,081 English adults; fieldwork: 9–26 March 2018, https://d25d2506s-fb94s.cloudfront.net/cumulus_uploads/document/7lnxwjw12j/BBC_EnglishIdentity_March18_Results_for_website.pdf

25 Castillo, A. (2012) 'Las Malvinas or Falkland Islands: British or Argentinean?', *The Conversation*, 2 April, https://theconversation.com/las-malvinas-or-falkland-islands-british-or-argentinean-6106

26 Kennedy, M. (2017) 'Cambridge academics weigh students' call for the de-colonisation of English literature', *The Guardian*, 26 October, https://www.theguardian.com/education/2017/oct/25/cambridge-academics-seek-to-decolonise-english-syllabus

27 Tolhurst, A. (2018) '"A DISGRACE": Oxford University will put portrait of Theresa May back on its wall after leftie students blasted for campaign to have it removed in protest at her policies', *The Sun*, 8 May, https://www.thesun.co.uk/news/6237918/oxford-university-will-put-portrait-of-theresa-may-back-on-its-wall-after-leftie-students-blasted-for-campaign-to-have-it-removed-in-protest-at-her-policies/

28 Although there is a team of robot Luxembourgian footballers who compete in the robot football tournament. See: *Grand Duchy News* (2017) 'Grand Duchy is European robot football champion', 7 May, http://www.luxembourg.public.lu/en/actualites/2017/06/12-robocup/index.html

29 Jarski, R. (2005) *Great British Wit: The greatest assembly of British wit and humour ever*, London: Ebury Press. From the frontispiece: 'The happiest moment of her life was when she finally twigged the rule of the game, Mornington Crescent. The ringtone on her mobile is "Always Look on the Bright Side of Life".'

30 The term 'small island' also refers to the distinction between small and big islands in the Caribbean.

31   Newsinger, J. (2010) *The Blood Never Dried: A People's History of the British Empire*, Stoke on Trent: Trentham Books.

32   Wright, P. (1991) *A Journey through Ruins: The Last Days of London*, London: Radius.

33   Shipman, T. (2017) *All Out War*, London: William Collins.

34   EU overseas countries, territories, and outermost regions, 2018, https://upload.wikimedia.org/wikipedia/commons/7/72/EU_OCT_and_OMR_map_en.png

35   Chu, B. (2017) 'Brexit: Is Owen Paterson talking nonsense about tariffs and the single market?', *The Independent*, 17 July, http://www.independent.co.uk/news/business/analysis-and-features/brexit-latest-news-owen-paterson-eu-single-market-access-pay-tariff-barriers-trade-goods-services-a7845776.html

36   Espinoza, J. (2016) 'Nigerian officials have made plans to travel to Britain to collect a controversial bronze statue', *Daily Telegraph*, 9 March, https://www.telegraph.co.uk/education/universityeducation/12189194/Nigerian-officials-have-made-plans-to-travel-to-Britain-to-collect-a-controversial-bronze-statue.html

37   Hope, C. (2018) 'Jeremy Corbyn says schools should teach children about the "grave injustices" of the British empire', *Daily Telegraph*, 11 October, https://www.telegraph.co.uk/politics/2018/10/10/jeremy-corbyn-says-schools-should-teach-children-grave-injustices/

38   Winder, R. (2013) *Bloody Foreigners: The Story of Immigration to Britain*, London: Abacus.

39   Brennan, Z. (2002) 'What are the Patten girls up to?', *London Evening Standard*, 7 August, https://www.standard.co.uk/news/what-are-the-patten-girls-up-to-6302164.html

40   Stembridge, J. H. (1956) *The World: A General Regional Geography*, Oxford: Oxford University Press, p. 347.

41   Evans, R. (2013) 'Michael Gove's History Curriculum Is a Pub Quiz Not an Education', *New Statesman*, 21 March, http://historyworks.tv/news/2013/03/09/history_curriculum_debate_updates/

42   Gove, M. (2009) 'Failing schools need new leadership', Conservative Party conference speech, 7 October, https://conservative-speeches.sayit.mysociety.org/speech/601288

43   *The Times* (2018) 'Know Your Place: Geography is the middle-class route to the top', 23 May, https://www.thetimes.co.uk/article/know-your-place-2mcz58m78

44   Bennett, R. (2018) 'Geography finds its place among elite', *The Times*, 23 May, https://www.thetimes.co.uk/article/geography-is-degree-for-the-well-off-b0gbc56zz

45   As a child, one of us would often see the dons naked as they bathed at this secluded area on the banks of the Cherwell, standing up to observe the young boys on the punts going by. They were an odd group of men.

46   Baker, O., Dimbleby, F., Gould, R., Morris, I., Ritchie, G. and Roller, M. (2018) 'Access denied: Oxford admits more Westminster pupils than black students', *Cherwell News*, 23 May, http://cherwell.org/2018/05/23/access-denied-oxford-admits-more-westminster-pupils-than-black-students/. Quote from this article: 'Of the 120 black students admitted to the University between 2015 and 2017, only one was admitted to Corpus Christi College, while seven other colleges – Balliol, Exeter, Jesus, Magdalen, New College, Univ, and Worcester – admitted just two.'

47   Freitag, C. and Hillman, N. (2018) 'How different is Oxbridge?', HEPI Report 107, Oxford: Higher Education Policy Institute, http://www.hepi.ac.uk/2018/05/24/5825/, pp. 11, 13, 28.

48   In 2018 'the happiness and confidence young people feel in their lives has fallen to their lowest levels since the study was first commissioned in 2009': The Prince's

Trust (2018) Youth Index, https://www.princes-trust.org.uk/about-the-trust/research-policies-reports/youth-index-2018

49 Wilkinson, R. and Pickett, K. (2018) *The Inner Level*, op. cit.

50 Dorling, D. (2018) *Peak Inequality*, op. cit., pp. 163–4.

51 Lawson-Walton, J. (1899) 'Imperialism', *Contemporary Review* LXXV, p. 306.

52 Mangan, J. A. (1986) 'The grit of our forefathers: invented traditions, propaganda and imperialism', in MacKenzie, J. M. (ed.), *Imperialism and Popular Culture*, Manchester: Manchester University Press.

53 Lloyd, T. O. (1984) *The British Empire 1553–1983*, Oxford: Oxford University Press.

54 Humphries, S. (1981) *Hooligans or Rebels? An Oral History of Working-Class Childhood and Youth, 1889–1939*, Oxford: Basil Blackwell.

55 Personal communication with Ian Ray, 19 October 2018. Many copies are available on the secondhand market, https://www.amazon.co.uk/New-Century-Geography-Readers-Greater/dp/B00BWOIL7W

Chapter 3: From empire to Commonwealth

1 Younge, G. (2018) 'Britain's imperial fantasies have given us Brexit', *The Guardian*, 3 February, https://www.theguardian.com/commentisfree/2018/feb/03/imperial-fantasies-brexit-theresa-may?CMP=twt_gu

2 This chapter is partly based on an academic article written two years ago and now much expanded upon: Dorling, D. and Tomlinson, S. (2016) 'The Creation of Inequality: Myths of Potential and Ability', *Journal for Critical Education Policy Studies*, Vol. 14, No. 3, http://www.jceps.com/archives/3204

3 El-Enany, N. (2017) 'Brexit is not only an expression of nostalgia for empire, it is also the fruit of empire', LSE Brexit blog, 5 November, http://blogs.lse.ac.uk/brexit/2017/05/11/brexit-is-not-only-an-expression-of-nostalgia-for-empire-it-is-also-the-fruit-of-empire/

4 Hirsch, A. (2018) 'Britain doesn't just glorify its violent past: it gets high on it', *The Guardian*, 29 May, https://www.theguardian.com/commentisfree/2018/may/29/britain-glorify-violent-past-defensive-empire-drug

5 El-Enany, N. (2017) 'Brexit is not only an expression of nostalgia for empire, it is also the fruit of empire', op. cit.

6 Brown, G. (2017) *My Life, Our Times*, London: Bodley Head, p. 27.

7 Hall, E. (2013) 'How Enoch Powell Got Vergil Wrong', The Edithorial, 20 April, http://edithorial.blogspot.co.uk/2013/04/how-enoch-powell-got-vergil-wrong.html

8 He just happened to be there at the right time, in the right place and with the right financial resources to travel and buy up samples of fossils, preserved plants and stuffed animals. See: Dorling, D. (2010) 'Commentary: The Darwins and the Cecils are only empty vessels', *Environment and Planning A*, Vol. 42, No. 5, pp. 1023–5, http://www.dannydorling.org/?page_id=769

9 Tomlinson, S. (2017) *A Sociology of Special and Inclusive education*, London: Routledge, p. 54.

10 Tomlinson, S. (2017) ibid., p. 71.

11 There are a huge number of sources that can be given, but perhaps the best is Wikipedia, where slowly and gradually more and more evidence of these crimes against humanity is being documented and presented for all to see, edit and add to, starting perhaps with: https://en.wikipedia.org/wiki/Racial_Integrity_Act_of_1924

12 Darwin quoted in Jamoussi, Z. (1999) *Primogeniture and Entail in England*, Paris: Centre de Publication Universitaire, p. 130.

13 Dorling, D. (2010) 'Commentary: The Darwins and the Cecils are only empty vessels', op. cit., p. 1024.

14 Reproduced from a study reported by Berra, T. M., Alvarez, G., and Ceballos, F. C. (2010) 'Was the Darwin/Wedgwood Dynasty Adversely Affected by Consanguinity?', *BioScience*, Vol. 60, No. 5, pp. 376–83. Available for free here: http://phylonetworks.blogspot.co.uk/2013/05/charles-darwins-family-pedigree-network.html

15 It is possible that he thought that he and his kind were not the principal achievement of the powers of nature as he stumbled around collecting his beetles. The beetles were far more beautiful and varied than man.

16 Kuper, A. (2010) *Incest and Influence: The Private Life of Bourgeois England*, Massachusetts: Harvard University Press, as quoted in http://phylonetworks.blogspot.co.uk/2013/05/charles-darwins-family-pedigree-network.html

17 Gorard, S. and Siddiqui, N. (2018) 'Grammar schools in England: a new analysis of social segregation and academic outcomes', *British Journal of Sociology of Education*, first published March 2018, https://doi.org/10.1080/01425692.2018.1443432

18 Pearson, K. (1892) *The Grammar of Science*, London: Walter Scott, p. 32.

19 Her anointment by the left-liberal *Guardian* is a useful proof of the fight of memory against forgetting; she 'was perhaps surprising as overall winner', the newspaper reported at the time, not realising that many of its readers would have voted for her to show support for the provision of Marie Stopes abortion services, with little known of her eugenic beliefs: Coward, R. (1999) 'There's something about Marie', *The Guardian*, 25 January, https://www.theguardian.com/world/1999/jan/25/gender.uk2

20 Sadler, M. (1916) 'Need we imitate the German system?', *The Times*, 14 January.

21 Ashton, E. (2013) 'Boris Johnson: Thickos Are Born to Toil', *The Sun*, 28 November.

22 Dorling, D. (2014) 'G is for Genes', *International Journal of Epidemiology*, Vol. 44, No. 1, pp. 374–8, https://academic.oup.com/ije/article/44/1/374/655644

23 One of the first scientists to note this was the biologist Raymond Pearl. Talking mainly of men (it was in the 1920s!) such as Michelangelo, Leonardo da Vinci, Shakespeare and Pasteur, he noted what is now widely understood by geneticists: 'I frankly do not see the usually alleged cause for eugenic alarm, for the reason that history demonstrates, I believe, that the superior people of the world have always been recruited from the masses, intellectually speaking, in far greater numbers than they have been reproduced by the upper classes.' Pearl, R. (1927) 'Differential Fertility', *Quarterly Review of Biology*, Vol. 2, No. 1, pp. 102–18.

24 Myall, S., Smith, M. and Bloom, S. (2017) '7 nasty or awkward DUP beliefs that show their deal with Theresa May could be a coalition of chaos', *Daily Mirror*, 9 June, https://www.mirror.co.uk/news/politics/7-nasty-awkward-dup-beliefs-10592322

25 At university in the 1980s, one of us was once taught of how ridiculous the idea of 'British birds' was – with its implication that these birds were different from those found in the rest of Europe, or became especially British at certain points in their annual migration from Africa.

26 Chitty, C. (2007) *Eugenics, Race and Intelligence in Education*, London: Continuum.

27 Gillborn, D. (2008) *Racism and Education: Coincidence or conspiracy*, London: Routledge.

28 Gillborn, D. (2016) 'Softly, softly: genetics, intelligence and the hidden racism of the new geneticism', *Journal of Education Policy*, Vol. 31, No. 4, pp. 365–88.

29 Hearnshaw, L. (1979) *Cyril Burt: Psychologist*, London: Hodder & Stoughton.

30 Kamin, L. J. (1974) *The science and politics of IQ*, New York: John Wiley & Sons.

31 Gould, S. J. (1996) *The Mismeasure of Man*, London: Penguin Books.

32 Montague, S. (1975) *Race and IQ*, New York: Oxford University Press.

33 Rose, S. (2014) 'Is Genius in the Genes?', *Times Educational Supplement*, 24 January.

34 Tomlinson, S. (2017) *A Sociology of Special and Inclusive education: Manufactured inability*, Abingdon: Routledge.

35 Evans, G. (2018) 'The unwelcome revival of "race science"', *The Guardian*, 2 March, https://www.theguardian.com/news/2018/mar/02/the-unwelcome-revival-of-race-science

36 Conley, D., Domingue, B. W., Cesarini, D., Dawes, C., Rietveld, C. A. and Boardman, J. D. (2015) 'Is the Effect of Parental Education on Off-spring Biased or Moderated by Genotype', *Sociological Science* 2, p. 82.

37 Conley, D., Rauscher, E., Dawes, C., et al. (2013) 'Heritability and the equal environment assumption: evidence from multiple samples of misclassified twins', *Behaviour Genetics*, Vol. 43, No. 5, pp. 415–26, https://www.ncbi.nlm.nih.gov/pubmed/23903437. This research showed that when identical twins did not look alike, their attainments were significantly different (despite being genetically identical) compared to other identical twins, but when non-identical twins looked very alike, their attainments were almost as similar as found in actual identical twins that looked alike, despite not being genetically identical. (Their similar appearance presumably being the cause of them being misclassified.)

38 'The recent revival of ideas about race and IQ began with a seemingly benign scientific observation. In 2005, Steven Pinker, one of the world's most prominent evolutionary psychologists, began promoting the view that Ashkenazi Jews are innately particularly intelligent – first in a lecture to a Jewish studies institute, then in a lengthy article in the liberal American magazine the *New Republic* the following year. This claim has long been the smiling face of race science; if it is true that Jews are naturally more intelligent, then it's only logical to say that others are naturally less so.' A quote appearing in: Evans, G. (2018) 'The unwelcome revival of "race science"', *The Guardian*, 2 March, https://www.theguardian.com/news/2018/mar/02/the-unwelcome-revival-of-race-science

39 Tomlinson, S. (1990) *Multicultural Education in White Schools*, pp. 85–6, London: Batsford.

40 See the graphs and tables in: Dorling, D. and Tomlinson, S. (2016) 'The Creation of Inequality: Myths of Potential and Ability', op. cit.

41 Dorling, D. (2013) 'Rising cornflakes – or Boris Johnson's faux pas', *New Internationalist* blog, 2 December, https://newint.org/blog/2013/12/02/boris-johnson-elite

42 Eyres, H. and Myerson, G. (2018) *Johnson's Brexit Dictionary: Or an A to Z of what Brexit really means*, London: Pushkin Press, p. 116.

43 As one commentator writing under one particular blog by a person who attempts to measure potential put it: 'Just so glad you've simplified the system so everyone knows the true value of the results… slightly tongue in cheek.' See: Jadhav, C. (2017) 'Setting grade 9 in new GCSEs', The Ofqual blog, 5 April, https://ofqual.blog.gov.uk/2017/04/05/setting-grade-9-in-new-gcses/

44 Admittedly one that now has actually officially decided that things can only get better. As David Dorling (the father of one of the authors) puts it: 'Watch the video on this blog. Key stage 2 results, years 3–6, age 7–10 are the gold standard for "potential". The government wants those to improve slightly year on year (thanks to teachers getting better at teaching to the test) and hey presto, GCSE results will also improve year on year!' See: Jadhav, C. (2017) 'Prediction matrices explained', The Ofqual blog, 21 April, https://ofqual.blog.gov.uk/2017/04/21/prediction-matrices-explained/

45 Dorling, D. (2017) *The Equality Effect: Improving life for everyone*, Oxford: New Internationalist.

46 Lusher, A. (2017) 'Who is the racist viscount jailed for inciting violence against Brexit campaigner Gina Miller?', *The Independent*, 14 July, http://www.independent.co.uk/ news/uk/crime/viscount-gina-miller-who-is-rhodri-colwyn-philipps-jailed-violence- abuse-online-a7842006.html

47 See: http://www.thepeerage.com/p5883.htm, citing *British Peerage 2003*, Vol. 3, p. 3470.

48 See: https://www.geni.com/people/Antonio-Correa-de-Acosta/6000060009893912983. And for more recent information see: http://www.thepeerage.com/p56806.htm

49 Savage, M. (2017) 'Theresa May faces new crisis after mass walkout over social policy', *The Guardian*, 3 December, https://www.theguardian.com/politics/2017/ dec/02/theresa-may-crisis-mass-walkout-social-policy-alan-milburn

50 Wilkinson, R. and Pickett, K. (2018) *The Inner Level*, op. cit.

51 OECD (2018) 'Key indicators on income distribution and poverty – latest years file', Paris: OECD, as downloaded in May 2018, data for December 2017, Israel most up to date, with data for 2016, http://www.oecd.org/social/income-distribution-data- base.htm

52 Joe Gastwirth, personal correspondence, 11 May 2018.

53 Cummings, D. (2013) 'Some thoughts on education and political priorities', paper delivered to the Secretary of State for Education, London: Department for Edu- cation, http://s3.documentcloud.org/documents/804396/some-thoughts-on-educa- tion-and-political.pdf. According to *The Guardian*, this '250-page screed sprawls across a vast canvas about the future, education, Britain's place in the world and disruptive forces ahead. Quite frankly, much will pass over the average reader's head. It is either mad, bad or brilliant – and probably a bit of all three.' See: Wintour, P. (2013) 'Dom- inic Cummings: genius or menace?', *The Guardian*, 11 October, https://www.the- guardian.com/politics/2013/oct/11/dominic-cummings-genius-menace-michael-gove

54 Wilby, P. (2014) 'Psychologist on a mission to give every child a Learning Chip', *The Guardian*, 18 February, https://www.theguardian.com/education/2014/feb/18/ psychologist-robert-plomin-says-genes-crucial-education

55 Wintour, P. (2013) 'Genetics outweighs teaching, Gove adviser tells his boss', *The Guardian*, 11 October, https://www.theguardian.com/politics/2013/oct/11/ genetics-teaching-gove-adviser

56 Elledge, J. (2018) 'If only we could all be as clever as Dominic Cummings', *New States- man*, 24 May, https://www.newstatesman.com/2018/05/if-only-we-could-all-be- clever-dominic-cummings

57 Labour Party (2015) Rule Book, Section 1, Chapter 1, London: Labour Party.

58 As our friend Carl Lee pointed out to us when commenting on a much earlier draft of this chapter. For instance, in the 1980s, A-level grades of CDE were enough to secure a place to read geography at Sheffield City Polytechnic (now Sheffield Hallam) and only about 80,000 students entered higher education around then (14 per cent). Today, the grades asked for are much higher (BCC for geography at Sheffield Hallam Uni- versity), and 49 per cent go: Department for Education (2017) 'Participation Rates in Higher Education: Academic Years 2006/2007–2015/2016 (Provisional)', London: Department for Education, https://www.gov.uk/government/uploads/system/up- loads/attachment_data/file/648165/HEIPR_PUBLICATION_2015-16.pdf

59 Very early on in her disastrous party conference speech of October 2017, The- resa mentioned that her grandmother 'boasts three professors and a Prime Minister' among her offspring. It is worth pondering why she thought that fact

important: May, T. (2017) 'Theresa May's Conservative conference speech, full text', *The Spectator*, 4 October, https://blogs.spectator.co.uk/2017/10/theresa-mays-conservative-conference-speech-full-text/

60   Kennedy, B. (1995) 'Obituary: Marjorie Sweeting', *The Independent*, 18 January, https://www.independent.co.uk/news/people/obituaries-marjorie-sweeting-1568531.html

61   Theresa May's tutor had lived very nearby and possibly even attended her father's church in Forest Hill, just outside the city of Oxford. The two may not have known each other, or they may well have met. As Theresa Brasier, she had been sent to a succession of schools, none open to all children, ending up in a grammar school that was in the process of turning into a comprehensive for children younger than her.

62   Meyer, H. D. and Benavot, A. (eds) (2013) *PISA, Power and Policy*, Didcot: Symposium Books.

63   Callender, C. and Thompson, J. (2018) 'The Lost Part-timers: the decline of part-time undergraduate higher education in England', London: Sutton Trust, pp. 3, 59, https://www.suttontrust.com/research-paper/lost-part-timers-mature-students/

64   Coughlan, S. (2018) 'Poor white schools "destroyed" by rankings', BBC News, 25 May, http://www.bbc.co.uk/news/education-44196645

65   Stotesbury, N. and Dorling, D. (2015) 'Understanding Income Inequality and its Implications: Why Better Statistics are Needed', Statistics Views, 21 October, http://www.statisticsviews.com/details/feature/8493411/Understanding-IncomeInequality-and-its-Implications-Why-Better-Statistics-Are-N.html

66   Common Ground blog (2017) 'A response from Common Ground', 15 December, https://commonground-oxford.com/response-to-nigel-biggars-article-dont-feel-guilty-about-our-colonial-history/

67   The African Society (2017) 'Against Biggar and "Recolonization"', press release, 19 December, http://www.oxforduniversityafricasociety.com/statement-19-12-17/

68   Drawn by Benjamin Hennig, with data kindly provided by the Oxford University admissions service.

69   Dorling, D., Smith, G., Noble, M., Wright, G., Burrows, R., Bradshaw, J., Joshi, H., Pattie, C., Mitchell, R., Green, A. E., McCulloch, A. (2001) 'How much does place matter?' *Environment & Planning A*, Vol. 33, No. 8., pp. 1335–69.

70   Tomlinson, S. (2013) *Ignorant Yobs?: Low attainers in a Global Knowledge Economy*, London: Routledge.

71   Schools Inquiry Commission (1886) The Taunton Report, Vol. 1, p. 93.

72   Beatty, C., Fothergill, S. and Gore, T. (2017) 'The Real Level of Unemployment 2017', Sheffield: Centre for Regional Economic and Social Research, Sheffield Hallam University, tp://www4.shu.ac.uk/research/cresr/sites/shu.ac.uk/files/real-level-unemployment-2017.pdf

73   Peachey, K. (2017) 'Council tax debt: Concern over use of bailiffs', BBC News, 14 November, http://www.bbc.co.uk/news/business-41974406

74   Allen, G. (2011) 'Early intervention: smart investment, massive savings', London: Cabinet Office, https://www.gov.uk/government/publications/early-intervention-smart-investment-massive-savings

75   Perry, B. D. (2002) 'Childhood Experience and the Expression of Genetic Potential: What childhood neglect tells us about nature and nurture', *Brain and Mind* 3, pp. 79–100, http://childtrauma.org/wp-content/uploads/2013/09/childhood_experience_expression_genetic_potential_perry.pdf

76   Shaw, M., Dorling, D. and Davey Smith, G. (2002) 'Editorial: Mortality and political climate: how suicide rates have risen during periods of Conservative government,

1901–2000', *Journal of Epidemiology and Community Health*, Vol. 56, No. 10, pp. 722–7, http://www.dannydorling.org/?page_id=1326

77 DWP (2015) 'Mortality Statistics: Employment and Support Allowance, Incapacity Benefit or Severe Disablement Allowance: Additional information on those who have died after claiming Employment and Support Allowance (ESA), Incapacity Benefit (IB) or Severe Disablement Allowance (SDA)', London: Department for Work and Pensions, August, https://www.gov.uk/government/uploads/system/uploads/attachment_data/file/459106/mortality-statistics-esa-ib-sda.pdf

78 Sahlberg, P. (2015) *Finnish Lessons: what the world can learn from educational change in Finland*, Columbia: Teachers' College Press.

79 Pearl, R. (1927) 'Differential Fertility', *Quarterly Review of Biology*, Vol. 2, No. 1, p. 116.

80 Turkheimer, E. (2000) 'Three laws of behavioural genetics and what they mean', *Current Directions in Psychological Science*, Vol. 9, No. 5, p. 160.

81 This is why Mendelian randomisation is such a good method of testing hypotheses, along with understanding that 'the basic notion that what is near-random at one level may be almost entirely predictable at a higher level is an emergent property of many systems, from particle physics to the social sciences'. Davey Smith, G. (2011) 'Epidemiology, epigenetics and the "Gloomy Prospect": embracing randomness in population health research and practice', *International Journal of Epidemiology*, Vol. 40, No. 3, pp. 537–62, https://academic.oup.com/ije/article/40/3/537/747708

82 'While all of you are brothers, we will say in our tale, God in fashioning those who are fit to rule mingled gold in their generation, for this reason they are most precious, but in the helpers are silver, and iron and brass in the farmers and craftsmen. You are all kin, but for the most part you will breed according to your kind.' Plato, *The Republic*, Book 3, Section 415a, quoted in Dorling, D. and Tomlinson, S. (2016) 'The Creation of Inequality: Myths of Potential and Ability', op. cit.

83 Smith, A. (1776) *The Wealth of Nations*, London: Strahan and Cadell.

84 Reay, D. (2017) *Miseducation: Inequality, education and the working classes*, Bristol: Policy Press.

85 Schatz, R., Staub, E., and Lavine, H. (1999) 'On the Varieties of National Attachment: Blind Versus Constructive Patriotism', *Political Psychology*, Vol. 20, No. 1, pp. 151–74, http://onlinelibrary.wiley.com/doi/10.1111/0162-895X.00140/abstract

86 http://www.loc.gov/pictures/item/2003675256/ and https://atomicink.files.wordpress.com/2016/07/british_empire_union_wwi_poster.jpg

87 Edith Cavell, whose grave is depicted in the poster, was a British nurse shot at dawn in 1915 by the Germans for helping Allied soldiers in occupied Belgium escape.

Chapter 4: High inequality and ignorant politicians

1 El-Enany, N. (2017) 'Brexit is not only an expression of nostalgia for empire, it is also the fruit of empire', op. cit.

2 Marquand, D. (2018) 'England, Ireland, Scotland, Wales – time for all to jump in to the debate', Open Democracy, 22 June, https://www.opendemocracy.net/uk/david-marquand/england-ireland-scotland-wales-time-for-all-to-jump-in-to-debate

3 This chapter is very much changed now, but it began its life as an article originally published as: Dorling, D. and Tomlinson, S. (2017) 'Beware of Kipling-spouting politicians: Britain's imperial mind-set is undermining its chances of Brexit trade success', *Prospect* magazine, 9 October, https://www.prospectmagazine.co.uk/politics/beware-of-kipling-spouting-politicians-britains-imperial-mindset-is-undermining-its-chances-of-brexit-trade-success

4   Dorling, D. (2018) *Peak Inequality*, op. cit.

5   Doward, J. (2014) 'Pay squeeze worst since Victorian age, study finds', *The Guardian*, 11 October, https://www.theguardian.com/politics/2014/oct/11/british-pay-squeeze-worst-150-years-tuc-study

6   On 16 November 2017, an article in the *British Medical Journal Open* concluded that severe public spending cuts in the UK were associated with 120,000 deaths between 2010 and 2017. The original article by ten researchers, mostly working in medicine, can be found here: Watkins, J., Wulaningsih, W., Da Zhou, C., et al. (2017) 'Effects of health and social care spending constraints on mortality in England: a time trend analysis', *British Medical Journal Open*, https://bmjopen.bmj.com/content/7/11/e017722, and longer explanation is given in the reference provided by the next endnote below.

7   Dorling, D. and Gietel-Basten, S. (2017) 'Life expectancy in Britain has fallen so much that a million years of life could disappear by 2058. Why?', The Conversation, 29 November, http://theconversation.com/life-expectancy-in-britain-has-fallen-so-much-that-a-million-years-of-life-could-disappear-by-2058-why-88063

8   BBC (2018) 'The English question: Young are less proud to be English', BBC News, 3 June, poll carried out across England, https://www.bbc.co.uk/news/uk-england-44142843

9   BBC (2018) ibid.

10   This poem by Rudyard Kipling was originally written for the Diamond Jubilee celebration of Queen Victoria, but was rewritten to support American colonisation.

11   Jacobson, D. (2007) 'Kipling in South Africa', *London Review of Books*, Vol. 29, No. 11, 7 June, https://www.lrb.co.uk/v29/n11/dan-jacobson/kipling-in-south-africa

12   Linstrum, E. (2017) 'The empire dreamt back: To help rule its empire, Britain turned to psychoanalysis. But they weren't willing to hear the truth it told', *Aeon* magazine, 4 December, https://aeon.co/essays/britains-imperial-dream-catchers-and-the-truths-of-empire

13   James, M. (2014) 'Cecil Rhodes and the Bullingdon Club', Rhodes Bishop's Stortford Museum News, 15 April, http://www.rhodesbishopsstortford.org.uk/museum-news/cecil-rhodes-and-the-bullingdon-club/

14   Brendon, P. (2007) *The Decline and Fall of the British Empire 1781–1997*, London: Vintage.

15   Gilbert, M. (1997) *A History of the Twentieth Century: Volume One, 1900–1933*, New York: William Morrow and Company, p. 11.

16   Hughes, G. (2010) 'South Africa and the British concentration camps', 16 June, https://christhum.wordpress.com/2010/06/16/south-africa-and-the-british-concentration-camps/

17   Moran, C. (2012) *Moranthology*, London: HarperCollins, in which David Cameron is said to resemble a slightly camp gammon robot, a C3PO made of ham.

18   John Bull locking the door to immigrants. A cartoon from page 4 of the *Daily Express*, 26 November 1901. The original can be found here: https://www.express.co.uk/paper-archive

19   The term fascism is thought not to have been used until Mussolini created a fascist organisation in Italy around the year 1914.

20   Benewick, R. (1969) *Political violence and public order: A study of British fascism*, London: Allen Lane.

21   Bar-Yosef, E. (2009) *'The Jew' in Late-Victorian and Edwardian Culture*, London: Palgrave Macmillan, p. 74.

22   Heffernan, E. (2005) 'The same old racist lies about immigrants and disease, a century on', *Socialist Worker*, No. 1940, 26 February, https://socialistworker.co.uk/art/5813/ The+same+old+racist+lies+about+immigrants+and+disease%2C+a+century+on

23   Rhodes, C. (1877) *Confession of Faith*. Source: Flint, J. E. (1974) *Cecil Rhodes*, Boston: Little, Brown, pp. 248–52. Also see: Lloyd, J. (2017) 'Dons, donors and the murky business of funding universities', *Financial Times*, 27 October, https://www.ft.com/ content/b6e358d8-ba2c-11e7-9bfb-4a9c83ffa852

24   This quote was first found at the very bottom of this webpage (when accessed on 30 October 2017): http://www.rhodeshouseoxford.com/the-venue/our-history/. That webpage has since been deleted, but you cannot rewrite history when you put something up on the internet. The original page can still be found here: https://web. archive.org/web/20171114201158/http://www.rhodeshouseoxford.com/the-venue/ our-history/

25   Rhodes, C. (1877) *Confession of Faith*, op. cit. See also: http://www.pitt.edu/~syd/ rhod.html

26   The statue of Cecil Rhodes in Cape Town University was removed in April 2015, and that has since been confirmed to be a permanent removal.

27   Morley, D. and Schwarz, B. (2014) 'Stuart Hall obituary: Influential cultural theorist, campaigner and founding editor of the New Left Review', *The Guardian*, 10 February, https://www.theguardian.com/politics/2014/feb/10/stuart-hall

28   Orwell, G. (1941) *The Lion and the Unicorn: Socialism and the English Genius*, London: Secker & Warburg.

29   The Morris Motors formal policy not to employ black people in Oxford ended in the 1950s, but the colour bar to working on the production line was maintained until 1967. Before then, black workers at the Oxford plant could only be cleaners. See: Thornett, A. (2014) 'Participation, resistance and betrayal among car workers', Revolutionary Socialism in the 21st Century, 7 February, https://rs21.org.uk/2014/02/07/ participation-resistance-and-betrayal-among-car/

30   Fazackerley, A. (2017) 'Universities deplore McCarthyism as MP demands list of tutors lecturing on Brexit', *The Guardian*, 24 October, https://www.theguardian. com/education/2017/oct/24/universities-mccarthyism-mp-demands-list-brexit-chris-heaton-harris

31   Dorling, D. (2017) 'Danny Dorling predicts "local nationalisation" of UK universities', *Times Higher Education*, 23 October, https://www.timeshighereducation.com/ news/danny-dorling-predicts-local-nationalisation-uk-universities

32   Tomlinson, S. (2017) personal communication with senior colleagues.

33   Welcome Europe (2016) 'Horizon 2020 – cost', last updated 20 December, https:// www.welcomeurope.com/european-funds/horizon-2020-cost-965+865.html

34   Stotesbury, N. and Dorling, D. (2015) 'Understanding Income Inequality and its Implications', op. cit.

35   Finding precise spending figures for China is not easy but we do know that 'the United States and China perform poorly when comparing their medal count to GDP, with 0.7 and 0.6 medals per £100bn of GDP respectively'. See: Kirk, A. (2016) 'Rio 2016 alternative medal table: How countries rank when we adjust for population and GDP', *Daily Telegraph*, 22 August, http://www.telegraph.co.uk/olympics/2016/08/21/ rio-2016-alternate-medal-table-how-countries-rank-when-we-adjust/

36   It is a moot point which country produces the most and/or the worst celebrities and the most crass celebrity culture. Occasionally Australia tries to outrank the UK for crassness.

37 http://www.migrationmuseum.org/no-turning-back-diverging-paths-in-brit-ains-migration-history/. Reproduced with the kind permission of the Jewish Museum, London, marked as drawn in 1906 from a scrapbook of newspaper cuttings donated to the museum, author and original publication unknown.

38 Coughlan, S. (2018) 'UK "missing out" on overseas students', BBC News, 4 September, https://www.bbc.co.uk/news/education-45398634

39 Dorling, D. (2011) *So you think you know about Britain?*, London: Constable.

40 Slack, J. (2016) 'Enemies of the people: Fury over "out of touch" judges who have "declared war on democracy" by defying 17.4m Brexit voters and who could trigger constitutional crisis', *Daily Mail*, 4 November (updated), http://www.dailymail.co.uk/news/article-3903436/Enemies-people-Fury-touch-judges-defied-17-4m-Brexit-voters-trigger-constitutional-crisis.html

41 White poppies were introduced in 1933 when the original Remembrance Day message of 'never again' was fading. See: http://www.ppu.org.uk/whitepoppy/index.html

42 Clark, D. (2011) 'Which nations are most responsible for climate change?', *The Guardian*, 21 April, https://www.theguardian.com/environment/2011/apr/21/countries-responsible-climate-change

43 The claim of second is made by 'UK Trade and Investment' in: Dunlop, T. (2016) 'The UK has become the world's second largest arms dealer, second only to the United States', *UK Defence Journal*, 5 September, https://ukdefencejournal.org.uk/uk-is-second-largest-global-arms-dealer/

44 Singman, B. and Burman, B. (2018) 'Trump imposes tariffs on steel and aluminium: Mexico and Canada exempt for now', Fox News, 8 March, http://www.foxnews.com/politics/2018/03/08/trump-imposing-tariffs-on-all-steel-aluminum-imports-exempts-mexico-and-canada-for-now.html

45 Elgot, J. (2018) 'Theresa May attacks Donald Trump's "unjustified" steel tariffs', *The Guardian*, 1 June, https://www.theguardian.com/politics/2018/jun/01/theresa-may-attacks-donald-trump-unjustified-steel-tariffs-eu

46 *Auf Wiedersehen, Pet*: a British TV series shown at various times from 1983 to 2004 as documented here: http://www.imdb.com/title/tt0086665/

47 Neate, R. (2018) 'Paper straw factory to open in Britain as restaurants ditch plastic', *The Guardian*, 17 June, https://www.theguardian.com/business/2018/jun/17/paper-straw-factory-to-open-in-britain-as-restaurants-ditch-plastic-mcdonalds

48 Elliott, L. (2017) 'Why the moaning? If anything can halt capitalism's fat cats, it's Brexit', *The Guardian*, 21 July, https://www.theguardian.com/commentisfree/2017/jul/21/capitalism-fat-cats-brexit-leaving-eu

49 Barnett, A. (2017) 'The lure of Lexit must be resisted – socialism in one country is a fantasy', *New Statesman*, 21 September, https://www.newstatesman.com/politics/uk/2017/09/lure-lexit-must-be-resisted-socialism-one-country-fantasy

50 Ballas, D., Dorling, D. and Hennig, B. (2017) *The Human Atlas of Europe*, Bristol: Policy Press.

51 Singleton, D. (2017) 'The "worrying truth" about Momentum – according to Theresa May's policy chief', Total Politics, 17 November, https://www.totalpolitics.com/articles/diary/%E2%80%98worrying-truth%E2%80%99-about-momentum-%E2%80%93-according-theresa-may%E2%80%99s-policy-chief. The worrying truth about Momentum was that it was appearing to be mainstream in its views as compared with the Conservative Party.

52 Luyendijk, J. (2017) 'How I learnt to loathe England', *Prospect* magazine, 6 October, https://www.prospectmagazine.co.uk/magazine/how-i-learnt-to-loathe-england

53 British Library Board, Source: '745.a.6, opposite 56'

54 Hope, C. (2017) 'Boris Johnson's 10-point plan for a successful Brexit', *Daily Telegraph*, 15 September, http://www.telegraph.co.uk/news/2017/09/15/boris-johnsons-10-point-plan-successful-brexit/

55 Hayward, E. (2018) 'Here's the truth about Brexit, the "punishment" some people claim the EU wants to inflict on us, the full horrific consequences of no deal, and the dangers lurking behind any deal we reach', Twitter, 14 October, https://twitter.com/uk_domain_names/status/1051411763680473090

56 Helm, T. and Savage, M. (2018) '"Stop Boris": MPs rally round May ahead of crucial Brexit vote', *The Observer*, 10 June, https://www.theguardian.com/politics/2018/jun/09/stop-boris-theresa-may-mps-backing-crucial-votes-brexit

57 BBC (2018) 'Boris Johnson challenged over Brexit business "expletive"', BBC News, 26 June, https://www.bbc.co.uk/news/uk-politics-44618154

58 BBC (2018) 'Johnny Mercer questions whether Tory party still shares his values', BBC News, 19 October, https://www.bbc.co.uk/news/uk-politics-45905581

59 Google 'Foreign Office Interior' images. There are a very large number to see. For example: https://openhouselondon.open-city.org.uk/listings/400

60 Which needs to be ratified by national and regional Parliaments in the EU next. See: CETA (2017) 'EU–Canada Comprehensive Economic and Trade Agreement', http://ec.europa.eu/trade/policy/in-focus/ceta/index_en.htm

61 BBC (2017) 'UK credit rating downgraded by Moody's', BBC News, 23 September, http://www.bbc.co.uk/news/business-41369239

62 Swinford. S. (2018) 'Davis in public battle with May over Brexit', *Daily Telegraph*, 7 June, https://www.pressreader.com/uk/the-daily-telegraph/20180607/281479277108429

63 Balls, K. (2018) 'What is Jeremy Hunt up to?', *The Spectator*, 25 June, https://blogs.spectator.co.uk/2018/06/what-is-jeremy-hunt-up-to/

64 Williams, S. (2018) 'Not again! BBC journalist accidentally calls Jeremy Hunt Jeremy C*** during BBC Radio 4 Broadcast', *London Evening Standard*, 25 June, https://www.standard.co.uk/news/uk/not-again-bbc-journalist-accidentally-calls-jeremy-hunt-jeremy-c-on-bbc-radio-4-broadcast-a3870856.html

65 Tharoor, S. (2017) *Inglorious Empire: What the British Did to India*, London: C. Hurst & Co. See also: Tharoor, S. (2017) '"But what about the railways…?" The myth of Britain's gifts to India', *The Guardian*, 8 March, https://www.theguardian.com/world/2017/mar/08/india-britain-empire-railways-myths-gifts

66 Maddison, A. (2007) *Contours of the World Economy, 1–2030 AD: Essays in Macro-Economic History*, Oxford: Oxford University Press, p. 382, Table A7. See also: https://en.wikipedia.org/wiki/List_of_regions_by_past_GDP_(PPP)_per_capita

67 Jeffries, A. (2017) 'Le Jaffa Cake fiasco – does Bake Off get lost in translation around the world?', *The Guardian*, 12 November, https://www.theguardian.com/tv-and-radio/shortcuts/2017/nov/12/jaffa-cake-fiasco-bake-off-lost-in-translation-around-world

68 First published 1950–52 with at least one reprint in 1960. He started writing geography textbooks in 1929. Presumably much was copied from previous volumes.

69 Ramsay, A. (2017) 'For Britain to solve its economic problems, it needs to stop lying to itself about its past', Open Democracy, 9 March, https://www.opendemocracy.net/neweconomics/trade-empire-2-0-and-the-lies-we-tell-ourselves/, in turn referencing *The Times* and Twitter: https://twitter.com/LiamFox/status/705674061016387584

70 Coates, S. (2017) 'Ministers aim to build "empire 2.0" with African Commonwealth', *The Times*, 6 March, https://www.thetimes.co.uk/article/ministers-aim-to-build-empire-2-0-with-african-commonwealth-after-brexit-v9bs6f6z9

71   https://data.imf.org/?sk=9D6028D4-F14A-464C-A2F2-59B2CD424B85

72   http://data.imf.org/?sk=9D6028D4-F14A-464C-A2F2-59B2CD424B85&sId=
      1515619375491

73   Boffey, D. and Topham, G. (2018) 'Aviation industry: EU blocks talks to avert
      "no-deal" Brexit crisis', *The Guardian*, 18 June, https://www.theguardian.com/
      business/2018/jun/18/aviation-industry-eu-blocks-talks-to-avert-no-deal-brexit-crisis

74   Dorling, D. (2017) Short Cuts, *London Review of Books*, Vol. 39, No. 22, p. 19,
      https://www.lrb.co.uk/v39/n22/danny-dorling/short-cuts. An illustrated and refer-
      enced version can be read here: http://www.dannydorling.org/?page_id=6211

75   This is disputed but the poem also speaks for itself, as does the line 'If any question
      why we died / Tell them, because our fathers lied'. See: Karlin, D. (2015) 'Our fathers
      lied: Rudyard Kipling as a war poet', Oxford University Press blog, 29 December,
      https://blog.oup.com/2015/12/rudyard-kipling-war-poet/

76   Southam, B. (2010) 'My Boy Jack', Kipling Society, 6 March, http://www.kiplingso-
      ciety.co.uk/rg_jack1.htm

Chapter 5: The fantasy and future of free trade

1   Hope, C. (2017) 'Foreigners charged £10 to enter UK under new Brexit visa pro-
      posal', *Daily Telegraph*, 23 December, https://www.telegraph.co.uk/news/2017/12/23/
      foreigners-charged-10-enter-uk-new-brexit-visa-proposal/

2   *Business Times* (2018) 'Brexit nightmare: 17-mile traffic jams at the Dover border', 4
      June, https://www.businesstimes.com.sg/transport/brexit-nightmare-17-mile-traffic-
      jams-at-the-dover-border

3   Oren, T. and Blyth, M. (2018) 'From Big Bang to Big Crash: The Early Origins
      of the UK's Finance-led Growth Model and the Persistence of Bad Policy Ideas',
      New Political Economy, May, https://www.researchgate.net/publication/325272450_
      From_Big_Bang_to_Big_Crash_The_Early_Origins_of_the_UK's_Finance-led_
      Growth_Model_and_the_Persistence_of_Bad_Policy_Ideas

4   Oren, T. and Blyth, M. (2018) ibid., p. 17, quoting Brian Griffiths and David Willetts.

5   As Wikipedia explains to any student who looks Mill up (or at least any student who
      did in November 2017): 'His influential History of British India contains a complete
      denunciation and rejection of Indian culture and civilization': https://en.wikipedia.
      org/wiki/James_Mill. Note that the term 'basket case' originated in the First World
      War for a soldier who had lost all four limbs and so had to be carried. Mill could not
      have used it as he was writing earlier than this, but his writings implied that India
      could not carry itself.

6   Ricardo's theory is worshipped among the far right, who repeatedly say that free
      un-tariffed trade 'will make us all richer, not poorer'. See: Worstall, T. (2017) 'Hard
      Brexit need not make us worse off', *The Guardian*, 6 November, https://www.the-
      guardian.com/politics/2017/nov/05/hard-brexit-need-not-make-us-worse-off

7   Sideri, S. (1970) *Trade and Power: Informal Colonialism in Anglo-Portuguese Relations*,
      Rotterdam: Rotterdam University Press. Quoted in Robinson, J. (1979) *Aspects of
      Development and Underdevelopment*, Cambridge: Cambridge University Press, p. 103.

8   Personal correspondence with Ann Pettifor, June 2018, director of Policy Research in
      Macroeconomics, author of *The Production of Money* (2017), London: Verso.

9   Dizikes, P. (2012) 'Economists find evidence for famous hypothesis of "compara-
      tive advantage"', MIT News, 20 June, http://news.mit.edu/2012/confirming-ricar-
      do-0620. Note: Arnaud Costinot and David Donaldson, working at the Massa-
      chusetts Institute of Technology, tried to find proof that David Ricardo's theory of

comparative advantage worked. They dated Ricardo's theory to 1817 and explained: 'Neat as this explanation may seem, it is by definition hard to prove. If England does not make wine, and Portugal does not make cloth, it is very hard to say how efficiently they could produce those goods. The same applies to any country not manufacturing any given product. So, does Ricardo's idea resemble reality?' Costinot and Donaldson used data from the UN Food and Agriculture Organization to look at seventeen types of crops grown in fifty-five countries. From this, they produced a model that found that Ricardo's theory did apply, but only to a relatively small extent. For it to be a complete explanation, there would have been a perfect correlation of 1.0 between how productive it was to grow a particular crop given underlying conditions and the output, the amount produced. As it was, they found a 'positive and statistically significant correlation' of only about 0.2. In other words, countries that have an advantage in producing a particular crop are a little more likely to produce it, but – surprisingly – not that much more likely than those with less of an advantage.

10 Redrawn using information in Martin, K. (2017) 'UK Budget: OBR pins growth forecast downgrade on productivity', *Financial Times*, 22 November, https://www.ft.com/content/ecfce415-44f5-377c-8fd4-30bd97fa2a50

11 Collingham, L. (2017) *The Hungry Empire*, London: Bodley Head, pp. 152–3.

12 Manning, S. (2013) 'Britain's colonial shame: Slave-owners given huge pay-outs after abolition', *The Independent*, 24 February, http://www.independent.co.uk/news/uk/home-news/britains-colonial-shame-slave-owners-given-huge-payouts-after-abolition-8508358.html

13 Lovell, J. (2011) *The Opium War: Drugs, Dreams and the Making of China*, London: Picador.

14 Collingham, L. (2017) *The Hungry Empire*, op. cit., p. 248.

15 https://en.wikipedia.org/wiki/Nation_of_shopkeepers

16 Dhingra, S. and Datta, N. (2017) 'How not to do trade deals', *London Review of Books*, Vol. 39, No. 18, 21 September, https://www.lrb.co.uk/v39/n18/swati-dhingra/how-not-to-do-trade-deals

17 Kamm, O. (2017) 'Face the facts: no deal over Brexit can only damage the economy', *The Times*, 16 October, https://www.thetimes.co.uk/article/face-the-facts-no-deal-over-brexit-can-only-damage-the-economy-w37crtbfn

18 González Durántez, M. (2017) 'How to beat the ticking Brexit clock: let British business leaders do the talking', *The Guardian*, 18 July, https://www.theguardian.com/commentisfree/2017/jul/18/brexit-british-business-leaders-legatum-eu

19 Geoghegan, P. (2017) 'Legatum: the Brexiteers' favourite think tank. Who is behind them?', Open Democracy, 26 November, https://www.opendemocracy.net/uk/peter-geoghegan/legatum-who-are-brexiteers-favourite-think-tank-and-who-is-behind-them. See also: Walters, S. and Owen, G. (2017) 'Secretive institute behind Boris and Gove's Brexit letter to "hijack" Number 10 faces probe by charity watchdog', *Mail on Sunday*, 2 December, http://www.dailymail.co.uk/news/article-5139897/Institute-linked-hard-Brexit-facing-charity-probe.html

20 North, R. (2017) 'Brexit: disaster capitalism', EUReferendum.com, 31 July, http://www.eureferendum.com/blogview.aspx?blogno=86556

21 *The Economist* (2016) 'Ulster evangelicals for Brexit: For hard-line Protestants, leaving Europe is a matter of eschatology', 24 July, https://www.economist.com/blogs/erasmus/2016/06/ulster-evangelicals-brexit

22 Ruddick, G. (2017) 'Brexit is the worst ever decision says Bloomberg', *The Guardian*,

24 October, https://www.theguardian.com/politics/2017/oct/24/michael-bloomberg-brexit-is-stupidest-thing-any-country-has-done-besides-trump

23   MI6 (2017) 'Trades and Services – careers information', Secret Intelligence Service, https://www.sis.gov.uk/trades-and-services.html

24   Leys, C. (1983) *Politics in Britain: An introduction*, London: Heinemann Educational Books, p. 82. Quoting in turn *The Times*, 8 June 1973.

25   The other part is feeling that their prime responsibility is to their shareholders rather than to their employees, customers or even the long-term future of their business; dividends and lucrative takeovers rather than investment and pay rises.

26   Ahmad, K. (2017) 'Bank of England believes Brexit could cost 75,000 finance jobs', BBC News, 31 October, http://www.bbc.co.uk/news/business-41803604. BBC Radio 4 (2018) *Today* programme, 9 November: a banker told his interviewer that some 10,000 bankers had already gone to work in Europe.

27   Fazi, T. and Mitchell, W. (2018) 'Why the Left Should Embrace Brexit', *Jacobin*, 29 April, https://www.jacobinmag.com/2018/04/brexit-labour-party-socialist-left-corbyn

28   Thanks to Claire Hann for finding these. For gluttons there are more here: http://www.economistjokes.com/jokes and here: https://www.barrypopik.com/index.php/new_york_city/entry/the_first_law_of_economists_for_every_economist_there_exists_an_equal_and_o/

29   https://en.wikipedia.org/wiki/Barclays#1690_to_1900

30   BBC (2008) 'What is a City trading job like?', BBC News, 24 January, http://news.bbc.co.uk/1/hi/business/7207543.stm

31   Staff Reporter (2009) 'Darling "blocked Barclays bid to take over failing Lehman"', *London Evening Standard*, 29 October, https://www.standard.co.uk/business/darling-blocked-barclays-bid-to-take-over-failing-lehman-6753348.html

32   https://en.wikipedia.org/wiki/Woolsack and in turn from here: http://www.parliament.uk/about/living-heritage/building/palace/architecture/palace-s-interiors/lords-chamber/

33   EU (2018) The Anti-Tax Avoidance Directive, Brussels: European Union, https://ec.europa.eu/taxation_customs/business/company-tax/anti-tax-avoidance-package/anti-tax-avoidance-directive_en

34   Zielonka, J. (2017) 'British leaders have lost the plot', Zeit Online, 14 November, http://www.zeit.de/politik/ausland/2017-11/great-britain-government-brexit-paradise-papers-sexism-english

35   See the Campaign Against the Arms Trade: https://www.caat.org.uk

36   Norton-Taylor, R. (2010) 'BAE tops global list of largest arms manufacturer', *The Guardian*, 11 April, https://www.theguardian.com/business/2010/apr/12/bae-systems-weapons-arms-manufacturers

37   Stone, J. (2016) 'Britain is now the second biggest arms dealer in the world', *The Independent*, 5 September, http://www.independent.co.uk/news/uk/home-news/britain-is-now-the-second-biggest-arms-dealer-in-the-world-a7225351.html

38   Borger, J. (2017) 'US nuclear plans will lead to arms race', *The Guardian*, 30 October, https://www.pressreader.com/uk/the-guardian/20171030/281865823728587

39   Leroux, M. (2017) '1,000 jobs at risk as BAE's fast jet runs out of orders', *The Times*, 10 October, https://www.thetimes.co.uk/article/1-000-jobs-at-risk-as-bae-gives-up-on-order-for-jets-77kb70g99

40   Evans, R. (2017) 'UK trade department draws half its secondees from arms industry', *The Guardian*, 8 October, https://www.theguardian.com/world/2017/oct/08/uk-trade-department-draws-half-its-secondees-from-arms-industry

41 Arias Sánchez, Ó. (2009) 'The global arms trade', *Harvard International Review*, 4 January, http://hir.harvard.edu/article/?a=1778

42 Foresight (2013) 'The future of manufacturing: a new era of opportunity and challenge for the UK project report', London: Government Office for Science, p. 15, https://www.gov.uk/government/uploads/system/uploads/attachment_data/file/255922/13-809-future-manufacturing-project-report.pdf

43 Various authors (2013) 'Collection: Future of manufacturing', London: Government Office for Science and Department for Business, Innovation and Skills, https://www.gov.uk/government/collections/future-of-manufacturing

44 Reuben, A. (2015) 'What's going on in UK manufacturing?', BBC News, 20 October, http://www.bbc.co.uk/news/business-34463597

45 Morris, N. (2017) 'Paupers' funerals rise by 50 per cent in four years', I-News, 16 April, https://inews.co.uk/news/uk/worrying-picture-isolation-numbers-paupers-funerals-soar/

46 Reuben, A. (2015) 'What's going on in UK manufacturing?', BBC News, 20 October, http://www.bbc.co.uk/news/business-34463597

47 Billy Bragg's song is 'Full English Brexit': https://www.youtube.com/watch?v=07X_yk1v8S4

48 Monaghan, A. (2017) 'Digital technologies offer antidote to Brexit, ministers told', *The Guardian*, 30 October, https://www.pressreader.com/uk/the-guardian/20171030/281986082812875

49 ONS (2018) 'UK manufacturers' sales by product: 2017 provisional results', Statistical Bulletin, 3 July, https://www.ons.gov.uk/businessindustryandtrade/manufacturingandproductionindustry/bulletins/ukmanufacturerssalesbyproductprodcom/2017provisionalresults

50 Corera, G. (2011) *MI6: Life and Death in the British Secret Service*, London: Phoenix, p. 5.

51 Poitras, L. (2014) 'GCHQ and NSA Targeted Private German Companies and Merkel', *Der Spiegel*, 29 March, http://www.spiegel.de/international/germany/gchq-and-nsa-targeted-private-german-companies-a-961444.html

52 Security and Intelligence Agencies (2016) 'Financial Statement 2015–16 (For the year ended 31 March 2016)', London: House of Commons, p. 16. https://www.gov.uk/government/uploads/system/uploads/attachment_data/file/540815/56308_HC_363_WEB.pdf

53 Boyle, A. (1979) *Climate of Treason*, London: Hutchinson, p. 33. Also see http://theinquisition.eu/wordpress/2009/history/meynell-nonesuch/

54 Rimington, S. (2001) *Open Secret*, London: Hutchinson.

55 Sanderson, D. (2017) 'We spied on Trotskyists who now advise Corbyn, says Stella Rimington, ex-boss of MI5', *The Times*, 14 October, https://www.thetimes.co.uk/article/we-spied-on-trotskyists-who-now-advise-corbyn-says-stella-rimington-ex-boss-of-mi5-55jg3lfpd

56 Dorling, D. (2018) 'Thank God for the House of Windsor (our museum future)', *London Review of Books*, 27 April, https://www.lrb.co.uk/blog/2018/04/27/danny-dorling/our-museum-future/

57 Davis, D. (2017) Letter to Baroness Verma, 30 October, http://www.parliament.uk/documents/lords-committees/eu-external-affairs-subcommittee/Brexit-trade-in-goods/Response-brexit-trade-in-goods.pdf

58 For instance, New Zealand invented the welfare state, not Britain: Carpinter, P. (2012) 'Summary – history of the Welfare State in New Zealand', Wellington: New Zealand Treasury, http://www.treasury.govt.nz/government/longterm/externalpanel/pdfs/ltfep-s2-03.pdf

59   http://www.parliament.uk/documents/lords-committees/eu-external-affairs-sub-committee/Brexit-trade-in-goods/Response-brexit-trade-in-goods.pdf

Chapter 6: How not to treat immigrants

1   Goodfellow, M. (2017) 'Labour isn't flip-flopping on Brexit – this is practical politics', *The Guardian*, 12 December, https://www.theguardian.com/commentisfree/2017/dec/12/brexit-jeremy-corbyn-keir-starmer-labour

2   Triggle, N. (2017) 'EU nurses "turning their backs on UK"', BBC News, 2 November, http://www.bbc.co.uk/news/health-41838426

3   Smith, A. (2018) 'Plea to bring back NHS bursaries for nurses after massive drop in applications', *The Metro*, 4 October, https://metro.co.uk/2018/10/04/plea-to-bring-back-nhs-bursaries-for-nurses-after-massive-drop-in-applications-8003557

4   RCM (2016) 'Midwife shortage could be huge if EU midwives unable to work in UK warns RCM', Royal College of Midwives press release, 12 September, https://www.rcm.org.uk/news-views-and-analysis/news/%E2%80%98midwife-shortage-could-be-huge-if-eu-midwives-unable-to-work-in-uk

5   Taylor-Robinson, D. and Barr, B. (2017) 'Death rate now rising in UK's poorest infants', *British Medical Journal*, 357, 11 May, j2258 doi: 10.1136/bmj.j2258

6   Siddique, H. (2018) 'Infant mortality in England and Wales could soar without action, study warns', *The Guardian*, 15 October, https://www.theguardian.com/politics/2018/oct/15/infant-mortality-in-england-and-wales-could-soar-without-action-study-warns

7   The UK already had the second lowest number of radiologists per head across all of Europe before the losses due to the immediate effects of Brexit. It probably now has the lowest number per head of all EU countries. See: FCR (2015) 'Clinical radiology UK workforce census 2015 report', London: Faculty of Clinical Radiology, September, https://www.rcr.ac.uk/system/files/publication/field_publication_files/bfcr166_cr_census.pdf

8   Onyanga-Omara, J. (2017) '"Brexodus": UK migration falls by biggest amount since records began', *Sydney Morning Herald*, 1 December, http://www.smh.com.au/world/brexodus-uk-net-migration-falls-by-biggest-amount-since-records-began-20171130-gzwfb4.html

9   Colthorpe, T. and Brown, R. (2018) 'Demography', in Colthorpe, T. and Brown, R. (eds), *The London Intelligence*, Issue 3, London: Centre for London, http://www.centreforlondon.org/reader/the-london-intelligence-issue-3/demography/#national-insurance-number-registrations

10   Colthorpe, T. and Brown, R. (2018) ibid.

11   Schraer, R. (2018) 'Is there a north–south divide in England's schools?', BBC News, 31 March, https://www.bbc.co.uk/news/education-43544255

12   ITV (2017) 'Immigrant children improve standards in London schools says Michael Gove', ITV News, 18 March, https://www.itv.com/news/london/2017-03-18/immigrant-children-improve-standards-in-london-schools-says-michael-gove/

13   See NHS (2018) 'Summary Hospital-level Mortality Indicator (SHMI) – Deaths associated with hospitalisation, England, October 2016 – September 2017' Funnel Plots', Leeds: NHS Digital, https://public.tableau.com/profile/waltworks#!/vizhome/SHMI_0/SHMIFunnelPlot accessed from here in May 2018: https://digital.nhs.uk/data-and-information/publications/clinical-indicators/shmi/current#Resources

14   Norton, P. (2012) Biographical note in Lord Howard of Rising (ed.), *Enoch at 100: a re-examination of the life, politics and philosophy of Enoch Powell*, London: Biteback.

15 what-when-how.com (undated) 'In Depth Tutorials and Information: Bradlaugh-Besant Trial (birth control)', http://what-when-how.com/birth-control/bradlaugh-besant-trial-birth-control

16 Quoted in Beers, L. (2016) *Red Ellen*, Massachusetts: Harvard University Press. Also see Wikipedia: https://en.wikipedia.org/wiki/Reginald_Sorensen,_Baron_Sorensen

17 Personal correspondence with Chris Lynch, 2018.

18 El-Enany, N. (2017) 'Things Fall Apart: From Empire to Brexit Britain', op. cit.

19 Winder, R. (2004) *Bloody Foreigners*, op. cit.

20 Kynge, J. (2018) 'Wealthy Chinese shrug off uncertainty to take lion's share of "golden visas"', *Financial Times*, 4 April, https://www.rte.ie/news/business/2018/0404/952023-today-in-the-press/

21 Dorling, D. (2018) 'Peak Inequality', *New Statesman*, 4 July, http://www.danny-dorling.org/?page_id=6678 or https://www.newstatesman.com/politics/uk/2018/07/peak-inequality

22 Hazeldine, T. and Rashbrooke, M. (2017) 'The New Zealand rich list twenty years on', *New Zealand Economic Papers*, doi: 10.1080/00779954.2017.1354907, https://www.tandfonline.com/eprint/EjSVceMfvCAqq2p8ZWMY/full

23 Byrne, L. (2018) 'Inclusive Growth', 4 April, London: House of Commons Library Research, https://www.inclusivegrowth.co.uk/house-commons-library-research/

24 Dorling, D. (2018) *Do We Need Income Inequality?*, Cambridge: Polity Press.

25 Byrne, L. (2018) 'Inclusive Growth', op. cit.

26 OECD (2018) 'Income inequality', doi: 10.1787/459aa7fi-en. At that point the only OECD country with rising inequality reported from 2016 onwards was Sweden (with an income inequality Gini of 0.282 which is still very low). Iceland, Israel, Italy, Korea, Lithuania, the Netherlands and Switzerland peaked in 2014. Most other OECD countries peaked before then, except for the UK in 2015 and the USA in 2013. The statistics showing income inequality now falling in most non-OECD countries are given in Dorling, D. (2017) *The Equality Effect*, op. cit.

27 Jones, R. (2018) 'Au pair shortage sparks childcare crisis for families', *The Guardian*, 9 June, https://www.theguardian.com/money/2018/jun/09/au-pair-shortage-prompts-crisis-for-families?CMP=twt_gu

28 *Truth* magazine (1893) 'Editorial', Vol. 34, No. 897, 2 November.

29 Jones, D. (2014) 'Joanna Lumley's legacy of misery', *Daily Mail*, 14 November, http://www.dailymail.co.uk/news/article-2835216/Joanna-Lumley-s-legacy-misery-fought-al-low-retired-Gurkhas-Britain-heart-right-place-Five-years-say-s-backfired-terribly.html

30 Winder, R. (2004) *Bloody Foreigners*, op. cit., p. 338.

31 Heffer, S. (2008) *Like the Roman: The life of Enoch Powell*, London: Faber and Faber; and, as an antidote to that: Tomlinson, S. (2018) 'Enoch Powell: empires, immigrants and education', *Race Ethnicity and Education*, Vol. 21, No. 1, pp. 1–14.

32 Norton-Taylor, R. and Milne, S. (1999) 'Racism: Extremists led Powell marches', *The Guardian*, 1 January, https://www.theguardian.com/uk/1999/jan/01/richardnortontaylor2

33 https://commons.wikimedia.org/wiki/File:Enoch_Powell_6_Allan_Warren.jpg

34 Manzoor, S. (2008) 'Black Britain's darkest hour', *The Observer*, 24 February, https://www.theguardian.com/politics/2008/feb/24/race

35 Manzoor, S. (2008) ibid.

36 Clarke, H. and Mezzofiore, G. (2018) 'Invited to the UK decades ago, now they must prove they're British', CNN, 17 April, https://edition.cnn.com/2018/04/16/europe/uk-windrush-generation-intl/index.html

37   Shipman, T. (2016) *All Out War*, op. cit.

38   Tomlinson, S. (1988) 'Clarifying the MacDonald Report', Letters, *The Independent*, 2 July.

39   Mould, W. (1986) 'No Rainbow Coalition on Tyneside', *Multicultural Teaching*, Vol. 4, No. 3, pp. 9–12.

40   DES (1985) 'Education for All: Annexe C, A report of visits to schools with few or no ethnic minorities', London: Department for Education and Science.

41   The last words Stephen Lawrence heard before he was killed. BBC (2011) 'Stephen Lawrence friend recalls attack on teenager', BBC News, 17 November, https://www.bbc.co.uk/news/uk-15769370

42   Pells, R. (2017) 'Parents urged to withhold personal data in latest school census targeting foreign-born children', *The Independent*, 16 May, https://www.independent.co.uk/news/education/education-news/government-school-census-parents-withhold-personal-data-foreign-born-children-passports-nationality-a7738486.html

43   https://twitter.com/ewa_jay/status/864087595659210753

44   Morris, S. (2003) 'Asylum seekers "were locked in during fire"', *The Guardian*, 23 July, https://www.theguardian.com/uk/2003/jul/23/immigration.immigrationandpublicservices

45   Sanghani, R. (2016) 'Home Office refuses to reveal if women in Yarl's Wood immigration centre have been raped', *Daily Telegraph*, 14 June, https://www.telegraph.co.uk/women/politics/home-office-refuses-to-reveal-if-women-in-yarls-wood-immigration/

46   Home Office (2002) 'Secure Borders, Safe Haven: Integration and Diversity in modern Britain', cm 5387, London: Home Office, Introduction.

47   Campbell, A. (2012) *The Burden of Power*, London: Arrow Books, p. 161.

48   Morris, N. (2003) 'Letwin pledges to send asylum seekers "far, far away"', *The Independent*, 8 October, https://www.independent.co.uk/news/uk/politics/letwin-pledges-to-send-asylum-seekers-far-far-away-90393.html

49   Staff Reporter (2006) 'Hanged detainee aimed to save son', BBC News, 19 September, http://news.bbc.co.uk/1/hi/england/beds/bucks/herts/5361324.stm

50   Peachey, K. and Palumbo, D. (2018) 'Tenants' tales – in five charts', BBC News, 11 May, http://www.bbc.co.uk/news/business-43799202

51   Hattenstone, S. (2018) 'Why was the scheme behind May's "Go Home" vans called Operation Vaken?', *The Guardian*, 26 April, https://www.theguardian.com/commentisfree/2018/apr/26/theresa-may-go-home-vans-operation-vaken-ukip

52   https://www.flickr.com/photos/oddsock/9376736345

53   Chorley, M. (2013) 'Home office vans telling illegal migrants to go home investigated by advertising watchdog', *Daily Mail*, 9 August, http://www.dailymail.co.uk/news/article-2387728/Home-Office-vans-telling-illegal-immigrants-Go-Home-investigated-advertising-watchdog-60-complaints.html

54   Baker, A. (2017) '97 per cent of international students leave UK after studies', The Pie News, 24 August, https://thepienews.com/news/government/97-international-students-leave-uk-studies/

55   McInerney, L. (2016) 'What society lets families fear deportation for sending their children to school?', *The Guardian*, 18 October, https://www.theguardian.com/education/2016/oct/18/deportation-boycott-school-census-data-nationality-parents

56   Lewis, E. (2018) 'Why we're asking MPs not to act as border guards', Global Justice Now, 19 June, https://www.globaljustice.org.uk/blog/2018/jun/19/why-were-asking-mps-not-act-border-guards

57   https://commons.wikimedia.org/wiki/File:Theresa_May_in_2007.jpg

58   Hill, A. (2018) 'At least 1,000 highly skilled migrants wrongly face deportation, experts reveal', *The Guardian*, 6 May, https://www.theguardian.com/uk-news/2018/may/06/at-least-1000-highly-skilled-migrants-wrongly-face-deportation-experts-reveal

59   Shirbon, E. (2018) 'May apologises to Caribbean countries for UK treatment of post-war migrants', Reuters, 17 April, https://uk.reuters.com/article/uk-britain-cho-gm-windrush/may-apologises-to-caribbean-countries-for-uk-treatment-of-post-war-migrants-idUKKBN1HO0OC

60   Gentleman, A. (2018) 'No clarity, no urgency, for Windrush case cancer patient', *The Guardian*, 20 April, https://twitter.com/guardian/status/987090672636383237

61   Shipman, T. (2016) *All Out War*, op. cit., p. 21.

62   Travis, A. (2017) 'More than 140,000 told by UK immigration they face removal', *The Guardian*, 2 November, https://www.theguardian.com/uk-news/2017/nov/02/more-than-140000-told-by-uk-immigration-they-face-removal-says-watchdog

63   Clarke, P. (2017) 'More deportees: Jamaica braces for their arrival from UK', *Jamaican Gleaner*, 8 March, http://jamaica-gleaner.com/article/lead-stories/20170308/more-deportees-jamaica-braces-their-arrival-uk-today

64   Samuel, J. (2018) 'How can a government so callous and chaotic be trusted with Brexit', *Daily Telegraph*, 30 April, https://www.pressreader.com/uk/the-daily-telegraph/20180430/281509341802830

65   Grierson, J. (2018) 'Hostile environment. Public opinion and Tory MPs still back a hard-line policy' (online as 'Rudd has gone but hostile environment policy set to stay') *The Guardian*, 30 April, https://www.theguardian.com/uk-news/2018/apr/30/rudd-has-gone-but-hostile-environment-policy-set-to-stay

66   Gentleman, A. (2018) 'What the victims say: I think the government has reignited the fires of racism' (online as 'I grew up with the National Front around my area. I thought these attitudes had been stamped out. The government has stoked it up again'), *The Guardian*, 1 May, https://www.theguardian.com/uk-news/2018/may/01/windrush-victims-voice-shock-scandals-political-consequences

67   Hirsch, A. (2018) *BRIT(ish): On race, identity and belonging*, London: Jonathan Cape, p. 25.

68   Jeory, T. (2016) 'Farage's fascist past? Nigel boasted about his NF initials and sang "gas them all", claims schoolfriend', *The Independent*, 11 August, https://www.independent.co.uk/news/uk/politics/nigel-farage-fascist-nazi-song-gas-them-all-ukip-brexit-schoolfriend-dulwich-college-a7185236.html

69   Farage as quoted in Bennett, O. (2016) *The Brexit Club*, op. cit.

70   Weaver, M. (2016) 'Polish Ambassador calls for unity against xenophobia as he visits scene of killing', *The Guardian*, 1 September

71   Adams, G. (2016) 'The great Brexit hate crime myth: How claims of an epidemic of race crimes since the referendum are simply false', *Daily Mail*, 24 September, http://www.dailymail.co.uk/news/article-3805008/The-great-Brexit-hate-crime-myth-claims-epidemic-race-crimes-referendum-simply-false.html

72   Schindler, J. (2017) 'Britain grows increasingly hostile to EU citizens', *Der Spiegel*, 2 December, http://www.spiegel.de/international/europe/as-brexit-nears-harrassment-of-eu-citizens-in-uk-rises-a-1181845.html

73   Boffey, D. and O'Carroll, L. (2018) 'Home office app for EU nationals fails to quell MEPs fears over Brexit' (online as '"Beyond belief": Brexit app for EU nationals won't work on iPhones'), *The Guardian*, 25 April, https://www.theguardian.com/politics/2018/apr/24/beyond-belief-brexit-app-for-eu-nationals-wont-work-on-iphones

74   Colson, T. (2018) 'This legal case could hand British people the right to remain

EU citizens after Brexit', *Business Insider*, 9 March, http://uk.businessinsider.com/british-people-keep-eu-citizenship-after-brexit-legal-case-crowdfund-2018-3

75   Iqbal, N. (2018) 'Top linguist: "I'm leaving the UK because of the disaster of Brexit"', *The Guardian*, 14 October, https://www.theguardian.com/politics/2018/oct/14/top-linguist-quits-uk-over-brexit-bad-atmosphere

76   Collins, L. (2018) 'Royal Pains: Marrying into the monarchy is no fairy tale', *New York Review of Books*, pp. 82–8.

77   Ormosi, P. (2016) 'The weight of Brexit', op. cit.

78   Ormosi, P. (2016) ibid.

79   Ormosi, P. (2016) ibid.

80   NHS (2017) 'National Child Measurement Programme – England, 2016–17', London: NHS, 19 October, https://digital.nhs.uk/catalogue/PUB30113 see Table 6a – the ratios are even higher by the postcode of the school, rather than the child's (table 6b).

81   Busby, E. (2018) 'Top private school holds "austerity day" with baked potatoes and beans for lunch', *The Independent*, 23 June, https://www.independent.co.uk/news/education/education-news/private-school-austerity-day-st-pauls-girls-london-potatoes-beans-poverty-a8411521.html

82   Redrawn from colour original provided by Mario Cortina Borja, Julian Stander and Luciana Dalla Valle (2016) 'The EU referendum: surname diversity and voting patterns', *Significance*, 18 July, https://www.statslife.org.uk/politics/2943-the-eu-referendum-surname-diversity-and-voting-patterns

83   Hirsch, A. (2018) *BRIT(ish)*, op. cit., p. 32.

84   Chakrabortty, A. (2018) 'Immigration has been good for Britain', op. cit.

85   Stewart, M. (2018) 'The 9.9 Percent Is the New American Aristocracy', *The Atlantic*, June, https://www.theatlantic.com/magazine/archive/2018/06/the-birth-of-a-new-american-aristocracy/559130/

86   The First Wave of immigrants (1820–60) came from western and northern Europe – Protestant, assimilated, similar culture. The Second Wave (1860–1920) came from Ireland, China, southern and eastern Europe. Culturally different – Orthodox, Jewish, Roman Catholic – they took low-paid jobs in urban areas.

87   Hutton, W. and Adonis. A. (2018) *Saving Britain: How we must change to prosper in Europe*, London: Abacus.

88   Shilliam, R. (2018) *Race and the Undeserving Poor (Building Progressive Alternatives): From abolition to Brexit*, Newcastle upon Tyne: Agenda Publishing.

Chapter 7: Imperially rooted education and bigotry

1   Guglani, S. (2017) 'The Notes: Doubt', *The Lancet*, Vol. 390, 14 October, p. 1731.

2   This chapter is based in part on an article we wrote for a newspaper prior to the 2017 general election: Dorling, D. and Tomlinson, S. (2017) 'Is Corbyn as lacking in drive and personality as Attlee? Let's hope so', *The Guardian*, 9 May, https://www.theguardian.com/commentisfree/2017/may/09/jeremy-corbyn-clement-attlee

3   Tony Blair attended Fettes. Sidney Webb was sent from London 'to school on the outskirts of Neuchatel in Switzerland and then on to Wismar on the Baltic in Germany'. See: Donnelly, S. (2015) 'Sidney Webb – the early years', LSE History blog, 13 July, http://blogs.lse.ac.uk/lsehistory/2015/07/13/sidney-webb-the-early-years/

4   Verkaik, R. (2018) *Posh Boys: How the English Public Schools Run Britain*, London: Oneworld.

5   Maley, J. (2006) '£45,000 damages for teacher who accused Prince Harry of cheating',

The Guardian, 14 February, https://www.theguardian.com/uk/2006/feb/14/schools.publicschools

6   Evans, A. (2017) 'Eton deputy head quits amid cheating scandal', *Daily Mail*, 25 August (updated online 29 August), http://www.dailymail.co.uk/news/article-4824050/Eton-deputy-head-quits-amid-claims-helped-pupils-cheat.html

7   Stephens, P. (2017) 'Brexit has broken British politics', *Financial Times*, 9 November, https://www.ft.com/content/8e592d24-c482-11e7-a1d2-6786f39ef675

8   Maidment, J. (2017) 'Almost two thirds of Conservative Party members want Theresa May to resign as Prime Minister', *Daily Telegraph*, 10 June, http://www.telegraph.co.uk/news/2017/06/10/almost-two-thirds-conservative-party-members-want-theresa-may/

9   Osborne, S. (2016) 'Stephen Crabb resigns as Work and Pensions Secretary citing family concerns', *The Independent*, 14 July, http://www.independent.co.uk/news/uk/politics/stephen-crabb-resigns-theresa-may-cabinet-latest-appointments-sackings-work-and-pensions-secretary-a7136651.html

10 Doward, J. (2017) 'Revealed: why Michael Fallon was forced to quit as defence secretary', *The Guardian*, 4 November, https://www.theguardian.com/politics/2017/nov/04/michael-fallon-defence-secretary-sexual-harassment

11 Osborne, S. (2016) 'Stephen Crabb resigns as Work and Pensions Secretary citing family concerns', op. cit.

12 Ryan, F. (2018) 'The new work and pensions secretary is an insult to disabled people, *The Guardian*, 16 January, https://www.theguardian.com/society/2018/jan/16/esther-mcvey-work-pensions-secretary-insult-disabled-people

13 Anonymous (2017) 'Capital Flight', *Private Eye*, No. 1457, 30 November, p. 7.

14 Elgot, J. (2017) 'Paradise Papers: Theresa May refuses to promise register of offshore trusts,' *The Guardian*, 6 November, https://www.theguardian.com/politics/2017/nov/06/paradise-papers-theresa-may-refuses-to-promise-register-of-offshore-trusts

15 Weaver, M. (2017) 'Damian Green denies making sexual advances towards young Tory activist', *The Guardian*, 1 November, https://www.theguardian.com/politics/2017/nov/01/damian-green-denies-making-sexual-advances-towards-kate-maltby-tory-activist; and Walker, P. (2017) 'Damian Green urged to step down during pornography inquiry', *The Guardian*, 5 November, https://www.theguardian.com/uk-news/2017/nov/04/damian-green-denies-pornography-was-found-on-his-commons-computer

16 Sparrow, A. (2018) 'May says she wants investigation into release of Damian Green information – as it happened', 14 February, https://www.theguardian.com/politics/live/2017/dec/21/damian-green-sacking-theresa-may-politics-live

17 http://mashable.com/2017/07/31/theresa-may-cabinet-the-scream-munch/#io9ddn-qBKsqb

18 Salmon, J., Sinmaz, E. and Steiner, R. (2016) 'Home Secretary Amber Rudd told to come clean over her embarrassing links to two firms set up in tax havens', *Daily Mail*, 22 September, http://www.dailymail.co.uk/news/article-3803116/Home-Secretary-Amber-Rudd-told-come-clean-embarrassing-links-two-firms-set-tax-havens.html. See also: Hughes, L. and Rayner, G. (2017) 'Revealed: Nine Tory MPs on the so called "sex dossier" – with some included for already known relationships', *Daily Telegraph*, 31 October, http://www.telegraph.co.uk/news/2017/10/31/tory-minister-mp-accused-paying-women-keep-quiet/

19 Sommerlad, N. (2014) 'Millionaire Tory Philip Hammond's £200 a month "tax dodge" – See video as our man confronts him', *Daily Mirror*, 11 March, https://www.mirror.co.uk/news/uk-news/millionaire-tory-philip-hammonds-200-3231876

20 Seamark, M. (2013) 'Boris's secret lovechild and a victory for the public's right to

know', *Daily Mail*, 21 May, http://www.dailymail.co.uk/news/article-2328067/Boris-Johnsons-secret-lovechild-daughter-Stephanie-victory-publics-right-know.html

21 Unite the Union (2014) 'Government links to private healthcare', 28 November, https://web.archive.org/web/20170415154126/http://www.unitetheunion.org/uploaded/documents/final%20mp%20dossier%2028%20nov%201411-20887.pdf. See also: Ellis-Gage, J. (2015) 'I Dislike Jeremy Hunt Because…', Huffington Post, 27 July, http://www.huffingtonpost.co.uk/joe-ellisgage/jeremy-hunt_b_7876164.html

22 McCann, K. (2016) 'Theresa May's new eight legged enforcer is Cronus the giant spider', *Daily Telegraph*, 16 November, http://www.telegraph.co.uk/news/2016/11/19/theresa-mays-new-eight-legged-enforcer-is-cronus-the-giant-spide/

23 Grant, K. (2017) 'New Justice Secretary David Lidington opposed gay rights and wanted to scrap Human Rights Act', *The Independent*, 11 June, https://inews.co.uk/essentials/news/new-justice-secretary-david-lidington-opposes-gay-rights-wants-scrap-human-rights-act/

24 By *Channel 4 News* on 9 November 2012: https://www.channel4.com/news/britain-to-scrap-financial-aid-to-india, and by the *Daily Mail*: 'Sacked Transport Secretary Justine Greening in furious rant at PM after being put in charge of overseas aid', *Daily Mail*, 8 September 2012, http://www.dailymail.co.uk/news/article-2200412/Sacked-Transport-Secretary-Justine-Greening-furious-rant-PM-charge-overseas-aid.html

25 Merrick, R. (2018) 'Education Secretary forced to admit that he wrongly claimed school spending is going up', *The Independent*, 14 March, https://www.independent.co.uk/news/uk/politics/education-secretary-damian-hinds-school-spending-increase-labour-a8255971.html

26 Unite the Union (2014) op. cit.

27 https://en.wikipedia.org/wiki/Liam_Fox.

28 Bloom, D. (2018) 'Who is Dominic Raab? Brexit secretary branded feminists "obnoxious bigots" and said foodbank users aren't "languishing in poverty"', *Daily Mirror*, 9 July, https://www.mirror.co.uk/news/politics/who-dominic-raab-brexit-secretary-12882420

29 BBC (2017) 'Tory MP under fire over "sinister" Brexit demand to universities', BBC News, 24 October, https://www.bbc.co.uk/news/uk-politics-41735839

30 Gregory, A. (2012) 'The most powerful unelected man in Britain… and you will never have heard of him', *Daily Mirror*, 5 March, https://www.mirror.co.uk/news/uk-news/sir-jeremy-heywood-the-most-powerful-751584

31 Clark, G. (2010) 'It's time for government to stop getting in your way', *Catholic Herald*, 30 July, /http://www.catholicherald.co.uk/commentandblogs/2010/07/30/it%E2%80%99s-time-for-government-to-stop-getting-in-your-way/

32 DfE (2011) 'Support and Aspiration: a new approach to special educational needs and disability', London: Department for Education: introduction, https://www.gov.uk/government/publications/support-and-aspiration-a-new-approach-to-special-educational-needs-and-disability-consultation

33 BBC (2018) '"Livid" Michael Gove rips up EU customs partnership report', BBC News, 30 June, https://www.bbc.co.uk/news/uk-44668572

34 Smith, M. (2017) 'The full list of Tory Chris Grayling's failures as Justice Secretary', *Daily Mirror*, 26 July, http://www.mirror.co.uk/news/politics/full-list-tory-chris-graylings-10873684

35 Batchelor, T. (2017) 'Transport Secretary Chris Grayling didn't give cyclist his details after knocking him off bike because "no one asked"', *The Independent*, 10 January, https://www.independent.co.uk/news/uk/politics/

transport-secretary-chris-grayling-doored-cyclist-road-accident-basic-rules-cy-cling-campaigners-a7519781.html

36 Freedland, J. (2017) 'The new age of Ayn Rand: how she won over Trump and Silicon Valley', *The Guardian*, 10 April, https://www.theguardian.com/books/2017/apr/10/new-age-ayn-rand-conquered-trump-white-house-silicon-valley

37 Saner, E. (2017) 'Theresa May's cabinet: pretty rich, but nothing on Trump's', *The Guardian*, 17 January, https://www.theguardian.com/business/shortcuts/2017/jan/17/theresa-mays-cabinet-pretty-rich-but-nothing-on-trumps

38 Sabbagh, D. (2018) 'Sajid Javid: combative capitalist and courtier of US neocons', *The Guardian*, 4 May, https://www.theguardian.com/politics/2018/may/04/sajid-javid-combative-capitalist-and-courtier-of-us-neocons. Additionally, in 2012 he is reported by a reliable source to have said that 'if he had to leave Britain to live in the Middle East, then he would choose Israel as home. Only there, he said, would his children feel the "warm embrace of freedom and liberty".': Bright, M. (2012). 'Muslim Tory MP: After Britain, Israel is best', *Jewish Chronicle*, 13 December, https://www.thejc.com/news/uk-news/muslim-tory-mp-after-britain-israel-is-best-1.39534

39 Which was set up in 2009 to support groups setting up free schools, which receive start-up grants and ongoing state funding without local authority control: https://en.wikipedia.org/wiki/New_Schools_Network

40 Baroness Evans of Bowes Park: http://www.parliament.uk/biographies/lords/baroness-evans-of-bowes-park/4329

41 Johnston, I. (2009) 'David Mundell: Claimed more than £3,000 on MPs' expenses to take photographs of himself', *Daily Telegraph*, 30 May, https://www.telegraph.co.uk/news/newstopics/mps-expenses/5413036/David-Mundell-Claimed-more-than-3000-on-MPs-expenses-to-take-photographs-of-himself.html

42 Press Association (2008) 'Tory candidate apologises for "greasy wops" comment', *The Guardian*, 14 June, https://www.theguardian.com/politics/2008/jun/14/conservatives.wales

43 Among her accomplishments Penny had previously said 'cock' six times and 'lay' or 'laid' five times in a parliamentary debate as a minister to win a bet: Walters, S. (2014) 'Minister staged obscene Commons debate... for a BET', *Daily Mail*, 30 November, http://www.dailymail.co.uk/news/article-2854421/Minister-staged-obscene-Commons-debate-BET-Tory-says-c-k-six-times-lewd-stunt-sailor-pals.html

44 Williams, C. and Foster, P. (2016) 'Black woman rejected for Channel 4 board was senior Arts Council executive', *Daily Telegraph*, 5 December, https://www.telegraph.co.uk/business/2016/12/05/black-woman-rejected-channel-4-board-senior-arts-council-executive/

45 Crace, J. (2018) 'Matt the blank makes few friends with genius take on NHS and Brexit', *The Guardian*, 23 October, https://www.theguardian.com/politics/2018/oct/23/matt-the-blank-made-few-friends-when-grilled-over-the-nhs-and-brexit

46 Butler, P. (2017) 'In David Gauke's world, Universal Credit is working well', *The Guardian*, 18 October, https://www.theguardian.com/society/2017/oct/18/david-gauke-universal-credit-working-well

47 Bloom, D. (2017) 'Where's David Gauke? Tory in charge of Universal Credit fails to turn up to emergency debate on bungled rollout', *Daily Mirror*, 24 October, http://www.mirror.co.uk/news/politics/wheres-david-gauke-tory-charge-11400282

48 Press Association (2018) 'Government faces £1.67bn bill for underpaying disabled benefits', *Powys County Times*, 17 October, http://www.countytimes.co.uk/news/national/16989630.government-faces-167bn-bill-for-underpaying-disabled-benefits/

49 Bowcott, O. (2017) 'Lord Chief Justice attacks Liz Truss for failing to back Article

50 judges', *The Guardian*, 22 March, https://www.theguardian.com//politics/2017/mar/22/lord-chief-justice-castigates-liz-truss-for-failing-to-defend-judges

50 Chambre, A. (2017) 'Liz Truss says she would now back Brexit', Politics Home, 11 October, https://www.politicshome.com/news/uk/foreign-affairs/brexit/news/89727/liz-truss-says-she-would-now-back-brexit

51 Mason, R. (2013) 'Edward Snowden NSA files: Guardian should be prosecuted, says Tory MP', *The Guardian*, 22 October, https://www.theguardian.com/politics/2013/oct/22/edward-snowden-guardian-should-be-prosecuted-tory-mp

52 Cole, H. (2017) 'Defending the indefensible: Theresa May backs Attorney General Jeremy Wright after he lands public with MASSIVE bill by losing Brexit case', *The Sun*, 24 January, https://www.thesun.co.uk/news/2697011/theresa-may-backs-attorney-general-jeremy-wright-after-he-lands-public-with-massive-bill-by-losing-brexit-case/

53 Smith, M., Blanchard, J. and Bloom, D. (2016) 'Highest-earning Tory MP claimed £1 on expenses for cheap bin bags', *Daily Mirror*, 13 May, https://www.mirror.co.uk/news/uk-news/highest-earning-tory-mp-claimed-7959693

54 McSmith, A. (2016) 'Geoffrey Cox: Tory MP has expenses claim for 49p pint of milk rejected by Commons', *The Independent*, 14 January, https://www.independent.co.uk/news/uk/politics/geoffrey-cox-tory-mp-has-expenses-claim-for-49p-pint-of-milk-rejected-by-commons-a6813131.html

55 https://en.wikipedia.org/wiki/Brandon_Lewis#Expenses

56 Dunt, I. (2012) 'The Ten Worst MPs on Twitter: 8 – Damian Hinds', Politics.co.uk, 15 May, http://www.politics.co.uk/comment-analysis/2012/05/15/the-ten-worst-mps-on-twitter-8-damian-hinds

57 Wilby, P. (2018) 'The European Research Group is the Tory group more powerful than Momentum', *New Statesman*, 4 February, https://www.newstatesman.com/2018/02/european-research-group-tory-group-more-powerful-momentum

58 Montgomerie, T. and Pancevski, B. (2017) 'May drafts Gove in to Brexit war Cabinet', *Sunday Times*, 3 November, https://www.thetimes.co.uk/article/theresa-may-drafts-michael-gove-into-brexit-war-cabinet-p6gordzz0

59 Hope, C. (2012) 'Exclusive: Cabinet is worth £70million', *Daily Telegraph*, 27 May, http://www.telegraph.co.uk/news/politics/9290520/Exclusive-Cabinet-is-worth-70million.html

60 Weaver, M. (2015) 'British slavery reparations Q&A', *The Guardian*, 30 September, https://www.theguardian.com/world/2015/sep/30/british-slavery-reparations-qa

61 Belltoons.co.uk, 21 November 2015.

62 BrexitCentral (2017) 'Brexit News for Wednesday 6 September', http://brexitcentral.com/today/brexit-news-wednesday-6-september/

63 Hope, C. (2012) 'Exclusive: Cabinet is worth £70million', op. cit.

64 Watkins, J. et al. (2017) 'Effects of health and social care spending constraints on mortality in England: a time trend analysis', *British Medical Journal Open*, pp. 7, 11, http://bmjopen.bmj.com/content/7/11/e017722

65 Lambert, V. (2014). 'Has the Minister for Magic Jeremy Hunt gone too far?', *Daily Telegraph*, 2 April, http://www.telegraph.co.uk/news/health/alternative-medicine/10739658/Has-the-Minister-for-Magic-Jeremy-Hunt-gone-too-far.html

66 Cowburn, A. (2018) 'Jeremy Hunt: Parliamentary authorities launch probe into purchase of luxury flats', *The Independent*, 18 April, https://www.independent.co.uk/news/uk/politics/jeremy-hunt-latest-probe-launch-luxury-flats-purchase-labour-health-secretary-investigation-a8310621.html

67 Goldsmith, Z. (2015) 'Zac Goldsmith: How my dad saved Britain', *The Spectator*, 28 February, https://www.spectator.co.uk/2015/02/zac-goldsmith-how-my-dad-saved-britain/

68 Chorley, M. (2014) '£250,000 bill for portraits of politicians is "chicken feed", claims wealthy Tory MP', *Daily Mail*, 14 January, http://www.dailymail.co.uk/news/article-2539190/Parliament-posers-Taxpayer-billed-250-000-MPs-order-paintings-statues-photographs-other.html

69 Oldroyd-Bolt, D. (2016) 'The many, many millions of Mogg: Behind the old-fashioned suits and perfect manners, Tory MP Jacob Rees-Mogg is a titan of high finance', *The Spectator*, 3 November, https://life.spectator.co.uk/2016/11/many-many-millions-mogg/

70 Bildt's tweet of 13 July 2016 is to be found here: https://twitter.com/carlbildt/status/753303826971713536

71 Simons, N. (2017) 'Boris Johnson Apologises And Admits He Was "Wrong" To Claim Nazanin Zaghari Ratcliffe Was Training Journalists In Iran', Huffington Post, 13 November, http://www.huffingtonpost.co.uk/entry/boris-johnson-apologises-and-admits-he-was-wrong-to-claim-nazanin-zaghari-ratcliffe-was-training-journalists-in-iran_uk_5a09bc2ce4b0b17ffcdf0eco

72 Travis, A. (2018) 'Theresa May cabinet process home-counties heavy', *The Guardian*, 12 January, https://www.theguardian.com/politics/2018/jan/12/theresa-may-cabinet-proves-home-counties-heavy

73 Benn, T. (1989) *Against the Tide: Diaries 1973–1976*, London: Hutchinson, p. 346 (18 March 1975).

74 Clarke, K. (2016) *A Kind of Blue: a political memoir*, London: Macmillan, p. 362.

75 Mason, R. (2014) 'PM backs Michael Gove but suggests former aide was a "career psychopath"', *The Guardian*, 1 July, https://www.theguardian.com/politics/2014/jun/18/david-cameron-dominic-cummings-career-psychopath

76 As reported in: Barnett, A. (2018) 'How to win the Brexit Civil War. An open letter to my fellow Remainers', Open Democracy, 6 June, https://www.opendemocracy.net/uk/anthony-barnett/how-to-win-brexit-civil-war-open-letter-to-my-fellow-remainers

77 As featured in *FE Week* magazine, 7 August 2014, and reproduced with permission.

78 The Legatum Institute, 'Creating the pathways from poverty to prosperity', https://www.li.com. According to Wikipedia, 'The Legatum Institute, together with the Centre for Social Justice, are considered to be the organisations central to the Conservative Party's case for Hard Brexit. The Institute is described as "a thinktank with unparalleled access to Davis and Theresa May".'

79 Singham, S., Tylecote, R., and Hewson, V. (2017) 'The Brexit Inflection Point: The Pathway to Prosperity', London: The Legatum Institute, November (was at this web address in November 2017, but now deleted): https://lif.blob.core.windows.net/lif/docs/default-source/default-library/brexitinflectionvweb.pdf?sfvrsn=0

80 Crookham Court Manor School was abandoned in 1989 after three members of staff and the owner were convicted of sexual abuse of the pupils following an investigation by BBC's *That's Life!* that exposed terrible abuse there.

81 Sloan, A. and Campbell, I. (2017) 'How did Arron Banks afford Brexit?', Open Democracy, 19 October, https://www.opendemocracy.net/uk/brexitinc/adam-ramsay/how-did-arron-banks-afford-brexit

82 Ramsay, A. (2017) 'What (precisely) is the Electoral Commission investigating Banks for?', Open Democracy, 1 November, https://www.opendemocracy.net/uk/brexitinc/adam-ramsay/what-is-it-electoral-commission-is-investigating-banks-for

83 Steerpike (2018) 'Watch: Arron Banks walks out of select committee', *The Spectator*, 12 June, https://blogs.spectator.co.uk/2018/06/arron-banks-walks-out-of-select-committee/

84 Brinded, L. (2017) 'The Brexit campaign got 61% of its funding from just 5 of Britain's richest businessmen', Business Insider, 23 April, http://uk.businessinsider.com/sunday-times-rich-list-2017-biggest-political-donors-to-the-brexit-campaign-2017-4

85 Wheeler, C. (2018) 'Farage's UKIP backer bolsters his DUP bid', *Sunday Times*, 14 May.

86 According to the Resolution Foundation think tank, 2.2 million families are expected to gain under Universal Credit, with an average increase in income of £41 a week. However, 3.2 million families are also expected to be worse off, with an average loss of £48 a week. See: Rogers, L. (2018) 'Universal Credit: Will benefit changes affect you?', BBC News, 26 October, https://www.bbc.co.uk/news/uk-45971686

87 Landman Economics (2018) 'Child poverty in working households up by 1 million children since 2010, says TUC', Trade Union Congress, 7 May, https://www.tuc.org.uk/news/child-poverty-working-households-1-million-children-2010-says-tuc

88 Personal communication (2018) Matt Barnes of City University, Living Costs and Food Survey Table 31, household expenditure by disposable income decile group, UK, financial year ending 2017, ONS, 18 January, https://www.ons.gov.uk/peoplepopulationandcommunity/personalandhouseholdfinances/expenditure/datasets/detailedhouseholdexpenditurebydisposableincomedecilegroupuktable31

89 Mudde, C. (2018) 'Orbán's Hungary is not the future of Europe: it represents a dying past', *The Guardian*, 10 April, https://www.theguardian.com/commentisfree/2018/apr/10/orban-election-hungary-europe-future-past

90 Clarke, H. D., Goodwin, M. and Whitely, P. (2017) 'Why Britain Voted for Brexit: An Individual-Level Analysis of the 2016 Referendum Vote', *Parliamentary Affairs*, Vol. 70, No. 3, pp. 439–646, https://academic.oup.com/pa/article/70/3/439/3109029

91 Dorling, D. (2017) 'Review of Brexit: Why Britain Voted to Leave the European Union, by Harold D. Clarke, Matthew Goodwin, and Paul Whiteley', *Times Higher Education*, 4 May, http://www.dannydorling.org/?page_id=6008

92 Bennett, A. (2016) 'Here's where Britain's newspapers stand on the EU referendum', *Daily Telegraph*, 21 June, https://www.telegraph.co.uk/politics/0/heres-where-britains-newspapers-stand-on-the-eu-referendum/

93 Pegg, D. (2017) 'Vote Leave inquiry: what is Electoral Commission investigating?', *The Guardian*, 20 November, https://www.theguardian.com/politics/2017/nov/20/vote-leave-electoral-commission-investigating

94 Lawford, M. (2018) 'Why are the Russians leaving London?', *Financial Times*, 25 October, https://www.ft.com/content/8685683e-d2b8-11e8-9a3c-5d5eac8f1ab4

95 Neate, R. (2017) 'Bet365 chief Denise Coates paid herself £217m last year', *The Guardian*, 12 November, https://www.theguardian.com/business/2017/nov/12/bet365-chief-denise-coates-paid-217m-last-year

96 Parris, M. (2018) 'Tories are lying to the voters and themselves over Brexit', *The Times*, 3 February, https://www.thetimes.co.uk/article/tories-are-lying-to-the-voters-and-themselves-over-brexit-r7nc79cw5?shareToken=6d0bda5d385ec-c04b74a5c20be04dbd0

97 Boyle, F. (2017) 'Is this the night of the living dead? No, it's Britain's Brexit team', *The Guardian*, 29 October, https://www.theguardian.com/commentisfree/2017/oct/28/night-of-the-living-dead-britains-brexit-team

98 Wintour, C. (2015) 'Jeremy Corbyn: I would never use nuclear weapons if I were

PM', *The Guardian*, 30 September, https://www.theguardian.com/politics/2015/sep/30/corbyn-i-would-never-use-nuclear-weapons-if-i-was-pm

99   Pickard, J. and Gordon, S. (2017) 'UK politics: can business learn to live with a "hard-left" Labour?', *Financial Times*, 7 December, https://www.ft.com/content/952bce9c-d9b6-11e7-a039-c64b1c09b482

100   Warren, I. (2018) 'Watch out, Tories. Your southern strongholds are turning red', *The Guardian*, 9 May, https://www.theguardian.com/commentisfree/2018/may/09/tories-southern-red-south-england-london

Chapter 8: A land of hope and glory?

1   Brown, G. (2017) *My Life, Our Times*, op. cit., p. 22.

2   BBC (2011) 'Euro crisis "opportunity for UK" to reclaim powers – PM', BBC News, 15 November, https://www.bbc.co.uk/news/uk-politics-15730084

3   Elliott, M. (2013) 'Matthew Elliott: Five language rules for the Right', Conservative-Home, 17 June, https://www.conservativehome.com/platform/2013/06/matthew-elliott-is-chief-executive-of-business-for-britain-founder-of-the-taxpayers-alliance-five-language-rules-for-t.html

4   Greener UK (2018) 'Brexit risk tracker, October 2017 – mid January 2018', http://greeneruk.org/resources/Greener_UK_risk_tracker_January.pdf

5   Bodkin, H. (2018) 'One in five British mammal species could be extinct within a decade', *Daily Telegraph*, 13 June, https://www.telegraph.co.uk/news/2018/06/12/one-five-british-mammal-species-could-extinct-within-decade/

6   Bodkin, H. (2016) 'Toads nearly endangered after suffering massive decline in 30 years', *Daily Telegraph*, 6 October, https://www.telegraph.co.uk/news/2016/10/05/toads-nearly-endangered-after-suffering-massive-decline-in-30-ye/

7   McKie, R. (2018) 'Where have all our insects gone?', *The Observer*, 17 June, https://www.theguardian.com/environment/2018/jun/17/where-have-insects-gone-climate-change-population-decline

8   Peter Rachman was a notorious slum landlord in the 1950s and early 1960s in Notting Hill, London, partly responsible for the Rent Act 1965 and rent regulation and secure tenancies, protections later removed by Margaret Thatcher.

9   Editorial (2017) 'Behind this disaster lies a brutal indifference to the lives of the poor', *The Observer*, 18 June, https://www.theguardian.com/commentisfree/2017/jun/17/observer-editorial-grenfell-tower-fire

10   Dorling, D. (2015) *All That is Solid: How the Great Housing Disaster Defines Our Times, and What We Can Do About It*, London: Allen Lane.

11   Mazzucato, M. (2017) 'After Irma, let those who use our tax havens contribute to the repairs', *The Guardian*, 10 September, https://www.theguardian.com/commentisfree/2017/sep/09/after-hurricane-irma-let-those-who-use-tax-havens-contribute-to-repairs

12   Erlanger, S. (2017) 'No One Knows What Britain Is Anymore', *New York Times*, 4 November, https://www.nytimes.com/2017/11/04/sunday-review/britain-identity-crisis.html

13   http://www.cer.eu/personnel/charles-grant and http://www.regents.ac.uk/events/senior-european-experts-the-uk-and-the-eu-are-there-alternatives-to-eu-membership/panel-details/

14   https://en.wikipedia.org/wiki/50_Most_Influential_(Bloomberg_Markets_ranking)#2014_ranking

15   Or he did in June 2018: https://www.cer.eu/personnel/charles-grant

16   Brown, G. (2017) *My Life, Our Times*, op. cit., p. 24.

17 The opposite is actually the case. Human beings are social animals who depend on co-operation and sharing for their survival.

18 Ashcroft, M. and Culwick, K. (2016) *Well, you did ask: Why the UK voted to Leave the EU*, London: Biteback.

19 Ashcroft, M. (2009) *Dirty politics, dirty times*, London: Biteback.

20 Ashcroft, M. (2009) ibid., pp. 2–10.

21 Anonymous (2013) 'How he made his pile: Lord Ashcroft, businessman/politician', *Management Today*, 9 October, https://www.managementtoday.co.uk/made-pile-lord-ashcroft-businessman-politician/article/940641

22 The Sunday Times Rich List 2017, http://features.thesundaytimes.co.uk/richlist/live/richlist

23 McCall, A. (2017) 'Britain's richest give £12m to parties fighting election', *The Times*, 21 May, https://www.thetimes.co.uk/article/rich-list-2017-britains-richest-give-12m-to-parties-fighting-election-jnodzpvms The most generous Tory donor was Subaskaran Allirajah, founder of Lycamobile.

24 MacAskill, E. (2017) 'Tory donor Ashcroft used offshore trust to shelter wealth while in Lords', *The Guardian*, 6 November, https://www.theguardian.com/news/2017/nov/05/lord-ashcroft-offshore-trust-wealth-tory-peer-paradise-papers

25 Belize is an independent Commonwealth realm, population 382,444 (2018), widely considered an offshore tax haven.

26 Bartlett, N. (2017) 'Watch as Tory donor Lord Ashcroft runs away and hides in the loo to avoid questions on paradise papers', *Daily Mirror*, 6 November, http://www.mirror.co.uk/news/politics/watch-tory-donor-lord-ashcroft-11476870

27 Ashcroft, M. (2015) 'A broken promise and why I wrote this book: Lord Ashcroft reveals how he went from supporter to critic of Cameron', *Daily Mail*, 20 September, http://www.dailymail.co.uk/news/article-3242581/A-broken-promise-wrote-book-LORD-ASHCROFT-reveals-went-supporter-critic-Cameron.html

28 Ashcroft, M. and Oakeshott, I. (2015) *Call Me Dave: The Unauthorised Biography*, London: Biteback. See also: Jack, I. (2015) 'Call Me Dave by Michael Ashcroft and Isabel Oakeshott review – a pig in a poke', *The Guardian*, 8 October, https://www.theguardian.com/books/2015/oct/08/call-me-dave-the-unauthorised-biography-michael-ashcroft-isabel-oakeshott-review

29 https://en.wikipedia.org/wiki/Piggate

30 Mediamonkeyblog (2017) 'Isabel Oakeshott runs squealing from David Cameron #piggate claims', *The Guardian*, 9 October, https://www.theguardian.com/media/mediamonkeyblog/2015/oct/09/isabel-oakeshott-david-cameron-piggate-call-me-dave. There is no evidence that he was a member of the tiny Piers Gaveston Society, that it had any initiation ceremony, or even that he went to their open parties, which are more exciting in the anticipation and the (un)dressing-up for it than the actuality.

31 Moore, M. and Ramsay, G. (2017) 'UK media coverage of the 2016 EU Referendum campaign', King's College London, Centre for the Study of Media, Communication and Power, May, p. 166, https://www.kcl.ac.uk/sspp/policy-institute/CMCP/UK-media-coverage-of-the-2016-EU-Referendum-campaign.pdf

32 Založnik, M. (2016) 'Here's what would have happened if Brexit vote was weighted by age', *The Independent*, 5 July, https://www.independent.co.uk/news/uk/here-s-what-would-have-happened-if-brexit-vote-was-weighted-by-age-a7120536.html and also available at: https://theconversation.com/heres-what-would-have-happened-if-brexit-vote-was-weighted-by-age-61877

33 Moore, P. (2016) 'How Britain Votes: Over-65s were more than twice as likely as under-25s to have voted to Leave the European Union', YouGov, 27 June, https://yougov.co.uk/news/2016/06/27/how-britain-voted/

34 'Tomorrow Belongs to Me' was a song in the musical *Cabaret* sung by Nazi Youth to stir up patriotism for 'the Fatherland'. It was not a genuine Nazi anthem but has been used subsequently at White Power rallies.

35 'For all the talk of liberal bubbles, it can't be said enough that the anti-immigrant panic is being led by people who have little personal experience living alongside immigrants and immigrant communities.' Matthew Yglesias, Twitter, 1 July 2018, https://twitter.com/mattyglesias/status/1013456427329957890

36 As Mehdi Hasan tweeted: 'This is a global phenomenon – AfD in Germany won big in the east of the country, where the fewest immigrants live. UKIP in the UK does best in the whitest, least-immigrant-filled areas, too', https://t.co/Pvuc7KLG4s

37 Staff Reporter (2017) 'When did schools ban corporal punishment?', *Schools Week*, 25 January, https://schoolsweek.co.uk/when-did-schools-ban-corporal-punishment/

38 Hosie, L. (2017) 'UK laws around smacking children are changing – everything you need to know', *The Independent*, 22 November, https://www.independent.co.uk/life-style/health-and-families/smacking-children-uk-law-change-ban-is-it-illegal-what-are-rules-parents-punishment-a8069436.html

39 UNICEF (2007) 'Innocenti Report Card 7', Unicef, 14 February, see Figure 5 on p. 26 of https://www.unicef.org/media/files/ChildPovertyReport.pdf

40 https://en.wikipedia.org/wiki/Special_member_state_territories_and_the_European_Union#Channel_Islands

41 Goodman, P. S. (2018) 'In Britain, Austerity Is Changing Everything', *New York Times*, 28 May, https://mobile.nytimes.com/2018/05/28/world/europe/uk-austerity-poverty.html

42 British Forces Network (2017) 'Meet the MPs with military careers', Forces Network News, 9 June, https://www.forces.net/news/meet-mps-military-careers

43 Quoted in Dean, A. (2017) 'Peering over the cliff-edge: why Dominic Cummings fears Brexit will fail', *Prospect* magazine, 11 October, https://www.prospectmagazine.co.uk/magazine/peering-over-the-cliff-edge-why-dominic-cummings-fears-brexit-will-fail

44 Jones, C. (2017) 'Bad news on Brexit will be better for businesses than no news at all', *The Times*, 14 October, https://www.thetimes.co.uk/article/bad-news-on-brexit-will-be-better-for-businesses-than-no-news-at-all-nslqqbqt5

45 Originally by Daniel Gordon Watts, who kindly gave permission for us to reuse – shaded in greys here. In colour: https://twitter.com/marwood_lennox/status/925760600755658752?s=03

46 Brexit has implications far and wide, including for the health of the nation as well as the medical work force.

47 Dorling, D. (2016) 'Brexit: the decision of a divided country', *British Medical Journal* 354, http://www.dannydorling.org/?page_id=5564

48 Detailed analysis by one of the authors, which takes up too many pages to be included here, has found that for each of these southern counties (and more) a set of districts can be identified in the north or Wales that all voted Leave in majority, that combined had a larger electorate than their southern counterpart, but because turnout in the periphery was lower, they were far less important in determining the final outcome and stacking up the votes. See Dorling, D. (2018) 'Brexit and Britain's Radical Right', *Political Insight*, December, pp. 16–18.

49 Skinner, G. and Gottfried, G. (2016) 'How Britain voted in the 2016 EU referendum',

Ipsos MORI, https://www.ipsos.com/ipsos-mori/en-uk/how-britain-voted-2016-eu-referendum

50 Rae, A. (2017) 'General election 2017: some maps and data', Stats, Maps n Pix blog, 17 June, http://www.statsmapsnpix.com/2017/06/general-election-2017-some-maps-and-data.html

51 Rosenbaum, M. (2017) 'Local voting figures shed new light on EU referendum', BBC News, 6 February, http://www.bbc.co.uk/news/uk-politics-38762034

52 Rae, A. (2017) 'A very late Brexity blog', Stats, Maps n Pix, 9 December, http://www.statsmapsnpix.com/2017/12/a-very-late-brexity-blog.html

53 The index is updated every year. In 2017: 'Norway is the overall happiest country in the world, even though oil prices have dropped. Close behind are Denmark, Iceland and Switzerland in a tight pack.' Next in Europe comes Finland, then the Netherlands, Sweden, Austria, Ireland, and Germany in Europe's top ten, The UK ranked 19th in the world, 13th in Europe in 2017: https://en.wikipedia.org/wiki/World_Happiness_Report#2017_report

54 Gregory, A., Smith, M. and Bartlett, N. (2018) 'Immigration cap on doctors and nurses to be axed IMMEDIATELY in humiliating U-turn for Theresa May', Daily Mirror, 18 June, https://www.mirror.co.uk/news/politics/immigration-cap-doctors-nurses-axed-12704643

55 Cowburn, A. (2018) 'Jeremy Corbyn to say there is "mounting evidence austerity is killing people"', The Independent, 1 July, https://www.independent.co.uk/news/uk/politics/jeremy-corbyn-mounting-evidence-austerity-is-killing-people-government-cuts-labour-welfare-a8424381.html

56 BBC (2018) 'NHS plan in case of no-deal Brexit, Simon Stevens says', BBC News, 1 July, https://www.bbc.co.uk/news/uk-politics-44672873

57 Which former Prime Minister Gordon Brown has recently hinted he has doubts about. See: Brown, G. (2017) My Life, Our Times, op. cit., p. 31.

58 Dickinson, K. (2016) 'MPs react after Vote Leave economist admits Brexit would "mostly eliminate manufacturing"', The Chronicle, 2 May, https://www.chroniclelive.co.uk/news/north-east-news/mps-react-after-vote-leave-11269819

59 Islam, F. (2018) 'Leaked Government analysis reveals post-Brexit impact on UK regions', Sky News, 7 February, https://news.sky.com/story/hit-to-northern-ireland-and-north-east-england-gdp-revealed-in-new-brexit-impact-papers-leak-11240254

60 Redrawn with permission from Rae, A. (2016) 'What can explain Brexit?', Stats, Maps n Pix blog, 25 June, http://www.statsmapsnpix.com/2016/06/what-can-explain-brexit.html and ONS Mid-Year Population Estimates 2016

61 Mullen, E. (2018) 'Jaguar Land Rover to move Discovery production to Slovakia', Birmingham Post, 11 June, https://www.birminghampost.co.uk/business/manufacturing/jaguar-land-rover-move-discovery-14770749

62 Gill, F. and Sakhuja, A. (2016) 'Who has the most to lose from Brexit? Introducing the Brexit Sensitivity Index', Standard & Poor's, http://www.agefi.fr/sites/agefi.fr/files/fichiers/2016/06/09_-_06_-_2016_-_brexit_sensitivity_index_sp.pdf

63 Gill, F. and Sakhuja, A. (2016) ibid.

64 Gudgin, G. (1999) Chapter 5: Discrimination in Housing and Employment under the Stormont Administration, in Roche, P. J. and Barton, B. (eds) The Northern Ireland Question: Nationalism, unionism and partition, Aldershot: Ashgate, https://web.archive.org/web/20160304193159/http://cain.ulst.ac.uk/issues/discrimination/gudgin99.htm

65 Gudgin, G. and Bassett, R. (2018) 'Getting Over the Line: Solutions to the

Irish border', Policy Exchange: https://policyexchange.org.uk/wp-content/uploads/2018/05/Getting-over-the-line.pdf

66   Demetriades, P. O. (2017) 'Why a no-deal Brexit doesn't even bear thinking about – let alone planning for', The Conversation, 11 October, https://theconversation.com/why-a-no-deal-brexit-doesnt-even-bear-thinking-about-let-alone-planning-for-85545

Chapter 9: Why not Brexit?

1   Dallison, P. and Khetani-Shah, S. (2017) 'Brexit quotes of 2017', Politico, 30 December, https://www.politico.eu/article/brexit-quotes-of-the-year-2017/

2   Bennett, O. (2016) The Brexit Club, op. cit.

3   Stone, J. (2017) 'David Davis's former chief of staff launches extraordinary tirade against "drunk, bullying and inappropriate" Brexit chief', The Independent, 15 August, https://www.independent.co.uk/news/uk/politics/david-davis-brexit-drunk-diane-abbott-james-chapman-farage-john-humphrys-andrew-neil-slovakia-a7893816.html

4   Dallison, P. and Khetani-Shah, 'Brexit quotes of 2017', op. cit. (You can make the calculation easily, given how long he was in office.)

5   Kentish, B. (2017) 'Tory MP who dismissed a disabled woman on live TV appointed as justice minister by Theresa May', The Independent, 13 June, https://www.independent.co.uk/news/uk/politics/tory-mp-dominic-raab-justice-minister-theresa-may-disabled-woman-spending-cuts-conservative-victoria-a7787206.html

6   Crerar, P. (2018) 'Dominic Raab: bullish Brexiter with outspoken reputation', The Guardian, 9 July, https://www.theguardian.com/politics/2018/jul/09/raab

7   Letts, Q. (2018) 'Dominic Raab – as he is interrupted by news of his own demotion', Daily Mail, 24 July, http://www.dailymail.co.uk/news/article-5988505/QUENTIN-LETTS-watches-Mays-increasingly-powerful-fixer-gives-evidence-alongside-Dominic-Raab.html

8   Peston, R. (2017) 'I don't appear to be living in the same Britain as much of the rest of the country', Daily Telegraph, 28 October, https://www.telegraph.co.uk/men/thinking-man/robert-peston-dont-appear-living-britain-much-rest-country/

9   Romei, V. (2017) 'How wages fell in the UK while the economy grew', Financial Times, 2 March, https://www.ft.com/content/83e7e87e-fe64-11e6-96f8-3700c5664d30

10   IPPR (2017) 'The IPPR Commission on Economic Justice', Institute for Public Policy Research, https://www.ippr.org/files/2017-09/cej-interim-report-summary-170911.pdf

11   Romei, V. (2017) ibid.

12   Chu, B. (2018) 'True financial squeeze on UK households bigger than previously thought, research suggests', The Independent, 3 July, https://www.independent.co.uk/news/business/news/minimum-income-standard-uk-households-inflation-benefits-joseph-rowntree-foundation-a8427151.html

13   Goodman, P. S. (2018) 'Theresa May Arrives in Davos as U.K.'s Post-"Brexit" Slide Continues', New York Times, 25 January, https://www.nytimes.com/2018/01/25/business/theresa-may-brexit-davos.html

14   Since 2007 the value of the pound against the dollar has fallen 35 per cent, and against the euro 23 per cent, as of 2018.

15   TUC (2014) 'UK workers suffering the most severe squeeze in real earnings since Victorian times', Trades Union Congress, 12 October, https://www.tuc.org.uk/news/uk-workers-suffering-most-severe-squeeze-real-earnings-victorian-times

16   Ford Rojas, J. P. (2018) 'Wage growth at strongest level for nearly a decade', Sky News, 16 October, https://news.sky.com/story/wage-growth-improves-to-strongest-since-2009-11527063

17 Savage, M. (2018) 'Coalition education reforms "fuelled inequality in schools"', *The Independent*, 30 June, https://amp.theguardian.com/education/2018/jun/30/coalition-education-reform-academies-fuelling-inequality

18 Watkins, J. et al. (2017) 'Effects of health and social care spending constraints on mortality in England: a time trend analysis', op. cit.

19 Hiam, L. and Dorling, D. (2018) 'Rise in mortality in England and Wales in first sixteen weeks of 2018', *British Medical Journal*, 8 May, https://www.bmj.com/content/360/bmj.k1090/rr-8

20 Dorling, D. (2017) Short Cuts, op. cit.

21 ONS (2018) 'Deaths registered in England and Wales (series DR)', Office for National Statistics, 23 October, https://www.ons.gov.uk/peoplepopulationandcommunity/birthsdeathsandmarriages/deaths/datasets/deathsregisteredinenglandandwalesseriesdrreferencetables/. The age-sex-adjusted mortality rate for the UK in 2017 was 0.97 per cent, still above the 0.95 per cent recorded in 2014. These were the very latest statistics. Both men and women were more likely to die having taken into account ageing. The rise in infant mortality was more sudden and shocking.

22 Elliott, L. (2017) 'Eurozone buoyant as Brexit talks resume', *The Guardian*, 10 November, https://www.pressreader.com/uk/the-guardian/20171110/282286730546375

23 De La Baume, M. (2016) 'Greenland's exit warning to Britain', Politico, 24 June, https://www.politico.eu/article/greenland-exit-warning-to-britain-brexit-eu-referendum-europe-vote-news-denmark/

24 Joint declaration by the European Union, on the one hand, and the Government of Greenland and the Government of Denmark, on the other, on relations between the European Union and Greenland. Brussels, 19 March 2015, https://ec.europa.eu/europeaid/sites/devco/files/signed-joint-declaration-eu-greenland-denmark_en.pdf

25 Buchan, L. (2018) 'Boris Johnson warns "Brexit dream is dying" in scathing resignation letter', *The Independent*, 9 July, https://www.independent.co.uk/news/uk/politics/boris-johnson-letter-resignation-latest-theresa-may-brexit-statement-a8439346.html

26 Osborne, S. (2017) 'Nigel Farage refuses to give up EU pension: "Why should my family suffer?"', *The Independent*, 3 December, http://www.independent.co.uk/news/uk/politics/nigel-farage-eu-pension-refuses-give-up-keep-britain-first-rise-far-right-a8089256.html

27 BBC (2017) 'German election: How right-wing is nationalist AfD?', BBC News, 13 October, https://www.bbc.co.uk/news/world-europe-37274201

28 https://en.wikipedia.org/wiki/European_Parliament_election,_2014_(United_Kingdom). In 2009, 27.5 per cent Conservatives were in the ECR group, UKIP got 16.0 per cent, BNP 6.0 per cent, English Democrat 1.8 per cent. In 2004, the Conservatives were in EPP-ED, UKIP got 15.6 per cent, BNP 4.8 per cent. In 1999, UKIP got 6.5 per cent, BNP 1 per cent. In 1994, UKIP got 1.0 per cent, National Front 0.1 per cent. In 1989, the National Front won less than 0.1 per cent. The first page in the series is: https://en.wikipedia.org/wiki/European_Parliament_election,_1979_(United_Kingdom)

29 Currently the best, most comprehensive and most easy to access data can be found here: https://en.wikipedia.org/wiki/European_Parliament_election,_2014_(United_Kingdom). See also: https://en.wikipedia.org/wiki/European_Parliament_election,_1979_(United_Kingdom)

30 At the time of Corbyn's comments, the EU was failing to respond fairly to the refugee crisis or to Greece's financial crisis, neither of which were entirely of Greece's own making. How could an honourable man unreservedly extol the virtues of the EU?

31 KPMG (2017) 'The Brexit Effect on EU Nationals: A survey on what European workers will do now', Klynveld Peat Marwick Goerdeler, https://assets.kpmg.com/content/dam/kpmg/uk/pdf/2017/08/the-brexit-effect-on-eu-nationals.pdf

32 https://en.wikipedia.org/wiki/British_Overseas_Territories

33 Shaw, M., Orford, S., Brimblecombe, N. and Dorling, D. (2000) 'Widening inequality in mortality between 160 regions of 15 countries of the European Union', *Social Science and Medicine*, Vol. 30, pp. 1047–58, http://www.dannydorling.org/?page_id=1462

34 Keating, J. (2009) 'Tuesday Map: Heineken's "Eurotopia"', *Foreign Policy*, 26 May, http://foreignpolicy.com/2009/05/26/tuesday-map-heinekens-eurotopia/

35 Heineken, Alfred (Freddy) H. (1992) *The United States of Europe, A Eurotopia?*, Amsterdam: De Amsterdamse Stichting voor de Historische Wtenschap.

36 Portes, J. (2018) 'Has the UK economy really shrugged off the impact of the Brexit vote?', *New Statesman*, 26 January, https://www.newstatesman.com/politics/staggers/2018/01/has-uk-economy-really-shrugged-impact-brexit-vote

37 Wallace, T. and McCann, K. (2018) 'Is Mark Carney right about Brexit?', *Daily Telegraph*, 22 May, https://www.telegraph.co.uk/business/2018/05/22/mark-carney-right-brexit/

38 BBC (2018) 'Boris Johnson says he "probably needs" a private plane', BBC News, 23 May, http://www.bbc.co.uk/news/uk-politics-44221524

39 Cockburn. P. (2018) 'Brexiteers like Boris Johnson must realise that past British successes were based on creating alliances, not breaking them up', *The Independent*, 21 July, https://www.independent.co.uk/voices/boris-johnson-brexit-churchill-ww1-napoleon-british-history-a8456916.html

40 YouGov (2018) 'Voting Intention: Conservatives 42 per cent, Labour 39 per cent (11–12 June)', https://yougov.co.uk/news/2018/06/15/voting-intention-conservatives-42-labour-39-11-12-/

41 Fransham, M. and Dorling, D. (2017) 'House prices can keep rising only if the Government backs mass buy-to-let', *Daily Telegraph*, 8 April, https://www.telegraph.co.uk/investing/buy-to-let/oxford-academics-house-prices-can-keep-rising-government-backs/

42 Britain Elects: 'Having greater control over immigration is more important than having access to free trade with the EU: Agree: 38% (-5), Disagree: 48% (+4), Record high for the % who disagree', https://twitter.com/britainelects/status/1016357278612623360?s=03

43 Hope, C. (2017) 'Foreigners charged £10 to enter UK under new Brexit visa proposal', *Daily Telegraph*, 23 December, https://www.telegraph.co.uk/news/2017/12/23/foreigners-charged-10-enter-uk-new-brexit-visa-proposal/

44 Khan, S. and Agerholm, H. (2017) 'Article 50 author calls for Brexit to be halted with a warning of "disastrous consequences"', *The Independent*, 18 July, http://www.independent.co.uk/news/uk/politics/article-50-author-lord-kerr-of-kinlochard-brexit-latest-news-warning-disastrous-consequences-a7846951.html

45 Kerr, J. O. (2017) 'Full text of Lord Kerr's Speech "Article 50: The Facts"', Open Britain, 10 November, http://www.open-britain.co.uk/full_text_of_lord_kerr_s_speech_article_50_the_facts

46 Stuart, G. (2017) 'Gisela Stuart: Ministers are mistaken. Regulatory alignment is Single Market membership in all but name. Here's why', ConservativeHome, 8 December, https://www.conservativehome.com/platform/2017/12/gisela-stuart-ministers-are-mistaken-regulatory-alignment-is-single-market-membership-in-all-but-name-heres-why.html

47   Brinkley, D. (1990) 'Dean Acheson and the "special relationship": The West Point speech of December 1962', *Historical Journal*, Vol. 33, No. 3, pp. 599–608, https://www.jstor.org/stable/2639732?seq=1#page_scan_tab_contents

48   Sachs, J. D. (2018) 'Europe Must Confront America's Extraterritorial Sanctions', Project Syndicate, 17 May, https://www.project-syndicate.org/commentary/europe-resist-american-iran-sanctions-by-jeffrey-d-sachs-2018-05

49   Also known as 'How to Fix America's Corrupt Political System', uploaded on 19 April 2016, https://www.youtube.com/watch?v=lhe286ky-9A

50   Gilens, M. and Pages, B. I. (2014) 'Testing Theories of American Politics: Elites, Interest Groups, and Average Citizens', *Perspectives on Politics*, Vol. 12, No. 3, pp. 564–81, https://scholar.princeton.edu/sites/default/files/mgilens/files/gilens_and_page_2014_-testing_theories_of_american_politics.doc.pdf

51   School Fees Independent Advice (2017) 'If you require help paying for college or private school fees, then the earlier you start the better. SFIA can help you Save 50% or more on the cost of College and Private School fees', accessed November 2017, http://www.schoolfeesadvice.org/landing28/?gclid=EAIaIQobChMIh-OP25PN-1wIVL5PtCh1kmQDXEAAYASAAEgLqr_D_BwE

52   Salem (2018) 'School and Boarding fees and other costs': 'The fee covers the services listed in No. V. of the General Terms and Conditions of contract (GTC). The additional costs listed in No. VII. of the GTC will be invoiced separately', https://www.schule-schloss-salem.de/fileadmin/user_upload/downloads/pdf/10_Downloads/Salem_School_and_Boarding_Fees_2017_2018.pdf

53   Renton, A. (2015) 'Rape, child abuse and Prince Charles's former school', *The Guardian*, 12 April, https://www.theguardian.com/society/2015/apr/12/child-abuse-at-prince-charles-former-school-scotland

54   Miller, T. (2018) 'Cisco and Microsoft – Their Part in My Downfall; or, the Lost Ethics of Higher Ed; or, Maybe, a Sob Story', *Los Angeles Review of Books*, 10 May, https://lareviewofbooks.org/article/cisco-and-microsoft-their-part-in-my-downfall-or-the-lost-ethics-of-higher-ed-or-maybe-a-sob-story/

55   Studemann, F. (2017) 'Schools provide a lesson in how to profit from Brexit: British institutions can meet the challenge of a City exodus by expanding overseas', *Financial Times*, 3 October, https://www.ft.com/content/4ba40d8a-a828-11e7-93c5-648314d2c72c

56   London's high housing-price rivals include Hong Kong, San Francisco and, at times, Tokyo. However, when you compare prices around major train stations in these cities, and account for the square metres that are inside dwellings, central London is often found to be the most expensive, at least for now – its prices are falling.

57   Macpherson, W. (1999) The Stephen Lawrence Inquiry, Cmnd 4262, London: The Stationery Office.

58   Adams, T. (2013) 'Doreen Lawrence: "I could have shut myself away, but that is not me"', *The Guardian*, 20 April, https://www.theguardian.com/uk/2013/apr/20/doreen-lawrence-stephen-lawrence

INDEX